The Transformation of UN Conflict Management

The world has vowed 'Never again' in memory of the 800,000 Rwandans and other groups slaughtered by *génocidaires*. Yet, ever since the Holocaust, the international community has repeatedly betrayed its pledge, most notably in 1994 with regard to the Rwandan Tutsi, and again ten years later in Darfur.

This book examines how the UN failed to prevent or halt the Rwandan genocide: the most efficient mass killing in history. It offers a new explanation, focusing on the structure of the UN and four mechanisms which were pertinent to UN conflict management at that time: early warning; bureaucratic rationalisation; organisational learning; and Western normalisation. The author sees the Rwandan case as a 'child of its time', or a focal point in which the dysfunctions of the ailing conflict management mechanisms of the 1990s combined with devastating consequences. The book proceeds to examine the transformation of these mechanisms from Rwanda to Darfur – a development which is regarded as indicative of a wider tendency, or direction – in UN conflict management over the past ten years and in the foreseeable future.

This book will be of great interest to students and scholars of political science, international relations, ethnic politics, international organisations and conflict studies.

Touko Piiparinen is currently a Postdoctoral Researcher at the Centre of Excellence in Global Governance Research in Helsinki. He is on leave of absence from the Ministry for Foreign Affairs of Finland, where he has been previously posted in the Unit for UN Affairs and as the Deputy Head of Mission at the Embassy of Finland in Riyadh, Saudi Arabia. He has also worked in the ISAF operation in Afghanistan, and in the KFOR operation in Kosovo.

Routledge research on international organisations

1 The Transformation of UN Conflict Management
Producing images of genocide from Rwanda to Darfur and beyond
Touko Piiparinen

The Transformation of UN Conflict Management

Producing images of genocide from Rwanda to Darfur and beyond

Touko Piiparinen

 Routledge
Taylor & Francis Group

LONDON AND NEW YORK

First published 2010
by Routledge
2 Park Square, Milton Park, Abingdon, Oxon OX14 4RN

Simultaneously published in the USA and Canada
by Routledge
270 Madison Ave, New York, NY 10016

Routledge is an imprint of the Taylor & Francis Group, an informa business

© 2010 Touko Piiparinen

Typeset in Times by Wearset Ltd, Boldon, Tyne and Wear
Printed and bound in Great Britain by TJI Digital, Padstow, Cornwall

British Library Cataloguing in Publication Data
A catalogue record for this book is available from the British Library

Library of Congress Cataloging-in-Publication Data
A catalog record for this book has been requested

ISBN10: 0-415-54408-4 (hbk)
ISBN10: 0-203-87067-0 (ebk)

ISBN13: 978-0-415-54408-5 (hbk)
ISBN13: 978-0-203-87067-9 (ebk)

Contents

List of figures   viii
Acknowledgements   ix
List of abbreviations   xi

Introduction   1

1   **Rwanda, the genocide of our time**   14

Introduction 14
Precolonial and colonial Rwanda 17
Hutu Republic and genocide 18
'Lessons learned', peoples betrayed: genocide ten years on 23
Conclusion 25

2   **A critical realist approach to conflict management**   26

Introduction 26
Developing critical realism for the study of international relations:
*   from philosophy to a methodological framework 29*
Devising the method of double movement 33
Mechanisms and possibilities: new ontological building blocks of
*   theory on conflict management 38*
Conclusion 42

3   **UN conflict management of the 1990s**   44

Introduction 44
Setting the scene for analysis: post-Cold War conflict
*   management 46*
Detection mechanisms of the UN 48
Securitisation mechanisms of the UN 51
Conclusion 57

4 Explanatory theories of the UN's failure   60

Introduction 60
Overview of the UN's failure 61
'First wave' of explanations: the role of member states 64
'Second wave' of explanations: the role of the Secretariat 69
Transcending the 'blame game': towards a deeper understanding
    of the UN's failure 74
Conclusion 76

5 Early warning   78

Introduction 78
Phenomenal level: the malfunctions of early warning 79
Structural level: the root causes of the malfunctions of early
    warning 83
Emancipatory move: locating possibilities for the early detection
    of genocide 90
Conclusion 95

6 Bureaucratic mechanisms   99

Introduction 99
Relationship between early warning and bureaucratic
    rationalisation 101
Dysfunctions of bureaucratic rationalisation during genocide 104
Mechanism of organisational learning 114
Emancipatory move: locating possibilities for transforming
    bureaucratic constraints 118
Tribalisation and the statist paradigm of Western thinking 123
Conclusion 128

7 Future visions of conflict management   131

Introduction 131
New division of labour as a counterstrategy for 'body-bag
    syndrome' 133
A pragmatic turn in peacekeeping 135
A functional shift in control mechanisms 136
Mainstreaming RtoP and thinking out of bureaucratic boxes 138
Defending the baseline of humanity as a future vision of the
    UN 148
Defender of truth: the second vision of a future UN 159
Conclusion 163

8 Conclusion 168

Notes 182
Bibliography 203
Index 219

Figures

2.1 Synthesis of Bhaskar's logic of scientific discovery and
    Sayer's method of double movement   35
2.2 Emancipatory windows   38
2.3 Structural embeddedness of the member states of the Security
    Council   39
2.4 The Security Council as an open system   41
3.1 Detection mechanisms of the UN   51
3.2 Securitisation mechanisms of the UN   57
3.3 Summary of the analytical framework: the Security Council as
    an open system   58
4.1 Decontextualised explanations of the UN's failure in Rwanda   75
5.1 Summary of the malfunctions of early warning mechanisms   97
6.1 Summary of the dysfunctions of organisational learning mechanisms   128
6.2 Summary of the dysfunctions of bureaucratic rationalisation   129
6.3 Summary of the dysfunctions of Western normalisation   130
8.1 Emancipatory windows to prevent the Rwandan genocide   177
8.2 Emancipatory windows to prevent present and future genocides   178

Acknowledgements

Rwanda of 1994 was the ground zero of a country and an organisation. It wrecked the lives of a million people. It also shattered the credibility of the UN conflict management system. It would not be an overstatement to argue that the UN has never been the same since its failure to prevent and manage the Rwandan genocide, neither in the imagination of people who had viewed the UN as a standard-bearer of humanity, nor institutionally, as the conflict management mechanisms of the UN have been drastically transformed since the disaster. The time has come to assess this structural development at the UN, which is the objective of the present book. For me, like many other researchers, the UN's failure in Rwanda is a place and time in history that manifests itself through indirect sources: through stories, archival records and interviews, as well as the unique opportunity I have had to observe the working methods of the UN and particularly that famous 'horseshoe-shaped table', a place in which the decision to withdraw the UN from Rwanda was made years earlier, and my visit to the International Criminal Tribunal of Rwanda in Arusha, Tanzania. The main driving force behind my decade-long journey has undoubtedly been a desire to understand humanitarianism and one of its greatest letdowns. This motivation made the University of Wales, Aberystwyth, a natural choice of the home institution for my PhD thesis, which I completed in autumn 2005 and is now transformed into a book.

During the ten years of writing this book I have become more and more convinced of a long-held wisdom of Critical Theory which has prevailed in the philosophy of science over centuries, that human beings are not only producers but also products of the social world to which they belong. Such an assertion could not be more apposite to this study, which is deeply indebted to the stimulating and warm social environment of the Department of International Politics at the University of Wales, Aberystwyth. Many individuals belonging to that environment deserve more gratitude than it is possible to express in this limited space. I feel similar gratitude to my colleagues at the Ministry for Foreign Affairs of Finland, particularly for providing me with opportunity and intellectual space to complete this book, which I hope combines practical experience and academic research in a mutually reinforcing way.

First and foremost, I would like to thank Nick Wheeler, who has been not only the best supervisor imaginable but also a friend from the very beginning of my PhD research. His invaluable support, encouragement and engagement in my PhD project frequently amounted to self-sacrifice, especially in summer 2004, when I provided him with a draft chapter of a hundred pages, which he nevertheless managed to read and return with meticulous comments like he always did. Many of my ideas, contacts and research visits I owe to him, as well as some of the more engaging discussions and debates informing this book, including that concerning the ontological nature of the 'horseshoe-shaped table'.

Throughout my project, I have been privileged to work with many of the foremost theorists in International Relations. I am especially grateful to Colin Wight, Jonathan Joseph and Hidemi Suganami, who have been part of my supervisory team at various stages of my research. They have without any doubt had a major impact on my thinking about critical realism. I have been extremely fortunate to have Andrew Linklater and Jennifer Welsh as the examiners of my thesis. They provided me with a number of new ideas to further elaborate my thesis, which have proven invaluable in writing this book. Moreover, one of the greatest pleasures afforded by my research has been the enthusiasm expressed on the part of many interviewed and consulted individuals, who have subsequently become actively engaged in my project, supplying me with suggestions and other support. In this regard, I would particularly like to thank Karel Kovanda, who has never tired of responding to my countless inquiries. Stefan M. Stec, Klaus Törnudd, Ben Klappe and many other individuals must also be credited for their detailed comments on various parts of my thesis.

A diverse group of people in Aberystwyth has proven that friendship and debate on IR research can go hand in hand and transcend philosophical boundaries. Although this group is too large to mention here, particular thanks go to Stig Hansen, Ching-Chang Chen, Lucie Dunn, Lynne Dryburgh, Alexej Behnisch, Sebastian Kaempf, Alastair Finlan, Milja Kurki, Adam Kamradt-Scott, Richard Shimooka, Tuncay Kardas, Silviya Lechner, Ilan Baron and Darren Conrad Brunk. The group of people to whom I feel deeply grateful for theoretical and practical insights extends beyond Aberystwyth; special thanks must go to Richard Gowan, Linda Melvern, Andrew Sayer, Heikki Patomäki, David Malone, Hazel Evans, Wilhelm Breitenstein, Olli Ruohomäki, Kai Sauer, Liisa Laakso, Mikko Santavuori, Jussi Saressalo and Ville Peltokorpi.

I am very thankful to all the colleagues at the International Peace Academy for hosting me in New York in December 2003, and for providing me with intellectual and material support and contacts for conducting interviews at UN Headquarters. Furthermore, I am grateful to the Nordic Africa Institute in Uppsala, where I benefited from the opportunity to gather source materials at the beginning of my project. The Centre of Excellence on Global Governance Research in Helsinki has provided me with an intellectually stimulating research environment to complete this book. In addition to intellectual contributions by many individuals and institutions, the material support provided by the Academy of Finland has been a necessary component of my research, without which this book would not have been possible.

Abbreviations

ACABQ	Advisory Committee on Administrative and Budgetary Questions
AMIS	African Union Mission in Sudan
APC	armoured personnel carrier
APROMOSA	*Association Pour la Promotion Sociale des Masses* (Association for the Social Promotion of the Masses)
AU	African Union
CDR	*Coalition pour la Défense de la République* (Coalition for the Defense of the Republic)
DHA	United Nations Department of Humanitarian Affairs
DMZ	demilitarised zone
DPA	United Nations Department of Political Affairs
DPKO	United Nations Department of Peacekeeping Operations
EISAS	United Nations Information and Strategic Analysis Secretariat
ESDP	European Security and Defence Policy
EUFOR DRC	European Union Force in the Democratic Republic of Congo
EULEX	European Union Rule of Law Mission in Kosovo
EUPOL	EU Police Mission in Afghanistan
FAR	*Forces Armées Rwandaises* (Rwandan army)
FYROM	Former Yugoslav Republic of Macedonia
ICC	International Criminal Court
ICISS	International Commission on Intervention and State Sovereignty
IDPs	internally displaced persons
IPEP	International Panel of Eminent Personalities to Investigate the 1994 Genocide in Rwanda and the Surrounding Events
IR	International Relations
ISAF	International Security Assistance Force
JEM	Justice and Equality Movement
LMRGA	*Linda Melvern Rwanda Genocide Archive*
MONUC	*Mission des Nations Unies en République Démocratique du Congo* (United Nations Mission in the Democratic Republic of Congo)

MRND	*Mouvement Révolutionnaire National pour le Développement* (National Revolutionary Movement for Development)
MSF	*Médecins Sans Frontières*
NAM	United Nations Non-Aligned Movement
NATO	North Atlantic Treaty Organisation
NGO	non-governmental organisation
NMOG	OAU Neutral Military Observer Group
OAU	Organisation of African Unity
OIOS	Office of the Internal Oversight Services at the UN Secretariat
ONUC	*Operation des Nations Units au Congo* (United Nations Operation in the Congo)
ORCI	United Nations Office for Research and the Collection of Information
OSCE	Organisation for Security and Co-operation in Europe
PARMEHUTU	*Parti du Mouvement de L'Emancipation des Bahutu* (Party of the Movement and of Hutu Emancipation)
PKO	peacekeeping operations
PRT	provincial reconstruction teams
RADER	*Rassemblement Démocratique Rwandais* (Rwandese Democratic Union)
RGF	Rwandan Government Forces
RPA	Rwanda Patriotic Army
RPF	Rwandan Patriotic Front
RSC	Reflexive Social Cube
RTLMC	*Radio Télévision Libre des Mille Collines*
RtoP	Responsibility to Protect
SLA/M	Sudan Liberation Army/Movement
SRSG	United Nations Special Representative of the Secretary-General
UNAMIR	United Nations Assistance Mission for Rwanda
UNAMSIL	United Nations Mission in Sierra Leone
UNAR	*Union Nationale Rwandaise* (Rwandese National Union)
UNDP	United Nations Development Programme
UNHCHR	United Nations High Commissioner for Human Rights
UNIFIL	United Nations Interim Force in Lebanon
UNITA	*União Nacional pela Independência Total de Angola* (National Union for the Total Independence of Angola)
UNITAF	Unified Task Force
UNMIS	United Nations Mission in Sudan
UNMO	United Nations military observer
UNOMUR	United Nations Observer Mission Uganda–Rwanda
UNOSOM	United Nations Operation in Somalia
UNPREDEP	United Nations Preventive Deployment Force
UNPROFOR	United Nations Protection Force

Introduction

> Europeans ... should ask themselves what were the psycho-political mechanisms
> which enabled German Nazis during the Second World War to cleanly remove
> from 'civilised' society five and a half million Jews ... without much protest
> from the local populace.
>
> (Gérard Prunier 1998: 148)

'Never again' has been voiced worldwide in memory of one million Rwandans
and other groups targeted by *génocidaires*. The slogan not only represents an
apology for past failures to stop mass killings, but also entails a promise to
prevent the recurrence of similar disasters. Yet, ever since the Holocaust, the
international community has repeatedly betrayed its pledge, most notably in
1994 with regard to the Rwandan Tutsi, and ten years later in Darfur. Although a
wide range of investigations already exists explaining these cases, less attention
has been paid to the ominous *persistence* of such 'betrayal'. The conspicuous
discrepancy between emotional condemnations of inaction in the face of genocide on the one hand, and the continuing re-emergence of merciless bystanders
on the other, signifies inconsistency in the collective 'conscience' of international society and double standards in humanitarian intervention. Seeking an
explanation for this incongruity is essential for the preservation of our moral
integrity in conducting international politics.

This book offers a critical realist explanation by reference to certain deep
structures pertaining to conflict management, whose 'troublemaking' mechanisms continue to produce devastating failures while 'faces change' in government offices and international organisations.[1] The concept of 'deep structure'
applied here immediately calls to mind the vocabulary of structural realism in
International Relations (IR) theory, in which it is understood as a fundamental,
relatively stable, durable or even self-producing feature of the international
system.[2] Although the term is not explicitly used in Kenneth N. Waltz's classic
realist text, *Theory of International Politics* (1979), it is implicit in his ideas of
the logic of anarchy and self-help, the organising principles of international relations.[3] The striving of state agents to gain and balance material power vis-à-vis
other, rival, actors in the arena of world politics (the level of deep structures)

persists independently of changes in particular institutional arrangements (the surface level). This logic, according to Waltz, pertains to all political systems, whether a feudal fiefdom of the Medieval era or the bipolar world order during the Cold War. This book retains the structural realist idea of the level of deep structures, which are understood as the root causes that produce observable events.[4] However, it importantly transcends the Waltzian political realist position, in which the examination of deep structures is typically reduced to a narrow sector of international relations, namely power politics.[5] A sufficient explanation for the UN's failures in Rwanda and Darfur cannot be based merely on the interests of great powers, but requires a holistic approach that considers the entire level of deep structures of our society, civilisation and decision-making, including bureaucratic rationalisation and normalisation processes.

At first glance, the promise of more holistic explanations appears to be nothing new in IR theory, which has already seen a post-positivist turn, or, rather, several divergent moves, beyond neo-realism; however, a deeper examination of the current literature on Darfur and Rwanda, and on conflict management in general, reveals a lack of encompassing structural analyses. Drawing upon Robert Cox's distinction between 'problem solving' and 'critical' theory (Cox 1981: 126–55), Alex J. Bellamy and Paul Williams criticise the current literature on international intervention for its ontological narrowness.[6] They argue that it is dominated by a 'managerialist or "problem solving" approach to improving peace operations that does not *fundamentally address structural issues* but instead attempts to deal with particular sources of trouble within contemporary political structures' (Bellamy and Williams 2004: 2; emphasis added by author). This book aims to advance a deeper understanding of interventionist policies by exploring key mechanisms that underlie humanitarian intervention. The 'lessons learned' reports regarding the Rwandan case and UN reforms, such as the then Secretary-General Boutros Boutros-Ghali's *An Agenda for Peace* (1992), will be examined here less as instruments by which practical problems of contemporary intervention could be solved, than as symptoms of a *particular type of rationality* behind the logic of interventionist practice.[7] Bellamy proceeds to argue that, 'Whilst there has been an explosion of literature on the strengths, weaknesses, and experiences of peacekeepers and peace operations per se, there has been very little reflection about what this tells us about global politics or the functions that peace operations fulfil within it' (2004: 17). Instead of a narrow technical and instrumental account of intervention, the objective of this book is to situate peacekeeping and conflict management in the material and social context of global politics; indeed, the operations of bureaucratic rationalisation, Western normalisation and other mechanisms pertaining to peacekeeping missions are not restricted to conflict management but form part of wider control processes at the global level. Revealing these mechanisms, therefore, has the potential to expose broader and deeper aspects of international relations.

Widening the ontological horizon of research, in turn, requires new methodological devices capable of transcending the technical concepts which are applied in problem-solving theory of peacekeeping, such as 'exit strategy' and 'national interest'. This book will draw upon the terminology of a wider philosophical toolbox provided by critical realism and IR theory, utilising concepts like 'emancipatory research' and 'method of double movement'. Although such a meta-theoretical 'mind-switch' puts research on conflict management at risk of becoming a complex endeavour, as a reward it has the potential to reveal methodological errors committed by previous accounts,[8] and to open up alternative ways of thinking. It may, for example, provide visions of better outcomes that would have been achieved in Rwanda, had certain 'troublemaking' mechanisms at the UN been transformed. The first part of the book in particular will be imbued by theoretical concepts, typically avoided in the mainstream literature, with a view to developing a new framework for analysis of an old topic; obtaining genuinely original findings on the Rwandan case requires seismic changes in research methods, as a wide range of investigations already exists on the topic. In sum, the value added by a holistic approach lies in its ability to situate the research object in the *ontological context* of world politics by analysing those control mechanisms that not only regulate peacekeeping, but also underlie all global politics; and to account for the *methodological context*, as the method applied here draws its argumentative power directly from the philosophy of science.

It is hard to imagine any worse example, or a better case study, with regard to the analysis of conflict management than the UN's failure in Rwanda. It cannot be considered as a mere 'prelude' to the similar tragedy in Darfur; on the contrary, the Rwandan case takes a central role in this book. If it is claimed here that Rwanda triggered an earthquake in the normative structure of international society by instigating an unprecedented number of proposals for the reform of humanitarian intervention, then massacres in Darfur must be portrayed as a series of ongoing shocks shattering our moral principles. Valuable studies on Rwanda published quite recently underline the fact that the story of the Rwandan disaster is far from over, but is in some respects only just beginning. Even now, a decade after the genocide, the difficulty of explaining the sheer evilness of the drama remains. In fact, the 'Rwanda debacle' provides a story of two parallel evils. On the one hand, it concerns the people of Central Africa. Between 7 April and 15 July 1994, approximately 800,000 Tutsi civilians and Hutu moderates were systematically killed by the extremist Hutu interim government (Des Forges 1999: 15). This makes the Rwandan genocide the most efficient mass killing ever known in history, even faster than the Holocaust (Berkeley 1998). On the other hand, the Rwanda debacle is a story about the international community and abandonment. Instead of strengthening its presence in the country, the United Nations Security Council *withdrew* the bulk of its peacekeeping force of over 2,000 troops from Rwanda on 21 April 1994 at the height of the killings.

This book will tackle the latter part of the story, i.e. the causes of the abandonment of Rwanda by the UN. In addressing this issue, it is important to recognise another puzzle concerning the case, one that is intrinsic to the literature surrounding the subject itself. A common characteristic in previous research projects on the UN's failure in Rwanda is a lack of methodological self-awareness. With only a few exceptions, such as Michael Barnett's book *Eyewitness to a Genocide* (2002), previous studies have not paid sufficient attention to the particular methodologies that underpin their propositions. This shortcoming has allowed certain methodological fallacies to creep in, most notably the empiricist fallacy, in which the cause of an event is derived from the regularity of events. It is understandable that early accounts, prompted by the shocking failure of the UN fresh in their minds, tend to commit such a fallacy by deducing the causes of international inaction in the face of genocide from a 'historically proven fact', namely, the selfishness of great powers in general, and of the United States in particular.[9] The explanation for the UN's failure is drawn from the empirical wisdom which holds that the superpowers have regularly paralysed the working of the Security Council, particularly during the Cold War.[10] Subsequent literature explaining the Rwandan case has somewhat widened the scope for blame by claiming that not only states, but also officials of the UN Secretariat bear some responsibility for the failure.[11] However, a critical literature review reveals that these accounts are, to a greater or lesser degree, exposed to another methodological fallacy, namely methodological individualism. In the latter, social phenomena are seen as resulting from the decisions of individual actors alone, as if the whole (organisation) was never more than the sum of its parts (members of an organisation). From the ringside seat he occupied at the US mission to the UN at the time, Barnett has pointed out that the faults and failings were not just on the part of individual UN diplomats and officials, but can also be located in the UN bureaucracy as a whole, for example in bureaucratic indifference (Barnett 2002: x–xi). Hence, methodological individualist approaches are somewhat misguided simply because they fail to see the wood (UN system) for the trees (members of the system).

The above summary of the literature review unavoidably entails rather crude generalisations, and its purpose is *not* to imply that previous accounts offer *nothing but* the two methodological fallacies; on the contrary, the literature on the Rwandan case that already exists is unusually precise and informative. It discloses almost all necessary empirical facts relevant to explaining the UN's failure in Rwanda, particularly those exposed by the investigative journalist Linda Melvern's detailed studies. Nor is the purpose here to force all previous accounts into the conceptual moulds of methodological fallacies, as if each and every study would neatly fit into a certain predetermined category. Instead, the aim here is to reveal common methodological fallacies, which are committed most probably unintentionally, possibly even unconsciously. Hence, the method of organising the literature here is the abstraction of certain methodological fallacies emerging from that literature, not its merits and arguments per se. This book itself is naturally not immune to such fallacies either. It may even open up further methodological errors to be discovered by subsequent accounts. There is no previous, present or future research project that can capture the perfect explanation of the UN's failure in Rwanda, and this realisation warrants continuous self-reflectivity and self-criticism.

Self-reflectivity may enable the improvement of already existing models and explanations, as demonstrated in Anthony Giddens' theory of modernisation.

The common methodological shortcomings, i.e. the empiricist fallacy and methodological individualism, have generated two theoretical problems in the existing research on the subject that this book aims to address. The first problem can be encountered in a tendency to *reduction of explanation*. The empiricist fallacy follows the political realist worldview in that the usual suspects, namely 'those betraying great powers',[12] are indicted, in the manner of a typical Hobbesian image of world politics. This assessment would not be problematic if the method of falsification was used, eliminating other possible or alternative causes of the UN's collapse in Rwanda and leaving the lack of political will on the part of member states as the only plausible explanation. Such method has not been applied. Subsequent records take institutional factors into account, but nevertheless tend to restrict argumentation to the actions and omissions of individual UN officials. Thus, the explanatory factors of the failure are reduced to the behaviour of either states or of individual UN officials, with no considerable (read: 'causally effective') role given to the wider socio-historical context within which these behaviours were situated.

This book views a contextual analysis of the early 1990s as an essential step in understanding the Rwandan case. No evidence has been produced to counter the presumption that both the causes of the UN's breakdown in Rwanda and the potential to avert the disaster lay in the socio-historical factors of UN conflict management specific to that time. This was the era during which the Security Council, in co-operation with the Secretariat, demonstrated an unprecedented willingness to monitor international conflicts with the aim of preventing their outbreak in the first place. The early 1990s saw a fleeting moment of optimism in the Council's long history of impasse: it was an interregnum between the Cold War paralysis, caused by the bipolarity of world politics in the 1980s, and the late 1990s paralysis, caused by the crushing disappointments of UN peacekeeping in the early and mid-1990s.[13] During that brief period of optimism, the Council invoked mechanisms by which to control international conflicts, the term 'mechanism' here meaning 'social control' by monitoring institutions. According to this definition, as Colin Wight describes, 'A mechanism, even a social mechanism, is a process or technique for achieving a desired end state or outcome' (Wight 2004: 288). In the case of an early warning mechanism, for example, the desired outcome was the early detection of potential genocides.

In the Security Council, such control mechanisms usually emerge through interaction between member states and the Secretariat. One example of this type of interaction took place in January 1992, when the President of the Council asked the Secretary-General to come up with recommendations for strengthening the conflict management capacity of the UN, and Secretary-General Boutros Boutros-Ghali responded to this by writing *An Agenda for Peace*. The Agenda, published in May 1992, envisaged the establishment of early warning mechanisms, which were supposed to move the focus of UN conflict management from previous reactive and *ex post facto* measures to more proactive and preventive strategies (Boutros-Ghali 1999: 23–6). It is essential to appreciate that the early warning mechanism was invoked by the Secretary-General only two years prior to the genocide, and ask how it is possible that this mechanism failed so disastrously at the moment when it was so desperately needed.

Reductive explanation underlies the most serious 'blind spot' in existing accounts, namely the *lack of emancipatory vision*. Such a vision would inform how agents could have liberated themselves from unwanted and suppressive constraints, such as those structural factors of the UN system which impeded the ability of individual diplomats and officers to raise concerns regarding Rwanda. However, most of the studies are underpinned by the political realist assumption that the Security Council could not have risen above the constraints set by the selfish great powers of the Council.[14] Other accounts view the Rwandan case through a neo-liberal prism which portrays UN institutions as merely the instruments or powerless servants of states. These studies therefore argue that, irrespective of whether the Secretary-General could have recognised the genocide at an early stage and lobbied for intervention, such efforts would have made little difference vis-à-vis the member states of the Council once they had made up their minds to freeze all humanitarian interventions, following their failure in Somalia in 1993.[15] Hence, the Hobbesian and neo-liberal theoretical underpinnings effectively nullify the possibility of finding a means of emancipation in the UN's conduct of the genocide: the Organisation is viewed either as a victim of the 'irresistible forces' of great powers or as a powerless servant of states.

It is argued in this book that an exploration of mechanisms might be the key to providing an emancipatory vision. *An Agenda for Peace* proves that there was a meaningful effort underway in the Security Council to monitor international conflicts at the beginning of the 1990s. If such monitoring mechanisms had worked properly, the Rwandan genocide might have been prevented. The final chapter of this book will take this emancipatory vision even further; it will examine the hypothetical, or counterfactual, impact of post-2005 conflict management mechanisms on the prevention of the Rwandan genocide. It will be claimed that the UN peacebuilding architecture and the mainstreaming of the responsibility to protect, both of which were initiated at the 2005 UN World Summit, could have played a significant role in preventing the Rwandan genocide, if they had already been in operation in the early 1990s. Widening the ontological horizon of research from states to control mechanisms yields a more complex view of the UN and the Security Council, but, as a reward, it may reveal unrealised possibilities of emancipation inherent in those mechanisms. It could thus be said that freedom lies within complexity. However, it is equally important to expose those dysfunctions and constraints that hampered the working of control mechanisms. These possible defects may, in turn, encompass not only the lack of political will on the part of member states and institutional malfunctions, but also factors such as human limitations in predicting events in complex civil wars; cognitive dissonance; the rigidity of bureaucratic procedures; the loose coupling of modern organisations; the ensuing fragmentation of worldview; and the reproduction of stereotypical images of African conflicts.

Any research question usually hinges on the philosophical foundation of research, which in previous studies of Rwanda has been positivism, the dominant epistemology in IR theory. Although social scientists tend not to explicitly state their adherence to positivism, they often implicitly base their propositions upon positivist assumptions, namely the belief that facts are theory-neutral and phenomenalism, i.e. reliance on observed events.[16] This is also the case with previous investigations of the Rwandan crisis, which generally prefer simple observation of events to any particular theory as a means of illuminating why the UN failed. Hence, existing accounts either do not define any theory or research question at all, or pose a straightforward question implicitly, along the lines of: 'Why did the Security Council not stop the genocide?' Such an approach resembles in many respects a Sherlock Holmes type of detective story, as it strives to investigate meticulously and thoroughly all events and persons involved in the UN debacle and to scrutinise all pieces of information surrounding the case. This common method typically results in accurate chronological reportages, which produce evidence of the 'crime of indifference' committed by certain members of the Council. A further feature of positivism is atomism, which means looking for the smallest observable units that cannot be broken down any further, such as individuals in society (Smith 1998: 76). In this manner, the objective of researchers is to find those individual culprits inside the UN system whose actions and omissions led to a betrayal of Rwanda.

However, quantity possesses no quality of its own: the power of pure information-gathering or fact-finding cannot provide a substitute for the power of theoretical thinking, simply because all facts are theory-laden to some degree. A theory is a set of concepts used to explain some phenomenon (Silverman 1998: 103), so taking stock of phenomena as such is not sufficient to explain anything. Explanation requires theory. As most of the previous studies tend to disregard or undervalue theory and, instead, rush to describe the events surrounding the Rwandan shambles, they often imply a simplified explanation in which individual 'betrayers' and 'betraying' are taken as given facts. This study invokes theory in order to open up *all possible causes* of the malfunctioning of the UN without taking any apparent causes, such as betraying states, for granted, on the grounds that there might also be other 'troublemaking' factors in the UN system that merit attention. The question can therefore be formulated as follows: 'How is it *possible* that the Security Council failed to prevent the Rwandan genocide?'[17] Such an approach resembles not so much detective work as criminal psychology, in which it is not sufficient to ask, 'Why did actor X commit the crime?', but is also necessary to enquire, 'How is it possible that actor X could commit the crime?' Sometimes the motive for a crime is easier to solve than to trace the factors that enabled its perpetrator(s) to commit it in the first place. The motives may be rooted in greed, incitement, or self-defence, but a different question is how an ordinary person could possibly commit a cold-blooded murder without feeling a bit of sympathy, or witness a brutal crime without making a sound to stop or prevent it.

The latter question widens the circle of investigation from the motives of an actor to the circumstances and context of the crime and to the 'nature' or 'state of mind' of the agent. In the same way, the motive of the Security Council in allowing Rwandans to die is quite obvious: it was the political refusal of member states to put their soldiers in harm's way to 'save strangers'.[18] However, a much wider question to ask is how it was possible for ordinary UN diplomats and bureaucrats to disregard the most efficient mass killing in history. What are the ethics of the Security Council such that it could continue with 'business-as-usual' while a genocide was happening? It would be understandable if the alarm bells failed to ring when an 'ordinary routine abuse of human rights' was happening, but it is much harder to comprehend how the Council could be so indifferent when a 'supreme humanitarian emergency'[19] was occurring. In sum, what structural conditions enable decent actors to commit such horrendous acts year after year, decade after decade, and persevere uninterrupted by devastating failures, while faces change in bureaucracies? Whilst the motive behind the UN's failure obviously lay in member states (which answers the Why-question), an understanding of the factors that enabled the UN to act with such indifference requires taking into consideration not only states, but also its institutions and mechanisms (addressing the How-question).[20]

The most obvious alternative to the empiricist approach of positivism is critical realism, because the latter initially emerged as a critique of positivism in the philosophy of science (see, for example, Bhaskar 1997). Thus, critical realism must be strictly separated from political realism encompassing classical and neo-realism in IR theory. While the latter contains substantial – and often fallible – axioms concerning the universal nature of human beings and the state-system, critical realism allows a socio-historical case study to reveal its particular nature. As opposed to positivism, critical realism deems that explanation based on events, phenomena and appearances is unsatisfactory. One should always go beyond events to explain and understand the structures and mechanisms that produced them (Collier 1994: 49). What this means in terms of the Rwandan case is that one should not restrict analysis to the sequence of events surrounding the tragedy. Instead, one should explore the 'troublemaking' structures and mechanisms operative within the UN system at the beginning of the 1990s.

The crux of the critical realist critique is directed against the empiricist fallacy of positivism, which erroneously assumes that a constantly occurring correlation between events A and B implies that the former is the cause of the latter in every instance (Bhaskar 1997: 34). In existing accounts, A refers to the selfishness of great powers while B denotes the UN's failure, and they are seen as bound together in the constantly occurring paralysis of the Security Council. Critical realism, however, deems that real causes cannot be found in regularities but in particular socio-historical contexts. Selfish great powers do not always constitute the sole cause of the malfunctioning of the UN, though this was certainly often the case during the Cold War. There may be other troublemaking factors within the UN system which also merit attention.

Reductionism tends to limit its view to a single explanatory factor emphasised by a particular theory. This reduction, in turn, leads to an overall fragmentation of explanation. By emphasising the material powers of states, most of the studies characterised by political realism tend to disregard or underestimate the role that UN institutions and the Secretariat could have played in lobbying for intervention in Rwanda (see, for example, Feil 1998: 4; Kuperman 2001: viii). Certain investigations underpinned by neo-liberal assumptions do take UN institutions into consideration but fail to conceive of how the Secretariat could have made a difference in rescuing Rwandans vis-à-vis states. Critical realism can serve as an 'umbrella meta-theory' or 'safety net' to prevent the occurrence of such reductionism, and therefore has the potential to provide a consistent, balanced and holistic view of the causes of the Rwandan drama. This expansion of worldview, in turn, paves the way for an emancipatory vision: if the efforts of individual states and UN officials would have been insufficient to save Rwandans, could states, institutions and mechanisms have made a difference by working together? Although IR research boasts of being inter-disciplinary in nature, compartmentalisation is still prevalent in the discipline and only a few IR approaches actually succeed in supplying a consistent, multi-theoretical methodology to a research topic. Critical realism can respond to that challenge.

Martin Hollis and Steve Smith argue that IR theory and social science in general have been characterised by a tension between two methodological positions. The 'explaining' position (*Erklären*) views the social world as composed of external structures, whereas the 'understanding' viewpoint (*Verstehen*) relies on hermeneutics and historical methods to explicate meanings and collective rules (Hollis and Smith 1990: 4–5; 1991: 408–9). Despite an impressive range of studies on Rwanda, all previous books on the subject, except for Michael Barnett's study *Eyewitness to a Genocide* (2002), have provided an explanatory approach. They have meticulously *explained* on whose desks and on which dates reports of genocide landed, and how desk officers responded to, or, in most cases, ignored these crucial pieces of information. But most of the analyses have not gone further to try to *understand* those reasons and mechanisms inside experts' minds, in inter-subjective rules and in organisational conventions that hampered the processing of such information. Critical realism deems this explanation-driven 'story-telling' insufficient. Understanding is also necessary in any piece of research simply because *reasons are causes* (Patomäki 1996a: 108). The *reasons* why UN officials saw the genocide stereotypically as 'just another instance of mad tribal violence in Africa' and why it did not deserve attention within the UN bureaucracy were *causes* of the UN's subsequent withdrawal from Rwanda.

Critical realism and hermeneutics are similar in the sense that they both ask the post-Kantian question of what the necessary preconditions are for knowledge to be possible (Patomäki 2002a: 9). However, critical realism and hermeneutics have different interests in knowledge in the sense that the latter views the *communication of knowledge* as an intriguing research object, whereas critical realism strives to take a step further and explore the *production of knowledge*. Critical realism draws upon the work of the Frankfurt School by emphasising that knowledge is produced in order to reinforce power structures in society and to serve hidden interests, which function through certain mechanisms. Communication and language games are set in motion and regulated by these underlying mechanisms. Thus, going beyond communication to explore them is more revealing than researching the language games as such. What this means in terms of the Rwandan case is that the hermeneutical approach would concentrate on the Security Council's language games through which Rwanda was excluded from the concerns and sympathy of the international community, whereas critical realism would go further and aim to expose those mechanisms that started this draconian language game in the first place and kept it in motion throughout the genocide.

So what are the fundamental principles constitutive of the Lakatosian 'hard core' of critical realist philosophy (Lakatos 1978: 4)? The term 'critical realism' emerged from the elision of two main philosophical principles, namely scientific *realism* and *critical* naturalism (Collier 1994: x–xi). As Copernicus removed the human being from the self-imposed centre-stage of natural sciences, critical realism strives to launch a similar Copernican revolution in the social sciences. Scientific realism views research based on individual human actions as insufficient and hence seeks to examine the structures and mechanisms that underlie and affect actors' decisions (Bhaskar 1997: 19). What this means in terms of research on the cases of Rwanda and Darfur is that less attention should be paid to the omissions and failures of individual UN officials. Instead, greater emphasis should be placed on the dysfunctions of the wider structural framework within which those individuals were situated, such as a bureaucratic culture breeding indifference. This non-anthropocentric approach has a smaller chance of allocating individual responsibilities and indicting those individual UN diplomats and officials who should be blamed for the debacle. Instead, the scientific realist approach possesses a greater potential of revealing 'troublemaking' factors in the structures and mechanisms of the UN.

Critical naturalism brings an important counter-balance to the natural-scientific sound of the terms 'mechanisms' and 'structures' by claiming that social objects, unlike natural ones, are concept- and activity-dependent and do not uphold the distinction between fact and value (Bhaskar 1998b: 38). Hence, a social scientist should always maintain a critical stance towards research objects and never take speeches, statements and narratives as 'objective truths', because they usually serve particular political purposes. The significance of this to understanding the Rwandan drama is that one should critically evaluate certain statements made by UN officials, according to which the UN's failure had nothing to do with its knowledge-production processes in general, or early warning in particular, but was caused by the political unwillingness of member states. Kofi Annan, the Under-Secretary-General for Peacekeeping at the time, formulated this claim as follows: 'If there was a problem, it was not one of information or intelligence. The problem was lack of political will.'[21] Similarly, the then Secretary-General Boutros-Ghali asserted to the author that,

> Member states were opposed to intervention in Rwanda, with early warning and without early warning. So the real problem is this: if there is no political will among the major actors in the Security Council, any [UN] system which we try to improve will be useless.[22]

On closer scrutiny, however, Annan's and Boutros-Ghali's arguments cannot be sustained, because the Secretariat did not convey any early warning signals of the genocide to the Security Council until the beginning of May 1994, one month after the massacres had begun. Nevertheless, both Annan's and Boutros-Ghali's statements have, unfortunately, managed to fulfil their ulterior motive: to lead researchers to indict the usual suspects, namely selfish states, and to exclude the Secretariat *as part of the UN's knowledge-producing system* from the sphere of blame.

The main methodological implication seems to be that unlike 'people sitting in offices',[23] which are the research objects of anthropocentric approaches, mechanisms are not directly observable. While the previous analyses of the Rwandan drama have concentrated on concrete, i.e. tangible and observable, factors, such as individual UN diplomats and officials, this book strives to examine control mechanisms that are abstract, non-observable. Being abstract, however, does not mean being somehow less real than concrete objects. When Secretary-General Boutros-Ghali proposed the early warning mechanism in 1992, he did not refer to a fuzzy object belonging to a wonderland or an empty conceptual shell, but to a real control mechanism belonging to the world of preventable conflicts.

The ontological nature of these mechanisms requires a particular *method*, namely abstraction. A method here is understood as a specific research technique (Silverman 1998: 103). In Andrew Sayer's critical realist method of double movement derived from Karl Marx, abstraction equates to the isolation of one-sided elements, such as mechanisms, through abstract thinking (*Begriff*) from the complex combination of various elements/mechanisms appearing in observation (*Vorstellung*).[24] In Sayer's method, this move *Vorstellung → Begriff* is followed by the return move *Begriff → Vorstellung*, when abstracted elements or mechanisms are situated back in their concrete setting in order to examine which alternative (better) outcomes could have been produced, had certain 'troublemaking' elements or mechanisms been eliminated (Sayer 1992: 86–91). The second move of Sayer's method thus refers to an emancipatory endeavour to explore alternative courses of action to those actually taken. In a nutshell, applying Sayer's method enables this study to examine the control mechanisms of the UN, and to attain an emancipatory vision of what more could have been done to save Rwandans.

The crux of the argumentation here will concern Rwanda; however, it will have major implications for the case of Darfur by revealing certain 'troublemaking' mechanisms which not only produced the UN's failure in Rwanda but also *persist* in the UN system today. These structural factors have compounded shortcomings in Darfur, and will almost certainly generate 'future Rwandas'. The book is structured in the following manner: before attempting to explain and understand the Security Council's shortcomings in preventing the genocide in Rwanda, it is first necessary to describe the conflict itself. Thus, Chapter 1 will provide a chronological narrative of the main events of the Rwandan crisis. The aim of Chapter 4, in turn, is to provide a critical review of the existing accounts of the UN's failures in the light of the theoretical framework developed in

Chapter 2. The main critique will be directed at the anthropocentrism of this literature, i.e. the belief that actors alone, rather than structures or mechanisms, played the primary role in the Rwandan case. This book will develop an alternative to the mainstream anthropocentric explanation, namely a possibilistic approach guided by a critical realist methodology.

Chapter 3 will scrutinise the socio-historical context of the 1990s with a view to exploring those mechanisms that were most pertinent to UN conflict management at that time. Four such mechanisms will be considered as possible explanatory factors of the Rwandan drama, namely early warning, bureaucratic rationalisation, organisational learning and Western normalisation. Chapters 5 and 6 will then examine the role that these mechanisms played in the UN's breakdown in Rwanda. Chapter 5 will analyse the early warning mechanism in more detail. Chapter 6 will examine bureaucratic rationalisation, organisational learning and the role of Western normalisation in the Rwandan case. In sum, this book seeks to approach the Rwandan case *indirectly* from the socio-historical context of UN conflict management in the 1990s. As a result, important clues will be found within that context indicative of certain dysfunctions of mechanisms that could help to explain the Rwandan drama.

Chapter 7 will invoke the lessons learned from the Rwandan tragedy as a reflective point against which to consider the implications of Darfur for humanitarian intervention, conflict management and PKOs (peacekeeping operations). Darfur and Rwanda will be regarded as two significant cases indicative of a wider tendency, or direction, in UN conflict management in the course of the past ten years and beyond. By investigating what has remained the same in the relevant UN structures since the 1990s, what advances have been made and what could still be improved, it is possible not only to assess the most recent progress made with regard to humanitarian intervention but also to anticipate future progress. This book will argue that, although political will on the part of member states remains the most crucial factor in explaining the success and failure of PKOs, structural transformations in conflict management strategies can considerably alter that will and enable a more rapid and desirable response to humanitarian crises of the future.

This book will apply the method of double movement. However, this approach is not so much a method as such but more an abstract 'meta-method', for it outlines only a general methodological framework of abstracting mechanisms from 'raw materials', i.e. from observations of events and phenomena. The Linda Melvern Rwanda Genocide Archive (henceforth: the *Melvern Archive*) in particular is the single most important source of these 'raw materials': the handwritten notes contained in the archive, which emanate from the Council's informal discussions on the Rwandan conflict, provide very accurate information on the events in the Council during the genocide. Thus, much of the information obtained through interviews in this book is corroborated and specified (e.g. dates) with the help of the *Melvern Archive*.[25] After publishing her groundbreaking book, *A People Betrayed* (2000), the investigative journalist and writer Linda Melvern collected the material used for her book in an archive, which was then donated to two universities for the sake of its preservation: the National University of Rwanda in Butare and the University of Wales in Aberystwyth. The *Melvern Archive* contains copies of dozens of authentic and previously unpublished internal UN documents, such as part of the cable traffic between UNAMIR[26] and UN Headquarters. The majority of the archive still remains to be analysed, and is not referred to in the existing literature except in Melvern's own books. This book aims to uncover new information on the Rwandan case by making use of the archive, and to offer an alternative viewpoint using the documents therein. The purpose is not to counter Melvern's interpretation of the archive's material but to add a new layer of 'understanding' to it. Two techniques will be applied here in order to interpret the documents: hermeneutics, which endeavours to elucidate the meanings of a text from the perspective of its author (Bryman 2001: 380–3), and the contextualised approach, which is used to understand effects wrought by the context (time and place) in which a text was written (Hodder 1994: 393).

Unlike the mainstream literature characterised by the 'blame game' aimed at the 'Permanent Five',[27] this book will focus on those who have been portrayed as 'a few good men' in the Rwandan drama, namely the non-permanent members of the Security Council, especially the role played by Nigeria and the Czech Republic. The purpose is neither to uncover new aspects of their blameworthiness nor to reinstate Edmund Burke's wisdom that, 'All that is required for evil to prevail is for good men to do nothing'. Instead, non-permanent members are studied here as a means of revealing the *striking consensus* prevailing in the Council on the way in which the Rwandan conflict was imagined and portrayed, a consensus that cannot be explained solely by the lack of political will or by the *Realpolitik* of permanent Council members. It can only be explained by certain *underlying mechanisms* that affected *all* members of the Council, Nigeria as well as the US. This methodological turn in the research on the Rwandan case calls for a shift from an individualist and atomistic ontology to a relational and holistic one; from explaining the policy of individual member states to understanding the UN system and its relationships as a whole.

1   Rwanda, the genocide of our time

Introduction

Before setting out to explain and understand how it is possible that the UN Security Council failed to prevent the massacres in Rwanda, it is first necessary to describe the crisis. The purpose of this chapter is to provide a chronological and narrative story of the events of the Rwandan conflict. It will thereby lay the groundwork for subsequent chapters, which will tackle the more fundamental questions concerning the failures of the UN. This chapter will contest the way in which mass killings are universally labelled as 'genocides' at the expense of analyses of their particular historical circumstances and social contexts. A comparative framework will therefore not be applied; instead, the following analysis aspires to explore the particular conditions and mechanisms that produced the devastating events in Rwanda.

The Rwandan genocide was conducted in a routine and mechanical manner not (only) by madmen but mostly by normal people. As Gérard Prunier notes, this confirms Hannah Arendt's adage that evil is extremely banal (Prunier 1998: xii). The *nettoyage*, or 'cleansing', of the minority Tutsi population became the civic duty of every Hutu in the country. Posters, leaflets and radio broadcasts had dehumanised the Tutsi into 'snakes', 'cockroaches' and 'animals' (Physicians for Human Rights (UK) 1994: 10). By the beginning of the genocide the Tutsi had become a socially dead people, like the Jews had become by the beginning of Hitler's Final Solution. Dehumanisation, among other factors, created the ideal conditions for genocide. Moreover, Hutu extremists portrayed Tutsi as *génocidaires* themselves, who were allegedly plotting the extermination of the Hutu. This was pure misinformation, but fear among Hutu spread rapidly. Thus, when the genocide finally began, the killed Tutsi accumulated at three times the rate of dead Jews during the Holocaust. By some accounts, as many Rwandans killed as were killed (Berkeley 1998).

The potential for genocide began to emerge gradually under the colonial rule of Germany from 1897 to 1919, and then under Belgian authority from 1919 to 1962. The pace of this dangerous development was intensified with the 1959 revolution and the birth of the Hutu Republic. However, the operational mechanisms of genocide, such as killing squads and executive plans, were created only from 1992 onwards. This acknowledgement of the complexity of the Rwandan crisis is necessary, as it prevents us from drifting into backward causalities,[1] where reconstruction of past events overcomes description of past events. To use Colin Wight's definition, backward causalities are complicit in the constitution of realities they merely claim to describe. They are similar to what John Shotter terms an *ex post facto* fallacy, which is committed as follows: being tempted to take one specific descriptive statement as true of a situation which is in fact subject to a number of possible interpretations, and then perceiving the constructed true statement retrospectively as quite definite (Shotter 1993: 85). Previous accounts have tended to commit an *ex post facto* fallacy by taking the term 'genocide' as the true and definite statement to describe the situation in Rwanda, without considering other possible interpretations.

Alain Destexhe begins his detailed account of the Rwandan conflict with the definition of three genocides in the twentieth century. Only then does he go on to elaborate the causes of the crisis, such as the aggravation of ethnic divisions and political extremism (Destexhe 1995). The Genocide Convention, which was signed by UN Member States on 9 December 1948, defines genocide as a criminal act with intent to destroy a national, ethnic, racial or religious group in whole or in part.[2] The Rwandan massacres undoubtedly amounted to a genocide, as there were massive crimes against humanity committed with the intent of destroying the Tutsi as an ethnic group. Destexhe is also right, at least in legal terms, as to what constituted the three genocides of the twentieth century, namely the massacres of Armenians by the Ottoman Turks from 1915 to 1916, the Holocaust and the Rwandan genocide.[3]

Where the above analysis might be somewhat misleading, however, is in prioritising 'genocide' over particular historical circumstances that led to the killings in Rwanda. It is true that *describing* the Rwandan conflict retrospectively as 'genocide' is the most adequate, evaluative, precise and accurate description of what actually happened there, as the judgemental rationality of critical realism also requires.[4] However, *beginning* the narrative history with 'genocide' carries a *wrong perlocutionary force*. For, to begin the story with 'genocide' is to ignore all the other possible interpretations and elements of the crisis in existence in 1994, such as 'civil war' and 'politicide'. What the perlocutionary force of the above investigation does is to create a sense of sensation: the genocide was occurring, the international community did nothing to stop it and, worst of all, the international community clearly *knew* in advance that it was going to happen. At the same time, the account conflates 'ways to talk about things' (transitive objects), i.e. 'genocide', with 'things' (intransitive objects), that is, the development of the situation in Rwanda. In short, one claims to see clearly the seeds of genocide in Rwandan history but begins his/her story by sowing them himself/ herself.

Therefore, judgemental rationality requires that this chapter will not begin with 'genocide' but with an analysis of the necessary relations that led to the Rwandan conflict, such as ethnic relations between the Hutu and Tutsi and the rise of political extremism. Thus far, researchers have come to a consensus that there was a causal complex at work leading to the genocide. Helen M. Hintjens divides these factors into three categories:

1   external influences of colonial and neo-colonial politics based on 'divide and rule', which created cleavages between the beneficiary Tutsi and suppressed Hutu;
2   domestic causes, including demographic and ethnic factors, such as overpopulation of a small country and the resulting struggle for scarce resources; and
3   psychological factors, such as deeply rooted social conformism and the blind obedience of Rwandans (Hintjens 1999: 243).

Three other prominent researchers on Rwanda, Filip Reyntjens, Gérard Prunier and René Lemarchand, agree that it was political factors, as opposed to ethnic ones, that formed the core group of causes in the causal complex leading to the genocide (Lemarchand 1999: 2; Prunier 1998: xiii; Reyntjens 1996: 240). Prunier best summarises this view: 'The ruling fraction of the country's elite manipulated the existing "ethnic" raw material into an attempt at political survival' (Prunier 1998: 141). The emphasis put on regime survival serves the purpose of downgrading the popular and fallible view of Rwanda and Africa in general as the Conradian 'Heart of Darkness', where tribal violence prevails and explains all troubles. The sense of belonging to an ethnic group, however, is not synonymous with conflict, nor does a political elite necessarily use ethnicity as a tool for violent purposes. Therefore, Lemarchand makes an important distinction between 'moral' and 'political tribalism', the latter meaning 'the use of ethnic identities in political competition with other groups' (Lemarchand 1999: 2).[5]

In order to unravel the complex dynamics of political tribalism, it is necessary to analyse ethnicity first as the 'raw material', then to examine its subsequent exploitation for political purposes, and finally to reveal the factors that ultimately triggered this explosive mix into genocide. Therefore this chapter will proceed as follows. The first section concerning precolonial and colonial Rwanda will address the invariant factor of ethnicity, which has been exploited for various political reasons, first by German and Belgian colonial administrators from 1897 to 1962. The second section will examine how ethnicity was subsequently manipulated by the Hutu rulers: the Kayibanda government (1962–1973) and the Habyarimana government (1973–1994). Although the reasons for ethnic manipulation vary between the colonial and Hutu rulers, its consequences were invariably detrimental, contributing to an increase in the potential for genocide. The second section will proceed to touch upon the mechanisms of mass extermination as well as the main triggers that activated the deadly combination of ethnic bipolarity and political extremism into genocide. Furthermore, it will provide an overview of conflict management in Rwanda. The aim, however, will not be to discuss the failure of conflict management, nor to explicate its causes, as these issues will be examined in subsequent chapters.

Precolonial and colonial Rwanda

> They were being killed for so long that they were already dead.
>
> (Laurent Nkongoli; quoted in Gourevitch 1999: 23)

Rwanda is among the few African countries that have only two significant ethnic groups. The Hutu group is by far the largest with 85–90 per cent of the population; the other major group, Tutsi, being a minority with 10–15 per cent. The Twa constitutes a marginal group of only 1 per cent (Reyntjens 1996: 244). Using the term 'group' here instead of 'tribe' refers to the fact that, in contrast to the popular image, the Tutsi and Hutu have none of the characteristics of tribes, which mean micro-nations. When the early explorers arrived in Rwanda in the 1890s, they realised that these groups were not hugely different, but not similar either. On the one hand, the Hutu and Tutsi share the same culture, religion and Bantu language, i.e. *kinyarwanda*, and they have traditionally intermarried, but still they have different somatic types. The physical appearance of the Hutu resembles the standard Bantu aspect, whereas the Tutsi are tall and thin, often displaying sharp facial features similar to Europeans. Furthermore, the Hutu have traditionally been peasants cultivating land, whereas the Tutsi have made their living as cattle-herders (Prunier 1998: 5).

The Hutu and Tutsi have also differed in terms of political power. In the fifteenth century the Tutsi arrived from the Horn of Africa, probably from southern Ethiopia, establishing feudal kingdoms in the lands now called Rwanda and Burundi (Prunier 1998: 16). The Tutsi formed an aristocracy with the king, *mwami*, at the top of the hierarchy. Through a complex feudal order the Tutsi ruled over the Hutu by controlling the land, cattle economy, the monarchy and religious life (Sellström and Wohlgemuth 1995: 10; Vassall-Adams 1994: 7). The binding force in this social order consisted of *ubuhake*, or clientship contracts, which were entered into by a patron and client. In return for the labour and services of a client, a patron provided his client with protection, the use of land and cattle. Although *ubuhake* evolved with time, in the classical form of *ubuhake* a patron gave a cow to his client. The Hutu were most likely to find themselves at the bottom of this system as clients, under the protection of Tutsi patrons (Prunier 1998: 13). However, *ubuhake* formed a complex network where virtually everyone, except *mwami*, could be a client to someone else at a higher social level (Sellström and Wohlgemuth 1996: 23).

Although *ubuhake* and the feudal order created unequal relationships between Hutu and Tutsi, as well as structural violence and even potential for genocide, neither of these systems was a sufficient condition for ethnic conflict. Wars were also fought in precolonial Rwanda, but they were not waged among different ethnic lineages but were mostly for the purpose of defending the kingdom against external enemies, for expanding the kingdom by conquest, or for stealing cattle from neighbouring non-Rwandan tribes (Prunier 1998: 14). In precolonial times Hutu and Tutsi lived side by side relatively peacefully. In fact, as Tor Sellström and Lennart Wohlgemuth point out, *ubuhake* was an important factor in keeping society together until it was brought to an end in the 1950s. It was during the colonial rule of Germany from 1897 to 1919, and then under the Belgian rule from 1919 to 1962, that ethnicity was politically manipulated, thereby creating an ethnic tinderbox ready to explode. An integral part in the birth of this new 'political tribalism' was the 'Hamitic thesis', a product of the nineteenth-century racial thinking that was rapidly introduced to Rwanda by Western explorers, missionaries and anthropologists. In this book the history of Central Africa is viewed as the conquest of inferior Bantu races by superior Hamitic or Semitic races, the former referring to the native Hutu race, and the latter being the pastoral Tutsi invaders from Ethiopia. The Tutsi were viewed as a relative race to the Europeans, both descending from the Caucasus, and therefore the Tutsi were 'bound' to lead and rule over the 'primitive' Hutu. Everything valuable in Rwanda, whether cultural, social or political, was attributed to Tutsi achievements. That the physical features of the Tutsi resembled those of the Europeans was seen as proof of their superiority (Sellström and Wohlgemuth 1996: 10–11).

The Hamitic thesis had dramatic consequences. First, it became an unquestioned scientific canon for German and Belgian colonial authorities, which determined that the political and administrative posts were exclusively granted to Tutsi. Furthermore, *ubuhake* was reinforced to benefit Tutsi. From the end of the 1920s, the Belgian colonial rulers executed an administrative reform, culminating in *Programme Voisin* in 1930, which stated that political posts had to be filled by Tutsi (Sellström and Wohlgemuth 1996: 11). Priority in education was given to Tutsi children in order to exclude the Hutu from the future political elite. This exclusion resulted in frustration and discontent among the Hutu, which, in turn, played a role in the 1959 violence against the Tutsi (Prunier 1998: 33). Second, the Hamitic thesis had a direct impact on the local population. As Prunier puts it, 'The result of this heavy bombardment with highly value-laden stereotypes for some sixty years ended by inflating the Tutsi cultural ego inordinately and crushing Hutu feelings until they coalesced into an aggressively resentful inferiority complex' (Prunier 1998: 9). There were other administrative reforms imposed by colonial rule that also contributed to the tearing apart of the traditional social fabric. The introduction of obligatory identity cards in 1933 deepened the cleavages between the ethnic groups, as they showed which group, i.e. Hutu, Tutsi or Twa, a person belonged to (Sellström and Wohlgemuth 1996: 11).

Hutu Republic and genocide

> For the crime of being a Tutsi, I had to beg pardon.
> (A survivor of genocide; quoted in African Rights 1995: 299)

The aggravation of ethnic cleavages and the subsequent resentment felt by the Hutu population had increased the potential for ethnic conflict throughout the colonial period, especially in the 1930s. They were actualised for the first time on a massive scale in 1959, triggered by a Hutu revolution and the abolition of the Tutsi monarchy. The Prosecutor of the International Criminal Tribunal for Rwanda traces the roots of the 1994 genocide back to that period: 'The revolution of 1959 marked the beginning of a period of ethnic clashes between the Hutu and the Tutsi in Rwanda, causing hundreds of Tutsi to die and thousands more to flee the country in the years immediately following.'[6] The manipulation of ethnic 'raw materials' for political purposes was not halted by the emergence of the Hutu elite. In contrast, the establishment of modern political parties in 1959 in effect reinforced the ethnic lineages. *PARMEHUTU, Parti du Mouvement de L'Emancipation des Bahutu* (Party of the Movement and of Hutu Emancipation) and *APROMOSA, Association Pour la Promotion Sociale des Masses* (Association for the Social Promotion of the Masses) were composed first and foremost of Hutu, whereas *UNAR, Union Nationale Rwandaise* (Rwandese National Union) and *RADER, Rassemblement Démocratique Rwandais* (Rwandese Democratic Union) were dominated by Tutsi. What is notable here is that both the Hutu and Tutsi parties soon adapted racial rhetorics from the colonial past, and that tensions and physical violence between, say, *PARMEHUTU* and *UNAR* in November 1959, were viewed not only in political terms but also in racial and ethnic terms. Thus the ensuing violence was mainly between Hutu and Tutsi (Prunier 1998: 45–8).

The two prominent Hutu parties *PARMEHUTU* and *APROMOSA* won 83 per cent of the popular vote in the first parliamentary elections on 25 September 1961 (Sellström and Wohlgemuth 1996: 11). Rwanda became formally independent on 1 July 1962 under Grégoire Kayibanda's presidency. Rwanda became republican, but the social and political system established by *PARMEHUTU* simply replaced the old Tutsi-dominated institutions with a new set of Hutu-dominated ones. Identity cards were retained and used for discrimination against Tutsi in education, the civil service and armed forces. Structural and physical violence against Tutsi forced many of them to move to the neighbouring countries of Zaire (the Democratic Republic of Congo), Burundi, Uganda and Tanzania. Once there, the exiled Tutsi formed guerrilla bands known as 'cockroaches', or *Inyenzi*, and launched attacks against the Rwandese army and Hutu officials hoping to return by force. The *PARMEHUTU* government exploited the *Inyenzi* threat by initiating reprisals against Tutsi civilians in order to gain popular support, which, in turn, caused more refugee flows (African Rights 1995: 12). The biggest killing of Tutsi followed an attack by *Inyenzi* from Burundi on 21 December 1963, which resulted in an estimated 10,000–13,000 Tutsi deaths.[7]

If the 1959 events depict a type of 'democratic' or 'demographic' revolution, then 1973 saw an example of what could be classified a 'moral revolution', as Major-General Juvénal Habyarimana instigated a coup d'état to restore peace and stability to the country. Indeed, under Habyarimana's rule the Tutsi felt less vulnerable to physical violence, compared to the turbulent years of the 1960s, but the disadvantage of Habyarimana's policy was the continuation of structural violence against the Tutsi. What Habyarimana established was an Albanian-style 'development dictatorship', where the values of economic development, progress and justice prevailed, accompanied by totalitarian control, spying and harsh punishments. Political parties were outlawed except one, *MRND, Mouvement Révolutionnaire National pour le Développement* (National Revolutionary Movement for Development) (Prunier 1998: 74–7). The Tutsi remained marginalised in the centrally controlled system. Habyarimana upheld Kayibanda's quota system where, for example, only a small percentage of Tutsi were allowed to attend schools and the Tutsi were granted only one seat in the nineteen-member cabinet (Melvern 2000: 25).

It was within this clandestine political environment characterised by secretive and corrupt policies and a total lack of transparency that the early forms of genocidal extremism began to develop. In addition to the presidency, another power base began to emerge. It was named the 'little house', *Akazu*, a term derived from the precolonial times when it meant a small circle of courtiers around the king. The *Akazu* was also known as '*Clan de Madame*', whose leading figure was the president's wife, Agathe Habyarimana, together with her three brothers Protais Zigiranyirazo, Colonel Pierre-Célestin Rwagafilita and Séraphin Rwabukumba. What enabled the *Akazu* to become even more powerful than the presidency itself was first and foremost the vast personal networks they were able to create in every sector of society, including politics, the army, finance, media, agriculture, science and religion (Melvern 2000: 42–3). Added to the relentless hatred of the *Akazu* against the Tutsi, the deadly combination of power and extremism was almost ready to explode.

The lethal mix of extremism and the political powers possessed by the *Akazu* was not triggered into genocide by one single spark. During the 1990s several triggering factors emanated from Uganda with *Inyenzi* attacks, from Burundi where 50,000–100,000 people were massacred only six months prior to the Rwandan genocide, and ultimately from within the country itself. On 1 October 1990 the Rwanda Patriotic Army (RPA), composed of Tutsi refugees who had fled from Rwanda to Uganda after the violence of 1959, carried out a major *Inyenzi* invasion of Rwanda with 10,000 well-armed refugee warriors aiming to depose the government (Otunnu 1999: 31). The Rwanda Patriotic Front (RPF) was beaten back, but the invasion was followed by recurrent RPF raids into Rwandan territory, as well as by counter-offensives of the *FAR, Forces Armées Rwandaises* (Rwandan army), thus provoking a protracted civil war from 1990 to 1994. The opposition to Habyarimana became emboldened by the civil war, which, alongside pressure from the international community and the RPF, forced Habyarimana to initiate political reforms. In April 1991 the single-party system was abolished, and by August 1991 about twelve new political parties had formed. The tense political atmosphere created by the civil war and the new political opportunities offered an ideal breeding-ground for extremism. The extremist Hutu *CDR, Coalition pour la Défense de la République* (Coalition for the Defense of the Republic) was founded in 1992 (Kakwenzire and Kamukama 1999: 66–9). Both the extremists and Habyarimana government exploited *Inyenzi* attacks in their political rhetoric to justify ethnic violence against Tutsi civilians, who were depicted as collaborators of the RPF and a menace to the Hutu power in Rwanda.

In the wake of political extremism the nascent mechanisms of genocide began to emerge. The Presidential Guard was created after the 1990 *Inyenzi* invasion, and it was the most trusted sector of the army, composed exclusively of Hutu extremists (Kakwenzire and Kamukama 1999: 78). Militias, or civilian terrorist groups to be more precise about their true nature, were set up in 1992. The most notorious militia group *Interahamwe*, meaning 'those who stand together' or 'those who attack together', was an armed youth wing of *MRND*. The young thugs of *Interahamwe* were recruited from among the unoccupied and disaffected youth, and they were trained, armed and led by the Presidential Guard, and supervised by the *Akazu*. Their intensive military training took place in different parts of the country, and the three-week programmes involved indoctrination in ethnic hatred against Tutsi and methods of mass murder. The aim of *Interahamwe* was to terrorise perceived enemies of the regime, whether opposition figures or Tutsi. Another militia group *Impuzamugambi*, meaning 'those who have a single aim', was created by the *CDR* but had similar activities, aims and structure to *Interahamwe* (Des Forges 1999: 4; Gourevitch 1999: 94–5; Kakwenzire and Kamukama 1999: 78–9; Physicians for Human Rights (UK) 1994: 10).

With time the mechanisms of mass murder were expanded to encompass the whole nation. In early 1993, Colonel Théoneste Bagosora, who had direct links to the *Akazu* and was later to become the main architect of the genocide, sketched out the programme of a 'civilian self-defence force' with the aim of recruiting local population to mass murders. The programme also provided their leaders and weapons. Large numbers of machetes were imported from China to arm every third adult Hutu male, as AK-47 assault rifles were too expensive for wider distribution (Des Forges 1999: 5). The media became a vital element in expanding the fear and hatred against the Tutsi. *Kangura*, a journal sponsored by the *Akazu*, published the 'Hutu Ten Commandments' on 10 December 1990, with the eighth commandment reading: 'The Bahutu [Hutu] should stop having mercy on the Batutsi [Tutsi]' (African Rights 1995: 43). The state-owned Radio Rwanda and the *Radio Télévision Libre des Mille Collines* (*RTLMC*), also funded by the *Akazu*, spread misinformation about the Tutsi. For example, in March 1992 the *RTLMC* announced the 'discovery' of a Tutsi plot to massacre Hutu, which was in fact pure misinformation, but it triggered the slaughter of 300 Tutsi by the Hutu militia in Bugesera (Gourevitch 1999: 93–4).

However, the international efforts remained preoccupied with tackling the triggering factors, i.e. the civil war, rather than the 'powder keg' itself, i.e. the potential of genocide. The United Nations became directly involved in the Rwandan situation on 22 June 1993, when the Security Council established the UN Observer Mission Uganda–Rwanda (UNOMUR) with Resolution 846. With 81 military observers, UNOMUR was to monitor the Uganda–Rwanda border. The purpose was to verify that no military assistance reached Rwanda, in the hope of supporting the ongoing peace talks in Arusha, Tanzania (Boutros-Ghali

1996: 19).[8] The Arusha peace process was facilitated by the Organization of the African Unity and the Tanzanian government, and its purpose was to bring about peace between the RPF and the Rwandan government. The formal negotiation phase started in June 1992 and ended with the signing of the peace accord on 4 August 1993, which determined power-sharing arrangements. The peace accord set up the transitional government that included the *MRND*, the opposition, as well as the RPF. It also determined that the two adversary armies were to be integrated into one national army, in which both the RPF and *FAR* would be given 50 per cent of the command positions (Jones 1999: 131–43). Extremists hardened their anti-Tutsi views, which further increased the probability of genocide. In order to safeguard the peace accord, the Security Council established the UN Assistance Mission for Rwanda (UNAMIR) on 5 October 1993 with Resolution 872. UNAMIR was composed of 2,548 military personnel, and its tasks were to monitor a demilitarised zone along the Rwanda–Uganda border, to assist in providing security in and around Kigali in a weapons-free zone, and to assist in maintaining security throughout the country (Boutros-Ghali 1996: 25–7).

The final triggering factor that sparked the genocide came on 6 April 1994, when the plane carrying the presidents of Rwanda and Burundi was shot down by a ground-to-air missile at Kigali airport. The genocide was not directed through one institutional channel, but involved various actors at different levels. On 7 April, prior to the formation of the interim government, members of the Rwandan army, including the Presidential Guard, killed the prime minister of the transitional government Agathe Uwilingiyimana and ten Belgian UNAMIR peacekeepers that were protecting her.[9] Within hours of Habyarimana's plane crash, *Interahamwe* and the army set up roadblocks, identified Tutsi with the help of their identity cards or from their physical characteristics, and killed them and opposition figures on the spot. The major massacres were usually directed and initiated by the Rwandese army, Presidential Guard, *Gendarmerie Nationale* (National Police) or communal police, who also possessed weapons including assault rifles, grenades, machine guns and even mortars. After the military had launched attacks on unarmed Tutsi, individual civilians were encouraged, ordered or forced to join the killings with machetes, hoes, axes, hammers and *masus*, i.e. clubs studded with nails (Des Forges 1999: 8).

The mechanisms of extermination exploited the strong central governance and social obedience of the Rwandese very effectively. Indeed, without these elements it would have been impossible to conduct large-scale massacres rapidly. The Prime Minister of the Interim Government incited and ordered the civilians to perpetrate massacres, and the orders cascaded down efficiently, from the top to the very bottom of local administration, from *préfets* and *bourgmestres* to *conseillers de secteur* and *responsables de cellule*. The mechanisms of genocide had to adapt with the passing of time. During the first days of killing in Kigali, death squads moved systematically from house to house and eliminated 'common enemies', i.e. Tutsi or opposition politicians named on the lists. By the middle of the first week, the local administrators, such as *préfets* and *bourgmestres*, lured or drove Tutsi from their homes and gathered them in government offices, churches, schools or other public sites, where they would subsequently be massacred en masse. Towards the end of April, greater control was brought over the killing, and by mid-May authorities ordered the tracking down of the last surviving Tutsi. All the way through the genocide, brutal and sadistic methods were applied. Maiming, torture, sexual abuse and coercing family members into killing each other was common (Des Forges 1999: 8–10). The role of the hate radio *RTLMC* in mobilising the whole nation into genocide cannot be underestimated. On 6 April, the first day of the genocide, the *RTLMC* announced that 'Tutsis needed to be killed', the widespread message that was repeated to the very end of the genocide (Keane 1996: 10).

The UNAMIR peacekeeping mission was not adjusted to an intensive conflict situation, let alone genocide, but to operate patrols in weapon-free areas and demilitarised zones regulated by the peace accord. As Force Commander Major General Roméo A. Dallaire describes the situation after the beginning of the genocide, 'We ran out of water, we ran out of food, we ran out of fuel, we had guys syphoning the fuel tanks in the vehicle park here just to keep some of [APCs] going.'[10] Initially, it was planned for UNAMIR to have twenty-two armoured personnel carriers (APCs) and eight military helicopters in order to enable rapid reaction operations, but no helicopters arrived and only eight APCs were provided, of which only a few were in operational condition (Melvern 2000: 85). The final attempt at intervention came on 22 June with Resolution 929 which authorised France and Senegal to conduct a humanitarian operation in Rwanda. From 23 June 1994, *Opération Turquoise* was launched, which saved approximately 12,000–15,000 lives in the safe humanitarian zones created in south-western Rwanda. However, it came far too late to save the hundreds of thousands who had perished in the genocide. Moreover, *Opération Turquoise* allowed some of the perpetrators of genocide to flee from advancing RPF troops to the neighbouring Democratic Republic of Congo (Klinghoffer 1998: 82–5). Meanwhile, the RPF continued to advance towards Kigali. It had initiated an invasion when the genocide had begun. Eventually, the RPF managed to establish military control over the whole country. By the time of the declaration of a unilateral cease-fire by the RPF on 18 July, at least 800,000 people had been killed (Boutros-Ghali 1996: 121). Ironically enough, it turned out that the most efficient instrument of the UN in protecting Rwandans had actually been the 444 troops left behind after the withdrawal of UNAMIR. During the genocide, they had been safeguarding a few humanitarian pockets established in places like the *Amahoro* Stadium, hotels and hospitals. This fact left Force Commander Dallaire, and the whole international community, to speculate about the possible capabilities of a strengthened UNAMIR force.[11]

'Lessons learned', peoples betrayed:[12] genocide ten years on

It is hardly a coincidence that calls for humanitarian intervention in Darfur in spring 2004 emerged simultaneously with the commemoration of the Rwandan genocide that took place ten years earlier. Images of razed villages and stories of killing and rape in Darfur immediately called to mind haunting memories of Rwanda, painful recollections of which were being repeated and relived in commemorative events all over the world. In Rwanda, the killing campaign was nurtured by the idea of Hutu Power and the dehumanisation of the minority Tutsi population, constructed as 'snakes' and 'cockroaches'. The (ir)rationale for atrocities was underpinned by racist supremacy and ethnic hatred. In Darfur, the idea of ethnic superiority of Arabs had already surfaced in the 1980s in conjunction with the formation of the so-called 'Islamic Legion' by Libyan Colonel Gaddafi. He recruited Sahelian Arabs, including those from Darfur, for his expansive plan of the Arab belt, arming his Legion and indoctrinating its members in Arab supremacy. Although the Legion was dismantled in the late 1980s, its legacy endured as some of its members became leaders of the infamous *Janjaweed* militia (De Waal 2004: 2).

It is exactly the *Janjaweed* which caught the attention of the international media and human rights organisations in 2004. Just as the machete-wielding, drunk and drugged *Interahamwe* militia quickly became the symbol of the Rwandan genocide, so too the eyes and imaginations of those watching CNN news coverage in the West fixed on the *Janjaweed* fighters, exotic killers riding on horseback and camels wielding AK-47s and G3 rifles. In co-operation with Sudanese government forces, the *Janjaweed* unleashed a campaign of terror, burning the villages of non-Arab communities, raping and abducting their inhabitants, looting their property, forcing them to abandon their homes, destroying their livestock, water points, mills and other village assets (Human Rights Watch 2004a: 14). Such a scorched earth campaign, taking aim not only at the lives of innocent civilians but also at their basic living conditions, intimates the 'ultimate crime', namely the genocide. Such a suspicion was confirmed by the close connection between the *Janjaweed* and the Sudanese government; the latter supplied uniforms, arms and financial assets to the *Janjaweed*. The government not only recruited the *Janjaweed* to fight non-Arab movements, but also launched indiscriminate aerial bombardments against civilian targets in Northern Darfur.[13]

In order to understand the current atrocities, it is necessary to explore their historical and socio-economic causes. Although the analogy between Rwanda and Darfur is somewhat problematic in terms of the nature of the conflicts, in both cases ethnic bipolarity provided the 'raw material' for political manipulation and supplied the 'tinder box' which hate-filled rhetoric would set alight. The term 'ethnic bipolarity' somewhat obscures reality, however, as the two main groups in both of these countries share important characteristics. In Darfur, both non-Arabs and Arabs are black, indigenous, African and Muslim. Nevertheless, whilst Arabs have traditionally been nomads, non-Arabs have made their living from farming, which explains the division of conflict in Darfur along ethnic lines. Following the draught and famine in Darfur from 1984 to 1985, local conflicts erupted over the scarce natural resources between these groups (De Waal 2004). Such a low-intensity conflict, however, soon broke into a larger war, as two non-Arab rebel groups, the Sudan Liberation Army/Movement (SLA/M) and the Justice and Equality Movement (JEM), began to accuse the government of backing the *Janjaweed* and neglecting the socio-economic conditions in the region. In February 2003, SLA/M and JEM launched an armed rebellion against the government. Like the so-called *Inyenzi* attacks on Rwanda by Tutsi refugees from Uganda, the rebellion by SLA/M and JEM triggered disproportionately harsh counter-insurgency strikes by the government on civilians of non-Arab communities.

Conclusion

In line with Critical Theory based on the work of the Frankfurt School, Alex Bellamy notes that knowledge of peacekeeping is never politically neutral. It is used in order to buttress certain belief systems and myths. Exposing these structures requires a new epistemological thinking of the way in which conflicts are conceptualised (Bellamy 2004: 28). The significance of a new epistemological thinking of conflict management to understanding the crises in Rwanda and Darfur is that one should critically evaluate certain theories produced and reproduced by researchers and practitioners, notably the prioritising of 'genocide' over particular historical circumstances that led to the killings. This chapter has demonstrated that the 'genocide narrative' adopted by previous accounts has generated an over-optimistic evaluation of the capacities possessed by the UN to predict the conflicts; one claims to see clearly the seeds of genocide in Rwandan history, but one begins the story by sowing them oneself. This book, by contrast, highlights the importance of an effective early warning mechanism in the 'post-Arusha' peace-building phase, which will be examined in more detail in Chapter 5.

2   A critical realist approach to conflict management

Introduction

Should the failure of UN diplomats and officials to prevent genocides be conceived of as largely self-inflicted, or should it be more reasonably attributed to the constraints of the surrounding structures and mechanisms which limited the political manoeuvring space of these actors? With regard to the UN's failure in Rwanda, only Michael Barnett has implicitly raised this question thus far (2002: xii), whilst most other authors working on the subject have not viewed it as relevant or problematic at all. However, the avoidance of this question has led to implicit answers, which indict the most obvious suspects, that is, the representatives of the great powers in general and the US in particular.[1] Hence, the blame is laid squarely on actors, not structures or mechanisms. This chapter will argue that the possibilistic methodology of critical realism seeks to open up all the *possible* causes of the UN inaction,[2] without automatically apportioning blame.

Although previous accounts provide detailed descriptions of the chain of events leading to the UN's failure in Rwanda and effectively expose culpable state representatives and UN officials, their tendency[3] to view individual events and behaviours as *sufficient* explanatory factors *in themselves* renders them ultimately superficial, and therefore deficient. The method of double movement based on critical realist philosophy views events and actors only as a starting point, not so much as explanatory factors per se but more as factors to be explained, because it considers the importance of the 'troublemaking' structures and mechanisms that generated those events in the first place and affected the behaviour of actors.

The chapter will be divided into three parts. The first section will present the ontological and epistemological positions of critical realism that are largely shared by all critical realist researchers. The second section will take as its point of departure the common theoretical grounding of critical realism established in the first section and, on that basis, will design an original critical realist approach to International Relations (IR) studies by synthesising Roy Bhaskar's theory with Andrew Sayer's method of double movement. The aim of this methodological framework is to supply an approach that is more capable of acknowledging the complexities of decision-making procedures with regard to conflict management, to provide a deeper and wider account of the causes of the UN's failures, and to offer a more emancipatory insight into the potential capacities of UN diplomats and officials to avoid such disasters. While the first and second sections will examine mechanisms in the context of social science in general, the third section will analyse mechanisms specifically in relation to the UN. The hypothesis here posits that the UN Security Council constitutes what Roy Bhaskar terms an 'open system': it is composed of fifteen member states, but what makes this group of state representatives the *Security* Council in control of international security threats, rather than a closed gentleman's club of ambassadors, is the surrounding framework of structures and mechanisms of the UN.

Before probing critical realism in more detail, it is appropriate to situate it in IR studies more broadly, which is the purpose of this introductory section. To use Martin Wight's famous characterisation, the 'old' debates in IR theory have been conducted by Machiavellians (political realists), Grotians (rationalists) and Kantians (liberal institutionalists). Machiavellians view states and state-systems as the proper levels of analysis. Grotians, in turn, emphasise the diplomatic and normative structures that bind states together, whilst Kantians prioritise transnational actors that enhance the emergence of international community. Since the end of the 1980s, a variety of new IR approaches has emerged, challenging and transcending the aforementioned 'Three Waves' of IR discipline (Wæver 1996: 149).

Viewed through the 'new' lenses, as Steve Smith characterises it, the 'old' appears as quite monovalent, composed of 'three versions of one world, rather than three genuine alternative views of international relations' (Smith 1996: 11). The common element shared by the three old IR approaches has been positivism, the dominant epistemology in IR, although not all traditional IR theories, such as the English School, have adhered to positivist principles. Positivism here is defined by the prevalence of the empiricist method in IR research and the belief in the existence of regularities in the social world. It also encompasses the adoption of methodologies from the natural sciences to explain the social world, the categorical distinction between facts and values, and the belief that facts are theory-neutral. These positivist assumptions, which underpin (neo-)realism and (neo-)liberalism, have been contested by post-positivist approaches, such as post-modernism, feminist approaches, Critical Theory and critical realism.[4]

The latter began to establish a niche in IR theory in the end of the 1980s. As a philosophy, critical realism initially emerged as a critique of positivism in the philosophy of science, which suggests that critical realist approaches in IR have close affinities with post-positivism. In common with post-positivist IR approaches, such as social constructivism, the critical realist methodology contests the way in which positivists pose 'Why?' questions, i.e. why one variable necessarily leads to another.[5] As opposed to this approach, critical realists and other post-positivists ask, 'How is it possible?', which allows them to be open to the possibility of multiple causes.[6] For this study, the evolution from positivist 'Why?' questions to post-positivist 'How?' questions means that the selfishness of great powers cannot be isolated as the only 'historically proven variable' causing the UN's failure, as presumed by the (neo-)realist axiom and some existing accounts of the Rwandan case. Instead, it argues that there were also other factors underlying the disaster.

Nevertheless, critical realism has a more ambitious standpoint than other post-positivist approaches in IR theory in the sense that it strives to transcend not only positivism but also the positivism/post-positivism debate itself. Critical realism rejects both positivist methodologies and the majority of post-positivist epistemologies in IR, on the ground that they are underpinned by the epistemic fallacy and anti-realism. The epistemic fallacy refers to the reduction of the theory of being and world (ontology) into the theory of knowledge (epistemology). Such a fallacy dictates that the world is defined solely in terms of linguistic conventions, images, beliefs, symbolic gestures and models, as if reality never existed beyond these concepts (Patomäki 2002a: 5; Wight 1998: 53).

Critical realists make no attempt to refute the existence of images, models or conventions. They do, however, strive to demonstrate that beyond these 'linguistic objects' there are structures, mechanisms and causes that produce events and generate linguistic objects in the first place. This ontic dimension, which both positivist and post-positivist IR approaches have largely ignored, constitutes the 'new' IR problem-field that critical realism aims to explore. One set of objects belonging to this 'new' problem-field, namely mechanisms, takes a central role here, as it forms the constitutive unit of the method of double movement and is therefore the ontological building block of this analysis. The value added that an exploration of generative mechanisms brings is that it is thereby possible to demonstrate *from where* the misleading images produced by the UN of the Rwandan genocide as 'anarchic, mad and tribal killing' came, and *to what* they refer: it will be suggested in this book that the images of security threats in Rwanda were generated by early warning mechanisms, bureaucratic control, and other securitisation and detection mechanisms, and that they referred to the actual and potential genocide. While the existing literature focuses on the level of misleading images, which indicates the apparent betrayal of Rwanda by the UN, a critical realist approach enables a deeper explanation by exploring the underlying level of reality, namely the causes (explanatory mechanisms) of such images.

At this point, however, we should step back and ponder mechanisms in more detail, because their status has been rather contentious in critical realist IR research. Although mechanisms hold a central position in Roy Bhaskar's philosophy, in critical realist IR theory they do not form part of the Lakatosian 'hard core' of fundamental concepts but, rather, belong to the outskirts of the 'protective belt' of critical realist discipline. In fact, the issue of mechanisms has, at least to some degree, divided the critical realist IR research community. Heikki Patomäki's as well as Colin Wight's early accounts represent those critical realist scholars who refute mechanisms as plausible research objects (see, for example, Patomäki 2002a: 82). Recent accounts by Branwen Gruffydd Jones, Alexander Wendt and Colin Wight explicitly advocate their application to critical realist IR (Jones 2002: 155; Wendt 1999: 81–2; Wight 2004: 287–8).

This study will defend the latter position, though acknowledges Patomäki's concern that 'mechanism' in the Newtonian sense erroneously implies that social mechanisms could be equated to machines. Mechanisms should be understood not in Newtonian but in Bhaskarian terms, as causal links. By elaborating on the latter, ontological, reading of mechanisms suggested by Bhaskar, Colin Wight maintains that they can in fact be understood in two senses: as *causal* processes in general, and as *control* processes in particular (Wight 2004: 287–8). *Both* descriptions of mechanisms will be employed in this study. According to the former definition, a mechanism is simply a way of acting or working of a struc-tured thing; for example, how bicycles or international organisations work in certain ways (Lawson 1997: 21).

The third section of this chapter will demonstrate how the critical realist framework developed in the first and second sections illuminates a novel way of understanding the Security Council as an *open system* and of conceiving the UN conflict management system as a *related whole*, in which control mechanisms play a central role. 'Control mechanisms' in the context of UN conflict manage-ment are understood metaphysically as causal linkages by which images of outside security threats are produced in the UN system. These linkages denote both the relationship between the 'two principal organs'[7] of the UN with regard to the maintenance of peace and security, namely the Security Council and the Secretariat, and their connection to the outside security environment: the Secre-tariat seeks to detect and issue warnings of forthcoming security threats under Article 99 of the UN Charter, whilst the Council bearing the greatest respons-ibility for peace and security under the Charter uses such information as raw materials for its conceptualisation of and reaction to conflicts.

Developing critical realism for the study of international relations: from philosophy to a methodological framework

> Now there is a chestnut that enjoys quite widespread popularity, not least in Megara, to the effect that x is capable of being/doing the F only when it actually is/does the F. So the non-builder is no bearer of a potentiality for building – the only such bearer is the builder *when engaged in his building* ... Exposing the idiocy of this buffoonery will not long detain us.
>
> (Aristotle, *Metaphysics*, Book Theta, Ch-3, 1046b)

The metaphysical arguments presented in the classical debate between Aristotle and the Megarians in the fourth-century BC, such as the relationship between the actual and the possible, not only precede but also to some extent directly corres-pond to the current conversation between critical realists and positivists. This section cannot examine these profound debates of Ancient Greece in any detail but will draw upon contemporary discussions in the philosophy of science, with the aim of creating a viable and innovative methodological framework for the study of international relations and conflict management. Roy Bhaskar's *A Realist Theory of Science* (1975) defends the commonsensical view, *contra* idealists, solipsists and phenomenalists, that a substantial part of reality exists independently of human minds (Niiniluoto 1999: 10; Patomäki 1992: 2). Critical realism rejects the human-centred philosophies that fall foul of the anthropocentric fallacy – that is, of reducing the theory of reality and being to the theory of nature or behaviour of men (Bhaskar 1997: 44). It is against positivism, however, that the main thrust of the critical realist challenge has been directed. That is because the first contributions to critical realism, especially *A Realist Theory of Science*, mainly concerned the philosophy of science where positivism, derived from Hume and Locke, has been the dominant approach. The recent variant of positivism, sometimes called the 'standard view' in the philosophy of science, emerged in the middle of the twentieth century. Its main contributors, Rudolf Carnap, Carl Hempel and Ernest Nagel, based their approach on the law-explanation orthodoxy according to which explaining an event denotes formulating a general law – that is, a universal generalisation (Outhwaite 1987: 5–7).

The ontological poverty of positivism derives mainly from the second type of fallacy, namely the *empiricist* fallacy. Such a fallacy defines reality merely in terms of experienced phenomena, constant regularities of events, theories, models and hypotheses. *A Realist Theory of Science* shows that the empiricist worldview is reduced to *closed systems*. An invariance of events is usually possible only in hermetic conditions produced artificially by scientists – that is, a closed system where a mechanism operates in isolation from other mechanisms, like in a scientific experiment. However, closed systems are rare in nature because, outside laboratory conditions, in *open systems*, events are caused and co-determined by a number of causal mechanisms (Bhaskar 1997: 34). The difference between open and closed systems can be exemplified by Karl Popper's distinction between 'clockwork precision' and 'vagaries of weather'. In this analogy, clocks represent closed systems. Both the clocks and closed systems are regular, orderly and predictable entities, as the singular mechanism of a clock is isolated from the disturbing effects of the outside world. Clouds here represent open systems because they both are irregular, disorderly and unpredictable. A particular form of clouds is a product of an indeterminate net effect of a large number of various mechanisms operating in the open atmosphere of nature (Collier 1989: 13–14).

Critical realism proposes an account of reality that is more comprehensive and etymologically correct than the reductionist and anti-realist conception offered by positivism. In philosophy, the term 'real', coined by medieval Schoolmen, derives from the Latin word *res*, meaning a 'thing' (Lucas 1990: 42). Etymologically, the word *res* means things both in the concrete and abstract senses. It thus refers to the totality of all real things (Niiniluoto 1999: 10). In critical realism, things refer not only to experiences, the course of actual events or constant conjunctions of events, as in positivist and other anthropocentric philosophies, but also to their underlying causes, structures, powers, possibilities, mechanisms and tendencies (Bhaskar and Lawson 1998: 5). Underlying mechanisms, structures and causes constitute *ontological depth*, which is characterised by stratification (Bhaskar 1998a: xi).

In *A Realist Theory of Science*, stratification usually implies the distinction between three ontological domains. The domain of the *real* consists of underlying causal powers, possibilities and generative mechanisms that cause, affect, enable and produce events. Counterfactuals are one intriguing form of possibilities, which Bhaskar defines as occurrences that would have ensued if certain conditions, which did not in fact arise, had done so (Bhaskar 1986: 31). In the domain of the *actual* there emerge the actualisations and events produced by their underlying mechanisms. Logically, the actual is less extensive than the real, as reality consists not only of actualised mechanisms but also of 'dormant', i.e. unactualised, mechanisms that 'wait' to be actualised by certain triggering conditions. The domain of the *empirical* covers only those objects that are empirically perceived by us. Therefore, the empirical is necessarily less extensive than the actual because there are many 'unperceived actualities', that is, events that go unperceived by anyone. In sum, these three domains constitute three overlapping layers where an underlying sub-layer is greater than a less extensive 'surface' layer: real > actual > empirical (Bhaskar 1975: 13; Sayer 1981: 9). In this regard, however, one should note a possible misunderstanding that the term 'domain of the real' may stir up. Bhaskar explicitly mentions that he does not intend to argue that the objects of the other two domains are less real (Bhaskar 1997: 58). Experiences and actual events are as real as mechanisms and structures; however, the domain of actual events is always smaller than the domain of the unactualised possibilities of the world.

While the above argumentation has concentrated on the first aspect of critical realism, i.e. transcendental realism, the second important phase in its development was Bhaskar's *The Possibility of Naturalism* (1979). This influential study situated transcendental realism in the social sciences and thereby established *critical naturalism*, according to which the social world can be studied in exactly the same sense, though not in exactly the same way, as the natural world (Bhaskar 1979: 203). The *critical limit* on naturalism entails the notion that the subject matter of social science includes not only social objects but also beliefs about them. Such beliefs are 'value-impregnated' in the sense that the subject matter of social science is itself in part constituted by values or things to which agents attach value (Bhaskar 1998a: xvii–xviii). The critical limit on naturalism concerns bridging the gap not only between fact and value in social science, but also between 'knowing' and 'doing', i.e. theory and practice. Bhaskar contends that the social sciences contain an essential emancipatory impulse. Emancipation here refers to the liberation of agents from unwanted states of affairs. Scientific explanation is a necessary, though in itself insufficient, condition for full human emancipation, as liberation requires not only cognitive enlightenment but also practice in order to transform suppressive structures (Bhaskar 1986: 169–71). For this study, the progression from theory to practice means addressing the crucial question as to what structural amendments or adjustments could have been made to the UN system in order to prevent past, present and future genocides.[8]

Since *The Possibility of Naturalism*, critical realism has been applied to various fields of human and social sciences, such as sociology, economics, political sciences, psychoanalysis, linguistics, history and feminist theory (Collier 1994: x–xi). This expansion in the application of critical realism from philosophical confines to the methodology of social sciences has also opened up prospects for critical realism to develop an innovative approach for the study of international relations. In 1987, Alexander E. Wendt brought critical realism into American political-scientist thinking with his essay 'The Agent–Structure Problem in International Relations Theory'. By then, only a handful of critical realist discussions were to be found in IR theory, all of them British (Wendt 1987: 336). Since then, American IR theory has seen critical realism developed at the margins of social-constructivist approaches of Wendt and a few other IR scholars, such as David Dessler.

What Wendt's account has faced, both within American and European IR theory, however, is that it appears to be insufficient to distinguish critical realism as an innovative and autonomous approach separate from alternative ones (Kratochwil 2000: 91; Suganami 2002: 29). European critical realist IR scholars, specifically Heikki Patomäki and Colin Wight, maintain that Wendt's social constructivism, or the 'middle ground' as they term it, does not adequately depart from the positivist IR tradition characterised by anti-realism. In fact, Wendt's approach strives less to establish a new critical realist problem-field than to *reconcile* the old ones, namely positivist epistemology and idealist ontology. This results in what Steve Smith deems a 'confusing and ambiguous picture of the relationship between the material and the ideational' (2000: 154).

Set against Wendt's theory, Wight and Patomäki propose a wholly new, critical realist, problem-field for IR study, based on the primacy of ontology to epistemology, and consisting of such objects of analysis as structures, mechanisms, causalities and underlying powers. The old IR problem-field remains, occupied by neo-realists, neo-liberals, linguistic constructivists and postmodernists. This old IR dimension is situated in the epistemic side of reality, and consists of such research objects as events, actualities, experiences, discourses and impressions. Wight and Patomäki's aim is not to refute the old IR problem-field, but to transcend it by demonstrating that beyond actual events and discourses there are real structures and mechanisms at work. As the 'old' approaches cannot make reference to the latter side of reality, they give only a partial picture of the world and are therefore insufficient to explain reality (Patomäki and Wight 2000: 223).

Whilst certain objects of the new critical realist problem-field have been elaborated and concretised in research of international relations, others have attracted scant attention. For example, Wendt has no hesitation in explaining international relations in terms of 'levels' and 'mechanisms' (Wendt 1999: 81–2), whereas Patomäki has objections to using these concepts and suggests applying 'contexts' instead of levels and 'social/causal complexes' as an alternative to mechanisms (Patomäki 2002a: 82). In Patomäki's 'critical social realism', mechanisms are regarded as uninteresting. Patomäki argues that social activity should be explained by social (causal) complexes rather than by mechanisms, on the grounds that mechanisms lack the intentionality that social activity always implies (Patomäki 1991: 224). Such a view could be denounced here on account of its adherence to a kind of anthropocentric fallacy in which all social activity is reduced to intentional activity, thereby excluding unintentional and unconscious mechanisms from explanation, as if unintentional activity never existed. A substantial part of social activity is caused by unconscious motivations and is characterised by unintended consequences (Bhaskar 1998a: xvi). As Bhaskar puts it, 'People do not marry to reproduce the nuclear family or work to sustain the capitalist economy. Yet it is nevertheless the unintended consequence (an inexorable result) of, as it is also a necessary condition for, their activity' (Bhaskar 1998b: 44). Patomäki later admits that, in addition to social complexes, there may also be some mechanisms at work in social activity, which lack human intentionality, such as economic tendencies and Freudian defence-mechanisms (Patomäki 1995: 71–2). While the examination thus far has touched upon ontology, i.e. the nature of the social world, the following section will proceed to address the epistemological question of how that world can be studied.

Devising the method of double movement

The critical realist emphasis on 'ontological depth' discussed above raises the question as to the means by which research objects situated in that depth, such as causal mechanisms, could be explored. Andrew Sayer provides a solution, namely the method of abstraction, which means isolating one-sided or partial aspects of a complex object. Those one-sided or partial, i.e. *abstract*, objects are usually necessary[9] features of a larger and complex system. For example, a respiratory system is a one-sided and necessary abstract mechanism in animals as larger organic complexes. *Concrete* objects denote combinations of diverse elements or forces, such as organic complexes, nations or an event containing various elements, of which abstract elements are part. Sayer suggests a method based on double movement: concrete → abstract, abstract → concrete. This means that in the first stage of research an adequate number of one-sided and necessary features or mechanisms is systematically abstracted from a diverse, complex and chaotic combination of events or elements. After isolating and examining each of the abstract features or mechanisms, it is necessary to move to the second phase, which combines the abstractions so as to conceptualise their combined effect, thus grasping the concreteness of the objects (Sayer 1992: 86–91).

Sayer's method of double movement is originally derived from Karl Marx's method of political economy, in which Sayer's two subsequent 'moves' are termed 'paths' (Joseph 2002: 33). The first path leads from the chaotic conception of the whole (*Vorstellung*), such as 'population', to ever more simple concepts (*Begriff*) concerning parts of the whole, such as 'social classes' and 'division of labour'. The second path then combines these parts to form a reorganised whole. 'I had finally arrived at the population again', as Marx describes the end result of the second path, 'but this time not as the chaotic conception of a whole, but as a rich totality of many determinations and relations' (Marx 1973:

100).[10] In the following paragraphs the method of double movement, as conceptualised in Sayer's novel representation of Marx's original method, will be synthesised with, and enriched by, the critical realist logic of scientific discovery and emancipatory inquiry presented in Bhaskar's *A Realist Theory of Science*. The value added by this synthesis lies chiefly in the fact that Sayer's method lacks an explicit emancipatory dimension.

Bhaskar maintains that scientific discovery moves through three consecutive levels (Collier 1994: 49). First at the Humean level of classical empiricism we can only identify the sequence or invariance of events. We may, to use Colin Wight's example, state that 'The 10.55 train from London is late' (Wight 1988: 57). Positivists would restrict themselves to the Humean level by reducing their explanation to a statement, 'It is always late'. Critical realists, by contrast, would find that explanation unsatisfactory and strive to move through the Lockean level of transcendental idealism to the Leibnizian level of realism in order to formulate a deeper explanation by uncovering malfunctions in the structures and mechanisms of the railway system (Wight 1988: 57). At the Lockean level, a researcher explores possible correct explanations for the analysed case, located in the nature of the thing or in the structure of the system. Eventually at the third, Leibnizian, level a researcher may seek to express the discovery in an attempted definition of a thing (Bhaskar 1997: 19).

Before synthesising Bhaskar and Sayer's methods, it is first necessary to reconceptualise the three levels presented in Bhaskar's model of scientific discovery, as the way in which Bhaskar names the levels after three prominent philosophers, Hume, Locke and Leibniz, is rather problematic. First, as Sayer himself pointed out to the author, his own model differs from Bhaskar's in not assuming that a researcher must start from Humean regularities.[11] As Sayer is held to be correct, the term 'sequence of events' is used here in place of 'regularity of events' and the concept of the 'Humean level' is replaced with the 'phenomenal level'.[12] Second, Bhaskar's inclusion of the three prominent philosophers into his model is undermined by the fact that his interpretation of the substance and meaning of the levels does not necessarily equate with the original philosophical positions of Hume, Locke and Leibniz. Therefore, in this book Bhaskar's definitions of 'Humean', 'Lockean' and 'Leibnizian' levels are replaced with the terms 'phenomenal', 'idealist' and 'realist' respectively.[13]

The purpose of the following synthesis is not to impose Bhaskar's theoretical model on Sayer's method, but to enrich the latter by demonstrating that it is built upon an identical critical realist logic of scientific discovery. The move from the phenomenal to the realist level suggested by Bhaskar underpins Sayer's first movement (concrete → abstract) in the sense that the aim is to move from analysing the diversity of elements that appear in the empirically observed event, most of which are irrelevant, to focus on only a few key mechanisms that are important for answering a research question. Following this move, Sayer's method is directed back towards the phenomenal level (abstract → concrete) with the aim of situating the abstracted mechanisms back in a new concrete setting of phenomena. In this phase, we may add an emancipatory insight informed by Bhaskar's theory. For example, we may try to state whether in improved conditions – in the 'other world' – the 10.55 train from London would be late as usual or not, if one or two structural malfunctions were not actualised. In sum, the first movement (concrete → abstract) examines which (abstract) mechanisms have caused a failure at a particular (concrete) moment. Then, we may proceed to the second movement (abstract → concrete) by examining whether that failure would (not) have happened, if some of these mechanisms had not been actualised. Thus, we may synthesise a basic methodological frame-work: phenomenal level (concrete) → realist level (abstract), realist level (abs-tract) → phenomenal level (concrete). Democritus' adage perfectly captures the essence of the method of double movement presented below: 'But in fact, we know nothing from having seen it; for the truth is hidden in the deep' (quoted in Popper 1983: 5).

It should be clarified here that associating the adjectives 'abstract' and 'meta-theoretical' to 'mechanisms' by no means signifies that the latter are somehow vague, ethereal or fuzzy objects, unrelated to the real world. In fact, even some critical realists would object to such linkage by arguing that mechanisms can also be concrete, in the sense of material objects such as an assembly line of a factory. The purpose here is not to refute this interpretation but only to claim that 'mechanism' is understood in the model below as a *one-sided entity* ('abstract'), whether material or not, belonging to a more complex combination of elements

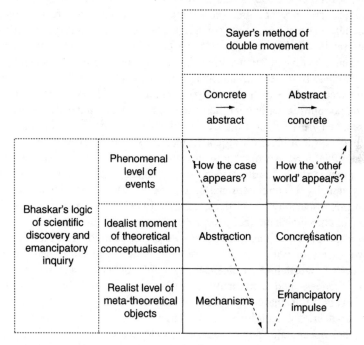

Figure 2.1 Synthesis of Bhaskar's logic of scientific discovery and Sayer's method of double movement.

('concrete'), as was elaborated in more detail earlier in this section. For example, an early warning mechanism of the UN is a very real and tangible thing belonging to a larger machinery of the UN system, and it can be identified and studied through abstraction, i.e. capturing its relevant patterns and components such as processes, structures, resources and outcomes from the complexity of appearances. In this regard, abstraction is similar to assembling together a mosaic; the pattern, and thereby the beauty and meaning, of the mosaic emerges from the chaotic pile of pieces. Both that organised pattern and the pile of pieces from which it emerges are real. In the same way, both a mechanism and the phenomena from which it is abstracted from are real, although the former is somewhat simpler, yet more meaningful, than the latter.

The second move demonstrated above denotes critical engagement, transformative praxis and a practical dimension in the sense that it strives to bridge the gap between theory and practice via an enquiry into how agents could emancipate themselves from material and social constraints to transform liberal institutions in order to achieve desired outcomes.[14] Bhaskar lays emphasis on the importance of avoiding the conflation of social or inter-subjective power relations and material ones. Similarly, *socially caused constraints* include, for example, oppressive norms of the international economic order that constrain the development of heavily indebted countries. These constraints can be absented, changed or removed through social (re-)construction or rational transformative praxis. The second type of constraint is *material* in nature; the ecological, physical, biological and psychological constraints to which social life is subject. Unlike socially caused constraints, material ones are often unsurpassable and only transformed with difficulty (Bhaskar 1993: 161). Critical realist approaches possess a transformative pulse to achieve human freedom from constraints, especially social ones, by revealing and analysing them (Collier 1995: 38). Therefore, in the second phase of the (revised) method of double movement we can examine the possibilities of doing otherwise to what actually happened. We may, for example, analyse whether a failure would have happened in an organisation if one or two of the troublemaking social mechanisms had not been allowed to actualise. Furthermore, we may draw lessons for the future by analysing the structure of these troublemaking mechanisms. Although a problematic event that has already actualised cannot be transformed, the underlying mechanisms generative of events, especially social ones, can be altered such that they would be prevented from producing another disastrous event in the future.

However, at the outset there seems to be a slight contradiction between the holistic worldview of critical realism implying totality and the transformative praxis concerning emancipation. There appears to be only a short step from conceding the openness and complexity of reality to submitting to its ultimate incomprehensibility. Richard Wyn Jones makes a similarly thought-provoking comment about critical security studies: 'There is the question of whether by expanding the conceptualisation of security, its study becomes the study of everything, and hence, effectively, nothing' (Wyn Jones 1999: 126). However, this study argues that there is a categorical distinction to be made between 'occupying' and 'opening up' totality. Whereas the former implies a positivist vision of a Grand Strategy, the latter refers to a critical realist method where totality is first scanned and then an emancipatory window is located within it.

What this study suggests is that all knowable material and social constraints of a particular case should be considered alongside the available possibilities at the time, both material and social. These considerations refer to a particular actor, individual or collective, and to a particular time sequence. Finally, we should situate this constraints/possibilities nexus into a wider totality in terms of space, time and/or actors. For example, when it comes to *material powers*, there is no doubt that Western states are powerful enough to launch wars unilaterally; yet in terms of *social, normative and moral powers*, they are usually obliged to seek legitimation from the United Nations due to its universal and impartial rational–legal authority. This particular constraints/possibilities nexus leaves room for what K.R. Brotherus describes as 'wise men':

> When discussing a hard and complex matter it might be of great benefit that besides power politicians there is a member sitting at the negotiation table, who does not represent power, nor particular state interests, but is solely a 'wise man', nothing further.[15]

Although Brotherus' wise words date back to the 1930s, they are still relevant for today's security experts, many of whom, from the UN Secretary-General to eminent personalities representing non-permanent members in the Security Council, have acquired their authority and powers by dint of their roles as 'wise men'. Eventually, we may be in a position to locate a 'rupture' of possibilities, or 'emancipatory window', between the constraints and in particular those emanating from the 'plate tectonics' of *Realpolitik*.

The 'rupture approach' here categorically opposes E.H. Carr's wisdom of political realism that 'Realism tends to emphasise the irresistible strength of existing forces and the inevitable character of existing tendencies … the highest wisdom lies in accepting, and adapting oneself to, these forces and these tendencies' (Carr 1946: 10). From the critical realist perspective, Carr's statement invokes an anti-realist vision, resembling more closely laboratory conditions, under which only the constraints emanating from superpowers are taken into account by isolating them from potential possibilities, rather than conditions in the real world. However, the critical realist path to emancipation does not lead to another anti-realist laboratory, constructed by certain neo-liberals apt to exaggerate possibilities and potentials of transnational actors, or by postmodernists inclined to reconstruct past events through backward causalities. In contrast, to close the whole argumentative circle thus far, we can state that the only way to emancipation is via the comprehending of reality, which begins with the identification of the real mechanisms of the world. Figure 2.2 demonstrates that the 'size' of emancipatory windows depends on three variables: the presence of possibilities (the breadth of the window), the absence of constraints (the height of the window) and time (Z-axis).

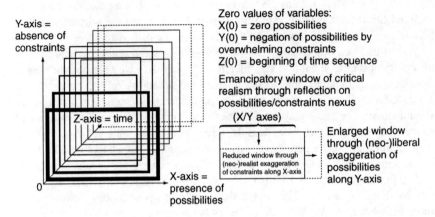

Figure 2.2 Emancipatory windows.

Mechanisms and possibilities: new ontological building blocks of theory on conflict management

It is now appropriate to tackle the ontological question as to how critical realism would consider the relationships between actors, structures and mechanisms within the framework of the UN and the Security Council. Roy Bhaskar's Trans-formational Model of Social Activity contends that, although an agent always has the power to transform a social structure, s/he cannot do so either in a vacuum or under conditions of their own choosing, as the activity of an agent is always enabled and constrained by prior conditions set by that structure (Bhaskar 1998b: 44).[16] With regard to the Security Council, the Transformational Model indicates that states do not constantly *create* but, more usually, just *transform* or reproduce certain pre-existing structures of the UN. In this Aristotelian sense, the members of the Council can be understood as sculptresses at work, fashion-ing the product, e.g. resolutions, decisions and presidential statements, out of pre-existing raw materials, such as norms, organisational culture and control mechanisms. Concrete structures here encompass the norms and institutions of the UN, such as the UN Charter and the Secretariat, which enable and constrain the activity of the fifteen member states by delineating the boundaries of proper state behaviour in the international community.

For example, the structural basis for the powers exercised by the Secretariat in relation to the Council is set out in Article 99 of the UN Charter: 'The Secretary-General may bring to the attention of the Security Council any matter which in his opinion *may* threaten the maintenance of international peace and security.'[17] Article 99 here represents a structure, which, on the one hand, *enables* the activity of state actors in the sense that they can receive information on potential conflicts through the Secretary-General's briefings. On the other hand, Article 99 *constrains* the activity of the member states: once state repre-sentatives are made aware of a conflict, they must either take action or choose

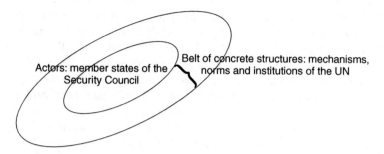

Figure 2.3 Structural embeddedness of the member states of the Security Council.

inaction in the public eye, with the potential damage to their international reputation as a consequence of choosing the latter option. Figure 2.3 illustrates this agent–structure relationship by demonstrating that state actors are always embedded within structures.[18]

Andrew Sayer's definition of structures is instructive here: '"Structure" suggests a set of internally related elements whose causal powers ... are emergent from those of their constituents' (Sayer 2000: 14). Hence, mechanisms *emerge* from their underlying structures as processes that realise the powers of structures and thereby produce events: structures → mechanisms → events (Sayer 2000: 15). In other words, structures may exist for a long period of time, but their causal powers remain *in potentia* until mechanisms realise those powers.[20] In the case in question here, the structure (Article 99 of the UN Charter) possessing the causal powers of early warning has existed since the UN Charter was signed in 1945. However, these powers were only realised for the first time in 1992, when Secretary-General Boutros-Ghali, in co-operation with the Security Council, invoked early warning mechanisms.

The aforementioned causal chain 'structures → mechanisms → events' implies that an examination of underlying structures can reveal even deeper causes of events than an examination of mechanisms. If 'troublemaking' mechanisms were causes of the UN's failure over Rwanda, then their underlying structures must have been the causes of those causes. So why not then examine structures instead of mechanisms? Though structures may, indeed, provide a deeper understanding of the *root causes* of the UN's failure, mechanisms are able to expose the *dynamics* of that failure due to their processual nature.[21] The question to be addressed, then, is: if certain disturbing factors in the deep structures of the UN system, such as Western biases, have existed for long periods of time,[22] why did they 'choose' to actualise during the Rwandan conflict? The answer lies in the dynamics and interaction of mechanisms. This could be illustrated by the following example or hypothesis, which will be elaborated in subsequent chapters of this book: the systematic and meticulously organised Rwandan genocide was erroneously categorised as 'mad tribal violence' by stereotypical normalisation (*mechanism*) emerging from underlying Western biases (*deep structure*); this normalisation process, in turn, was aggravated by the previous chastening experiences and organisational learning of the UN (*interacting mechanism*) gained in the course of the Somalia conflict (where the description 'mad tribal violence' was more apposite) only six months prior to the Rwandan genocide (*time sequence of the interaction of the two mechanisms*). Hence, this study views both structures and mechanisms as important and complementary research objects, because the former provide a deeper, though more static, explanation, while the latter can explain the case in procedural terms.

Bhaskar's notion of 'open systems' implies that social mechanisms seldom emerge or work in isolation from other objects belonging to the surrounding environment, such as actors, structures, and interacting mechanisms (Bhaskar 1997: 47). Similarly, Milja Kurki's idea of 'related wholes' in critical realist IR theory implies that social structures cannot include material causes alone but must also encompass three other Aristotelian causes, i.e. the formal, final and efficient ones (Kurki 2003: 13; 2006: 206–9). What these critical realist definitions of 'open system' and 'related whole' mean in terms of the subject matter of this book is that the reduction of the understanding of UN conflict management to the fifteen member states of the Security Council is inadequate, because the Council cannot be isolated from the control mechanisms of the UN system, such as early warning, or from the institutional structures embodied in the Secretariat.

The crux of the meaning of the Security Council as an open system can be encapsulated by the term 'holistic ontology': it widens the conception of the nature and operations of the Council from states to a triangle of powers encompassing also institutions and control mechanisms. Each of its vertices (actors, structures and mechanisms) is both necessary and interrelated to the others, for without any one of these components the proper functioning of the UN conflict management system would not prove possible. Without the material powers of states, the Security Council would lack 'teeth' in the same way as its predecessor the League of Nations did. Without the UN Charter and other normative and institutional powers of the UN, the actions of the Council, such as collective military intervention, would be groundless, aimless and even illegal. Without establishing and maintaining control mechanisms, the Council would soon begin to lack legitimacy, because it could neither perceive the threats of the outside security environment nor win the 'hearts and minds' of the international community. The value added by this innovative three-tiered approach is its ability to demonstrate that the UN conflict management system constitutes more than the sum of its parts (states).[23]

From a critical realist standpoint, there is, in fact, a *dual emergence* of mechanisms out of structures at two levels: they arise from structures both in the concrete sense, e.g. from UN agencies; and in the abstract sense, such as from the social relations of modern society and Western civilisation and from human resources. It can therefore be said that concrete structures are visible 'traces' or 'reflections' of more profound structures and problems deeply rooted in our society and civilisation. The method of abstraction discussed in the second section allows us to follow such traces from the concrete 'surface level' to the abstract 'deep level'. Just as Karl Marx construed capitalism as one trait of industrialised society abstracted from the concrete appearances of working life, so too could the working of the UN reflect the state of affairs in modern society and Western civilisation. Revealing the deep 'sediment' of abstract structures could clarify the often repeated, but seldom explained, slogan according to which we are all responsible for the disaster in Rwanda.[24] Indeed, if the failure of the UN reflects certain deeper and wider problems in our society and civilisation, then we are all guilty of reproducing those structures and the problems they entail, which may not only have been the case in the Rwandan tragedy, but may also be the case for us all in different contexts. Figure 2.4 illustrates control mechanisms as arrows, which emerge from the 'structural belt' of norms and institutions linking actors to an outside security environment *and* from certain deep structures belonging to social and human strata. The deep structures, such as human resources and the social relations of modern society, are partially

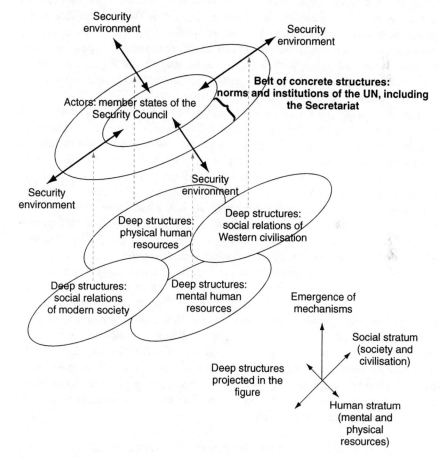

Figure 2.4 The Security Council as an open system.

overlapping, in order to emphasise that in the social world, mechanisms do not usually emerge from an isolated structure but from various structures.

Conclusion

This chapter has demonstrated that, unlike political realism which contains substantial – and often fallible – axioms concerning human nature and state-systems, critical realist approaches endeavour to maintain their role as an 'underlabourer' in, and an 'occasional midwife' to, the sciences (Bhaskar and Norrie 1998: 567). As argued in the first part of the chapter, critical realism allows a particular case study to reveal its nature without hampering it with prior ontological assumptions, which often lead to anti-realism, i.e. answers being given before questions have been asked. It seems necessary to view the actual behaviour of states as problematic rather than to take actors and their properties as given. It is more relevant to ask, 'How is action X of a state/organisation Y possible?' rather than, 'Why did X happen rather than Y?' (Wendt 1987: 362–3). If we reduced our horizon of view to actual happenings alone, seeing only those observable events that come to the fore in diplomacy or via the media, we would create an already apparent and given explanation devoid of any deeper scientific meaning. Most probably we would end up with the (neo-)realist image according to which international organisations are simply the servants of states or prisoners in the straitjacket of betraying great powers.

That is certainly the image conveyed in the existing literature on Rwanda, as will be analysed in more detail in Chapter 4. In reality, however, international organisations can also be uninterested bureaucratic institutions, which themselves misuse their possibilities, or 'rent-seeking' actors spending their resources on those instances that bring profit instead of those that risk loss. Critical realism enables us to explore these new 'candidates' and possible 'co-existing' causes of problems, instead of accepting explanations generated through a face-value analysis of the regularity of events. This is the single most important advantage that critical realism holds over alternative methodologies: it bestows the possibility of *revealing previously hidden explanatory mechanisms* underlying the Rwandan crisis.

In order to realise the above-mentioned possibility, this chapter has outlined an original methodological framework developed by incorporating Bhaskar's theory into Sayer's method of double movement. The product of this synthesis bears a close resemblance to the Rubik's Cube. In the latter, the departing point is a mixed-up cube, that is, a haphazard constellation of coloured squares, and the objective is to form a re-organised whole with single-coloured cubelet faces. Within the revised method of double movement, there is a similar move away from the diversity and chaos of various elements appearing in a particular event towards single elements. This first movement (concrete → abstract) corresponds to the following phases of research:

1   abstracting single mechanisms that generate an event; and
2   analysing their processes.

In the second move back from abstract to concrete, the intention is to totalise a reconstructed whole – like the rearranged Rubik's Cube with six single-coloured faces. This movement (abstract → concrete) corresponds to the following measures:

3   totalisation, i.e. scrutinising the combined effect of mechanisms and situating them in a wider social context in terms of time, space and/or actors; and
4   scanning their emancipatory possibilities to do otherwise than actually happens or happened.

Positivist, idealist and post-modern IR approaches tend to adopt the fallible starting-point of a re-organised whole. Indeed, by beginning with single-coloured cubelet faces already in place, the Rubik's Cube becomes less arduous to solve, but it implies the primacy of the researcher (player) over the analysed research object (Rubik's Cube). The debate between neo-realists and neo-liberals has, in fact, been merely a 'pushing and pulling exercise' between two extreme prejudices: 'Realists answer no. They believe that institutions cannot get states to stop behaving as short-term power maximizers. ... Institutionalists answer yes' (Mearsheimer 1995: 82). Instead, critical realism allows a particular case study to reveal the real balance between possibilities and constraints, and proceeds to invoke transformative practice to invert this possibilities/constraints nexus into practical suggestions to change the world.

The method of double movement has the potential to provide a holistic and reflective device for IR research. Originally, Robert Keohane's call for a 'reflective' account of international relations was based upon the assertion that 'rationalists' deal only with 'one dimension of a multidimensional reality' (Keohane 1989: 171). However, the problem of unreflective, i.e. impoverished and narrow, worldviews is wider than Keohane imagined. Considering the Rwandan case, it is tempting, for example, to presume that the misleading representation of the conflict as 'chaotic and anarchic tribal killing' was a deliberate attempt on the part of the UN to distract attention away from the systematic, well-organised genocide that was taking place. As Chapter 4 will show in more detail, such a presumption is indeed prevalent in the existing literature (see, for example, Melvern 2000). The method of double movement, by contrast, allows for an exploration that goes beyond the most apparent causes and uncovers the underlying explanatory mechanisms. Only then is it possible to judge whether the Rwandan fiasco was a result of deliberate action or human error. Only then can we grasp the whole nature and complexity of the problem, i.e. its mechanisms, its necessary and accidental components, and its triggering conditions.

3 UN conflict management of the 1990s

Introduction

> The Rwandan genocide, probably more than any other event, shattered humanitarianism's self-confidence in its own virtue and opened the floodgates to critical interpretations.
>
> (Barnett and Weiss 2008: 6)

Rwanda of 1994 was the ground zero of UN conflict management and perhaps humanity as a whole. The damage it wrought on the UN's credibility was so devastating that subsequent stock-taking reports, notably the so-called Brahimi report (2000), suggest wholly new structures of conflict management in place of old ones. The UN architecture has consequently changed almost beyond recognition in some sectors, as will be examined in more detail in the following chapters. A new set of control mechanisms has been erected on the rubbles of old ones. However, the UN has never been reinvented, but its new capacities have usually been built by strengthening or developing already existing ones. Therefore, understanding the landscape of the 1990s is the necessary starting point for the examination of both the Rwandan disaster and the case of Darfur a decade later. Critical realism offers an effective methodology to study this development, for it emphasises the analysis of underlying structures of phenomena, mechanisms and their transformation. Viewed from the critical realist lenses, the cases of Rwanda and Darfur appear as snapshots of history which indicate the direction of the longer-term transformation of the UN conflict management architecture.

The *relational* ontology suggested by the previous chapter stands in opposition to the *atomistic* ontology by demonstrating that not only individuals and state actors but also 'troublemaking' structures and mechanisms intrinsic to the UN system, such as Western normalisation and bureaucratic indifference, constitute *possible* loci of its failure. This chapter will locate those 'troublemaking' factors within the relevant structures and mechanisms of the UN that were prevalent in the 1990s, whilst the ensuing analysis in Chapters 5 and 6 will proceed to examine whether these possible structural causes were actual causes of the Rwandan drama. Such a possibilistic methodology, which approaches the

Rwandan case *indirectly* from its socio-historical context, offers an opportunity to reveal unrealised, even surprising, causes. Previous investigations rush directly to examine the events of the Rwandan failure, thereby taking the apparent suspects, i.e. selfish states, as a given explanatory factor.

As opposed to the Kantian idea of universal structures and to the positivist belief in universal covering-law explanations, critical realism assumes that mechanisms in the social world are always *socio-historical*, shaped by surrounding conditions in a particular time and place.[1] This chapter will therefore explore the control mechanisms that typified UN conflict management in the early 1990s. Such an examination will make important inroads into unravelling the Rwandan case, because the hypothesis here posits that the UN's failure in Rwanda in 1994 was a 'child of its time', or, perhaps more accurately, its 'enfant terrible'. This study holds that the Rwanda debacle constituted a prime example of the ailing conflict management mechanisms of the 1990s, whose dysfunctions intertwined and combined with devastating consequences. A review of the socio-historical context therefore leads us halfway to understanding and explaining the Rwandan case. The point of departure for such a socio-historical examination will be furnished by two groundbreaking reports on UN conflict management covering the period from 1992 to 1995, namely Secretary-General Boutros Boutros-Ghali's *An Agenda for Peace* (1992) and the *Supplement to an Agenda for Peace* (1995). The method used in this analysis will be the *abstraction* of mechanisms, the first step in the method of double movement. It will draw upon various relevant sources, practical and theoretical, as raw materials for abstraction, such as Boutros-Ghali's *Agenda* and *Supplement*, theories of bureaucratisation and realist cultural studies.

This chapter will abstract four control mechanisms: two pertaining to detection, namely early warning and organisational learning, and two with regard to securitisation,[2] that is, bureaucratic rationalisation and Western normalisation. The functions, dysfunctions and structures of these mechanisms will be investigated both at the *concrete level* (the norms and institutions of the UN from which these mechanisms emerged) and particularly at the *abstract level* (the deep structures of society and human stratum from which they emerged). Previous accounts, informed by (neo-)realist/(neo-)liberal ontological assumptions, tend to resort to simplistic explanations of the UN's failure in Rwanda, according to which states just pulled the plug on the institutions and mechanisms so that they failed to work properly. This book will oppose such reductionism by arguing that these explanations based on the (mis)behaviour of states must be supplemented by an analysis of the dysfunctions of mechanisms. This chapter will demonstrate that, during the 1990s, the Security Council was:

1   facing complex civil wars that were humanly impossible to predict (overload of the *early warning* mechanism emerging from the material stratum of human resources);
2   stumbling in human errors while 'learning to walk' following the end of the Cold War (cognitive dissonance of the *organisational learning* mechanism arising from mental resources);

3   attempting to visualise the world through rigid self-constructed categories, but was itself misled and blinded by them (dysfunction of *bureaucratic rationalisation* operating on the social plane of modern society); and

4   imposing double-standards and stereotypical images of the 'Other' (dysfunction of the mechanism of *Western normalisation* working on the social plane of Western civilisation).

In short, a socio-historical analysis of mechanisms might offer the prospect of providing a deeper and wider understanding of the causes of the UN's failure than do previous studies.

Setting the scene for analysis: post-Cold War conflict management

A wise man is strong; yea, a man of knowledge increaseth strength.

(Francis Bacon)

This and the next sections will carry out the first move of the method of double movement, namely abstraction, which will yield four different control mechanisms as the result of four abstraction processes. Because these mechanisms illustrate the workings of the Security Council in the 1990s, it can be said that the dysfunctions of these mechanisms were *possible* causes of the UN's failure in Rwanda in 1994. Thus, the four abstraction processes must be repeated in subsequent chapters in relation to the Rwandan case in order to verify/falsify these possibilities and conclude whether they were the actual causes of the Rwandan tragedy. It therefore seems incorrect to assume that the two moves of the method of double movement are strictly linear steps. Double movement may also be cyclical in the sense that abstraction can be first conducted in terms of a wider socio-historical context (the 1990s), and the result of this first 'round' of abstraction can give some lead or starting point for a second 'round' focused on a specific case study.

As explained in the previous chapter, each abstraction process begins with phenomena, which here refers to an overview of the important events of the UN conflict management in the 1990s. The beginning of the 1990s saw the renaissance of the Security Council. For the forty years following 1945, the Council had remained at an impasse due to the lack of co-operation between member states, which, in turn, was caused by the prevalence of ideological mistrust between the Eastern bloc and the Western powers. Nevertheless, the collective security system existed as an 'unrealised ability', to use Justin Morris' phrase, until it was activated at the end of the 1980s (Morris 2000: 266; Parsons 1993: 105–17). This 'post-Cold War' renaissance of UN conflict management is evidenced by the Security Council's authorisation of the use of military force on five occasions during the early 1990s, which stands in stark contrast to the previous forty years, during which the Council resorted to military force only three times (Koskenniemi 1998: 37). There were as many as thirteen new peacekeeping operations initiated by the Council between 1988 and 1993, equalling *all* previous peacekeeping operations from 1945 to 1987 (Bourgi and Colin 1993: 581). In December 1994, seventeen operations were underway, compared to only five in 1985 (Tardy 2000: 390). The new missions launched in the 1990s were not traditional military peacekeeping in the strict sense as previously, but they often constituted multifunctional operations including civilian and humanitarian components. Therefore, the increase in the number of peacekeepers in the field was even more dramatic, rising from about 11,000 at the beginning of 1992 to approximately 82,000 in 1993 (Evans 1993: 124). The Council, previously constrained by the bipolar rivalry between permanent members, began to work efficiently.[3]

In terms of the Related Powers model presented in the previous chapter, it can be said that the end of the Cold War converted the disunited conflict management system of the UN into a related one: it released the mutual-interaction process between member states and UN institutions, which, in turn, materialised and energised control mechanisms. As a consequence, Secretary-General Boutros-Ghali, who was in office from 1991 to 1996, found himself in charge of a global armada of UN peacekeeping operations and other conflict management mechanisms established by the Security Council. The Secretary-General began to exercise considerable rational–legal powers, not only as the executive manager of peacekeeping missions, but also as the conceptual architect of the new conflict management system, for example in the drawing up of an influential document called *An Agenda for Peace*, which will be examined at length below.

Michael N. Barnett and Martha Finnemore's theory provides a viable starting point from which to explain the sources of these bureaucratic powers. Drawing upon Max Weber's theory of bureaucratisation, Barnett and Finnemore discern two important sources of autonomous power for bureaucracies, namely the rational–legal authority they embody and their control of technical expertise and information. With regard to the former, the impersonal procedures and technical rationality of bureaucracies are viewed as particularly good and legitimate in modern life. Therefore, bureaucracies appeal to modern subjects (Barnett and Finnemore 1999: 708). At the surface level, bureaucracies appear as powerless servants obeying the rules and nothing further, but this appearance in fact provides a cover that enables bureaucracies to wield considerable power as technical experts, specialists, advisers and so on. Bureaucracies exert their extensive authority by classifying and organising information, fixing meanings and defining the norms of proper behaviour (Barnett and Finnemore 2004: 29–33).[4] To use Francis Bacon's aphorism dating back to the sixteenth century, 'knowledge is power', and control over knowledge through rational–legal authority is more powerful still.

Barnett and Finnemore's view of rational–legal authority appears compelling, especially when applied to relations between the UN Secretariat and the Security Council. As Roger A. Coate *et al.* point out, 'The strength of the office of the Secretary-General lies in its impartiality, which is derived from the lack of vested interests' (2001: 105). The normative basis for the powers of the Secretary-General in relation to the Security Council lies in Article 99 of the UN Charter: 'The Secretary-General may bring to the attention of the Security Council any matter which in his opinion may threaten the maintenance of international peace and security' (De Cuéllar 1993: 130). Secretaries-General have, however, exercised powers beyond those granted by Article 99 through informal channels particularly since Hammarskjöld's period of office (1953–1961). Such measures include providing the Council with regular briefings and reports on UN peace operations and conflicts, good offices and diplomatic persuasion, and suggesting initiatives to the Council (Karns and Mingst 2000: 67–8).

Detection mechanisms of the UN

On 31 January 1992, the President of the UN Security Council asked the Secretary-General to elaborate recommendations on strengthening the UN conflict management capacity, and making it more efficient. As Boutros-Ghali describes this unique occasion, 'The Security Council had delegated a responsibility that hitherto had belonged to the Security Council itself' (Boutros-Ghali 1999: 26). Boutros-Ghali accomplished his task by writing *An Agenda for Peace* (henceforth the '*Agenda*'), published in May 1992. With the help of the *Agenda*, Boutros-Ghali effectively exercised bureaucratic powers of a type which Barnett and Finnemore term 'classification', that is, the categorisation of information. Boutros-Ghali emphasises one key category of conflict management in the *Agenda*, namely 'preventive diplomacy'. He argues that, 'In the past, UN forces had been sent only after a conflict had occurred and a cease-fire had been agreed on. Preventive deployment meant that UN forces could be dispatched quickly, *at the earliest warning of serious trouble*' (Boutros-Ghali 1999: 27; emphasis added by author). Section 23 of the *Agenda* captures the relationship between preventive diplomacy and early warning mechanisms.[5]

Relying on the rational-legal authority of the Secretary-General, Boutros-Ghali embarked on promoting the establishment of early warning mechanisms. 'You will pay the price sooner or later if you don't intervene', he reasoned to state representatives, 'and later it could cost you 10 times more' (quoted in Newman 1995: 192). Boutros-Ghali's statement echoes the efforts of his predecessor Dag Hammarskjöld and his *chef de cabinet* Sir Brian Urquhart decades earlier to persuade state representatives that the future of the UN lay in 'preventive' rather than 'corrective' action, 'which was far less effective and in the long run far more expensive' (quoted in Schechter 2001: 56). Yet, despite the success of the first-ever preventive peacekeeping force UNPREDEP (United Nations Preventive Deployment Force) in the Former Yugoslav Republic of Macedonia (FYROM), the Security Council did not establish any more preventive peacekeeping missions in the 1990s. Meanwhile, the negative experiences with early warning mechanisms were mounting, not least the failure to foresee the Rwandan genocide in 1994. UNPREDEP reveals one obvious cause of such failure: states are unwilling to spend resources on those operations in which there is *no actual proof* of a tangible threat. Only strategically and geo-politically important areas, such as FYROM on account of its proximity to European states, are exceptions to this rule.

However, there was an even deeper and more fundamental material cause for the failure of the UN early warning mechanisms. Marrack Goulding, Under-Secretary-General for Peacekeeping Operations from 1986 to 1993, describes his failure in late 1991 to predict ethnic cleansing performed by the Serbian army in the eastern part of Bosnia:

> My poor understanding of the deeper currents of Yugoslavia's ethnic politics at this time was symptomatic of a persistent weakness in the UN's efforts to prevent and resolve conflicts ... most of the conflicts which the Security Council wanted the Secretariat to tackle in the nineties were new to the United Nations.
>
> (Goulding 2002: 299)

Previously, the Security Council had been called upon to tackle largely inter-state conflicts with clearly defined boundaries between belligerent governments. In the 1990s, by contrast, the majority of conflicts were internal and intra-state in nature; from 1945 to 1989, most substantial conflicts were inter-state, whereas *all* of the thirty-four major conflicts that occurred in 1993 were intra-state (Bercovitch 1998: 49).

The new intra-state conflicts were usually caused by 'state failure'. This phrase denotes the causal complex of a democracy deficit and ethnic struggle, the subsequent collapse of state structures, and the ensuing protracted conflict between sub-state actors, such as refugee warriors, guerrilla movements and armies. In the 1990s, the Secretariat and the Council faced what J. 'Bayo Adekanye calls a 'ubiquity of armed conflicts', which is distinct from, and more challenging than, a typical 'fog of war' situation. As evidenced not only in the Balkans, but also in Liberia, Somalia, Sierra Leone, Rwanda and Burundi, the interplay between the structural causes of conflicts, their triggering conditions and accelerating factors constituted a complexity whose outcome was more difficult to predict than that of previous inter-state conflicts. Early warning mechanisms became overloaded, as the structural causes of conflicts, such as the oppression of minorities and the socio-economic burden of debt, compounded one another in an unpredictable manner (Adekanye 1999: 103–4).

Situational triggers heightened the complexity of these 'new conflicts', as they usually came from obscure and unforeseen sources, which, in Adekanye's words, 'may be unpredictable and seem fortuitous and *beyond human agency*' (Adekanye 1999: 114; emphasis added by author). The statement 'beyond human agency' captures the heart of the problem: although the dramatic increase in peacekeeping operations drained the resources of the Secretariat, the overload was not merely symptomatic of meagre institutional adjustments within the Secretariat or a scarcity of organisational resources at the *level of concrete structures*. It was, more alarmingly, a demonstration of the limitations of the human ability to control and predict events befalling the new and more complex conflicts at the *level of deep structures of human resources*. Indeed, some institutional adjustments were made. Javier Pérez de Cuéllar, who preceded Boutros-Ghali in the office of the Secretary-General, established the Office for Research and the Collection of Information to provide background information on conflicts. Nevertheless, the Secretariat and the Council found themselves obliged, in accordance with the description of their remit in the UN Charter, to become involved in almost all erupting conflicts, even the most complex ones. States, in contrast, had the luxury of being more selective; they could withdraw or abstain from the most complex crises, as no constitution of any state demands that a government be concerned with all international security threats. Also in pre-genocide Rwanda, the complexity of the evolving potential for conflict crossed ethnic, political, economic and social sectors and interacted between intra-state, state, regional and global levels (Uurtimo and Väyrynen 2000: 15). It is possible that the sheer complexity of the situation did not allow security experts to appraise it accurately, a factor that will be taken up as one possible cause of the UN's failure in Rwanda to be examined in more detail in Chapter 5.[6]

In addition to early warning, another type of detection mechanism characteristic of UN conflict management in the early 1990s appears to be organisational learning, whose function was to support the detection of new conflicts by reference to 'lessons learned'. As one former UN diplomat explains, 'The Secretariat, like the UN as a whole, was going through a hectic *learning process* in the 1990s. A lot of things had to be improvised.'[7] In fact, 'conventional wisdom' or simply 'drawing lessons from the past' could be more accurate descriptions of the mechanisms of organisational learning, because, as W. Andy Knight points out, 'Learning is generally very rare in any organization' (Knight 2001: 33). Moreover, learning lessons from the past may only mislead judgement in new situations. By the beginning of the 1990s, the Security Council had achieved the successful resolution of the Iran–Iraq war, the Namibian conflict and the Gulf war. However, as the international security environment was changing dramatically, the lessons learned from these occasions proved inapplicable to, and misleading for, subsequent conflict management initiatives in other contexts.

As Goulding describes the change, 'The successes also bred over-confidence, which caused the United Nations – member states and Secretariat alike – to make mistakes in a number of new peacemaking and peacekeeping initiatives' (Goulding 2002: 269). For example, many UN officials, such as Secretary-General Pérez de Cuéllar's right-hand Álvaro de Soto, contributed to the successful peace settlement of the civil war in El Salvador in 1989. Later, de Soto worked for DPA, briefing the Security Council on the situation in Rwanda in 1994. It is *possible* that de Soto's perception of the Rwandan civil war was distorted by his prior experience in El Salvador, which may have produced a misplaced over-optimism about the development of the political situation in Rwanda. Positive memories of El Salvador may have encouraged de Soto and other UN officials and diplomats to expect the improvement of the security situation in Rwanda after the Arusha peace accord, thereby preventing them from discerning the impending genocide. Such a phenomenon represents so-called 'cognitive dissonance', in which new information (obtained from Rwanda) was in increasing dissonance with lessons learned (from El Salvador, Namibia and other positive experiences), causing psychological stress.[8] This will be taken up as another possible cause of the UN's shortcomings in Rwanda to be analysed in Chapter 6.

The present chapter has thus far explored two types of control mechanisms and their underlying structures. They are presented in Figure 3.1.[9] Generally, the objective of early warning mechanisms is the prediction of conflict, and their function is to activate at the earliest warning of genocide, but they may also lead to overload and failure. The function of the mechanisms of organisational learning is to adapt to the outside security environment in accordance with 'lessons learned', but they may also produce a dysfunction, namely cognitive dissonance.

Securitisation mechanisms of the UN

It would be interesting here to examine Boutros-Ghali's *Agenda* as an output of the mechanism of bureaucratic rationalisation and to evaluate its functions and dysfunctions. Boutros-Ghali's classification of UN conflict management into three main categories can be regarded as a forceful imposition of rational–legal authority, as these categories proceeded to be commonly used in the Security Council, gradually becoming intersubjective properties of the Council and a fixed rulebook in the Secretariat. Boutros-Ghali invented the new category 'peace-enforcement units', much as 'peacekeeping' had been devised by Hammarskjöld. According to the *Agenda*, peace-enforcement units would be more

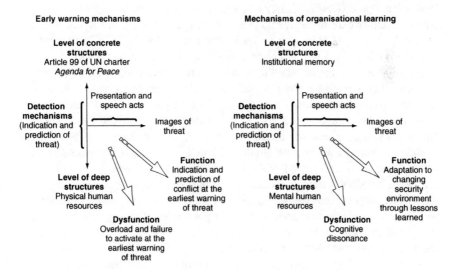

Figure 3.1 Detection mechanisms of the UN.

heavily armed than peacekeeping forces, and they would be made available by member states at the call of the Secretariat. Boutros-Ghali justifies the establishment of such troops with technical and historical reasons: 'Cease-fires have often been agreed to but not complied with, and the United Nations has sometimes been called upon to send forces to restore and maintain the cease-fire. This task can on occasion exceed the mission of peace-keeping forces...' (Boutros-Ghali 1992: 26). In this regard, Boutros-Ghali stresses the unpredictability of intra-state conflicts, whose nature requires 'extra muscles' (peace-enforcement units) in addition to traditional peacekeeping forces.

The *Agenda* states that, 'Peace-enforcement units should not be confused with the forces that may eventually be constituted under Article 43 to deal with acts of aggression or with ... peace-keeping operations' (Boutros-Ghali 1992: 26). Thus, the *Agenda* defines three categories of UN peace operations: peacekeeping forces, peace-enforcement units and coercive military action under Article 43. Interestingly, in Boutros-Ghali's *A Supplement to An Agenda for Peace* (henceforth the '*Supplement*'), published in January 1995, these three categories are reduced to two. The category of 'peace-enforcement units' vanishes, whilst the two other categories remain unchanged, although the 'forces under Article 43' mentioned in the *Agenda* are now termed 'peace-enforcement' in the *Supplement*.[10] The *Supplement* imposed a radical and uncompromising distinction between peacekeeping and peace-enforcement, whereas the *Agenda* had earlier implied that peace-enforcement units could fill the gap between peacekeeping and more coercive peace-enforcement. What could explain the strict division made by the *Supplement*?

At the time of writing the *Agenda* (1992), nobody could anticipate the magnitude of the crisis into which UN peacekeeping was about to plunge. Contrary to the wishes of the Secretariat, the Security Council launched the United Nations Protection Force (UNPROFOR) in 1992. UNPROFOR was deployed in a hot conflict zone 'where there was no peace to be kept', namely in Croatia and subsequently in Bosnia-Herzegovina under the name UNPROFOR II (henceforth 'UNPROFOR'). As a lightly armed peacekeeping force, it had neither the military equipment nor the mandate to respond to the harsh conditions of its area of responsibility. Consequently, UNPROFOR failed to protect civilians in numerous 'safe havens', took casualties for no strategic purpose,[11] and found its soldiers taken hostage by Serb forces (Economides and Taylor 1996: 59–93). 'Introducing the concept of "peace-enforcement",' as one former UN diplomat explained, 'was an attempt by Boutros-Ghali to derive something useful from the sad experiences of UNPROFOR in former Yugoslavia.'[12] In separating 'peace-enforcement' from 'peacekeeping', the Secretariat highlighted the need for a more forceful intervention in places like Bosnia-Herzegovina. Eventually, such interventions were carried out in Bosnia-Herzegovina by certain member states and the NATO Alliance. This took place in 1995, to the benefit of both local people and the UN peacekeeping force.

There was a further reason for introducing the concept 'peace-enforcement' with a longer historical echo. The United Nations Operation in Congo (*ONUC*) from 1960 to 1964 provided the first lesson in so-called 'mission creep' or 'creeping escalation', which refers to the way in which a peacekeeping operation gradually turns into an effort to enforce political order, thereby losing its major asset, impartiality (see, for example, Economides and Taylor 1996: 85). Usually this escalation also results in 'body-bag syndrome', as lightly-armed peacekeepers begin to fight a conventional war against well-armed combatants and suffer heavy military losses. This culminates in political tensions and a desire to pull back troops (Ryan 2000: 69; Thakur 1998: 5). In sum, distinguishing between 'peace-enforcement' and 'peacekeeping' already at the outset of conflict management served to prevent mission creep in general.

As Marrack Goulding describes, 'For a long time the United Nations' peacekeeping doctrine was that coercion cannot be combined with consent-based peacekeeping ... "there is no halfway house", I would say, "between peacekeeping and peace enforcement"' (Goulding 2002: 17). At the same time, however, in becoming a fixed canon to which all members of the bureaucracy were obliged to adhere in every situation, this categorical dichotomy engendered severely dysfunctional behaviour within the UN bureaucracy, and particularly the Secretariat. Peacekeeping operations are usually dispatched only after consent for deployment from the belligerent parties is received. Previously, such consent could be relied upon, as belligerents were usually internationally recognised governments. Since 1990, however, hostile parties have more typically been guerrilla movements and other extremist sub-state actors whose consent was uncertain and rarely absolute. In the 1990s, therefore, peacekeepers were likely to face continued armed resistance from the parties regardless of their prior consent. What was consequently required was a new peacekeeping doctrine that could provide the flexibility to adjust peacekeepers' rules of engagement and to ensure sufficient firepower with which to attain military superiority, or, put simply, the flexibility to move from peacekeeping to peace-enforcement.[13]

Barnett and Finnemore's definition of the 'irrationality of rationalisation' seems apposite here: 'The "rationalization" processes at which bureaucracies excelled could be taken to extremes and ultimately become irrational if the rules and procedures that enabled bureaucracies to do their jobs became ends in themselves' (Barnett and Finnermore 1999: 720). The old peacekeeping doctrine fostered this kind of organisational pathology. Based on the rigid and unquestioned distinction between 'peacekeeping' and 'peace-enforcement', the doctrine did not allow for a change of peacekeeping mandates or rules of engagement from traditional peacekeeping to peace-enforcement where it would have been possible and appropriate. Due to this bureaucratic inflexibility, peacekeeping operations could not properly adapt to the 'rhythm' of new conflicts. Such a detrimental side-effect will be taken up as another possible cause of the UN's breakdown in Rwanda. Subsequent chapters will examine whether this strict bureaucratic categorisation pre-empted the option of strengthening UNAMIR's mandate and equipment from traditional peacekeeping to peace-enforcement in order to respond to the changed circumstances, in which civil strife had turned into genocide.

According to Weber, the 'irrationality of rationalisation' is a logical consequence of *Zweckrationalität*, which can be translated as 'instrumental rationality'. *Zweckrationalität* is a particular kind of rationality prevalent in the deep structures of modern societies. In *Zweckrationalität*, everything is harnessed to profit-making and viewed as means of gathering optimum benefits for an organisation. According to *Zweckrationalität*, accounting is not only a suitable metaphor but an ideal way of working for an organisation: everything has to be systematically and accurately calculated to examine its net benefit to a bureaucracy. This profit-driven rationality gradually leads to a moral vacuum, as ethical considerations must yield to the gathering of ever-increasing profit. Means thereby overcome ends by becoming ends in themselves (Patomäki 1996b: 83–4; Weber 1948: 120). *Zweckrationalität* will be adopted as another possible cause of the dysfunctioning of UN conflict management in Rwanda. The aim will be to investigate the way in which the risks and benefits of intervention in Rwanda were calculated in relation to the overall net profit for the UN bureaucracy *as a whole*, and whether such risk calculations actually took precedence over the moral imperative to save Rwandans.

A further defect mentioned by Barnett and Finnemore is 'bureaucratic universalism'. Bureaucracies strive to orchestrate several local contexts at the same time. Their belief that technical knowledge is transferable across local circumstances licenses the creation and application of universal models to control local contexts. Such universal models, however, sometimes lead to critical misjudgement, as knowledge gained in one location is often not applicable in another. Barnett and Finnemore view the failure of the UN Special Representative in Yugoslavia as one such example. As the UN envoy in Cambodia, Yasushi Akashi learned to employ traditional peacekeeping – commitment to impartiality and avoidance of military force – which fitted well with the requirements of the local context. However, Akashi was then assigned to former Yugoslavia, where he continued to apply lessons learned in Cambodia whilst failing to recognise that Bosnia differed substantially from Cambodia. In Bosnia, an avoidance of military force caused a failure to protect safe havens when it would have been appropriate and effective (Barnett and Finnemore 1999: 721). Barnett and Finnemore, however, uncritically attribute Akashi's failure to the dysfunctions of bureaucratic rationalisation, without considering whether it was instead a symptom of cognitive dissonance. The main cause of Akashi's failure (Cambodia → Bosnia) may have been more closely related to the cognitive dissonance of learning (mental layer) than to bureaucratic mechanisms as such (social stratum),[14] much like Álvaro de Soto's possible failure (El Salvador → Rwanda) mentioned in the previous section.

Ilkka Heiskanen's realist cultural study of international politics demonstrates another type of function – dysfunction nexus derivative of the mechanism of bureaucratic rationalisation. Drawing upon Karl E. Weick's organisational theory, Heiskanen contends that one special feature of modern civilisation is 'loose coupling', meaning that modern systems are composed of independently responsive components, such as specialised agencies (Heiskanen 2000a: 19).

Weick asserts that loose coupling 'simply connotes things, "anythings," that may be tied together either weakly or infrequently or slowly or with minimal interdependence' (Weick 1976: 5). Modern civilisation has been successful in expanding its boundaries partly by dint of its loose coupling, which has facilitated enhanced efficiency through specialisation, the rise of expert communities, and the sophisticated division of labour (Heiskanen 2000a: 18). Loose coupling has however simultaneously produced a severe dysfunction. The UN, for example, can be viewed as a modern, loosely coupled organisation. The UN Commission on Human Rights is loosely coupled to the Security Council and the Secretariat, which reveals the central problem of loose coupling, namely a fragmentation of worldview: the Commission's area of specialisation was 'human rights', whereas that of the Council was 'international peace and security'. Subsequent chapters will investigate whether this contributed to the failure of conflict prevention in the Rwandan case.

Heiskanen's realist cultural account also draws upon Samuel Huntington's 'clash of civilisations' theory, which makes a distinction between modern and Western civilisations. Huntington points out that Western civilisation emerged during the eighth and ninth centuries and developed its distinctive characteristics in the centuries that followed, but only began to modernise in the eighteenth century (Huntington 1996c: 30). In this reading, it becomes possible to separate the 'Western' layer of the social stratum from the layer of 'modern' society. Huntington approximates Hans Morgenthau's political realist position in the sense that both view self-interest as the driving force of international politics (Huntington 1996c: 43). Self-interest, however, does not make Western civilisation unique amongst other civilisations. Rather, its uniqueness lies in a missionary zeal to universalise its own values and properties. 'Universalism', as Huntington notes, 'is the ideology of the West for confrontations with non-Western cultures' (Huntington 1996a: 66). The Western ideology maintains that all other civilisations should commit themselves to the Western values of liberal democracy, free markets, individualism, human rights, the separation of church and state and so on (Huntington 1996c: 40). When self-interest and universalisation converge, the result is often the upholding of hypocritical 'double standards' by Western civilisation, which epitomise the gulf between Western principle and Western practice. As Huntington remarks, 'Democracy is promoted, but not if it brings Islamist fundamentalists to power' (Huntington 1996c: 41). Heiskanen describes these dysfunctions as the 'wild forces' and 'dark side' of Western civilisation (Heiskanen 2000b: 11). They are the systematic, necessary and intrinsic dysfunctions of the mechanisms of Western civilisation, not its accidental, contingent or temporary malfunctions.

The Security Council is one arena in which the clash of civilisations occurs, as Huntington notes:

Decisions made at the UN Security Council ... that reflect the interests of the West are presented to the world as reflecting the desires of the world community. The very phrase 'the world community' has become the euphemistic collective noun ... to give global legitimacy to actions reflecting the interests of the ... Western powers.

(Huntington 1996b: 16)

Although Carl Schmitt's famous dictum, 'Whoever invokes humanity wants to cheat' (1976: 54) may be too cynical a description of Western intentions, African governments have indeed criticised the Western-dominated Security Council for the 'double standards' it routinely applies to European and African conflicts. For example, only six days after the Council reduced the UNAMIR operation in Rwanda from 2,539 to 270 troops, it strengthened the UNPROFOR operation in Bosnia by 6,500 extra troops.

Huntington, however, overlooks another considerable dysfunction of the mechanism of Western civilisation, namely the 'normalisation of deviance', by reducing the 'dark side' of the West to 'tangible' or 'hard' material factors, such as economic and military ones. *Contra* Huntington, critical realism emphasises that reasons are also causes. It follows that intangible and seemingly harmless discourses can wield considerable powers through the normalisation of deviance; they can, in fact, wreak devastating consequences for those constructed as 'deviant' or 'abnormal'. Normalisation here refers to the way in which the 'West' reproduces stereotypical images of the 'Rest', for example, by visualising Africa as the Conradian 'Heart of Darkness'. According to Michel Foucault, power in Western societies is exercised not only through the military and within political circles but also in schools, prisons and expert communities, where those subjects labelled 'abnormal' are systematically isolated, marginalised and excluded from the 'normal' sphere of life (see, for example, Foucault 1989a: 32–3; see also Dreyfus and Rabinow 1982: 184–5). The criteria determining which cases deserve attention and which are bluntly excluded depend less on the case itself (the 'Other') than on the insider account (the 'Us').

Mai Palmberg argues that the normalisation of deviance currently produces images of tribal warfare lurking around every corner of the African continent. 'Tribal warfare' constitutes a universal explanation for African conflicts, thereby conveniently obliterating the need to determine other causes of any particular crisis which could involve the 'West', such as the arms trade or arms exports from Western countries to Africa (Palmberg 2001: 10). This observation already provides a clue as to how it is possible that the Rwandan conflict was described by the UN Secretariat as 'mindless and tribal', conducted by 'unruly elements', when in reality it was neither tribal nor anarchic but political, systematic and well-orchestrated. The Secretariat created the false impression that no grounds for intervention existed in what was described as a senseless and irrational chaos with insurmountable difficulties and considerable risk of casualties. In other words, the Rwandan conflict was dumped into the category of 'hopeless, lost cases' providing no basis for intervention.[15] At the same time, the attention of Security Council discussions was distracted from French exports of weapons and other military assistance to the genocidal Rwandan government, even after the genocide had commenced. The most influential African delegate in the Council,

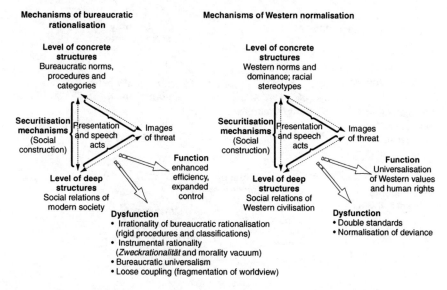

Figure 3.2 Securitisation mechanisms of the UN.

Nigeria, was not even aware of the French arms deliveries. 'If we were,' as the Nigerian representative Ibrahim Gambari noted to the author, 'we would have spoken up [against them].'[16] Figure 3.2 summarises the discussion of the mechanisms of Western normalisation and bureaucratic rationalisation in this section.[17]

Conclusion

According to a predominant concept in IR literature, there is not one, but two United Nations. This dichotomy is divided by the so-called 'neo–neo debate' between neo-realists and neo-liberals. The widely quoted UN scholar Inis L. Claude, Jr. describes the 'first' UN, which is emphasised by liberal institutionalists: 'The First UN is constituted by its staff, an international secretariat ... located in New York.' Claude continues by saying that, 'The Second UN is a collectivity formed by almost all the states of the world' (Claude 1996: 290–1), which captures the political realist conception of the UN. The previous chapter did not refute this well-established distinction but maintained that there is, in fact, a third UN. The latter is evidenced in the mechanisms that the UN Organisation initiates through co-operation between the Security Council and the Secretariat in order to control the international security environment.

This chapter has argued that four mechanisms in particular were characteristic of UN conflict management in the early 1990s. Each of these was triggered at the end of the Cold War: the subsiding of bipolar political squabbling in the Council raised optimism about the increasing use of *bureaucratic rationalisation* to not only resolve and manage conflicts but also to prevent their outbreak,

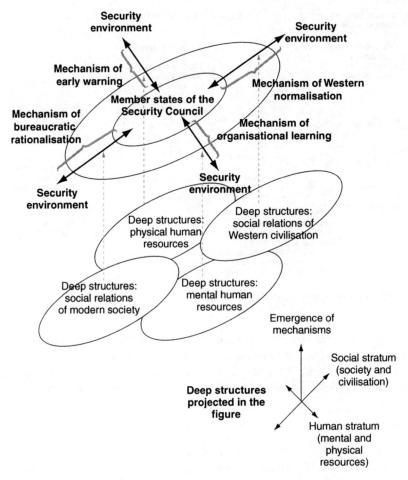

Figure 3.3 Summary of the analytical framework: the Security Council as an open system.

which, in turn, presupposed the application of *early warning* mechanisms. Simultaneously, the international security environment was dramatically shifting from a dominance of inter-state to intra-state conflicts, which prompted an unprecedented *organisational learning* process in an attempt to adapt to changing circumstances. At the same time, most of the 'new' conflicts were emerging in the Third World, but they were, unfortunately, often excluded from the concern of the Council by *Western normalisation*.

This chapter has shown that, although the political unwillingness of states can go some way to explaining the failure of the Council in the 1990s, it is also deficient in important respects. For, during the 1990s, the Council confronted puzzles that were humanly impossible to solve (overload of the mechanism of early warning), committed human errors whilst 'learning to walk' after the end of the Cold War (cognitive dissonance of the mechanism of organisational learning), visualised the world through rigid, self-constructed categories which proved misleading and obfuscating (dysfunction of the mechanism of bureaucratic rationalisation), and imposed double-standards and stereotypical images on the 'Other' (dysfunction of the mechanism of Western normalisation). In short, it is the very *complexity* and *contextuality* of social reality that must be conceded. This acknowledgement does not however sanction the primacy of control mechanisms over state actors. It merely serves to point out that actors, structures and mechanisms do not function in a *vacuum* but form *contexts* for one another. The mechanisms of early warning, organisational learning, bureaucratic rationalisation and Western normalisation combined together to form an epistemic complex, which both enabled and constrained the decision-making of the member states of the Security Council in the early 1990s. They also constituted an epistemic context, within which that decision-making was embedded. The following chapters will proceed to analyse their role in the Rwandan case: Chapter 5 will concentrate on the malfunctions of early warning, whilst Chapter 6 will examine the dysfunctions of bureaucratic rationalisation, cognitive dissonance in organisational learning and Western normalisation.

4   Explanatory theories of the UN's failure

Introduction

The purpose of this chapter is to provide a critical literature review of the accounts that discuss the UN's failure to prevent and halt the Rwandan genocide. The first section of the chapter aims to give a descriptive overview of the key events in the Rwandan case, a task which will be realised using the existing literature on the subject. The second and third sections will examine the way in which the causes of the UN's inaction are explained in the existing analyses. It will be claimed from the critical realist perspective that the previous investigations are characterised by positivist features similar to those outlined in Chapter 2, namely methodological individualism, empiricist fallacy, actor-centrism (anthropocentrism) and phenomenalism.[1]

Methodological individualism seems to have been adopted as a result of a popular 'hunt for individual responsibilities'; the common opinion held that a second holocaust in our times should never have been allowed to happen again. Therefore, those politicians, diplomats and other individuals who were guilty of such a devastating abdication of responsibility were to be exposed and held accountable. Furthermore, the sheer magnitude of the failure, particularly the withdrawal of UN troops from Rwanda in the midst of genocide, seemed to imply a deliberate plot to betray Rwandans. The dramatic appearance of events induced analysts to take the culpability of certain individuals as given without going deeper to examine the underlying reasons for, and causes of, their failure. 'Lynching' may not be a wholly accurate metaphor for this type of methodology, because all major inquiries into the Rwandan shambles are justifiable. However, such a description would not be entirely misleading either, as early accounts in particular take the guilt of the 'major culprit', the US, at face value.[2]

Methodological individualism stems also from another source, namely the empiricist fallacy. Early investigations tend to commit such a fallacy by drawing upon the past conjunction of events to illuminate the UN's failure in Rwanda. To grasp the connection between the empiricist fallacy and individualism in the existing literature, take, for example, the following statement published in 1995, which is bracketed into three parts below for the sake of clarity:

[S]ince events in Iraq, Somalia and even Bosnia [constant conjunction of events], no international action can be taken without the leading role of the United States [empiricist fallacy] who, this time, were unwilling to act as police force to the world [the methodological individualist explanation of the UN's failure].

(Destexhe 1995: 49)

In this account, individualism is blended with empiricism via the exclusive attribution of both the principal cause of the UN's failure and any possibilities for its avoidance to the US *as an empirical law*. It is such a 'covering-law explanation', coupled with individualism, that pervades existing literature. Samantha Power's account elaborates this explanation beyond the Rwandan case to encompass similar instances yet to ensue: 'For the foreseeable future, American leadership will be necessary to stop or punish genocide' (Power 2002: 262). Such methodological individualism has engendered two detrimental side-effects. First, it undermines a coherent understanding of how the individual actors were interrelated within a common structural framework. The above accounts, for example, fail to comprehend, or perhaps simply ignore, the existence of the potential powers of the Security Council as a collective actor, and the possibilities of the Belgian, Ghanaian and French UN forces situated in Rwanda at the time. This atomistic worldview, in turn, effectively nullifies the potential of emancipatory inquiry, for the possibilities of preventing the disaster did not lie in atomistic ontology (the efforts of individual member states and officials), but in relational ontology (relations between the Council and the Secretariat through control mechanisms). Thus, the purpose of this book is to 'piece together' actors, structures and mechanisms in order to construct a coherent outline of their emancipatory possibilities during the Rwandan genocide.

Overview of the UN's failure

This section will draw upon existing literature in order to provide a generic description of the main events in the abandonment of Rwanda by the Security Council and the Secretariat. The inaction and omissions of the Council during the genocide have been well-documented by previous investigations. Each of the fifteen member states of the Council has assumed, or been fitted into, a certain role in this story. If there are no heroes to be found, at least there are fellow sympathisers: a group of non-permanent members of the Council, including New Zealand, the Czech Republic, Nigeria and Spain, is presented as a vocal minority for action among indifferent 'by-standers'. The group of 'evil-doers' include three permanent members of the Council, namely the US, the UK and France. Although this book argues for a less simplistic story, the existing literature points to the fact that placing an element of blame with the three aforementioned countries is not unreasonable.

The role of the great powers in the UN's malfunction can be traced to the very beginning of UN involvement in Rwanda. When UNAMIR was established in October 1993, Boutros Boutros-Ghali requested the deployment of two battalions composed of 5,000 troops to Rwanda. However, the US suggested a force of only 500 soldiers. As a compromise, the Security Council authorised the sending of only one battalion to Rwanda, until in January 1994 Boutros-Ghali managed to persuade the Council to approve the deployment of the second infantry battalion. Moreover, the US and the UK repeatedly argued for the cheapest possible peacekeeping force in Rwanda and lobbied the Council to keep UNAMIR as cost-effective as possible. Consequently, UNAMIR suffered from severe shortcomings in equipment, personnel, training, intelligence and planning, which proved fatal both to peacekeepers and Rwandans when the genocide erupted (Boutros-Ghali 1999: 130; Melvern 1995: 4; Shawcross 2001: 107–8).

During the first week of the genocide, the discussion in the Security Council was characterised by ambiguity towards what was happening in Rwanda and indecisiveness as to what should be done about it. Linda Melvern and Human Rights Watch sharply illustrate the way in which the Council concentrated on the civil war as opposed to the genocide. The Council was concerned with the question as to how UNAMIR could assist in obtaining a cease-fire, but rarely touched upon the fate of Rwandans or how UNAMIR could respond to the crimes against humanity being perpetrated, except for those small 'humanitarian pockets' that were under its control and where Tutsi civilians had sought refuge (Des Forges 1999: 625–8). Eventually, it was the British UN Ambassador, David Hannay, who came up with four possible solutions to deal with the situation. Hannay's initiative, however, turned out to be a Trojan horse: it appeared as a rational framework to manage the Rwandan situation, but its ulterior motive was to justify the withdrawal of the bulk of UNAMIR from Rwanda.

The first of Hannay's solutions was to increase the number of peacekeepers and to strengthen the mandate of UNAMIR to include peace-enforcement, but Hannay deemed this option would lead to a repetition of Somalia. Hannay's reminder invoked the worst collective memories of the Somalia conflict, in which the UN had taken the highest casualties since *ONUC* (United Nations Operation in the Congo) in the early 1960s. Alternatively, UNAMIR could stay on without changes in its composition and mandate, but Hannay questioned the value of retaining UNAMIR, as he argued that UNAMIR was in no position to save civilians. As to the two remaining options, UNAMIR could be pulled out completely, or it could retain a small skeletal force in Rwanda. Hannay viewed the latter as the safest option. The US agreed, arguing that there was a serious risk for peacekeepers in an environment where there was 'no peace to be kept' (Melvern 2000: 153–4).

On 21 April 1994 the Council agreed Resolution 912, which reduced UNAMIR to 270 troops.[3] The above discussion clearly demonstrates that the Security Council, and its permanent members in particular, had 'blood on their hands'[4] in the Rwandan tragedy. But what role did the Secretariat play in this outcome? This section will proceed to address this question with reference to the existing literature. A week into the genocide, the non-permanent members began to request recommendations from the Secretariat on how to proceed in the

Rwandan situation, but no advice was forthcoming. In this vacuum, Ambassador Hannay presented the four options mentioned earlier, to strengthen or to withdraw UNAMIR (Melvern 2000: 153). But these options were, in fact, a means of disguising the desire to cut down the number of peacekeepers in Rwanda. If the Secretariat had decisively redeemed its role as an impartial expert by bringing forward proposals before Hannay's initiative, instead of following on from UK and US policy, the result might have been different. However, the Secretariat was not only indecisive but also reluctant to act. For the first two weeks of the genocide, Secretary-General Boutros-Ghali was on a tour of European capitals (Melvern 2001b: 108). Cancelling his tour would have been appropriate not only morally, due to the death of ten Belgian peacekeepers, but also politically, as Boutros-Ghali's absence from New York led to a lack of political leadership in the Secretariat. This seems to have paralysed the Secretariat, since the Secretary-General's powers were not sufficiently delegated to UN officials.

Suspicions about UN officials' mishandling of information were raised by the exposure of a piece of documentation known as the 'genocide fax' (Gourevitch 1998: 42). This cable was an internal UN report sent from Major-General Roméo A. Dallaire, the Force Commander of UNAMIR, to DPKO on 11 January 1994, three months before the beginning of the genocide. The cable reports a secret meeting between UNAMIR officials and a Hutu informant, who was a government politician working as a top-level trainer in the *Interahamwe* militia. What has captured the attention of most of those analysing the cable is its sixth section, which states that, 'He [the informant] has been ordered to register all Tutsi in Kigali. He suspects it is for their extermination. An example he gave was that in 20 minutes his personnel could kill up to 1000 Tutsis.'[5] The informant disagreed with the extermination of the Tutsi and was therefore willing to provide UNAMIR with the location of a major weapons cache delivered from the Rwandan Government Forces to the *Interahamwe* militia. The 'genocide fax' proves that the Secretariat had received warning signals of the forthcoming genocide three months prior to its beginning, but failed to present this crucial information to the Security Council. In fact, DPKO informed neither the Council nor the Secretary-General of the existence of the cable.[6] DPKO also rejected the request of the informant for protection from UNAMIR. Moreover, the Secretariat at first rejected the request from the UNAMIR Force Commander to seize the arms cache, again without consulting the Council, although stockpiling weapons clearly violated the provisions of the Arusha peace agreement concerning the Kigali Weapons Secure Area.

Institutional mismanagement was not restricted to the conflict prevention phase but also extended to conflict management during the crisis. Throughout the first month of the genocide, the Secretariat provided the Security Council with erroneous and misleading reports and briefings on the Rwandan conflict. On 12 April 1994 Assistant Secretary-General for Peacekeeping Operations Iqbal Riza addressed the Council and described the conflict as 'chaotic, ethnic, random killings' (Melvern 2000: 153; 2001b: 108). Similarly, Secretary-General Boutros-Ghali's reports to the Council on 20 April 1994 and 13 May 1994 claim that the killings were perpetrated by 'unruly elements'[7] and 'unruly members of the Presidential Guard'.[8] Riza and Boutros-Ghali thereby confused the disciplined, systematic and well-organised genocide with anarchic, tribal and mindless killing characterised by unruliness. On 29 April 1994, Boutros-Ghali's letter to the Council described the crisis as 'deep-rooted ethnic hatreds, which have plagued Rwanda in the past and which have again led to massacres of innocent civilians on a massive scale'.[9] Boutros-Ghali's statement carried a wrong perlocutionary force in at least four different respects.

First, the main proximate cause of the killing was not ancient tribal hatred but political manipulation and hate rhetoric from the *Akazu*. Boutros-Ghali's description erroneously implied that there was no possibility of intervening in such a 'mindless ethnic killing' without a high risk of casualties to UN troops. Second, it invoked the 'shadow of Somalia' by incorrectly equating the Rwandan crisis to the frenzy of ethnic violence in Somalia only six months earlier, where the UN took the heaviest casualties since the *ONUC* operation in the 1960s.[10] Third, Boutros-Ghali's attempts to associate the genocide with the previous sequence of conflicts in Rwanda was like comparing a hurricane to a seasonal autumn whirlwind, which served to undermine the severity of the crisis and the sense of urgency to intervene in Rwanda. What was most detrimental, however, was the way in which the genocide was conflated with the ongoing civil war. In the Secretary-General's reports, the explanation for the massacres was deemed to lie in the 'resumption of the civil conflict', that is, the 'resumption of fighting between the Rwandan Government Forces (RGF) and the Rwandese Patriotic Front (RPF)'.[11] As the Ambassador of New Zealand Colin Keating pointed out, 'The negative was that the members of the Security Council came to see Rwanda not as the smouldering volcano that it really was, but rather as a small civil war.'[12] The Secretariat's avoidance of describing the killings as genocide enabled the complete silencing of the magnitude of the conflict: during the first three weeks of genocide the Council did not discuss the systematic slaughter of Tutsi civilians by Hutu extremists at all, but instead considered the civil war between the RGF and RPF (Melvern 2001b: 108).

'First wave' of explanations: the role of member states

> But tellers of fables are prone to love a genre which focuses on the irresponsible cops (in this case, the U.S.A.), the simple hero who takes direct action (Paul Kagame) and a horrific villain – the genocidists.
>
> (Adelman 2000: 9)

After the generic description of main events conducted in the previous section, it is now possible to proceed to explore the causes of the UN's failure as proposed by existing literature. However, it is first necessary to clarify the terminology, particularly the terms 'first and second waves of literature', applied in the causal analysis below. As already mentioned in the introduction, the existing accounts are categorised in accordance with their methodological approaches, not the merits and value of their argumentation as such; rather, these categories represent Weberian ideal types, i.e. abstractions of the main methodological approaches applied in each of these groups of literature. Such abstractions unavoidably lead to crude generalisations at the expense of certain particularities and individual parts which are highly valuable in the existing literature. *The Joint Evaluation of Emergency Assistance to Rwanda* published in 1996, for example, includes some parts that amount to sophisticated structural analyses and make its categorisation as a 'second-wave study' somewhat unjustified. The term 'first wave' applied below refers to the literature of a certain time period, namely the earliest elucidations written during the first two years following the genocide. At the same time, it also denotes the dominance of a certain type of explanation still prevalent in the literature on Rwanda: by emphasising the 'lack of political will', the mainstream literature tends to attribute the explanatory factors of the tragedy to (state) agents and their volition, without considering that their will and behaviour was, to a greater or lesser degree, enabled and constrained by certain structures and mechanisms.

The 'first wave' of analyses focuses on states and the great powers in particular as the referent objects of explanation. These investigations are typically presented by UN officials, professionals, humanitarian workers and human-rights experts, such as Alain Destexhe (*Médecins Sans Frontières*) and Alison des Forges (Human Rights Watch). They were often eyewitnesses to the genocide and had first-hand information about the conflict. They also had high hopes for US action, which had previously shown both ability and willingness to conduct forcible humanitarian interventions, most notably in Somalia in 1993. Therefore, it is understandable that the first wave is susceptible to an empiricist fallacy, in which expectations are mixed with explanation. Oxfam's (UK and Ireland) account in 1994, for example, states of the UN's breakdown in Rwanda that, 'The United States, the world's only remaining superpower, took the lead in this shameful abdication of responsibility' (Vassall-Adams 1994: 56–8). Thus, the US was given the thankless task of bearing the banner of world police, simultaneously functioning as the scapegoat for any failure to 'save strangers'.[13] However, reducing the cause of the UN's failure to the actions of the US is bizarre, because this type of explanation ignores the potential powers of the Security Council as a collective actor; the potential abilities of the French, Belgian, Ghanaian, Senegalese, Polish and Tunisian UN forces; the French, Belgian and Italian evacuation troops situated in Rwanda at the time; the unused powers of the Secretariat to legitimise intervention in Rwanda through its rational–legal authority; and the responsibility of other states to conduct such intervention.

The first wave of accounts often draws upon the earlier statements of UN officials, particularly those of Secretary-General Boutros-Ghali and the UNAMIR Force Commander, Major-General Dallaire. Boutros-Ghali derives the explanation of the UN's breakdown mainly from its member states: 'The capacity of the United Nations to reduce human suffering in Rwanda was severely constrained by the unwillingness of Member States to respond to the changed circumstances in Rwanda...' (Boutros-Ghali 1996: 4).[14] In his letter addressed to the Security Council on 29 April 1994, Boutros-Ghali notes that the intervention in Rwanda 'would require a commitment of human and material resources on a scale which Member States have so far proved reluctant to contemplate'.[15] One month later, Boutros-Ghali phrased this complaint against member states as the 'absence of the collective political will'. This term appears in a report from the Secretary-General to the Council concerning the situation in Rwanda, a report in which Boutros-Ghali also for the first time applies the word 'genocide' in an official document to describe the events in Rwanda.[16]

Later, in May 1994, Boutros-Ghali attributed the UN's shortcomings in Rwanda to the 'donor fatigue' of Western countries. Boutros-Ghali noted that while Western countries had previously often been willing to assign troops and equipment to UN operations, the number of UN missions had dramatically peaked since the end of the Cold War. As a consequence, contributing countries became increasingly tired of strengthening any new operations (Lewis 1994). This explanation sounds convincing, as there were thirteen new peacekeeping operations initiated by the UN from 1988 to 1993, equal to the total number of all previous operations between 1945 and 1987. As a result, the UN faced over-stretched peacekeeping budgets. While the *total cost* of peacekeeping up until 1993 had been approximately ten billion dollars, in 1993 costs were forecast to rise to three billion dollars *per year* (Bourgi and Colin 1993: 581). Bound by the quota system, where Western countries are liable to pay more than developing countries with a lower GNP, the US paid 31 per cent of the whole peacekeeping bill. Thus, the US and its main political ally in the Council, the UK, were the most vocal opponents of UNAMIR from the time when France first suggested its launch in March 1993 (Melvern 2000: 77).

Boutros-Ghali's view is by and large shared by senior officials in the Department of Peacekeeping Operations. The then Under-Secretary-General for Peacekeeping Kofi Annan contended that, 'If there was a problem, it was not one of information or intelligence. The problem was lack of political will.'[17] Annan based his argument on the unwillingness of member states to contribute troops to UNAMIR II after the 'first' UNAMIR was withdrawn on 21 April 1994: 'Those who were critical did not offer ... the sceptical did not offer, and the silent did not offer. What choice did we have?' (quoted in Melvern 2000: 235). None of the Western countries responded favourably to the request by the Peacekeeping Department to send troops to UNAMIR II. In fact, on 29 April 1994 the US and the UK informed Boutros-Ghali that any action to stop violence in Rwanda should be taken primarily through the efforts of African countries (Boutros-Ghali 1996: 45). This left the Secretary-General with no option other than to write to more than thirty, primarily African, heads of state requesting troops. As a result, UNAMIR II came to be composed of African troops, with Western countries providing equipment.

On the ground in Rwanda, Force Commander Dallaire came to a similar cynical conclusion about the unwillingness of Western governments. Within days of the beginning of the genocide, nearly 1,500 highly capable troops from

France, Italy and Belgium landed in Kigali and began air evacuations of foreign expatriate communities. Several hundred US marines were stationed at the Burundian border, while the Americans were evacuated by land. Although UNAMIR assisted in the evacuation, the poorly equipped UN mission received no reciprocal assistance or supplies from the national evacuation forces, nor did the evacuation troops stay to support UNAMIR in peacekeeping efforts. As Dallaire describes their abandonment, UNAMIR was left 'with only survival rations that were rotten and inedible' (Dallaire 1998: 79). Dallaire's cynical impression was reinforced by the fact that the capitals of the troop-contributing countries of UNAMIR frequently ordered their national contingents within UNAMIR to limit their activities and not to use force to intervene in order to avoid the risk of casualties. Ultimately, the majority of the contingents were withdrawn. Only the governments of Ghana, Senegal, Uruguay, Congo and Tunisia left their contingents in place throughout the genocide. In Dallaire's words, their commitment stood out as 'sterling examples to the rest of the world' (Dallaire 1998: 79–80).

While UN officials tend to highlight the 'absence of collective political will' as the explanatory factor of the Rwandan tragedy, humanitarian and human-rights experts are in a position to criticise the political unwillingness of certain individual states. The Secretary-General of *Médecins Sans Frontières*, Alain Destexhe, lays the blame for the UN's disappointment squarely with the US: 'The Security Council left the Tutsi to their fate. Why? Because the United States was "haunted by the ghost of Somalia", where thirty of its soldiers had died' (Destexhe 1995: ix). On 3 October 1993 alone, eighteen US Rangers were killed in the single most lethal incident of the UN peacekeeping operation in Somalia, which triggered fierce domestic criticism of the Clinton administration. Republican hardliners, the US Senate and Congress sought a pledge from the president not to commit more troops to UN operations (Melvern 2000: 78). Thus, the Somalia debacle had repercussions for UNAMIR, which was established only two days later on 5 October 1993. The tragedy in Somalia gradually led to a new restrictive policy of the US towards UN peacekeeping missions.

More detailed information about US policy on Rwanda was obtained in autumn 2001, when the National Security Archive published declassified US government documents. Basing her findings on these documents, investigative journalist Samantha Power argues that it was not until 21 May 1994, six weeks after the genocide began, that the Secretary of State Warren Christopher permitted US diplomats to use the term 'genocide', or a 'type of genocide', in connection with the Rwandan crisis (Power 2003: 361–2). It was a further three weeks before US officials began using the term in public (Klinghoffer 1998: 100).

If the US contribution to the abandonment of Rwanda took place in an interest vacuum, that cannot be said of the other main player in the drama, namely the French government.[18] Following the *Inyenzi* raid of the RPF in Rwanda in October 1990, France sent not only weapons but also a small contingent of troops to assist President Habyarimana's government to repel the invaders. Within days of the *Inyenzi* raid, French troops in Rwanda stood at 600. The military assistance of France continued throughout the civil war and even after the beginning of the genocide, despite the UN weapons embargo. The Hutu government had developed a 'special relationship' with the French government. French political circles saw Rwanda as part of '*le pré carré*', that is, 'our own backyard' in Africa (Prunier 1998: 101–5). The political ties between the two regimes were strengthened by the strong personal relationship between President Mitterand's son Jean-Christophe, who was in charge of the Africa Office at the Elysée, and President Habyarimana's son Jean-Pierre (Clapham 1998: 199).

This 'special relationship' can be understood, on the one hand, using the theory of the 'Fashoda Syndrome'. As Gérard Prunier describes, the Fashoda Syndrome is a persistent French mindset, according to which 'the whole world is a cultural, political and economic battlefield between France and the "Anglo-Saxons"' (Prunier 1998: 105). According to this thinking, the English-speaking RPF represented the reincarnation of '*les Anglais*', attacking the French-speaking Hutu government with the support of the Anglophonic Ugandan government. In Mitterand's eyes, the *Inyenzi* attack was part of the Anglo-Saxon plot to destabilise and invade 'one of ours', and so the Habyarimana government had to be supported despite its human rights violations.

On the other hand, the French military support to the Rwandan Hutu government can be understood as a policy to expand the French sphere of influence over the former Belgian colonies of Rwanda, Burundi and the Democratic Republic of Congo. Although the Habyarimana government had enjoyed the 'special relationship' with Belgium as its former colony, in October 1993 Belgium cut off its arms deliveries to Rwanda. This withdrawal signalled an opening for France, which strived to incorporate Rwanda into its Franco-African family. Central Africa had become important to French political prestige, because in that corner of the world France could still be a superpower (Klinghoffer 1998: 17–18).

Moreover, it is interesting to note that France administered Rwanda as if it were a former French colony. Therefore, the key departments in the French establishment were the Ministry of Cooperation and Development regarding economic matters, the General Directorate for External Security in terms of arms deliveries, and the Africa Office for the maintenance of general political relations. As Arthur Jay Klinghoffer points out, 'This meant that the foreign ministry did not really control policy' (Klinghoffer 1998: 88). The way in which the foreign ministry was bypassed in French political relations with Rwanda could partly explain why the French government was not responsive to public criticism of French arms deliveries to the Rwandan government, which continued despite the latter's human rights abuses.

To speak of the 'first wave' or 'early' accounts in this context is in fact misleading, as the individualist type of explanation they favour has become the prevailing and commonly accepted norm of explanation. UN officials and academic researchers alike have continued to derive the explanation for the UN's failure in Rwanda from a lack of political will on the part of member states; mainstream literature tends particularly to invoke opinions expressed by Boutros-Ghali, Annan and Dallaire to emphasise political unwillingness as the crucial explanatory factor. The term 'political unwillingness', which is commonly applied in the existing literature, encapsulates two elements: methodological individualism and state-centrism. There is nothing wrong with this kind of explanation per se: the lack of political will on the part of member states must be a central consideration in explaining the Rwandan tragedy. However, many accounts erroneously imply that it is this factor alone that explains the shortcomings of the UN to prevent the genocide. Philip Gourevitch (1999), for example, claims that 'The desertion of Rwanda by the UN force was Hutu Power's greatest diplomatic victory to date, and it can be credited almost single-handedly to the United States' (Gourevitch 1999: 150). Set against this, it is argued here that political reluctance is a necessary but insufficient factor in itself by which to explain the Rwandan disaster. There is a fine line, but a crucial one, between 'flogging a dead horse' (judging 'Clinton and Co.' single-handedly) and analysing events realistically by judging the US and other states only *after* situating their actions in the structural context within which they were embedded.

In contrast to the first wave of explanations considered above, this book claims that the Secretariat played an important supportive role for the Security Council, because UN institutions formed a *context* for the decision-making of state actors by producing information (and misinformation) on the Rwandan conflict for the consumption (and manipulation) of state representatives. Most 'first wave' accounts, however, tend to play down the importance of institutional structures. Bruce Wallace, for example, deems it a '*silly* assumption' that 'UN staffers withheld crucial information from the Security Council until it was too late to stop the killing …. The main players in the drama – the French, American and Belgian governments – *all knew exactly* what was unfolding' (Wallace 2000: 34; emphasis added by author). By reducing their explanation to state actors, Wallace and most other authors fail to realise the value added by the institutional context within which the member states of the Council were situated during the Rwandan crisis. In contrast, Anders Bjurner perfectly captures the importance of such a relationship: 'Political will … will be dependent on the depth and relevance of the analysis, the time perspective and the dynamism of the process presented and not least in what fora the government was faced with the case for prevention' (1998: 288). Moreover, considerations about the political will and national politics of individual states do not satisfactorily answer the question as to why all the great powers and international society as a whole were not responsive to the genocide. This being the case, it is necessary to shift the level of analysis from states to UN institutions, which will be the focus of the next section.

'Second wave' of explanations: the role of the Secretariat

'Why me? And why us? And why America?' And the only answer is, 'Because destiny put you in this place in history, in this moment in time, and the task is yours to do'.

(Tony Blair; quoted in Jeffery 2003)

Kofi Annan and Boutros-Ghali have proven themselves unprepared to fill this position by refraining from using the power entrusted in them.

(Willum 1999: 28)

This section will examine the 'second wave' of explanations that has emerged in the existing literature, which widens the sphere of blame from states to institutional actors. Howard Adelman's view vividly illustrates this shift from one-dimensional explications based on the lack of political will to more complex accounts. Adelman criticises both Arthur J. Klinghoffer and Philip Gourevitch for simplicity: the latter for holding the US almost singularly responsible for the genocidists' success, and the former for removing all responsibility from the shoulders of UN officials. This study concurs with Adelman's view that 'There were many actors and all played their respective parts in the disaster' (2000: 9). It is at least understandable that states felt hesitant to 'send their boys into harm's way', whereas telling the truth about the conflict would not have directly harmed anyone. 'Telling stories' about what was happening in Rwanda was virtually the only power resource that the Secretariat possessed, but it was a powerful one, and the Secretariat misused and underused it. As Linda Melvern points out, the debate in the Security Council is often shaped by recommendations from the Secretary-General (Melvern 2001b: 104). In the case of Rwanda, however, the Secretariat fell silent.

This book maintains that the importance of UN institutions was accentuated in the Rwandan case for four reasons. First, there was the 'dilemma of lead agency'. Oxfam (UK and Ireland) is right in claiming that 'France, and now the USA and the UK, have proved that it is possible to send troops within days if there is the political will' (Vassall-Adams 1994: 59). However, only a handful of strategically or geopolitically important nations can enjoy the luxury of such automatic protection on the part of the great powers, while others are dependent on the collective opinion of states and the lobbying of independent institutions for sending troops to rescue strangers, as in Somalia and Rwanda. Hence, the importance of institutions is accentuated when the decision-making of the Security Council concerns a politically unimportant country. As a geopolitically distant country, Rwanda faced indifference from all the permanent members of the Council, with the exception of France. Virtually all Council members appeared reluctant to step forward and emphasise those pieces of information that pointed to genocide. That is because such an initiative, showing special concern for Rwanda, would have implied willingness on the part of that state to lead or to actively engage in conflict management efforts in Rwanda. In this stalemate, the institutional structure, and particularly the Secretariat, had a special role and responsibility to bring forward and highlight crucial information, because all the others were hesitant to do so.

Second, the constitutive and regulative rules of the UN define the Secretariat's role as an impartial actor. Equipped with rational–legal authority, the Secretariat could have recognised and 'publicised' the 'objective truth', that is, genocide, more credibly, rapidly and powerfully than state representatives concerned with their vested national interests, such as France with known pro-*MRND* interests and the US with 'disinterest' in basically anything relating to Rwanda. Thus, rational–legal authority is a considerable power resource as such, and its use/misuse constitutes as valid a basis for judging responsibilities as political willingness/unwillingness

Third, empirical evidence indicates that the Secretariat's rational–legal authority could have made a difference. For example, in October 1993 the Security Council authorised the deployment of only one of the two UNAMIR battalions proposed by Secretary-General Boutros-Ghali. In December 1993, however, Boutros-Ghali was able to persuade the Council to authorise the deployment of the second battalion to Rwanda. Boutros-Ghali succeeded in this by invoking his rational–legal authority, namely by justifying the deployment of troops by highlighting the fragility of the security situation in Rwanda and the failure of the parties of the Arusha peace accord to establish the Broad Based Transitional Government (Shawcross 2001: 109).

Fourth, the conventional wisdom maintains that the local embassies of France, Belgium and the US possessed 'superior' local intelligence (see, for example, Wallace 2000: 34), but this is only partially true. Within six days of the beginning of the genocide, all embassies in Kigali, except that of China, had closed. Similarly, all the aid agencies and development co-operation missions had closed their offices (Melvern 2001b: 107). It was UNAMIR that stayed in Rwanda and regularly conveyed first-hand information to the UN Secretariat. Thus, the Secretariat possessed valuable intelligence information concerning the deterioration of the security situation in Rwanda, at least in the Kigali section.[19] Moreover, if the Security Council had possessed better information and a clearer sense of the ongoing genocide in Rwanda, it is possible that, at the least, the non-permanent members would have pressured the Council to strengthen UNAMIR instead of withdrawing it. Furthermore, they could have affected public opinion in the international community to support greater efforts to save threatened civilians in Rwanda.

As UN institutions seem to merit attention with regard to the Rwandan case, it is now appropriate to examine the way in which the existing literature explains the causes of the Secretariat's failings. Three profound international inquiries and numerous other academic studies have striven to explain these shortcomings. The most recent extensive inquiry, The Report of the International Panel of Eminent Personalities (IPEP) to Investigate the 1994 Genocide in Rwanda and the Surrounding Events, was presented by the Organization of African Unity (OAU) in May 2000.[20] The IPEP attributes some of the Secretary-General's failures to his ill-advised strategic decisions, such as the marginalisation of sub-regional and continental actors, including the OAU, in conflict management in Rwanda (IPEP 2000: 101). However, the IPEP falls into the same reductive fallacy that is characteristic of early accounts, as it diminishes the importance of the institutional structure of the UN. The IPEP holds that the problem of early warning lay with the states, particularly Belgium, France and the US, which received substantial early warning signals but lacked the political will to act upon such information. The IPEP points out that, 'When they are motivated, western powers can mobilize troops in a matter of days rather than weeks or months' (IPEP 2000: 100). However, the IPEP ignores the fact that the less influential or 'attractive' a country is on the political landscape of the international community, the more importance UN institutions have for that country in terms of raising awareness and concern for its people. And the fewer incentives there are for individual states to bring forward information that requires action in that country, the more relevant independent institutions become in distributing such information. The final chapter of this book will elaborate these arguments into a model of the 'UN safety net'.

Existing explanations for the Secretariat's shortcomings in conveying early warning signals to the Security Council seem to fall into two categories: intelligence failure produced by individual officials or deliberate political decision to withhold information. In the former category, there was a problem with 'messengers', as another major international inquiry, the Joint Evaluation of Emergency Assistance to Rwanda (1996) points out. The Secretariat paid inordinate attention to distorted and misleading media reporting of the Rwandan conflict while discounting the information flowing from the field and warnings from its own system. The Secretariat's briefings to the Security Council therefore reflected the popular media image rather than the analysis of more informed and professional observers. Moreover, the relevant units of the Secretariat were thinly staffed. Only one person in DPKO consistently monitored Rwanda, and this official was also burdened with heavy operational duties (Adelman and Suhrke 1996: 66–9).

Nonetheless, intelligence failure alone cannot explain the Secretariat's omissions, given that UN officials did possess crucial information, including the 'genocide fax'. This begs the question as to what the Secretariat's intentions were in not bringing these crucial pieces of information to the attention of the Security Council. Bruce D. Jones is inclined to take a rather sympathetic position: although the Secretariat's intentions were good, the results were poor. Jones points to the fact that there was a meaningful effort underway by the international community to prevent and mitigate the Rwandan conflict for three-and-a-half years prior to the genocide, including the Arusha peace process. As Jones summarises his view, 'The crisis in Rwanda illustrates not only the failure to act but also the ultimate failure of actions taken. It is the story of the failure of intervention as well as non-intervention' (1995: 233). Jones raises two major themes in the overall dynamics of failure: the weakness of international institutions and the paucity of coordination between them. As for the first factor, the perception of early warning signals was not only hampered by the weak political support of states but also by various other 'blinders', such as the failure of the UN bureaucracy to fully understand the cultural legacy of Rwandan history (Jones 2001: 127–9). With regard to the latter factor, Jones notes that there was a breakdown in coordination between the mediation and implementation phases of the peace process. If the mediation process was to exclude and isolate extremists, as was the case with the Arusha process, then the implementation phase (UNAMIR) should have been equipped with enough powers to contain the extremists (Jones 2001: 170).

While Jones tends to have an overtly benevolent stance on the Secretariat's intentions, Bjørn Willum is inclined to take a wholly contrasting viewpoint. Willum uses the Popperian method of falsification to show that the Secretariat officials were neither the 'ambassadors of goodwill', as Jones implies, nor the 'powerless scapegoats' that UN officials portray themselves to be. Nor was the lack of information the cause of the disappointment. Instead, Willum claims that the top Secretariat officials took a deliberate political decision to withhold information regarding the Rwandan conflict. However, there remain problems with Willum's account. First, after spilling ink to negate the three aforementioned alternative explanatory factors, Willum cannot come up with a better rationalisation as to why the Secretariat should have chosen the draconian policy of withholding information.[21] Second, Willum overlooks a fourth factor in his method of falsification, namely what this book calls the 'troublemaking' mechanisms. Willum is correct in stating that the lack of information is not a credible stand-alone explanatory factor, but what Willum ignores is that there were bureaucratic and other mechanisms which severely hampered the processing of such information in the Secretariat.

It could be said metaphorically that the second wave of inquiries reached its peak when Secretary-General Kofi Annan set up the Independent Inquiry into the Actions of the United Nations during the 1994 Genocide in Rwanda. The 'Carlsson Inquiry', as the Independent Inquiry is also known,[22] was unprecedented because the UN Secretariat for the first time reflected on its own conduct. The reason for this new openness and self-reflectivity was the embarrassing documents that leaked out from the Secretariat, such as the 'genocide cable', provoking widespread criticism of the Secretariat and thereby placing the credibility of the UN in question. In its conclusions, the Carlsson Inquiry states:

> The responsibility for the failings of the United Nations to prevent and stop the genocide in Rwanda lies with a number of different actors, in particular the Secretary-General, the Secretariat, the Security Council, UNAMIR and the broader membership of the United Nations.[23]

The Carlsson Inquiry stands out from simplistic early accounts in the sense that it does not merely shift responsibility onto the member states. The Secretariat and other institutional actors are also 'put on line'. For example, the Inquiry finds it disturbing that the Secretary-General could have done more to argue for the reinforcement of UNAMIR in the Council.[24] On the other hand, the Carlsson report echoes the methodological individualism of previous examinations in the way in which responsibilities are allocated to individual actors. The conclusions of the report are also organised according to this individualistic principle.[25] As the last exhaustive inquiry into the role of the UN in the Rwandan genocide,[26] the Carlsson Inquiry illustrates where the research on the subject currently stands.

The next section will address the crucial question as to what can be made of the existing literature, and in which direction research should proceed. Despite an impressive amount of studies on the subject, the majority of the existing accounts, with the exception of Michael Barnett's book *Eyewitness to a Genocide* (2002), have sought only to describe the Rwanda debacle. As demonstrated above, previous investigations have meticulously *explained* on whose desks and on which dates reports of genocide landed, and the way in which desk officers responded to, or, in most cases, ignored these crucial pieces of information. They have not gone further to try to *understand* these actions by reference to those structures and mechanisms that affected the decision-making, and operated within the UN Organisation and bureaucratic culture to hamper the processing of such information. This study maintains that the explaining type of story-telling concentrating on events and individual behaviours is inadequate, as it largely ignores the structural factors that affected and constrained the decision-making of diplomats and security experts.[27]

Transcending the 'blame game': towards a deeper understanding of the UN's failure

This book endeavours to understand the actions of UN officials and diplomats by situating them within the social context, i.e. the conglomeration of structures and mechanisms which contributed to the fatal mistakes made by those individuals, and to their betrayal of Rwandans. How, then, does the model of structural embeddedness outlined in Chapter 2 relate to the existing literature on Rwanda analysed above? Figure 4.1 portrays the main argument of this chapter, according to which the existing literature tends to commit an anthropocentric fallacy by decontextualising the actions of the members of the Security Council and Secretariat officials to the exclusion of the wider structural framework of the UN, i.e. 'carving' actors out of the social context. The 'first wave' of investigations reveals only two major factors by which to explain the UN's failure, namely the *Realpolitik*[28] of states and national factional politics. The 'second wave' uncovers certain structural malfunctions that played a part in the failure, but still demonstrates methodological individualism by focusing on the behaviour of individual UN officials. The role of the structures and mechanisms of the UN in the Rwandan disaster has been largely ignored. The aim of the following chapters is therefore to examine those themes that have been characterised by question marks in the existing literature; that is, to explore and understand the structural context within which the decision-making of the Council and the Secretariat was embedded.

It is only in recent years that research on the Rwandan case has seen a push towards a more structural direction, spearheaded by three authors, namely Michael Barnett, Howard Adelman and Astri Suhrke. They can be viewed as the forerunners of a third, structuralist wave of themes. Their accounts stand out as exceptions from the individualistic story-telling of the existing literature, as they detail certain structural causes underlying the UN's failure. However, none of

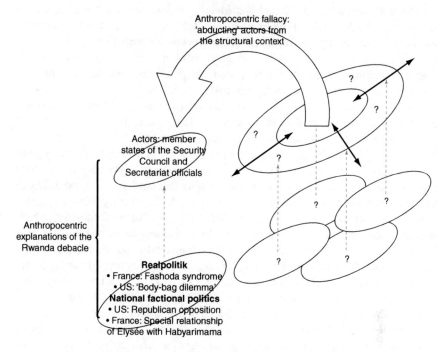

Figure 4.1 Decontextualised explanations of the UN's failure in Rwanda.

them have applied an extensive theoretical framework to fulfil that task. This book strives to both develop and move beyond these accounts and thereby add to the nascent third-wave literature. As will be demonstrated in this section, the main value this book can bring to the third wave lies in the application of a critical realist methodology.

Barnett can be conceived of as the foremost author of the 'third wave'. Unlike the mainstream literature on Rwanda, his account does not so much concentrate on registering individual omissions and inaction on the part of UN diplomats and officials, but rather focuses on the rules and norms of the UN bureaucracy that affected the decision-making of these actors. Barnett examines the way in which the bureaucratic culture of the UN shaped the behaviour of diplomats and officials by alienating them from their original ethical positions and socialising them to a different, organisationally situated morality. Hence, Barnett sharply illustrates how concerns regarding Rwanda were replaced with a more or less heartless bureaucratic logic (Barnett Barnett 2002; 2003: 174–91). According to Barnett, the rules of peacekeeping functioned as social optics through which the possibilities of intervening in Rwanda were viewed: those rules excluded the possibility of peace-enforcement and restricted the normative boundaries of responsible peacekeeping to merely monitoring cease-fires and peace agreements, as more robust peace-enforcement measures would put the lives of peacekeepers at risk and were therefore deemed irresponsible (Barnett 2003: 176–7).

The Somalia debacle in 1993 had considerably tightened these rules. As a consequence, UNAMIR was prohibited by the UN bureaucracy from taking any enforcement action against Hutu militias to prevent the genocide.

However, Barnett's analysis is illustrative of a *reductive ontology*, which uncompromisingly accounts for only socio-cognitive and bureaucratic factors, but at the same time discredits human and material ones. Barnett does, indeed, recognise the need for 'organizational and sociopsychological theories' (Barnett 2002: 114) to explain the Rwandan fiasco, but fails to specify which theories and what psychological mechanisms. Moreover, Barnett ignores the lack of human resources to predict the genocide, cognitive dissonance and those psychological mechanisms that are *un*related to bureaucratic processes as possible explanatory factors. This book endeavours to produce a more balanced, holistic and differentiated account of the Rwandan crisis by providing a deeper insight into particular explanatory theories and by invoking the critical realist methodology, which accounts not only for social processes (securitisation mechanisms), but also human ones, such as the resources enabling humans to foresee events and the deep psychological structures underlying an individual's perception and misperception of conflicts (detection mechanisms). The main value added through this holistic approach is the realisation that the UN's collapse in Rwanda was not produced by a single mechanism, i.e. bureaucratic rationalisation, but was also generated by the malfunctions of other mechanisms and in a wider psychological sense than merely the socio-cognitive processes of a bureaucracy. With regard to the analysis of bureaucratic rationalisation as one of the four mechanisms to be examined in the subsequent chapters, this book will not only expand upon Barnett's conception of bureaucratic rationalisation but also transcend it in some respects. For example, this book will add certain aspects of bureaucratic rationalisation that are not considered by Barnett, such as *Zweckrationalität*, or the instrumental rationality of modern organisations, and their loose coupling and fragmentation of worldview.

While Barnett concentrates on bureaucratic rationalisation, the two other harbingers of the structuralist approach to the Rwandan case, Astri Suhrke and Howard Adelman, pave the way towards understanding the Security Council's role in the Rwandan crisis from a structural viewpoint. Adelman and Suhrke's 2004 account explores certain 'structural weaknesses of the Council' that contributed to the Rwandan fiasco, such as the lack of accountability and transparency of the Council, its failure to affirm the legal principles of international law, which culminated in the undermining of the Genocide Convention, and the unrepresentative nature of the Council's composition (Adelman and Suhrke 2004: 484).

Conclusion

This chapter argues that the 'missing part' in the Rwandan story is the complexity of structures and mechanisms of the UN that contributed to the failure. The second section of this chapter showed that the majority of studies believe the main explanatory factor of the tragedy to be the political unwillingness of the member states of the Security Council, and particularly the apparent selfishness of the permanent members. However, if it is correct to say that the Council's policy was dominated by the US, then it is also true that the academic debate on the Rwandan catastrophe has been dominated by an emphasis on *Realpolitik*, which has limited and precluded analysis of other possible causes of the UN's failure.

The third section claimed that more recent literature sheds light on the role of the Secretariat in the drama. Even more importantly, it exposes not only individual mistakes but also certain *structural* malfunctions, such as the fact that the Secretariat was too thinly staffed to deal with the complexity of the Rwandan crisis. These occasional explications of structural causes notwithstanding, the second wave of literature is still characterised by methodological individualism and a certain simplicity of analysis into the causes of the failure. For example, Bruce Jones is correct in claiming that there was a disparity between the mediation and implementation efforts of the Arusha peace process, but he fails to explain more fully which mechanisms caused such disparity. One answer could be that the mechanism of organisational learning misled mediation experts to expect positive results from the Arusha process, as they had previously been involved in the successful resolution of the civil wars in El Salvador and Namibia, so thinning down the implementation troops (UNAMIR) seemed logical at the time. This underlines the need for a systematic analysis of generative mechanisms, which will be the subject of subsequent chapters.

This chapter has shown that previous accounts are 'heavy on the *descriptive* and *explaining* side of story-telling', as they meticulously detail events and the behaviour of UN diplomats and officials. However, this comes at the expense of a deeper *understanding* of the mechanisms embedded in the mindsets and bureaucratic structures which were the underlying cause of the dysfunctional behaviour of those actors. Michael Barnett's recent account stands out from the previous literature for the way in which it goes beyond the descriptive level of explaining to a deeper level of understanding. This is facilitated by Barnett's privileged access to the insider account, as he worked as a political officer at the Permanent Mission of the US to the UN from 1993 to 1994. However, while Barnett's account offers an extremely useful starting point by examining bureaucratic rationalisation, there is a need to consider other mechanisms that may have had an effect on the UN's actions. This book will follow Barnett's 'understanding' method, but will strive to go beyond it by opening up the whole spectrum of 'troublemaking' mechanisms. These will be systematically analysed in the following chapters.

5 Early warning

Introduction

This chapter will set out to explore the uncharted waters of the Rwandan drama, namely the mechanisms and structures that explain the failures of UN officials and diplomats. Chapter 3 located these in the socio-historical context of UN conflict management in the 1990s, whilst this chapter and the next one will put that structural framework into practice by means of an inquiry into the role of these mechanisms in the Rwandan case. The primary methodological tool will be the *first phase of the method of double movement*, that is, abstraction. As outlined in Chapter 2, abstraction moves beyond the 'surface level' of describing phenomena and events to the 'underlying level' of understanding the mechanisms and structures in which these are rooted. Within the theoretical framework employed here, abstraction refers to the retroduction of mechanisms from events. This chapter will concentrate exclusively on early warning, surely the mechanism that harboured the greatest potential to detect the genocide.

The secondary methodological tool derives from the *second phase of the method of double movement*. Chapter 3 demonstrated that the two phases of double movement are not strictly linear steps. The search for an emancipatory vision delineating outcomes which would have been more desirable in the Rwandan case must not, therefore, necessarily be delayed until the net effect of all four mechanisms has been assessed. This chapter and the next one will thus contain sections that will address the intriguing questions pertaining to how agents could have transformed the UN system in order to liberate themselves from the dysfunctional effects of a particular mechanism, and what positive outcomes such transformations could have produced.

The first section of the chapter will draw upon new evidence from the *Melvern Archive* to reveal the diverse ways in which the malfunctions of the early warning mechanism actually contributed to the UN's failure. The second section will explore the institutional weaknesses underlying the shortcomings of early warning. It will be argued that the vacuum of early warning structures was so profound that it obstructed not only proactive conflict prevention in the pre-genocide phase, as certain previous studies maintain (Adelman 1998a: 56), but also reactive conflict prevention during the early weeks of the genocide.

Phenomenal level: the malfunctions of early warning

No, we were not aware of this [January] cable, but we as non-permanent members of the Security Council were aware that something dangerous was happening ... So I think, in my own view, the importance of that telegram may have been overblown.[1]

(Ambassador Ibrahim Gambari)

This chapter will establish an interesting contrast between two sets of data: on the one hand, interviews with non-permanent members of the UN Security Council indicate that the UN bureaucracy possessed sufficient information to detect the genocide at an early stage; on the other hand, documentary sources reveal that the shortcomings of early warning were deeper than the interviewees acknowledge. The reasons for this contrast lie in the persistent efforts of political actors and the research community to downplay the lack of early warning in the Rwandan tragedy. In the case of decision-makers, such efforts seem partly attributable to the belief held by many non-permanent members in the untested potential of the UN to prevent the genocide, particularly in terms of the unused capacities of permanent Council members. Such a retrospective belief, coloured by idealism, recalls the so-called 'backward causalities' described in Chapter 1. In the case of researchers, it will be claimed that their motivation lies in a desire to apportion blame exclusively to individual actors, thereby diverting attention away from other possible explanatory factors, such as the lack of early warning.

On closer scrutiny, the backward causalities committed by the reconstruction of past events cannot be sustained. It was not until 28 April that a crucial distinction was employed which changed the course of the Security Council's discussion. It was the separation between what Under Secretary-General Ibrahim Gambari, Nigeria's Permanent Representative to the UN at the time, called 'two types of fighting' in Rwanda: civil war between armed forces, and the systematic slaughter of innocent civilians.[2] The importance of this 28 April meeting is accentuated by the fact that it heralded the shift in focus of the Council's discussion from the former type of killing to the latter, although the genocide had begun three weeks prior to this date. In this meeting, Gambari pointed out that the Council's discussions had thus far concentrated on only the civil war. The Czech Ambassador Karel Kovanda agreed, adding that 20 per cent of the Council's discussions were preoccupied with the cease-fire and 80 per cent on withdrawing UNAMIR. Meanwhile, the slaughter of civilians was largely ignored.[3] The New Zealand Ambassador Colin Keating also noted that the so-called 'second level of killing' had not been addressed in the Council's discussions. In order to highlight the difference between the two levels of killing, Keating reminded the Council that the threat to civilians behind enemy lines would continue even if a cease-fire was concluded between the parties of the civil war.[4] By that junction, even the most unwilling permanent members of the Council had to assent to a differentiation between the two levels of killing. The US finally acknowledged the main culprit of the massacres by admitting that the Rwandan government was actively seeking to purchase arms to kill civilians.[5] Even China conceded that the 'second level of killing' had to be addressed in a presidential statement of the Council.[6]

These informal Security Council meetings of 25 and 28 April 1994 were ground-breaking in two respects. First, the Council for the first time differentiated the Rwandan conflict. The differentiation between the 'two levels of killing' was crucial, as the Council had thus far confused the massacres of civilians with civil war. The latter form of killing and the necessity and potentiality of a cease-fire to arrest it had heretofore dominated Council discussions. Second, the Council for the first time clearly identified and named the killers, i.e. the Rwandan Government Forces. Together these two breakthroughs in recognising the real nature of the Rwandan conflict opened up the possibility of describing it as a genocide, although another week expired before the first Council member, namely the Czech Republic, publicly used the word 'genocide' in connection with the Rwandan crisis. This first acknowledgement of genocide by the Czech Republic took place in an open meeting of the Council concerning the situation in Mozambique on 5 May 1994.[7] Nevertheless, the initial *public* recognition of the large-scale killings of Tutsi civilians by Hutu forces in a formal meeting on 5 May and in an informal meeting on 25 April did not necessarily constitute the first time that the Czech delegation *actually* perceived the true nature of Rwandan events, as evidenced by the following:

> 25 April is fairly late. I don't think that it would have taken that long to figure it out. Especially with the information from non-governmental organisations, to my delegation at least, and I'm sure the New Zealand delegation having been in constant contact especially with the Africa Watch. So I don't think that 25 April would have been the first time that we realised it.[8]

Kovanda's statement reveals that the intent behind his question regarding the perpetrators of the Butare massacres in the Security Council's informal meeting on 25 April was not so much concerned with receiving information, as the Czech delegation was obviously already well-informed of the massacres by human rights organisations. Rather, Kovanda's question seems to have been intended more as a speech act aimed at shifting the focus of Council discussion from the context of civil war to that of government-directed massacres of civilians. Assuming that the Czech delegation had already been rendered aware of the systematic massacres of Tutsi civilians by 25 April, when and exactly how did this realisation take place? To this crucial question, Kovanda gave the following answer:

> For me, the critical moment was reading an article in the *New York Times* written by Frank Smyth, which made so much sense. And not only internally in terms of the article making sense itself, but also it helped shed light on the discussions in the Council which I didn't quite understand completely while I was in the Council.[9]

Frank Smyth's article was published in the *New York Times* on 14 April 1994, prior to the crucial meetings of the Security Council which acknowledged the genocide. However, it draws a more confusing picture of the Rwandan conflict than Kovanda acknowledges in retrospect. The article neither recognises the genocide nor explicates the nature of the killing in more detail; rather, it focuses primarily on French arms deliveries to Rwanda. The article fails to identify the systematic and organised nature of the killing and the coordination between the different actors involved in it: 'Hours after the President was killed last Wednesday, his Presidential Guard went on a rampage ... Militiamen and soldiers under irregular command randomly attacked Tutsi or anyone suspected of being one' (Smyth 1994: 21). In this regard, the article actually endorses the stereotypical image of the Rwandan conflict as spontaneous and 'random' attacks by 'irregular' forces. Thus, the information that Kovanda gleaned from the article could hardly amount to an accurate picture of the scale and organised nature of the killing in Rwanda.

The closest estimate that this book can present of the crucial date when the Czech delegation became aware of the Rwandan genocide is 25 April 1994, when Ambassador Kovanda for the first time applied the term 'genocide' in his communication with the Czech Foreign Ministry. On that day, Kovanda wrote to Prague: 'This [Rwandan conflict] is clearly a genocide, of governmental and presidential Hutu units against the Tutsis. Whichever way one looks at the numbers, there had been some 1.2 million Tutsis before the war, of which certainly 100,000 have been killed.'[10] What is noteworthy in this regard is the short time-span in which the Czech delegation was able (and willing) to convert its perception of the genocide into political pressure applied on Security Council members to take necessary actions in Rwanda. Immediately after Kovanda's report to Prague, the Czech delegation entered consultations with other non-permanent members as to whether the Council could react to the genocide in some way other than by simply withdrawing UNAMIR. The Czech delegation also set in motion the drafting of a presidential statement describing the situation as a genocide which was presented to the Council on 28 April 1994.[11]

Although it is virtually impossible to validate the exact date when the representatives of the non-permanent members of the Security Council *personally* recognised the widespread and systematic killing of Tutsi by Hutu forces, two important conclusions can be drawn from the above examination. First, both the Nigerian and Czech representatives faced more substantial difficulties in perceiving the genocide than they openly admit. When archival sources were compared to results of semi-structured interviews, an interesting contrast was found. On the one hand, interviews with Gambari and Kovanda reflected their firm belief in the Council's ability to detect the Rwandan genocide *even before the last week of April 1994*. On the other hand, archival records served to reveal that these two representatives and other members of the Council lacked a clear picture of fighting in Rwanda *until 25 April 1994*. They were particularly bewildered over the coordination between the killers and the scale of the killing.

A second and related matter concerns the time perspective, for the window of opportunity to strengthen UNAMIR was effectively closed on 21 April 1994 with the adoption of Resolution 912 to withdraw the bulk of UNAMIR. Had non-permanent members possessed a definite sense of the genocide by 21 April, they might have been able to persuade (or shame) other Security Council members into action in Rwanda. What is particularly interesting to note is that the fate of UNAMIR and tens of thousands of Rwandans was sealed by just a few crucial days whose course could have been radically different: Kovanda was able to perceive clearly the genocide only four days after the withdrawal of UNAMIR. Most importantly, he was able to transform his individual perception into a collective one (Presidential Statement of the Security Council) in three days through vigorous political pressure and lobbying. Had the UN early warning system enabled him and other non-permanent members to grasp the Rwandan disaster in its entirety only a few days earlier than they actually did, they might have been able to persuade the Council to strengthen UNAMIR with a similar level of energy and conviction as employed by Kovanda in pressing the Council to take action.

One indication of the severity of structural shortcomings in the UN early warning system is evidenced by the extent to which non-permanent members were obliged to resort to sources outside the UN Organisation in order to obtain vital information. The disappointment experienced by non-permanent members over the Secretariat's failure to convey early warning information is reflected in the following statement by Kovanda:

> In a draft presidential statement which we put forward on 28 April, we very purposefully highlight and recognise the importance of the information that we had been given from non-governmental organisations. And this is sort of an indirect jab at the Secretariat for the Secretariat not having been providing information.[12]

In fact, certain malfunctions of the early warning mechanism appear to have been generated through a three-phased causal chain, in which mistakes were transferred in turn from the ground (UNAMIR) to the Secretariat and finally to the Council. This chain effect is sharply evidenced by the way in which the misleading image of highly organised *génocidaires* as 'unruly elements' was produced. First, on 17 April 1994 UNAMIR's cable to the Secretariat described the militia fighters as a 'totally irrational group of people' having 'no particular respect for anyone', which subsequently appeared in the Secretary-General's report to the Council three days later. In that report, Boutros-Ghali describes the perpetrators of the killing as 'unruly elements' and 'unruly members', terms which effectively obscure the organised and systematic nature of the massacres. Finally, these descriptions emerged in the Council's discussions. The draft presidential statement presented by the Czech delegation on 28 April points to the fact that, 'The current wave of killings was started by unruly members of the Presidential Guard, joined by elements of the Rwandese Government Forces (RGF), over which the interim Government ... had failed to establish its authority.'[13] The statement from the Nigerian delegation to the Council's formal meeting on 21 April describes the Rwandan conflict as 'vicious rage and mindless violence of some of the elements of rival parties and groups'.[14]

Such a causal chain was also related to an inability to comprehend the scale of the killing: as UNAMIR was restricted to the Kigali section and therefore lacked resources to observe the planning, preparation and implementation of the nationwide killing campaign, so too did the Secretariat and the non-permanent members of the Council. This lack of awareness led Nigeria to grossly underestimate the scale of the killing in the Council's formal meeting on 21 April 1994, claiming that 20,000 deaths had been recorded in Rwanda.[15] However, one week later the true scale of the massacres had become evident. The Czech draft presidential statement presented in the Council's meeting on 28 April is particularly revealing in this regard, as it speaks of 'Rwanda's killing fields'.[16] What is most striking is that the word 'genocide' appears no fewer than *five* times in the Czech draft.[17] In the final, watered-down Presidential Statement, the Czech draft's five-time assertion of genocide was eliminated. Kovanda describes the drafting of the presidential statement in the following terms:

> [W]e presented our draft, and Gambari presented the African Group's thoughts at the same meeting of April 28, and Keating blended the two plus elements of the discussion together, to produce his own draft. It was dated April 29 because we got to that point only past midnight.[18]

What is most revealing, however, is that Secretary-General Boutros-Ghali first used the term 'genocide' in a broadcast of *Nightline* on 4 May 1994 (Boutros-Ghali 1996: 51). This means that the Czech delegation informally applied the word 'genocide' nine days *earlier* than the Secretariat, although the latter possessed greater early warning capacities than any of the non-permanent members. What can be concluded from this evidence is that certain of the Secretariat's failures can be traced to the defects of the early warning mechanism, whilst the late recognition of the genocide by Boutros-Ghali indicates that a substantial proportion of the Secretariat's failures was unrelated to the early warning mechanism and remains yet to be explained. The next chapter concerning bureaucratic rationalisation, organisational learning and Western normalisation will strive to expose and explore these remaining 'troublemaking' factors.

Structural level: the root causes of the malfunctions of early warning

As demonstrated in the previous chapter, the anthropocentric fallacy in existing literature on Rwanda has engendered an ontology that is not only narrow but also biased and sometimes even illusory: by missing out the role played by structures and mechanisms, researchers have been able to embroider that part of the story. This problem has been aggravated by the fact that early accounts in particular were influenced by a 'hunt for individual responsibilities'. Researchers have tended to turn a blind eye to structural constraints that imposed limits on the action of UN diplomats and officials, because admitting to those constraints could have revealed unwelcome mitigating factors and thus hindered the process of attributing individual responsibility. In fact, this has even led to the *fabrication of structural possibilities* available to actors at the time (see Piiparinen 2006a: 335–9). The latter point is illustrative of the epistemic fallacy at its starkest, namely, the confusion between transitive and intransitive objects of research – where intransitive objects refer to 'things' existing independently of the researcher's viewpoint and transitive objects denote the researcher's own viewpoint and the 'way to think and talk about things'.[19]

As Chapter 3 of this book demonstrated, Secretary-General Boutros-Ghali's *An Agenda for Peace* (1992) introduced 'preventive action' as an innovative tool of conflict management, which opened up the possibility of instituting early warning practices and structures in the UN. Boutros-Ghali's initiative, however, fell somewhat by the wayside, as evidenced by the following statement from a senior UN official:

> There was no specific structure set up in the aftermath of *An Agenda for Peace*, but all the operational departments, like DPA [the Department of Political Affairs], DPKO [the Department of Peacekeeping Operations], and [the Department of] Humanitarian Affairs, these were asked to have all their field offices alerted to inform us [the Secretariat] of whatever signals there were that could be treated as early warning.[20]

This statement exposes two major problems at the level of concrete structures with regard to early warning. First, the early warning system was fragmented across different units in the Secretariat. Boutros-Ghali's predecessor, Javier Pérez de Cuéllar, had centralised fact-finding and the gathering of early warning information in the Office for Research and the Collection of Information (ORCI) established in 1987. However, in 1992 ORCI was abolished and its functions were distributed between the newly established Department of Political Affairs (DPA) and the Department of Humanitarian Affairs (DHA) (Adelman 1998a: 55). It was only *after* the Rwandan conflict, in 1995 and 1998, that the early warning functions were centralised, when DPA, DHA and DPKO formed inter-departmental institutions to exchange early warning information (Adelman 1998b: 47; Kanninen 2001: 40–1).

Second, and most importantly, the above statement is indicative of severe inadequacies in, or a complete deficiency of, early warning structures in 1994. Such a view, commonly entertained among UN officials, is echoed by Ambassador Keating:

> An operations centre has been set up, but here [at UN Headquarters] is no system for disseminating the information that exists in the operations centre to the Security Council .... Perhaps over the years France and Belgium have had good sources of information about Rwanda, but I think the reality is that

the other permanent members of the Security Council are in no better position to get information on Rwanda than any of the rest of us [non-permanent members].[21]

Researchers in the field of conflict prevention, on the other hand, contend that while there was not a complete dearth of early warning structures in the Secretariat as UN officials imply, the existing UN early warning mechanism was distinguished by severe inadequacies and shortcomings. In 1994, Jürgen Dedring observed that the early warning practices of the UN were epitomised by 'incomplete designs and half measures' (Van Walraven 1998: 21). Howard Adelman also judges that '[UN] agencies used to possess an inadequate *coordinating* mechanism for receiving and evaluating information about an impending conflict ... Until 1994, attempts to develop such a system were totally inadequate' (Adelman 1998a: 55). Consequently, the UN had been confronted with serious difficulties in effecting early warnings by the beginning of the Rwandan conflict: following the demise of ORCI in 1992, the first considerable early warning structure, the DPA Policy Analysis Team, was established only *after* the Rwandan conflict in 1995.

What implications, if any, did this scarcity of early warning structures have for the prevention of the Rwandan genocide? Reflecting on interviews with UN officials, this study maintains that the lack of early warning structures impeded not so much information-gathering as such, but more the capacity to analyse information and develop policy options. As a consequence of the lack of these structures, the Secretariat became too reliant on UN field offices for analyses of early warning signals and for elaboration of suitable policy options. This dependence is reflected in the aforementioned statement by the senior UN official: 'All the operational departments ... were asked to *have all their field offices alerted* to inform us [the Secretariat] of whatever signals there were that could be treated as early warning.'[22] On the one hand, such an arrangement represents what Connie Peck terms the 'on-call eminent persons model' in which the UN early warning capacities rest with the ad hoc Special or Personal Representatives or Envoys of the Secretary-General (Peck 1996: 146). By appointing Special Representative Jacques-Roger Booh-Booh to Rwanda, Secretary-General Boutros-Ghali transferred early warning functions from UN Headquarters to his French-speaking personal representative who could be in touch with key persons and observe developments 'on the ground' in Rwanda.

On the other hand, 'Although it may provide a useful adjunct', as Peck notes, 'this model cannot substitute for a more comprehensive and permanent preventive diplomacy capacity' (Peck 1996: 147). Peck's argument seems apposite to the Rwandan case. Although Booh-Booh was head of UNAMIR, he failed to fulfil his duties to convey urgent early warning signals and to ring the alarm bells with regard to the forthcoming genocide.[23] As the Secretariat lacked comprehensive and institutionalised early warning structures, Booh-Booh's messages could not be supplemented, corroborated, analysed or contested to a sufficient degree at UN Headquarters. The lack of 'backup structures' to save early warning from failing is evidenced by another statement by the senior interviewee on the role of the head of a UN field mission:

> We [the Secretariat] have to depend on his assessment, on his advice ... [he] should be the one to inform the Secretary-General of what might happen, what was happening, what the implications were, what his analysis was, and what his advice would be.[24]

There were some 'backup structures' that might have ameliorated the scarcity of early warning signals, such as Secretary-General Boutros-Ghali's private information-gathering operation within the folds of the Arab League,[25] but these individual efforts could not amount to a sufficient and systematic information-gathering channel. As a result of an inherent poverty of information analysis capacities, the Secretariat was severely impaired in preventing the Rwandan conflict. It was conducive to a dilemma in which the Secretariat, on the one hand, relied on UNAMIR, and the Special Representative of the Secretary-General in particular, to analyse early warning signals, whilst UNAMIR, on the other hand, depended to a similar degree on the Secretariat's information-analysis capacities because of its own material constraints and its withdrawal to the Kigali section. This vicious circle, in which the weaknesses of UNAMIR and the Secretariat compounded each other, is dramatically illustrated in the following extract deriving from a cable conveyed from UNAMIR to the Secretariat on 17 April 1994, which has not been mentioned in the existing literature on Rwanda:

> UNAMIR has lost its eyes and ears outside of Kigali with the concentration or withdrawal of its UNMOS [United Nations military observers], the withdrawal from the DMZ [demilitarised zone] and its inability, due to security tasks in Kigali, to conduct patrolling outside of the Kigali area. Whereas in the first few days of the conflict we had a clear picture of the situation throughout Rwanda, we now are limited to knowledge of the Kigali area and RPF zone. *We are rapidly entering a phase where UN New York [the Secretariat] may very well know more about what is going on than UNAMIR...*[26]

Dallaire was accurate in his assumption that, at least hypothetically, the Secretariat possessed greater capacities to process early warning information than UNAMIR. Due to the deterioration of the security situation, UNAMIR had withdrawn to the Kigali section and was too burdened by heavy operational duties to produce any in-depth analyses. Of all the documentary sources, Dallaire's memoir (2003) provides the most compelling illustration of UNAMIR's daily struggle to, on the one hand, keep up with dangerous military tasks ranging from the evacuation of expatriates to the protection of Rwandan civilians and, on the other, to complete the necessary paperwork for 'New York' following each long day of operational duties. The Secretariat, by contrast, could have gathered information from various sources, such as non-governmental organisations, and analysed, corroborated and combined these pieces of information with a view to producing early warning analyses, just as the non-permanent members of the Security Council actually did. Moreover, even if bureaucratic obstacles prevented the distribution of the January cable to the Council when it arrived at UN Headquarters, it could, and should, have been re-examined in early April 1994, integrated into the overall information analysis process in the Secretariat, and conveyed to the Council, once its predictions of mass killing had actually materialised. Such a procedure would, however, have required early warning structures, particularly a coordination mechanism and an information-sharing framework between different departments of the Secretariat, institutions regrettably established only *after* the Rwandan conflict.

Documentary sources disclose that the Secretariat itself conceded to the Council its own limitations in analysing early warning information. On 28 April 1994, the Senior Political Adviser and Special Representative of the Secretary-General to the Security Council, Chinmaya Gharekhan, noted in an informal meeting of the Council that it was entirely appropriate for members of the Council to pool information from sources outside the UN, such as the International Committee of the Red Cross and *Médecins sans frontiers*. The Secretariat justified this by reference to its own rather limited capacity to gather first-hand information from other regions of Rwanda, given that UNAMIR had withdrawn to the Kigali section.[27] This 'apology' came in the wake of heightening criticism and indirect 'jabs' by non-permanent Council members towards the Secretariat which was assailed for its failure to bring information to the Council's attention. Nevertheless, it has been argued here that the embryonic or defective character of early warning structures did pose severe *human constraints on UN officials at the time of the Rwandan conflict*, as had been the case since the failure to implement *An Agenda for Peace*. However, such human constraints could and should have been avoided by *socially constructing* and enlarging the material capacities of early warning structures *prior to the Rwandan conflict* in the aftermath of the publication of the *Agenda* in 1992.

But why did early warning matter with regard to the management of the Rwandan conflict in particular? And why was the importance of a functioning early warning mechanism accentuated in this case? As demonstrated in Chapter 1, the regional context is the key to answering these questions. The African Great Lakes region is an example of the so-called 'regional security complex' where the security concerns of one state are inherently linked to those of its neighbouring countries.[28] The neighbouring states of Rwanda and Burundi form parts of this system, for they share not only a border but also the same ethnic composition, culture and colonial history.[29] Thomas Ohlson describes the main characteristic of a regional security complex: 'Events and dynamics in the context of intra-state security, such as processes of internal war or war termination, are both influenced by and influence the surrounding regional complex' (Ohlson 1998: 15). In this way, the violence in one country in the African Great Lakes has frequently been projected into another country through family ties, ethnic affinities, kinsmen and refugee warriors.

The sheer complexity of attempting to detect causal linkages in the security complex of the African Great Lakes, and the consequent need for functioning early warning structures, arises from the fact that interethnic conflicts in that region are not structurally deterministic but produced through endogenous and contingent relations. Therefore, mass killings are not necessarily preceded by any prior indications. For example, the Burundian massacres in 1972, which claimed 80,000–200,000 lives, were not preceded by any detailed plot to massacre Hutu (Bhavnani and Backer 2000: 283–7). What is noteworthy in considering the perception of the 'radiation effect' of Burundian massacres on Rwandan violence in 1993 is that the UN did detect this causal linkage, but perhaps failed to grasp its proportions and impact on structural violence in Rwanda. The following empirical examination will test this hypothesis.

In its Presidential Statement on 16 November 1993, the Security Council expressed its concern over the movement of more than 700,000 Burundian refugees into neighbouring countries and appealed to the international community to provide humanitarian help. However, the Presidential Statement does not link the refugee crisis with any security concerns.[30] The UN raised its concern over regional security later in the Secretary-General's report on UNAMIR on 30 December 1993:

> Although the southern region [of Rwanda] is at present reasonably quiet, the relative ease of access to considerable arms and the ethnic tensions amongst and around the refugees have created a potentially destabilizing situation which had not been foreseen in my initial assessment of requirements for the mission ... [T]he situation in Burundi has created a new source of tension in the south.[31]

Hence, the UN was able to detect the causal linkage between the Burundian and Rwandan violence, but could not fully grasp the gravity and implications of such radiation effects for the structural violence in Rwanda. In fact, the Security Council failed to adopt a single resolution to condemn the Burundian violence, issuing only a presidential statement. The Secretariat's report depicts the radiation effect as merely a local and temporary destabilising factor in southern Rwanda, not as pertinent to the possibility of genocide or to nation-wide interethnic violence. A further, and even more illustrative, example of these limitations was the reaction of the international community to the possible effects of Rwandan massacres in Burundi in April 1994. Initially, the possibility of these effects was raised in an informal meeting of the Security Council on 13 April 1994. On that occasion, the Nigerian and French representatives pointed out that the worsening of the security situation in Rwanda combined with the withdrawal of UNAMIR would lead to an even more serious spread of violence to Burundi.[32] However, these early comments hinting at the necessity of preventive action were isolated, and their purpose was more to oppose the total withdrawal of UNAMIR than to raise real concerns over the possible projection of violence from Rwanda to Burundi.

The Security Council began to study seriously the possibility of a preventive deployment to Burundi only after the Rwandan genocide had spread across the country. On 28 April 1994, Nigeria introduced the idea of a preventive deployment as part of the African Group's overall plan to manage the Rwandan conflict. It was to be similar to UNPREDEP in the Former Yugoslav Republic of Macedonia, and its purpose would have been to prevent the Rwandan conflict from engulfing the whole Great Lakes region. Nigeria emphasised that the situation in Burundi remained quiet but dangerous.[33] The African Group's proposal was greeted with enthusiasm by France, New Zealand and Russia.[34] It also gave rise to other similar suggestions, such as the use of preventive diplomacy, as proposed by China[35] and Brazil.[36] The US also responded positively and proposed a plan in which a preventive deployment figured as one component of the 'protective zone' to be established on the border between Rwanda and Burundi. The dual function of this protective buffer was to assist in refugee repatriation and to use, if necessary, 'preventive capacity' to deter the spread of violence to Burundi.[37]

As for the potential spread of the Rwandan genocide to Burundi, the Security Council seriously entertained the idea of a preventive deployment, but unnecessarily, as the predicted violence in Burundi never took place. Instead, the genocide 'found its way' into the Democratic Republic of Congo. Ironically, in the case of the radiation effect of the Burundian massacres on Rwanda six months prior to these discussions, violence in one state in the security complex actually did incite violence in another, but the Security Council never considered a preventive deployment. The Security Council was clearly struggling to predict the 'path of genocide'[38] in the African Great Lakes. However, the Security Council was not alone in its miscalculations. As the Special Representative of the Secretary-General to Burundi, Ahmedou Ould-Abdallah, points out, 'Everyone expected the country [Burundi] to ignite. Headlines such as "Burundi Is Next," "Countdown for Burundi," "Burundi: A Ticking Time Bomb" were to be seen and heard everywhere' (Ould-Abdallah 2000: 60). Experts and news agencies speculated on new genocidal killing, this time in Burundi (see, for example, Legum 1995: 31). An officer in the Bureau of Intelligence and Research of the US Department of State put it bluntly: 'We have predicted ten of the last three crises [in the African Great Lakes]' (quoted in Evans 1997: 79). In sum, what the UN found in common with non-governmental organisations and international news agencies with regard to early warning was, first and foremost, the limitations of the human capacity to predict conflicts in the security complex of the African Great Lakes.

In this regional 'open system', conflict potential crossed regional, state and sub-state levels, and interacted across political, economic and social sectors. The global level also played a role within this causal complex: the national economy of Rwanda depended heavily on the export of coffee, and the crash of coffee prices in the late 1980s undermined the Habyarimana government and fuelled extremism. As a result of this complexity, all actors were susceptible to making erroneous predictions. Subsequent to the Rwandan genocide, the international community was inclined to predict that Burundi would be next to succumb to a crisis; a warning which did not come true. In contrast, the international community could not fully grasp the radiation effect that the Burundian massacres had on the Rwandan conflict since their beginning in October 1993, although it was a major contributing factor to the eruption of the Rwandan genocide in April 1994.

Emancipatory move: locating possibilities for the early detection of genocide

The previous section and Chapter 3 initially identified the possibilities of Secretary-General Boutros-Ghali's *An Agenda for Peace* (1992) in inaugurating early warning structures, which could have been utilised to prevent the Rwandan genocide. However, failure to implement the *Agenda* entailed that a paucity of early warning structures endured. This observation immediately calls forth the question as to whether the genocide could have been detected at an earlier stage if the *Agenda*'s suggestions had been realised. In order to address this question, the following section will take as its point of departure Boutros-Ghali's successor Kofi Annan's initiative of a 'culture of prevention', which is similar to Boutros-Ghali's *Agenda* in terms of its intention to create structures for early warning.

Much as his predecessor, Annan's initiative elevated conflict prevention and early warning to a position of priority on the UN's agenda. The Secretary-General's Annual Report on the Work of the Organization in 1999 states that, 'For the United Nations, there is no higher goal, no deeper commitment and no greater ambition than preventing armed conflicts' (Annan 1999: 10). Boutros-Ghali and Annan's initiatives also resembled each other in that both were intended as political signals emitted by senior UN officials in the hope that the UN bureaucracy would develop early warning mechanisms, whilst neither initiative proposed any meticulous plans or guidelines that would assist in the realisation of such a goal. However, unlike the *Agenda*, Annan's initiative did not remain zealous but empty rhetoric; instead, it engendered tangible results in establishing early warning structures. This interesting contrast raises the following counterfactual[39] to be addressed below: had such structures for early warning existed in 1994 could they have contributed to the prevention of the Rwandan genocide, given that Boutros-Ghali's *Agenda* might have generated similarly positive outcomes as Annan's initiative? The final part of the chapter will also examine the political and bureaucratic obstacles that hampered the implementation of the *Agenda*, thereby indirectly contributing to the UN's failure in Rwanda.

The 'culture of prevention' promoted by Annan essentially denotes what Tapio Kanninen, the Head of the Policy Planning Unit in the Department of Political Affairs (DPA), terms an 'improved culture of information-sharing among departments and agencies' (Kanninen 2001: 40). This novel culture inspired the establishment of two major inter-departmental institutions with regard to early warning. In mid-1998, the Interagency Framework Team for Coordinating Early Warning, Prevention and Preparedness was created. Henceforth, the membership of the Framework Team has included various departments of the Secretariat, most notably the Departments of Political Affairs, Peacekeeping Operations, and Humanitarian Affairs, and other UN organs, such as the UN High Commissioner for Human Rights (UNHCHR). Another enhancement in early warning capacities also took place in 1998 with the launch of the UN-wide training programme, 'Early Warning and Preventive Measures: Building UN Capacity'. The programme aimed to change the culture of the UN system from a reactive to a more proactive mode (Kanninen 2001: 41). By 2001, 250 UN staff members from 22 departments, agencies and offices had received training through the programme.

How, then, could early warning structures such as those described above have enabled UN officials to adopt alternative routes of action to prevent the Rwandan genocide? The so-called 'black file' episode furnishes an interesting vantage point from which to address this question: an individual desk officer in DPKO received a response of inertia from the UN bureaucracy when it was suggested that the January cable be considered as an early warning signal.[40] As the following chapter will seek to explain more carefully, the *bureaucratic culture* in DPKO determined that the cable be processed as *nothing more than* an operational report concerning UNAMIR's activity; in terms of UN procedures, the fax had nothing to do with early warning or the detection of genocide. An awareness-raising scheme, such as the UN-wide training programme described above, could have provided UN officials with an additional 'cognitive prism' through which to consider the January cable. Such inter-departmental training could have sensitised Secretariat officials to detect early warning signals within the entire range of duties they performed. As a consequence, the January cable might have been recognised as an early warning signal in the wider context of the UN bureaucracy, not only in DPA which has been primarily responsible for early warning,[41] but also in DPKO where the January cable first arrived.

Furthermore, the institution of an interagency framework for coordinating early warning information, such as the Framework Team described above, could have significantly altered the outcome of conflict prevention in the Rwandan case. The Special Rapporteur of the UN Commission on Human Rights had already argued in October 1993 that the Genocide Convention was applicable in Rwanda. By combining UN departments, human rights experts and humanitarian organisations, the Interagency Framework could have offered the requisite forum for raising awareness of concerns about human rights violations in Rwanda and for calling early indications of the potential for genocide to the attention of the wider UN bureaucracy before the eruption of the massacres. Moreover, such a forum would have enabled DPKO to distribute the contents of the January cable to a wider audience in the Secretariat, given that this cable should have been initially detected as an early warning signal in DPKO.

The strengthening of information-sharing between local representatives of the UN and the Security Council can be viewed as a further possibility which would have permitted the detection of the genocide at an earlier stage. The Special Representatives of the Secretary-General regularly visit UN Headquarters in order to brief the Council in advance of reports by the Secretary-General to the Council. Such periodical briefings were already being held at the time of the Rwandan genocide, but did not constitute an *institutionalised* practice. The institutionalisation of this arrangement would have facilitated the prevention of the Rwandan crisis, as Special Representative Booh-Booh never showed up in the Council.[42]

Force Commander Dallaire agreed on the potential merits of a direct information channel between local UN representatives, such as force commanders, and the Security Council: 'I think it would have been useful. One of my major feelings was that I wasn't able to convince them.'[43] Although Dallaire courageously accepts personal responsibility for the failure to convince the Council of the seriousness of the Rwandan crisis, it is obvious that the majority of the blame was attributable to the UN structure, such as the division of labour, which effectively isolated Dallaire from the Council and allowed the UN bureaucracy to dilute his messages to the Council. Ambassador Kovanda elaborated from an 'insider's perspective':

> Such a briefing would without any question have been useful .... It was extremely important for the Council that Special Representatives would from time to time visit the Council and give their first-hand impression about situation in the crisis area that they were responsible for.[44]

Interestingly, during Secretary-General Annan's tenure the direct reporting to the Council by Special Representatives has become an institutionalised and frequently used practice (Peck 2004: 331), which would have been beneficial in the Rwandan case, as the above statements by Kovanda, Dallaire and Gambari demonstrated.

Information-sharing could have been further enhanced by the creation of 'backup channels', for example by the nomination of two deputy Special Representatives. Such arrangements may have permitted the UN system to bypass Special Representative Booh-Booh's failure to convey early warning signals. Consider, for example, the following statement by one UN official:

> I can readily tell from the field that the structure has been greatly improved recently. There used to be one deputy SRSG [the Special Representative of the Secretary-General]. Now you may notice, like in the mission in Sierra Leone and Liberia, there are two deputy SRSGs: one for administration, and the other one for humanitarian ... And they bring both into one fold under the leadership of the SRSG.[45]

Such an arrangement would have been beneficial in the Rwandan case, as all UNAMIR's decision-making occurred within an exclusive group centred around Booh-Booh. This monopolised control of the information flow from UNAMIR to UN Headquarters and isolated itself from other agencies, and the military command of UNAMIR in particular. The institutionalisation of two deputy Special Representatives could, in hindsight, have ruptured this hermetic circle of information-production. The inclusion of the United Nations Development Programme (UNDP) representative in UNAMIR as the deputy Special Representative on humanitarian affairs could have positively affected UN decision-making, as UNDP would most probably have portrayed a more alarming picture of the Rwandan situation than did Booh-Booh's group. In fact, the responsiveness of UNDP was so widely recognised by other agencies that it was at times even perceived as a 'claim jumper'[46] for its active efforts in alleviating suffering in Rwanda. The information-production capacities were concentrated in the hands of a closed, isolated circle around the Secretary-General not only at the field level but also at UN Headquarters. The day-to-day operations between the Secretariat and the Security Council were managed by the Senior Political Adviser and Special Representative of the Secretary-General to the Security Council, Chinmaya Gharekhan. As Gambari describes, Gharekhan's briefings to the Council were characterised by serious shortcomings:

> He [Secretary-General Boutros-Ghali] had Ambassador Gharekhan to brief on all issues to the Council. That was not very helpful, because you could be an expert or not. And he was the former Ambassador of India, very competent man, but he didn't know the technicalities of peacekeeping and peace-enforcement. And he treated all issues alike with little or no emotion.[47]

Gambari's statement illustrates the way in which the isolation of information-production in the small group around the Secretary-General contributed to the lack of urgency concerning the Rwandan situation. Since the Rwandan genocide, the UN system has shifted from this bureaucratic 'closure' in the direction of a more diverse, open system, both in terms of early warning and peacekeeping operations in general. Currently, briefing the Council on peacekeeping missions is not exclusively entrusted to the Secretary-General's closest political advisers, but is usually assigned to a team composed of the senior leaders of DPKO.[48] The exact composition of the team depends on the particular issue arising on the Council's agenda.[49] This would have been beneficial in the Rwandan case, as Special Representative Gharekhan's briefings on UNAMIR lacked not only urgency regarding the situation in Rwanda but also expertise in peacekeeping and peace-enforcement matters. In sum, the more diversified and flexible channel through which to convey information that exists presently could have bridged these gaps in early warning and expertise. Most importantly, such a system would have allowed the detection of early warning signals in a wider sphere of early indications of the potential for genocide, such as human rights and economic indicators. The consultation mechanism of the Council has only recently been enlarged from a hermetic circle relying merely on member states' own information sources and briefings by a small group of Secretariat officials to encompass a wide range of other relevant actors, such as the High Commissioner for Human Rights and non-governmental organisations (Hulton 2004: 241–4). The Council would have greatly benefited from briefings by these actors in the Rwandan case, as they could have drawn the Council's attention to the conflict potential residing for example in human rights violations.

The UN took a further step in a more desirable direction with regard to conflict prevention on 12 July 2004, when the first Special Adviser on Genocide was appointed, employed to act as an early warning mechanism to the Secretary-General and the Security Council. The purpose of the Special Adviser is to monitor and collect data on potential conflicts that could evolve into genocide, and draw up recommendations to the Council on how these crises can be prevented. According to one instructive hypothesis raised in the current debate, the genocidal violence in Darfur, Sudan might have been discussed in the Council at an earlier date, if the recently established Special Adviser on Genocide had been invested with more authority to access the Council directly.[50] In the Rwandan case, both UNAMIR and UN Headquarters faced severe restrictions in analysing and gathering early warning information, as demonstrated in the second section of this chapter. Any capacity-building measure, such as the Special Adviser, would have alleviated this dearth of resources in the Secretariat by offering a focal point around which the January cable and other crucial pieces of information from UN agencies and non-governmental organisations could have been assembled with a view to producing coherent early warning analyses and recommendations to the Council.

In light of the above considerations, it seems evident that the enhancement of human resources in the Secretariat would have increased detection capacities and contingency planning in relation to the Rwandan genocide. Between 1994 and 2000, the number of DPKO staff officers increased from 300 to 465. By 2003, the number had risen to 630.[51] The human-resources situation continues to improve. For example, the number of military officers working in the Office of Military Affairs in the DPKO rose from 54 to 92 from the beginning of July to the end of October 2008.[52] Thus, the human resources of DPKO have more than doubled since 1994, which, in turn, has had an advantageous effect on the material capacity of DPKO to conduct contingency planning. In 1994, DPKO was hardly coping with the day-to-day executive command of the global armada of peacekeeping operations whose number had doubled since 1988. In 2003, by contrast, DPKO had considerably more staff and fewer operations to direct. Therefore, DPKO has been able to release resources from operational duties to contingency planning: in 2003, the monitoring mechanism of DPKO had constantly six or seven possible 'hot spots', i.e. potential conflicts, around the world under its surveillance for possible peacekeeping operations or interventions. 'As soon as we've seized some smoke beyond the horizon,' as Special Assistant to the Military Adviser of the Secretary-General, Lieutenant-Colonel Ben Klappe explained, 'then we basically start planning.'[53] At the time of the Rwandan crisis, such an extensive monitoring mechanism was inconceivable in the resource-starved UN Secretariat, which partly explains the complete lack of contingency planning of UNAMIR for the possibility of genocide. The increase in human resources is also reflected by the fact that, since the Rwandan crisis, DPKO has been able to develop its own early warning structures, such as the Oversight Group (Adelman 1998b: 47). Without such resources, detection mechanisms cannot function properly, as the Rwandan case illustrates.

In sum, the construction and development of the early warning system could have significantly altered the outcome of conflict prevention in the Rwandan case, a possibility opened up by the 1992 *Agenda*. This, in turn, invites the question as to why the *Agenda* was not implemented. Interviews with UN officials uncovered that objections to the implementation of the *Agenda* concerned less its overall conceptual framework than its specific recommendations on new institutions. Boutros-Ghali noted that, 'There were many meetings of the Security Council approving [the *Agenda*], but approval and implementation are two different things. It was a great success, but purely on a theoretical basis, and it was never applied.'[54] One Secretariat official, working as the secretary in the Drafting Committee of the Agenda for Peace and of the General Assembly Working Group on the Agenda,[55] elaborated this observation by identifying those reforms envisaged in the *Agenda* that aroused reluctance regarding its implementation:

> One idea we had was to integrate the information management in the house [UN Headquarters] concerning peacekeeping, humanitarian affairs and political affairs. We drafted a blue print, but it was not really accepted by all of our superiors.... So it could have led to an early warning system, if that kind of route had been taken.[56]

This statement reveals the lack of interest on the part of member states to implement the *Agenda* in the early 1990s, which stands in stark contrast to positive reactions to Annan's similar initiative in the late 1990s. In its Presidential Statement[57] of 30 November 1999, the Security Council 'invites the Secretary-General to present to the members of the Council periodic reports on ... disputes, including, as appropriate, early warnings and proposals for preventive measures'. Other UN organs also expressed their readiness to implement the Secretary-General's initiative. In response to the Secretary-General's report[58] on the prevention of armed conflict, the General Assembly adopted Resolution 337[59] on 3 July 2003, which has been hailed as the 'landmark resolution' on the prevention of armed conflict.[60] Had UN member states responded to Boutros-Ghali's *Agenda* with similar enthusiasm, the UN system would have been better placed to detect the Rwandan genocide at an earlier stage.

Conclusion

In accordance with the possibilistic methodology of critical realism outlined in Chapter 2, the defects of the early warning mechanism identified in Chapter 3 have been considered as possible permissive causes of the UN's failure in Rwanda. The aim of this chapter has been to test that possibility by scrutinising the Rwandan case. In general, the conclusions indicate that the malfunctions of the early warning mechanism indeed formed part of the causal complex which generated the Rwandan disaster. Although the malfunctions of early warning were not in themselves sufficient to cause the abandonment of Rwanda, they certainly facilitated such an outcome by enabling the emergence of the so-called 'perception gap', i.e. by nourishing a political atmosphere in the Security Council characterised by confusion, misperceptions and a consequent reluctance to engage in the Rwandan crisis in the run-up to the Council's critical decision on UNAMIR's future. Most crucially, this chapter has demonstrated the particular ways, i.e. the *causal chains*, through which the inadequacies of the early warning mechanism hampered decision-making. However, the relationships of this mechanism with other mechanisms, such as bureaucratic rationalisation, as well as the 'net effect' of all 'troublemaking' mechanisms, remain yet to be examined in the next chapter.

The first section uncovered the 'backward causalities' by which indefinite, ambiguous or complex events that occurred in the past are reconstructed as definite, clear or simple in hindsight. Attaching the label 'genocide fax' to the January cable is one clear example of this process. Philip Gourevitch's description of the January cable as the 'genocide fax' (Gourevitch 1998: 42) and the *Observer* article's characterisation of the content of the cable as a 'warning of Rwanda genocide plan' (Hilsum 1995: 23) are misnomers for three reasons. First, the term 'genocide' does not appear anywhere in the cable. Second, individual and scattered bits and pieces of information, such as the January cable, do not automatically amount to a coherent picture of early warning, which requires a relevant institutional structure; there is a difference between sufficient information being available and that information being available in a form and within a structure to give it utility.[61] Third, the complexity of past events which backward causalities aim to diminish specifically refers to a multifaceted decision-making environment. Such an environment, in turn, requires that the structural capacity of early warning and other detection mechanisms that strive to make sense of complexity is taken seriously. Although Boutros-Ghali, along with the authors of existing literature, largely belittled the importance of such mechanisms in the Rwandan case, his statement to the author supports the argument advanced here that the complexity of UN decision-making requires the development of an early warning mechanism that would enable officials and diplomats to prioritise those situations that demand urgent action:

> When you are doing a study of what happened there, it is already artificial, because you are paying one hundred per cent of your attention to Rwanda, but we responsible [UN officials] were paying only ten. [The remaining] ninety per cent was dealing with Yugoslavia, Angola, Salvador, Mozambique, South Africa or the problem of the UN budget. We had the sanctions against Libya and the dispute between Israel and Arab countries. Now we are talking about spending all our energy on Rwanda, so it is already a different approach …. Today it is easy, but on the spot, we did not have that vision to [distinguish] the bigger crime from a smaller one.[62]

The first section demonstrated the way in which the malfunctions of this mechanism contributed to the Security Council's shortcomings through a 'three-phased causal chain': UNAMIR → the Secretariat → the Council. After this generic description at the phenomenal level, the second section proceeded to discuss the underlying structural level in a bid to understand the causes of the weaknesses, inadequacies and fragmentation of the mechanism. It was the conclusion of this section that at the outset of the proactive conflict prevention phase (January 1994) the necessary components of an early warning system were not in place, which severely reduced the capacities of UN officials to analyse early warning information about Rwanda. The failure of early warning between January and April 1994 does not, therefore, reflect damage in the making but damages already occasioned.

The third section embraced this conclusion as its point of departure and, on that basis, analysed the particular ways in which the enhancement of early warning capacities in the aftermath of the *Agenda* could have contributed to the prevention of the genocide. The conclusions of this analysis confirm the idea put forward by the 'Related Powers' model outlined in Chapter 2, which argues that emancipatory potential to prevent the Rwandan disaster resided in *co-operation* between three components of the UN system: member states; institutional structures, including the Secretariat's capacities; and control mechanisms, such as early warning arrangements, emergent from the interaction between institutional structures and state actors.

The following illustration, which elaborates on the model of detection mechanisms presented in Figure 3.1 (Chapter 3), summarises the principal arguments of this chapter. Its findings intimate the commonsensical yet important fact that the Rwandan fiasco was not only *socially constructed* by UN officials and diplomats (the social stratum), but also that those individuals who dealt with the January cable and other early warning signals were subject to *human*

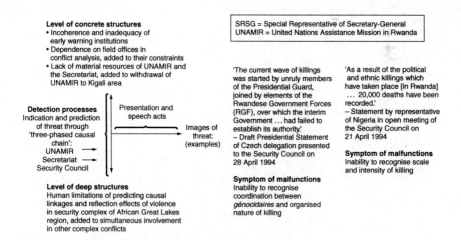

Figure 5.1 Summary of the malfunctions of early warning mechanisms.

limitations affecting their capacity to predict the genocide (the material stratum of human resources). The complexity of the decision-making environment imposed a considerable burden on the *material stratum* of human resources, upon which the early warning mechanism was based, as this mechanism was not sufficiently built up to meet these challenges in the Rwandan case.

However, the Rwandan drama cannot be explained by 'human limitations' and the material restrictions of early warning alone. The securitisation mechanisms based on social construction, namely bureaucratic rationalisation and Western normalisation, also played a part. In fact, the malfunctions of early warning were compounded by other interacting mechanisms. Thus, the next chapter will proceed to explore bureaucratic rationalisation as one type of securitisation mechanism that worked in convergence with the early warning mechanism, hampering the proper functioning of the latter.

6 Bureaucratic mechanisms

Introduction

> The bizarre thing is that in the preface of the blue book on Rwanda, Boutros-Ghali asserts that, 'Yes, the Council was informed about this [January] cable' [see Boutros-Ghali 1996: 32]. And then in December 1995, I wrote him a letter saying, 'How do we explain that your recollection and my recollection differ so greatly?' He invited me over to his office, and Chinmaya Gharekhan, who was his representative and briefed the Council very frequently, said: 'Well, alas, there's no record of it, so, we just differ in our memories.'[1]
>
> (Ambassador Karel Kovanda)

To label the Rwandan failure as merely a malfunction of early warning would serve to conveniently relieve the UN bureaucracy of political responsibility. However, such a reductive explanation emerges as manifestly blinkered in light of evidence which reveals that 'New York', as UN Headquarters is commonly termed at the level of UN field offices, pursued a bureaucratic policy of its own which frequently collided with suggestions of UNAMIR and the non-permanent members of the Security Council. These internal contrasts signal the presence of another important mechanism, namely bureaucratic rationalisation. As the critical realist notion of 'open systems' demonstrates, the early warning mechanism cannot be conceived of as permitting the 'pure detection' of potential conflicts, in splendid isolation from other mechanisms. Instead, early warning is always influenced and inhibited by bureaucratic calculations of what it may cost the bureaucracy as a whole. In this sense, the mechanisms of early warning and bureaucratic rationalisation are interrelated, working in conjunction with each other. This chapter will provide an important supplement to the previous one, its intention being to focus on the interrelation of early warning and bureaucratic rationalisation (the first section) and the transformation of bureaucratic rationalisation during the genocide (the second section). The implications of the 'open systems' model for this book go even further. It opposes the reduction of analysis to the institutional sphere and obliges a researcher to look for explanatory causes of social phenomena outside bureaucratic factors. Therefore, the overall

picture of the Rwandan case will be added by the analysis of two further mechanisms, namely organisational learning (the third section) and Western normalisation (the fifth section).

An ancillary methodological tool will be employed here by means of a supplement to Andrew Sayer's method of double movement: Tony Lawson's
method of contrastive explanation. As with Sayer's approach, Lawson's method
derives from critical realist philosophy. In simple terms, contrastive explanation
poses the question, 'Why this rather than that in these conditions?' (Bhaskar and
Lawson 1998: 12). Its first step involves the identification of two groups of
objects whose causal histories might be expected to be the same, but which nevertheless produce divergent outcomes. The second, and related, task is to attempt
to uncover the underlying mechanism explaining these intriguing and unexpected differences in outcomes (Lawson 1998: 151). Such a method will be put
to use in this chapter which will identify interesting contrasts between
UNAMIR's policy suggestions to the Secretariat and options presented by the
latter to the Security Council. These contrasts disclose the workings and dysfunctions of bureaucratic rationalisation.

The previous chapter provided an extensive overview of the January cable
and the overall failure of proactive conflict prevention. As the primary events of
the *pre-genocide phase* have therefore been described, the present chapter will
commence by interrogating the bureaucratic structures that contributed to the
UN's failure during that period. The second section will examine the role of
bureaucratic rationalisation during the *genocide phase* and expose interesting
contrasts in the policies of diverse UN organs. It will be argued that there were
three main areas of disagreement between New York and the military command
of UNAMIR: the appropriate strength of UNAMIR, the priority to be accorded
to the protection of civilians, and UNAMIR's mandate and function. The second
section will also explore the structures of bureaucratic rationalisation that produced these discrepant policies.

The notion of bureaucratic rationalisation calls forth the further question as to
the motivations behind the perceptual biases of the UN bureaucracy. If miscon-
ceptions surrounding the genocide were purely attributable to bureaucratic and
political calculations, the blame should be placed squarely on the shoulders of
bureaucrats themselves. But if their biases were psychological in nature, it would
be appropriate instead to invoke 'diminished responsibility', their misconcep-
tions being more or less unavoidable human errors. Robert Jervis' conception of
'motivated and unmotivated biases' clarifies such a distinction; in line with his
conceptual framework to be applied later in this chapter, motivated biases occur
as a result of the workings of the mechanism of bureaucratic rationalisation,
whilst unmotivated biases refer to the functioning of another mechanism, namely
organisational learning.

As for the motivated biases generated by bureaucratic rationalisation,
entrenched belief systems and policies of bureaucracies, for example, may
induce policy-makers to over- or under-estimate threats (Jervis 1985: 24–5).
Unmotivated biases produced by psychological learning mechanisms, on the

other hand, surface because of the complexity and ambiguity of information regarding the decision-making environment. The distorting effect occasioned by recent events on the perception of threats will be discussed in the third section as a dysfunction of organisational learning, namely cognitive dissonance. In the Rwandan case, the latter functioned as a cognitive filter: it imposed tolerable limits on the great variety of inputs to perception issuing from the Rwandan conflict by including only those elements that were consonant with prior experiences in Somalia. This engendered the (mis)perception of the genocide as a Somalia-type of unmanageable, tribal chaos, and served to recall the lesson well-learnt in Somalia that peace-enforcement would be highly dangerous in Rwanda. At the same time, such a cognitive filter excluded certain pertinent elements of the Rwandan conflict from the attention of the UN bureaucracy, such as early warning signals indicative of genocide and the possibility of robust peacekeeping. The stereotypical image of a chaotic Africa, however, seems to stem not only from our past experiences but also from our deep social prejudices. The last section of this chapter will argue that 'body-bag syndrome' has a specific meaning in relation to African crises since the early 1990s: popular imagination in the West has 'normalised' conflicts in Sub-Saharan Africa as chaotic, mindless and irrational, thus posing insurmountable risks for any intervention attempts.

Relationship between early warning and bureaucratic rationalisation

Whilst Chapter 3 has delineated the common features, structures, and dysfunctions of bureaucratic rationalisation in general, this section will examine such aspects with specific reference to the pre-genocide phase of the Rwandan case, and the ensuing sections will proceed to analyse them in the genocide phase. This section will investigate the role played by two dysfunctions of bureaucratic rationalisation in pre-genocide Rwanda: instrumental rationality (*Zweckrationalität*) and loose coupling.[2] According to *Zweckrationalität*, everything must be accurately assessed to calculate its net benefit to the bureaucracy as a whole. In the context of pre-genocide Rwanda, *Zweckrationalität* could be seen in the way in which risk-free means (the aversion of peace-enforcement) gradually overcame ends (the maintenance of peace and security) by becoming ends in themselves. Consider, for example, the following statement by a senior UN official, which provides a valuable insight into the bureaucratic considerations that regulate early warning:

> The Secretary-General is facing a risky situation if he goes regularly to the Council with early warning signals, because that could very easily create tension between the Security Council members, particularly the permanent members, and himself or herself. He might try that, but then he might lose political capital in doing so. There are also these kinds of concerns which have to be taken into account: if the Secretary-General says that this small

country in Africa or the Caribbean is facing problems, the country's credit ratings might go down. So in going to the Security Council he might just exacerbate the situation.... Before he brings information to the Security Council, he has to have almost certainty that it's accurate and that the consequences of not acting are terrible.... And then if you give false alarm, then no-one is taking you seriously in the future.[3]

Whilst this statement does not explicitly allude to the Rwandan case, it illuminates at least three aspects of the underlying bureaucratic logic which informs decisions on early warning in any context. First, to sound the alarm in the Security Council is not only a matter of the 'pure' detection of potential conflicts, but is governed by careful and complex calculations of what the costs of warning signals might be for the bureaucracy as a whole. In theoretical terms, the statement illustrates the relationship between the early warning mechanism and the mechanism of bureaucratic rationalisation: if the former fails to furnish overwhelming evidence of potential conflict, as occurred in the Rwandan case due to incomplete early warning structures, bureaucratic rationalisation usually determines that the risks of conveying alarm signals are too high for the bureaucracy. If the early warnings in the January cable had, in fact, turned out to be spurious, the Secretariat would have found it hard to deliver any credible early warning signals afterwards. These doubts were reinforced by Dallaire's suspicions regarding the credibility of the informant. As another senior UN official remarked, 'It was simply that we had some doubts about the information [in the cable].'[4] Thus, bringing the crucial piece of information contained in the sixth section of the cable to the attention of the Security Council was calculated as simply too great a risk for the UN bureaucracy as a whole.[5]

Second, the dilemma between risk calculation and early warning was exacerbated by the vehement opposition on the part of the US and other permanent members to allowing UNAMIR to overstep their restrictive interpretation of its mandate. If the Secretariat had warned the Security Council of the January cable and allowed peace-enforcement actions to be implemented against the Hutu, it would have jeopardised its working relationship with the US, the UK and particularly France, given the latter's pro-Habyarimana bias. Setting itself on a collision course with the permanent members of the Council would have been detrimental to the Secretariat as a whole, as its political credibility with the Council was already low as a consequence of the Somalia debacle of 1993. Secretary-General Boutros-Ghali had actively persuaded the Council to engage in ambitious peace-enforcement and nation-building efforts in Somalia. The Council had responded positively to these requests by launching UNOSOM II (United Nations Operation in Somalia) under Resolution 814.[6] Unfortunately, however, this operation led to the largest number of casualties among UN peacekeepers since the 1960s. Boutros-Ghali was therefore deemed partly responsible for the Somalia debacle, particularly in the minds of US representatives.

Third, conveying of the January cable to the Security Council risked, to a greater or lesser degree, the stability of Rwanda itself: publicising information on malicious intentions of the Hutu side could have contributed to the derailment of the Arusha peace process, thereby provoking a plummeting in the price of Rwandan coffee and a crash in its credit ratings. As a consequence, the UN would have been held accountable for Rwanda's demise. Adding to this dilemma, a senior UN official pointed out that simply starting the process of contingency planning either on the part of UN troops or the Secretariat gives the impression of a problem in the country and that its government might not be willing to admit that.[7] Hence, the risks attaching to the activation of contingency planning for the possible breakdown of the Arusha Accord were deemed too high not only for the UN bureaucracy but also for Rwanda.

As noted in Chapter 3, bureaucratic rationalisation is also characterised by the *loose coupling* typical of modern organisations. In the words of Bruce Russett, 'The UN and its family of component or related organizations is hardly tightly coupled; at best it may become a very loosely coupled security community' (1998: 383). The division of modern bureaucracies into independently responsive units enables increased efficiency through specialisation, but unfortunately also facilitates a *fragmentation of worldview*. In the case of pre-genocide Rwanda, perhaps the most disenchanting consequence of this dysfunction was that human rights violations failed to be regarded as part of the Security Council's agenda despite their exposure by UN human rights organisations.

China reminded other Council members in an informal meeting on 13 April 1994 concerning the situation in Somalia that while the Council's mandate encompassed international peace and security, there had been no intention to include human rights in its remit.[8] Moreover, the 'specialisation' of the Security Council in international peace and security, coupled with the simultaneous exclusion of human rights from its horizon, was evident not only in the conduct of those countries that are resistant to the issue of human rights in general, but in the Council as a whole. All members of the Council completely ignored the Special Rapporteur's view expressed in the UN Commission on Human Rights in August 1993, in which he insisted that the word 'genocide' was applicable in relation to the violence in Rwanda.[9] Even non-permanent Council members were not concerned with, and perhaps not even aware of, the alarming report by the Special Rapporteur.[10]

An exhaustive explanation of this common lack of awareness cannot be provided simply by signalling either political unwillingness or normative constraints, for the early 1990s had already witnessed a normative shift in state practice and *opinio juris*. Groundbreaking precedents had placed human rights concerns on the Council's agenda, most notably via Resolution 794[11] which deemed human rights violations inside Somalia a threat to international peace and security. Moreover, with Resolution 688[12] the Council had described the consequences of Kurdish repression by Iraqi forces and the flow of refugees to international frontiers in similar terms (Stromseth 1993: 85). Hence, the convincing explanation here is that the Council was so preoccupied with its area of 'specialisation', i.e. international peace and security and the Arusha peace process, that it simply overlooked human rights violations which were seen as falling outside that area. The ultimate dysfunction was, of course, discernible in the fact that these excluded issues actually had the greatest repercussions on peace and security in the region.

Loose coupling and a consequent fragmentation of worldview constituted obstructive factors not only in the Security Council but also in the Secretariat. UNAMIR Force Commander Dallaire, for example, was not briefed by the Secretariat on the aforementioned report by the Special Rapporteur on Human Rights (1993) or provided with other relevant information on the human rights situation in Rwanda.[13] Moreover, it is noteworthy that Dallaire sent the crucial January cable and other early warning signals to the Department of Peacekeeping Operations (DPKO), not the Department of Political Affairs (DPA) or the Department of Humanitarian Affairs (DHA). After the abolition of ORCI in 1992, its early warning functions were transferred to DPA and DHA, not to DPKO. The attempts of an individual desk officer in DPKO to call attention to Dallaire's cables, and the ultimate failure of these acts, reflect the exclusion of DPKO from the early warning system in 1994. In DPKO, Dallaire's cables were treated as part of UNAMIR's reports on its *operational* duties, rather than as *early warning* signals as such. Only *after* the Rwandan disaster was DPKO incorporated into the 'loop' of early warning information diffusion in the Secretariat. DPKO assumed a greater role in the early warning system, as it became part of an Inter-departmental Task Force with DPA and DHA and developed its own early warning structures, such as the Oversight Group (Adelman 1998b: 47). As demonstrated in the previous chapter, the outcome of UN conflict prevention in Rwanda might have been different if such structures had already existed in 1994.

Dysfunctions of bureaucratic rationalisation during genocide

UN policy was distinguished by three major contradictions between its diverse bodies during the Rwandan genocide. On 10 April 1994, Force Commander Dallaire informed the Secretariat that with 4,000 operational troops UNAMIR would be able to bring the killing in Rwanda to a halt (Dallaire 2003: 289). At that time, the genocide was still preventable. However, the Secretariat failed to inform the Security Council of Dallaire's request.[14] On the contrary, it issued orders to Dallaire four days later to examine two options for *withdrawing* UNAMIR from Rwanda, despite his vociferous objections to any such withdrawal (Dallaire 2003: 294–5). Nor did the Secretariat inform the Council of the severe lack of resources and logistical problems facing UNAMIR, despite being regularly informed by the Force Commander of the urgent need for greater material support. As the Deputy Force Commander of UNAMIR, Major-General Henry K. Anyidoho described:

> Immediately after the killing started, we were talking to the [UN] Headquarters, our commanders, that if we could only carry out reinforcement, *not only in troops but also in armament, our capabilities*, we would be able to address the situation.[15]

When asked by the author whether UNAMIR's material inadequacies, such as lack of ammunition and even drinking water, presented an even greater problem than the shortage of professional troops, Force Commander Dallaire answered: 'Yes. It prevented us from even maximising the troops I had. It was the Achilles heel.'[16]

Strengthening UNAMIR's material base would not only have maximised its efficiency; it would also have reduced the risks to its soldiers. Increasing the number of peacekeepers in Rwanda would not have been incommensurable with security concerns, provided that UNAMIR's material capacities had been simultaneously reinforced by, for example, the provision of operational armoured personnel carriers for the protection of UNAMIR troops. However, the UN bureaucracy failed to seize this basic point and regarded any strengthening of UNAMIR as fundamentally incompatible with the safety of its troops. In the Security Council as in the Secretariat, the option of strengthening UNAMIR was misleadingly portrayed as a fatalistic gamble likely to merely endanger a greater number of UN peacekeepers, given that ten soldiers had already died on 7 April 1994.

Bureaucratic rationalisation in New York was fundamentally flawed not only in terms of the bolstering of UNAMIR but also with regard to the protection of civilian lives. The *Melvern Archive* dramatically reveals that on 11 April 1994 in an informal meeting of the Security Council, the Secretariat[17] argued that the protection of civilians was not within UNAMIR's mandate, despite the fact that the peacekeeping mission was indeed carrying out this task. The Secretariat also held that the UN's first priority was to protect UN personnel and to assist in the evacuation of foreign nationals. It is instructive that these priorities did not include the safeguarding of 'humanitarian pockets', namely the 6,000 Tutsi civilians sheltering in the Amahoro Stadium and the 8,000 people located in the King Faisal Hospital.[18] The logic underlying these statements seems somewhat peculiar and contradictory. On the one hand, the evacuation of foreign nationals was *not* part of UNAMIR's mandate, but the Secretariat nevertheless insisted that it was one of the duties to be carried out by UNAMIR. On the other hand, the Secretariat contended that the protection of civilians was not part of UNAMIR's mandate, despite the moral and procedural dubiousness of this claim. One DPKO officer and legal expert in rules of engagement pondered:

How can a peacekeeping mission ever be successful, if they [peacekeepers] are not allowed to act in case of an imminent threat to innocent civilians ...? When you are sending troops, they always should have at least the possibility of acting beyond self-defence.[19]

Force Commander Dallaire raised a similar question in Kigali on 14 April 1994:

I scanned the attached transcript of the Security Council meeting of the day before to find that [the Secretariat] had raised an even more disconcerting point. On the issue of protecting the civilians in our care, [the Secretariat] noted that, 'The Council should consider whether PKOs [peacekeeping operations] should be assigned such tasks.' On humanitarian and moral grounds, I had taken the safeguarding of civilians as a given, and here my superiors were questioning the whole concept.... [S]o far the security at the sites had been working fairly well.

(Dallaire 2003: 295–6)[20]

Dallaire's latter point indicates that bureaucratic rationalisation at UN Headquarters not only militated against humanitarian considerations but also contradicted instrumental rationality itself: the small humanitarian pockets established by UNAMIR in the Amahoro stadium, King Faisal hospital and elsewhere *were working*. If UNAMIR had been equipped with adequate material resources and the necessary troops with which to establish further humanitarian pockets, they would have served as a *cost-effective* means of protecting tens of thousands of civilians, thereby satisfying the imperatives of instrumental rationality. The Secretariat, however, was of the opposite opinion, which wrought a detrimental effect on Security Council deliberations in at least two ways. First, the Secretariat's failure to portray safe areas as a viable means of protecting civilians enabled, and perhaps even provoked, the Council's overtly negative stance towards them. Lord Hannay, the then UK Ambassador to the UN, described this pervasive mindset among Council members: 'Many members thought that safe areas were of no value.'[21] Such a depressing image of safe areas stood in direct opposition to Dallaire's more optimistic assessment of their possibilities, as mentioned above.

Second, by referring to the humanitarian pockets as 'concentrations of refugees' in Security Council meetings, the Secretariat effectively stripped these protective zones of the status of 'supreme humanitarian urgency'[22] that was required to protect them. The expression 'concentrations of refugees' sounds peculiarly hygienic and carries a misleading perlocutionary force, as it fails to imply that people sheltering in them faced imminent danger. In accordance with the dialectical critical realism outlined in Chapter 2, it could be said that silence, the absence of self-evident descriptions, was the loudest voice in the Rwandan case. Imagine, for example, if the transportation of Jews to concentration camps was termed merely 'relocation of internally displaced persons' as opposed to 'campaign of mass killing'; in the same way, the words chosen by the Secretariat to describe the humanitarian pockets in Rwanda missed the severity of their situation and were thereby cynically anti-realist. Even worse, the 'dubbing' of these humanitarian spaces as nothing but refugee areas partially *enabled* the shameful abandonment of certain safe havens without protest from the international community. Most notably, the Belgian and French forces withdrew their troops from the humanitarian pocket at the École Technique Officielle on 11 April 1994, although the soldiers in that area were not in danger. As a result, over 2,000 Tutsi civilians were left unprotected and subject to subsequent slaughter. No condemnation of the Franco-Belgian action was forthcoming from the UN.

One particular aspect of the protection of civilians brought the contrast between suggestions of UNAMIR's military command and the policy of UN

Headquarters to a climax, namely the contingency planning for safe humanitarian areas. One of the most striking empirical findings of this book, not discussed in the existing literature, demonstrates that UNAMIR had already begun planning secure humanitarian zones by 15 April 1994. Major Stefan Stec, a Polish officer working as the head of UNAMIR's humanitarian assistance cell at the time, describes these contingency plans:

> By 15 April we had this plan which exactly called for the secure zones in the north of the country, which was safe militarily speaking, providing the water, the food, getting the coordination with relief agencies, because they could deliver everything to the Ugandan border, if they didn't want to enter Rwanda. Or even they could deliver actually through Uganda, whatever they wanted, frankly speaking. So the plan was doable and good without much resources, but because exactly of the political pressure, we had been literally told: 'Wait and do nothing, negotiate cease-fire, evacuate expatriates, do nothing serving the local population.[23]

As Stec proceeds to elucidate, the Secretariat's response to UNAMIR's requests was even more revealing:

> They [the Secretariat] actually reacted in a very interesting way by completely ignoring every fax about humanitarian assistance. There was a number of other faxes which I sent through General Dallaire, and there had been questions like, 'Do you have a manual about humanitarian assistance?', 'How much water?', 'How much food do you need for how many people?' For example things like these we had been asking. 'Send us the data how to organise it', because we didn't have experience in that area. So to all of these faxes we never received the answering, to the point that, in a sarcastic way, we sent the last fax: 'immediate help necessary'. And the General signed, we sent it, and we never sent anything else about that to New York.[24]

This stark disparity culminated in the fact that no mention of the term 'safe havens', or anything resembling it, appeared in the Secretariat's reports to the Security Council or in the Council's discussion until the beginning of May 1994, although UNAMIR had actually been studying and preparing for the possibility of establishing safe havens by 15 April. The Council did discuss the situation in the 'concentration of refugees' at the King Faisal Hospital and the Amahoro stadium, areas which were also called 'pockets of civilians'.[25] Nigeria in particular emphasised the importance of protecting the tens of thousands of civilians sheltering in these areas.[26] However, no member of the Council or the Secretariat suggested establishing *further* safe areas or humanitarian zones, although these plans had already been sketched out by UNAMIR by 15 April.

It was not until 5 May that the possibility of setting up humanitarian corridors in Rwanda was raised for the first time in the Security Council, when France outlined plans for areas similar to those established by Operation Provide Comfort in Northern Iraq in 1991.[27] The following week, the Council engaged in a debate on that scenario. On 11 May, the US expressed its willingness to explore the idea of a 'protective zone' along the border between Burundi and Rwanda.[28] Russia agreed and suggested the establishment of one or two such zones.[29] The non-permanent members of the Council, on the other hand, entertained discrepant opinions on safe havens. Spain wished to explore the possibility of setting up humanitarian zones around Rwanda's frontiers with Uganda and Tanzania.[30] New Zealand also noted that humanitarian zones should be situated in areas in the heart of the fighting.[31] The Czech Republic pointed out that there were civilians in a vulnerable position all over Rwanda, not merely in the border areas.[32]

The Secretariat pronounced its opinion on safe sites on 13 May, when the Military Adviser to the Secretary-General, Major-General Maurice Baril, briefed the Security Council. Baril recognised that dozens of areas identified by non-governmental organisations were at risk. The most vulnerable sites were not necessarily situated in border areas.[33] This time the Secretariat's policy was in line with Force Commander Dallaire's position, which could have been a result of Dallaire's discussions with the Secretariat:

> The Americans wanted me to set up a safe haven area just like they did with the Kurds. I said to Maurice Baril: The guys can't get there, cause they were being slaughtered all the way down. So you had to set up these different sites and then with helicopters and observation we would be able to protect them in these sites.[34]

The only silver lining in the cloud of the issue of safe havens was that the Secretariat, together with certain non-permanent Council members and the Force Commander, confirmed the viability of *functional* bureaucratic rationalisation. They were successful to some extent at least in promoting the idea of an 'inside-out' approach, i.e. establishing several safe havens inside the Rwandan killing zone, as opposed to the US proposal of an 'outside-in' version, which envisaged only one large safe haven located on its outskirts. The latter was logistically easier to implement and less risky to soldiers, but would have endangered the lives of fleeing Tutsi civilians. However, the *dysfunctional side* of bureaucratic rationalisation had already damaged the situation by that time anyway: UN Headquarters had 'dehumanised' safe havens by categorising them merely as 'concentrations of refugees' in April 1994. The emergence of safe havens on the Council's agenda in early May 1994 simply arrived too late to alter the course of events.

The collapse of the UN safe haven in Goražde, Bosnia, in April 1994, which coincided with the Security Council's informal meetings on Rwanda, further exacerbated the situation. The Goražde incident severely undermined the credibility of those who *could* have advocated the establishment of similar safe areas in Rwanda, as the Czech Ambassador Kovanda explains:

We talked about safe havens in Bosnia, and I was one of those who argued for extending the number of safe havens to some other cities in Bosnia, feeling, naïvely, as I realised later ... that the sheer moral standing of the UN and the UN Security Council would prevent the Serbs from attacking them. Of course this didn't happen, so safe havens wouldn't have done much good anywhere. Or rather generally speaking, safe havens do zero good anywhere, if, on the one hand, the adversary has the determination to go against them, and if, on the other hand, the safe haven promoters don't have the military wherewithal and the political will to defend them .... I don't recall anybody ever having suggested that safe havens might even be considered in Rwanda.[35]

This statement exposes an additional dysfunction intrinsic to bureaucratic rationalisation, namely the failure to grasp the differences between *actual* safe havens in Bosnia and *potential* safe areas in Rwanda. The former were systematically attacked by the well-equipped and disciplined Serb army, whereas the latter were sporadically assaulted by drunk and drugged machete-wielding thugs. In contrast to Bosnian 'safe' areas, humanitarian pockets in Rwanda could have been secured by reasonably well-equipped UN peacekeepers. However, this crucial distinction was never apprehended by the UN bureaucracy.

In addition to disagreements over UNAMIR's strength and the protection of civilians, the third main point of contention between New York and UNAMIR concerned the mandate and function of peacekeepers. Until 20 April 1994, both of the Secretariat's existing options regarding the future of UNAMIR were predicated on the establishment of a cease-fire and the withdrawal of UNAMIR. On 20 April, however, the Secretariat introduced a third option proposing the shoring up of UNAMIR. This option was included as 'Alternative I' in the Secretariat's report to the Security Council, and called for a

massive reinforcement of UNAMIR and a change in its mandate so that it would be equipped and authorized to coerce the opposing forces into a cease-fire, and to attempt to restore law and order and put an end to the killings.[36]

In this scenario, UNAMIR was to be granted enforcement powers under Chapter VII of the UN Charter.[37] To Dallaire's amazement, the Secretariat informed the Council that Alternative I would require several thousand additional troops, even in excess of 10,000 soldiers.

The provisions of Alternative I stood in stark contrast to Dallaire's suggestions on the future of UNAMIR (Dallaire 2003: 320). First, Dallaire had never requested such a dramatic reinforcement of UNAMIR as 10,000 troops. Instead, his final appeal to the Secretariat on 17 April 1994 called for merely 1,300 troops,[38] scaled down from his original request of 10 April for 4,000 troops. Second, Dallaire had never asked for the Chapter VII mandate or peace-enforcement powers (Dallaire 2003: 320), in the knowledge that it would have been neither acceptable to the Security Council nor operationally necessary, as UNAMIR was able to protect civilians under the Chapter VI mandate, or what Dallaire termed 'Chapter Six Plus'.[39] Indeed, a Chapter VII mandate would have nourished mistrust towards UNAMIR unnecessarily on the part of the Hutu militias and the Presidential Guard, thereby increasing risks to UN troops. Third, Dallaire had never wished that UNAMIR 'coerce the opposing forces into a cease-fire'. In his recommendation, the objectives of UNAMIR comprised humanitarian support tasks, the securing of the Kigali airfield for humanitarian relief efforts, and the maintaining of the political mediation process between the RGF and RPF.[40] In conclusion, the Secretariat's sole option which discussed bolstering UNAMIR was over-ambitious; none of the three options it presented to the Council included suggestions to protect civilians or construct safe havens. As Major Stefan Stec observed from the perspective of a UNAMIR soldier, 'The dilemma was either we pull out, or we do everything. What about doing something in the middle?'[41]

The following analysis will explain the contradictions between the various organs of the UN by reference to their underlying structural causes. The first section already outlined two dysfunctions of bureaucratic rationalisation, i.e. instrumental rationality (*Zweckrationalität*) and loose coupling. It will be argued in this section that these dysfunctions, which emerged in the pre-genocide phase of conflict prevention, persisted during the genocide phase, albeit in a different form. The structural root causes of such 're-emerged' forms of dysfunctions will be examined below.

As the first section demonstrated, *Zweckrationalität* constituted one factor that induced the UN bureaucracy to discredit early warning information in the pre-genocide phase. The 'new' form of instrumental rationality that surfaced in the genocide phase, 're-emerged *Zweckrationalität*', explains why the UN bureaucracy assumed a cautious stance on the possibility of intervention in Rwanda. The most detrimental effects of re-emerged *Zweckrationalität*, much as those of its earlier form, were felt by the relationship between the Secretariat and the great powers. As Boutros-Ghali explained to the author, his decision *not* to convene the Council to discuss intervention in Rwanda was determined less by conditions in the country than by calculations of the possible costs of such a decision for the UN bureaucracy as a whole, particularly its potential counter-productive effect on the funding of other UN operations elsewhere and on the prospect of resolving the problem of UN budget arrears:[42]

> The fact that you are taking into consideration only Rwanda is artificial, because at the same time I was asking for assistance to Somalia, Mozambique, Angola or even Salvador, or I was asking that they [member states] pay their contributions. So they would tell me: 'You want the money, don't provoke us now.' ... I had a contact with the American representative, and I said: 'We want to convene the Security Council to discuss the situation in Rwanda.' And their representative said: 'I would not advise you, because you will obtain nothing.' Immediately after, I received the British one, who

came to see me: 'Don't do it, because this will be *counter-productive* for what you are asking for somewhere else.' *Then, here is your responsibility: you are supposed to have enough energy to say, 'No, in spite of this I will convene the Security Council.* '[43]

So how does such a 'risk calculation' manifest itself in the Secretariat's options regarding UNAMIR's future which were presented to the Security Council on 20 April 1994? The first step in answering this question requires the unveiling of the source from which the peculiar Alternative I envisaging a massive reinforcement of UNAMIR was derived. Using a Popperian method of falsification, this can be carried out by eliminating possible alternative sources. First, Alternative I could not have emanated from UNAMIR, as it crucially differed from Dallaire's suggestions for a less ambitious and more realistic strengthening of UNAMIR. In addition, all permanent Council members were opposed to a massive reinforcement of UNAMIR; they are also thereby eliminated as a potential source. Nor did any of the non-permanent members of the Council present such an option.[44] Hence, the only possible remaining source is the Secretariat. This demonstrates in turn that Alternative I did not constitute a Trojan horse on the part of any member state determined to withdraw UNAMIR, unlike the four options presented to the Council a week earlier by Ambassador Hannay. Instead, Alternative I must be seen as a product of bureaucratic rationalisation in general, and *Zweckrationalität* in particular. *Zweckrationalität* underlay the formation of the Secretariat's options on UNAMIR in the following manner: if the UN was to intervene in Rwanda, the intervention force had to be *massively reinforced in order to* eliminate the risk of a failure on the scale of that in Somalia, as a further major failure could have heralded the collapse of the UN. Thus, Alternative I, which envisaged the reinforcement of UNAMIR with up to 10,000 troops, was *instrumental* to the survival of the UN bureaucracy as a whole. However, the ultimate irrationality of such instrumental rationality resided not only in its fundamental contradiction with Dallaire's suggestions, which were based on first-hand knowledge of the situation, but also in the Secretariat's awareness that Alternative I was never acceptable to the Council.

Zweckrationalität also contributed to the reluctance of the Secretariat and the Security Council to articulate the word 'genocide'. The UK Ambassador David Hannay famously predicted that the Council would become a 'laughing stock' if the term 'genocide' was employed in an official UN document at a time when the Council could not support such a strong statement with appropriately robust measures.[45] The existing literature, such as Linda Melvern's account, emphasises that the US, China, Rwanda and Djibouti also wished to avoid the term 'genocide' for political reasons (Melvern 2000: 180). However, what is left unmentioned is that countries such as Spain, devoid of any vested political interests, held similar views. Spain pointed out in an informal meeting of the Council on 13 April 1994 that more should not be promised than could be delivered with the available means. Otherwise, Spain reasoned, the Council would risk jeopardising its own credibility.[46] Political disinclination cannot provide an exhaustive explanation for Spain's reasoning, as it was not among those countries actively seeking convincing reasons to withdraw UNAMIR. What the Spanish statement rather illustrates is the logic of instrumental rationality that was prevalent in the Council *as a whole*. Although Spain explicitly called for 'proportionality between ends and means',[47] implicitly this signified prioritising risk-free means over realistic means of curbing Rwandan violence. Certain means thus overcame ends by becoming ends in themselves.

The 'dark side' of *Zweckrationalität* can be summarised by the following statement from Major Stefan Stec: 'This is one of the UN typical tactics: Do not reply, then the problem does not exist. If you reply, you admit you [need to] solve it.'[48] Although Stec specifically refers to the Secretariat's ignorance of or refusal to acknowledge every fax that UNAMIR sent to UN Headquarters concerning humanitarian assistance, it also perfectly captures the logic underlying Alternative I and the evasion of the word 'genocide': if the UN had decided to 'answer' calls for humanitarian intervention in Rwanda either by dispatching troops or by acknowledging the genocidal nature of killings, the expectations of the international community regarding the ability of the UN to solve the crisis would have been increased. The Secretariat thus felt it *safest for the UN bureaucracy* to raise the level of requirements for an intervention to the point where the Security Council would find it unacceptable, which provoked the Secretariat to present the overambitious Alternative I. The Council, for its part, tacitly accepted the exclusion of realistic means for intervention in Rwanda. By 'not responding' to the humanitarian crisis in Rwanda, the UN faced zero expectations, and therefore zero risks. But this rationalisation proved irrational in the long run: rather than safeguarding the credibility of the UN, its inaction in Rwanda compounded the damage already effected by the Somalia crisis.

Nevertheless, to attempt to explain the irrational nature of the UN's three options regarding the future of UNAMIR solely by appeal to *Zweckrationalität* leaves too many questions unanswered. It does not, for example, account for the fact that none of the alternatives included a means of protecting civilians. The reasons for this can instead be uncovered through an examination of *irrationality of bureaucratic categorisation*. A useful starting point from which to study this dysfunction is furnished by the taxonomy of UN peacekeeping operations outlined by Marrack Goulding in 1993. Although the taxonomy does not directly represent the official policy of the UN, it does provide valuable insights into UN procedures at the time of the Rwandan conflict, as it was written by an experienced UN official only one year prior to the Rwandan genocide. Goulding worked as Under-Secretary-General for Peacekeeping Operations from 1986 to 1993 and then as Under-Secretary-General for Political Affairs from 1993 to 1995.

Goulding's taxonomy delineates six discrete categories of peacekeeping operations according to the functions they perform. It is interesting that Alternative I of UNAMIR discussed above falls into two categories of UN operations, both of which denote peace-enforcement: 'Type Five' peace-enforcement operations whose purpose is peace-building in a country where state institutions have largely collapsed; and 'Type Six' peace-enforcement missions whose purpose is the enforcement of cease-fire (Goulding 1993: 459). In Goulding's taxonomy, Type Five and Six peace-enforcement operations are strictly separated from peacekeeping missions. To quote one of Goulding's favourite phrases of the early 1990s, 'There is no halfway house between peacekeeping and peace enforcement' (Goulding 2002: 17). For the UN bureaucracy, Dallaire's suggestion of a modest strengthening of UNAMIR by up to 4,000 troops on 10 April 1994 was exactly what was implied by the unwanted 'halfway house'. Dallaire's proposal of what he called a 'Chapter Six Plus' or 'Chapter Six and a half' type of peacekeeping was viewed as an unwelcome 'half-measure' and uncategorised 'hybrid' falling between the stools of peace-enforcement (Chapter VII) and peacekeeping (Chapter VI).

Even worse, Dallaire's suggestion was seen as *dangerous* to the UN. The Secretariat believed the strict separation between peacekeeping and peace-enforcement to be indicative of an unassailable bureaucratic wisdom. 'Creating [a] grey area between peacekeeping and peace-enforcement', as Goulding deliberated in 1993, 'can give rise to considerable dangers ... [i]n political, legal and military terms, and in terms of the survival of one's own troops' (Goulding 1993: 461). This statement is underpinned not only by bureaucratic categorisation but also by another kind of bureaucratic rationalisation, namely *bureaucratic universalism*. Goulding's view epitomises a belief in the universal truth that crossing the line between peacekeeping and peace-enforcement spells danger, regardless of local context. Perhaps the greatest irrationality of such bureaucratic universalism in the Rwandan case was the inability to spot the differences between the requirements of local security environments: unlike in Bosnia, 'creating a grey area' in Rwanda, i.e. protecting civilians under the 'Chapter Six Plus' or 'Chapter Six and a half' mandate, would have saved tens of thousands of lives without incurring unreasonable risks for UN soldiers.[49]

The combination of bureaucratic categorisation and bureaucratic universalism required that UNAMIR would have had to be either *massively* strengthened, 'painting the country blue',[50] as peace-enforcement was described, or not strengthened at all. Dallaire's proposed 'middle option' was not conveyed to the Security Council until it was too late, simply because his plan did not comply with the UN categories, bureaucratic wisdom and organisational procedures. Alternative I, by contrast, fell neatly into the category of peace-enforcement operations and fulfilled its requirements, namely overwhelming troops, firepower, and a peace-enforcement mandate to impose law and order, yet it was understood from the outset that the Council would never accept it as a viable option.

Another peculiar feature in Goulding's categorisation is that *none* of the seven types of peacekeeping operations mentioned involve the protection of civilians or creation of safe havens. To understand this omission, an overview of UN conflict management in the early 1990s is necessary. The concept of safe havens dates back to April 1991, when France, the US and the UK intervened in Northern Iraq to provide safe areas for Kurds fleeing repression by the Iraqi army.[51] Despite Security Council Resolution 688, which defined the consequences of the Kurdish oppression as a threat to international peace and security, the Secretariat was cautious about Western plans to set up safe havens in Iraq for its own bureaucratic reasons, fearing that the Western action could jeopardise the delivery of UN humanitarian relief in Iraq (Wheeler 2000: 155). Secretary-General Javier Pérez de Cuéllar also entertained reservations regarding the legality of such actions, warning that the presence of foreign troops on Iraqi territory required Iraq's consent or an express authorisation from the Security Council (Stromseth 1993: 90). The Iraq case demonstrates that safe havens were not among the 'grand strategies' of the Secretariat at the time. The concept of safe areas is also absent from *An Agenda for Peace* written by Pérez de Cuéllar's successor Boutros Boutros-Ghali. Unlike the Somalia conflict, which functioned as a laboratory for the nation-building strategies envisaged in the *Agenda*, the Rwandan conflict lacked the potential to serve as a testing-ground for any 'greater purpose' of the UN. The effects of this dysfunction may, of course, have been compounded by cognitive dissonance of organisational learning from the Somalia example; a possibility which will be examined in the following section.

Mechanism of organisational learning

This section marks a shift in the focus of analysis from motivated biases caused by bureaucratic calculations to unmotivated psychological biases produced by cognitive dissonance. The role of the latter has not been studied in the previous literature on Rwanda. This section will attempt to fill that gap by drawing upon theories of cognitive dissonance and particularly on Robert Jervis' book *Perception and Misperception in International Politics* (1976). This classic explores the role of psychology and cognitive factors in international relations. Jervis defines cognitive dissonance in the following terms: 'Two elements are in a dissonant relation if, considering these two alone, the obverse of one element would follow from the other' (Jervis 1976: 382). In the Rwandan case, cognitive dissonance surfaces in the discrepancy between the reality on the ground in Rwanda and the mental images produced of that reality. The Rwandan conflict was imagined as the mindless, anarchic, unruly, tribal killing; in reality, such killing was systematic, well-organised and political in nature.

Cognitive dissonance is psychologically uncomfortable for an individual. As a consequence, actors will endeavour to reduce such discomfort, not by conforming to new information, but by avoiding and discrediting information that increases the dissonance (Jervis 1976: 382). UN officials and diplomats surely felt increasingly restive about the dissonant images they were producing, particularly as human rights organisations were uncovering new evidence negating the UN portrayals of the Rwandan conflict. In compliance with the expectations of cognitive dissonance, UN officials and diplomats did not strive to adjust their misleading images as new information filtered in on the Rwandan conflict. On the contrary, they discounted and denigrated such information.

This section will analyse four different aspects of cognitive dissonance which help to explain misperceptions of the Rwandan conflict: post-decisional rationalisation, aggravation of cognitive dissonance, dissonance reduction, and the boomerang effect. A useful starting point may be encountered in observations of the Secretariat's conduct. Unlike the Czech Republic, Nigeria and other non-permanent members of the Security Council that assumed their responsibilities in the Council in January 1994, the Secretariat possessed a long organisational memory as the executive director of UN peacekeeping operations. UN officials were therefore particularly susceptible to the dysfunctions of organisational learning, including cognitive dissonance emerging from the disjuncture between organisational memory on peacekeeping operations and new information that contradicted the lessons learned.

According to the theory of *post-decisional rationalisation*, cognitive dissonance is always preceded by the *decision* of a person or bureaucracy to adhere to certain (consonant) information confirming their beliefs. At the same time, contradictory or dissonant information is downplayed (Lebow 1984: 58). Before examining the process of post-decisional rationalisation in more detail, it is necessary to question exactly when the Secretariat came to such a crucial decision. Certainly, as Robert Jervis points out, an exact moment of decision proves more tricky to trace scientifically in the social world than under laboratory conditions. Moreover, political decisions are typically characterised by a gradual 'build up' of determination (Jervis 1976: 385). This book, however, maintains that in the Rwandan case, the critical moment of decision can be traced to an exact date, namely 11 January 1994. On that day, the Military Adviser to the Secretary-General, Maurice Baril, brought the infamous January cable to Assistant Secretary-General Iqbal Riza and the Director of the Africa Division, Hedi Annabi, in the Department of Peacekeeping Operations. They then decided to call a meeting to consider Dallaire's message.

In his cable, Dallaire informed the Secretariat of his intention to conduct search and cordon operations to seize arms caches from Hutu militias who were allegedly plotting the extermination of Tutsi civilians. The meeting at UN Headquarters was convened to reach a decision as to whether or not to allow Dallaire's action. Riza, Annabi and Baril refused Dallaire permission for his initiative, albeit not without reservations. The decision was not taken lightly, as Riza describes: 'It [the January cable] alarmed us, it alarmed us. But there were certain clarifications that we felt were essential .... We said, "Not Somalia, again"' (Frontline 1999b: 1–3). It is obvious that Dallaire's plans triggered painful recollections of UNOSOM II and initiated the lessons of an organisational learning process. Dozens of UN soldiers had been killed in similar search and cordon operations conducted by UNOSOM II in Somalia. In one crucial incident, twenty-four Pakistani peacekeepers were killed in an attempt to inspect one of Mohamed Farah Aidid's arms depots on 5 June 1993 (Hirsch and Oakley 1995: 117). It is also obvious that Riza was referring to the ongoing Arusha peace process when he mentioned the 'essential clarifications': 'We rated the chances as fair, simply because the successes ... really depend on the will of the parties [of the peace agreement]' (Frontline 1999b: 1). Thus, the experiences of Somalia and Arusha outweighed Dallaire's call for action and early warning signals.

The theory of post-decisional rationalisation contends that following a crucial decision, such as that taken on the January cable, decision-makers strive to convince themselves that they were constrained by overwhelming factors which left them little option other than to reach the decision they did (Lebow 1984: 58). This phenomenon is illustrated by the Secretariat's conduct in the wake of its pivotal decision of 11 January 1994, particularly in the way in which it appealed to analogies of 'anarchy' and 'chaos' in relation to the Rwandan conflict. The production and reproduction of such analogies can be interpreted as a means of retrospectively justifying the Secretariat's decision on 11 January to follow the 'Arusha route' of (passive) impartiality rather than the 'Somalia route' of robust peacekeeping in Rwanda. By understanding and portraying the Rwandan conflict as an impenetrable Somalia-like 'chaos' with little possibility of resolution, the Secretariat, as well as the Security Council, reassured itself with the idea that following the 'Somalia route' would inevitably lead to a disaster in Rwanda. Their decision to choose the 'Arusha path' was thereby rationalised *a posteriori* in accordance with the theory of post-decisional rationalisation. Hence, none of the key actors in the UN wished to forsake the 'Arusha mode', that is, the constant discussion of 'cease-fire' and 'civil war', despite the fact that this discourse became increasingly detached from the reality in Rwanda.

Symptoms of post-decisional rationalisation can even be discerned in the Secretariat's recent comments. Consider, for example, the following statement by a senior UN official:

> There is no doubt that in any peacekeeping mission, whose mandate is founded on an agreement signed by two parties or more, *the only way* the UN can work in implementing such an agreement is to assume that there is good faith of the parties who have signed it. If there is not good faith, there is no way of implementing it. So let us take another example in Angola, where *UNITA* signed an agreement but then sabotaged it. So it didn't work, and this is what happened in Rwanda also. Yes, we thought that parties who had signed the Arusha agreement did mean to implement it.[52]

Two major conclusions can be drawn from this statement. First, it falsifies the hypothesis advanced in Chapter 3 of this book, which suggested that the positive experiences of the UN in resolving civil wars in the early 1990s, for example in Namibia and El Salvador, generated cognitive dissonance with regard to the Rwandan case by producing over-optimism concerning the Arusha peace process. As the above statement illustrates, the early 1990s were distinguished not only by successes but also by major setbacks such as the Angola case, where the peace agreement signed on 31 May 1991 was torn to pieces only eighteen months later by the eruption of fighting between *UNITA* rebels and government forces. However, the hypothesis outlined in this section concerning post-decisional rationalisation is supported by the above statement. On the one hand, it reflects the way in which the UN peacekeeping doctrine required uncompromising impartiality on the part of Secretariat officials in implementing a peace agreement at the time of the Rwandan conflict.[53] On the other hand, it illuminates the fact that UN officials continue to believe that they were subject to overwhelming constraints which impelled them to act as they did. They still maintain the view that averring trust in the good faith of the parties that signed the Arusha agreement constituted the '*only way*' to proceed. However, it must be noted that such rationalisation of decision *a posteriori* is common to all people and to all decision-making (human stratum), not solely to the UN bureaucracy (social stratum).

In addition to post-decisional rationalisation, cognitive dissonance is typically facilitated by *aggravating factors*. Dissonance theory assumes that the higher the costs and risks to which a person or bureaucracy is subject as a result of discrepant information, the greater the dissonance becomes (Jervis 1976: 387). In the Rwandan case, this equation refers to interaction between two mechanisms, namely organisational learning and bureaucratic rationalisation: from the viewpoint of instrumental rationality, the risks of responding to early warning signals (pre-genocide phase) and portraying the conflict as 'manageable' (genocide phase) were simply too high for the organisation, which further intensified the Secretariat's reluctance to accept new information. Conforming to the new, discrepant information, such as the January cable and other early warning signals, would have risked both UNAMIR's mandate and the impartiality of the UN in the Arusha peace process. It would also have jeopardised the series of painstaking efforts achieved by the international community since June 1992, which had culminated in the signing of the peace accord on 4 August 1993.

Third, the Secretariat's conduct was characterised by *dissonance reduction*, which refers to the avoidance of new information likely to augment dissonance. As cognitive dissonance is psychologically distressing and generative of internal conflict, a person or bureaucracy will strive to reduce it by disparaging discrepant information (Jervis 1976: 382). The following discourse between the New Zealand delegation and the Secretariat in the Security Council's informal meeting on 12 April 1994 is especially illustrative of dissonance reduction: at the outset of that meeting, the President of the Security Council, the New Zealand Ambassador Colin Keating, briefed the Council on a press statement issued by the Rwandan Patriotic Front (RPF). Keating noted that the press statement accused the media of inaccurately depicting the Rwandan conflict as tribal when in reality it was political in nature. By making this remark, Keating probably aimed to undermine the popular image which unfairly equated the situation in Rwanda with that of Somalia. Nonetheless, what is most revealing is the Secretariat's prompt reaction, which came immediately after Keating had spoken. The Secretariat's representative embarked on a briefing of the Council by employing the language of 'chaotic, ethnic and random killings'.[54] Such an image was further reinforced by the Secretariat's assertion that the interim government of Rwanda had left Kigali,[55] thus highlighting the sense of disorder in Rwanda.

By producing these images of chaotic tribal violence, the Secretariat was weakening Keating's attempt at persuading the Security Council to view the

Rwandan conflict as political, as opposed to tribal. With recent experiences of Somalia still fresh in their minds, Secretariat officials perceived another tribal war, chaos and the collapse of state institutions in Rwanda. However, Keating's briefing offered an unwelcome surprise for the prefixed mindset of the Secretariat because it challenged the presumption of similarity between the Rwandan and Somalia conflicts which styled both as instances of insane, and thus, 'unmanageable' killing. The Secretariat's reaction to Keating's statement is indicative of its endeavour to refute unwelcome information which caused dissonance in its established mindset. By doing this, the Secretariat reconfirmed its image of the Rwandan conflict as chaotic and mindless. Such an act, by which dissonant or discrepant information is dismissed, downgraded, misinterpreted or overlooked in favour of consonant information, supplies an example of what dissonance theory refers to as 'selective exposure' (Jervis 1976: 387).

The fourth aspect of cognitive dissonance that seems pertinent to the Rwandan case is the *boomerang effect*. A recurrent process of dissonance reduction, exemplified by the Secretariat's continuous efforts to resist Keating and Kovanda's 'jabs' and to discredit information pointing to genocide, induces an actor to intensify his or her commitment to a particular belief or a previous dysfunctional attitude. This 'boomerang dissonance reduction', as Jervis reflects, actually engenders the opposite outcomes to those predicted by learning theories: dissonant information does not lead actors to adjust behaviours or modify mindsets to comply with the new information, but, on the contrary, provokes them to intensify adherence to existing beliefs (Jervis 1976: 404–5).

Such a boomerang effect seems to have been at work in the UN Secretariat over Rwanda. The Secretariat's actions evidence no attempt to respond to new information indicating genocide. On the contrary, resistance to, and avoidance of, new information heightened and reached its apex on 20 April 1994, when the Secretariat presented its three options on UNAMIR's future. In its statement on Alternative I, the Secretariat *explicitly* mentions the Somalia conflict in relation to Rwandan violence. In its previous reports and briefings to the Security Council, such a connection had solely been posited *implicitly* via analogies, such as the terms 'anarchic', 'chaotic' and 'tribal'. Thus, the Secretariat's stereotypical image of the Rwandan conflict seems to have been *consolidated* throughout April 1994. This is a counterintuitive conclusion in light of traditional organisational learning theory, which assumes that increased information on the Rwandan conflict would have *undermined* such a platitudinous image.[56]

Emancipatory move: locating possibilities for transforming bureaucratic constraints

While the previous section implies, rather pessimistically, that a considerable part of the UN's failure in Rwanda was psychological in nature, and therefore to a greater or lesser degree unchangeable,[57] such a conclusion cannot be advanced with regard to the dysfunctions of bureaucratic rationalisation discussed in the preceding two sections. The flexibility of social factors permits their transformation through social construction; the crucial question regards how such a transformation could have been achieved in the Rwandan case. This question will be addressed below. The first section presented the strict bureaucratic distinction between peacekeeping and peace-enforcement as an obstacle to the prevention of the Rwandan conflict. Interestingly, the UN system has recently transcended this bureaucratic barrier, through its frequent inclusion of elements from Chapter VII of the UN Charter concerning peace-enforcement within the mandates and rules of engagement for peacekeeping operations.[58] Furthermore, as one DPKO official observed, 'It appears now that there's even much more flexibility than before [to move from peacekeeping] into peace-enforcement.'[59] This notion stands in stark contrast to Under-Secretary-General Goulding's view in the early 1990s that, 'There is no halfway house ... between peacekeeping and peace enforcement' (Goulding 2002: 17). The interviewee pondered the functional and historical reasons for such a shift:

> It is a better mechanism to control situations when the belligerents know that [the UN mission] can be enforced, that there will be firepower. When they know that there can never be firepower, then the situation goes out of hand. And there is another term which has been used recently which is called 'robust UN peacekeeping mission'. So if you look at the genesis of this term 'robust', you see it related to enforcement. The setbacks that DPKO had over years in Bosnia, Somalia and Rwanda had a major impact on this. Those three setbacks did make the Organisation change a lot in terms of the way it does its business.[60]

The term 'robust mandates' is derived from the so-called Brahimi report published in August 2000, which provides recommendations on strengthening UN peacekeeping.[61] Other ideas recently added to the UN's conceptual tool-box are the notions of peacekeeping as 'dynamic police work' and 'strong policing' (Samuels 2004: 7). The purpose of this reconceptualisation is the creation of a 'middle ground' between peacekeeping and peace-enforcement, much as Boutros-Ghali's *Agenda* (1992) aimed to bridge the gap between traditional peace operations (Chapter VI) and coercive military action (Chapter VII) via the establishment of what he called 'peace-enforcement units', although such attempts proved unsuccessful at the time. On the one hand, it is acknowledged today that such a middle ground would enable peacekeeping missions to conduct those imperative and robust military tasks that previously fell outside their mandate. On the other hand, this type of robust peacekeeping is clearly differentiated from large-scale enforcement actions and the waging of war. This transformation of peacekeeping has three important 'retrospective' implications for the Rwandan case, which will be addressed below: the deterrence effect, the protection of civilians and the discretionary powers to use force.

First, the authorisation to use peace-enforcement as part of UNAMIR's mandate could have functioned as a credible *deterrent*: although UNAMIR possessed considerable military capacities before the eruption of genocide, particularly the well-equipped and well-trained Belgian contingent, it was widely known within extremist Hutu circles that UNAMIR lacked teeth to engage in robust action on account of its restrictive mandate. Had UNAMIR been authorised to use peace-enforcement, this deterrent could, to a greater or lesser degree, have prevented Hutu militias from organising the genocide. Such an authorisation would at least have increased the political price to be paid by the potential aggressor.

In the current debate on peacekeeping, it is broadly understood that the potential or actual use of vigorous military force does not necessarily jeopardise the security of peacekeepers. On the contrary, missions that include Chapter VII elements tend to be even safer than Chapter VI operations, as they possess greater political manoeuvring space and military capacity with which to respond to violence. Moreover, the show of robust force also deters further attacks and violent behaviour on the part of so-called 'spoilers' of the peace process. According to some recent estimates, casualty rates for those operations which act under Chapter VII mandates have been several times *lower* than those under Chapter VI missions (Langille and Keefe 2003: 6). This contradicts the common belief based on bureaucratic rationalisation of the early 1990s that 'Creating grey area between peacekeeping and peace-enforcement', as Under-Secretary-General Goulding claimed in 1993, 'can give rise to considerable dangers ... in terms of the survival of one's own troops' (Goulding 1993: 461). In this respect, the following remark by one peacekeeping expert seems apposite to the Rwandan case:

> One of the most critical lessons is that peacekeepers have to start on the right track from the very beginning, with overwhelming and intimidating military power, at the same time using that power only when necessary. Exactly this language and message will be well understood by the dozens of rebels and criminals, terrorizing the countryside and jeopardizing a fragile peace process.[62]

As the second major contrast between past and contemporary peacekeeping, the *protection of civilians* currently belongs to the mandates and tasks of *all* operations, be they peacekeeping or peace-enforcement missions, whether officially stated in the mandate or not.[63] This, in turn, may entail the use of enforcement action even in peacekeeping operations against the belligerent parties who threaten civilians or UN troops. At the time of the Rwandan genocide, by contrast, the protection of civilians occurred mainly as a result of personal initiatives of individual peacekeepers rather than as a consequence of compliance with specific UN guidelines for commanders and troops. In fact, such guidelines did not exist at the time. Two years later, James Mayall observed that,

> If by 'new world order' is meant structural change in the nature of international relations to allow effective coercive intervention on the side of the victims in civil conflicts, then the first and most obvious conclusion is that no such change has occurred.

(Mayall 1996: 18)

There is still no military doctrine for the protection of civilians in UN missions (Langille and Keefe 2003: 20). However, presently a broad emphasis is laid on the protection of civilians in UN peacekeeping, which is reflected by the tendency of the Security Council to include this aspect in the mandates of missions. The following statement, for example, is extracted from the report of the tenth-anniversary seminar of DPKO organised in 2002, which brought together highly reputed UN officials, including the Secretary-General and all former Under-Secretaries-General who have headed DPKO: 'Today, maintaining international peace and security cannot be separated from protecting the individual security of civilians. The UN must put the protection of civilians at the center of its peacekeeping and peace-building activities.'[64] If such a transformation in the bureaucratic mindset had occurred by the time of the Rwandan crisis, it would have constrained and perhaps even forestalled the comments made by the Secretariat in the Council to the effect that the protection of civilians did not fall under UNAMIR's remit. Moreover, it could have precipitated Council discussion of the issue of safe havens from early May to mid-April 1994.

Third, the authorisation of peace-enforcement as part of UNAMIR's mandate would have transferred *discretionary powers* from UN Headquarters to the field level. The strict separation between peacekeeping and peace-enforcement in the early 1990s served to retain executive control of peacekeeping operations at the Headquarters level.[65] This, in turn, prevented the discretionary powers from entering the hands of individual force commanders. But imagine the following counterfactual: if force commanders had been entrusted with independent discretionary powers permitting them to take enforcement actions, it is likely that UNAMIR Force Commander Dallaire would have used such powers to conduct search and cordon operations against Hutu militias in January 1994, which might have helped impede the genocide. Interestingly, this counterfactual, i.e. possible action by UNAMIR against Hutu militias, seems to have been retrospectively approved by the UN bureaucracy, as it has been assimilated into the UN's organisational learning process following the Rwandan case. For example, a DPKO expert in the rules of engagement described one session of the United Nations Training and Assistance Teams organised by the Training and Relations Office of DPKO:

The former Force Commander of UNIFIL [United Nations Interim Force in Lebanon], General Erskine from Ghana, was there as well. And I asked him the question: 'If you had been in the position of Force Commander Dallaire by the time, would you have sent the code cable to New York asking for permission, or asking for guidance?' 'No, I wouldn't have sent the code cable', he said, and he reflected upon his experience as the UNIFIL Force Commander: 'A) You never know when you'll have the response from UN Headquarters; and B) It may not be the answer that you're looking for. I read the situation on the ground, and if it's the wise thing to do, that I'm the responsible person to act on this information, I will do so, and I may inform Headquarters later.' And I asked a few more force commanders whether they would have sent the code cable to New York, and some said that, 'Well, I wouldn't have sent code cables to New York.'[66]

At first sight, the critical reaction of force commanders to Dallaire's conduct implies that the latter erred in informing UN Headquarters of his intention to raid the arms caches of Hutu militias. From that viewpoint, Dallaire could be rebuked for lacking the following characteristics of a force commander: initiative and courage to 'act first and inform later', pragmatism and ability to 'read between the lines' of UNAMIR's mandate loosely enough to justify enforcement actions, when the situation in Rwanda so required. Upon closer inspection, however, Dallaire's conduct seems perfectly understandable, when two bureaucratic impediments characteristic of the 'pre-Brahimi' era are taken into consideration: the uncompromising separation between peacekeeping and peace-enforcement, and the vagueness of the terms of mandates. The latter compounded the obscurity of UNAMIR's executive direction. As a consequence, Force Commander Dallaire wrongly presumed that certain peace-enforcement measures, such as the use of force to confiscate illegal arms and the protection of civilians, formed part of UNAMIR's mandate. Such a presumption was vigorously rejected by UN Headquarters on 11 January 1994 to Dallaire's great surprise and disappointment. These structural constraints afflicting the 'pre-Brahimi' era are reflected in Dallaire's response to the author's question as to whether he regrets sending the January cable to the Secretariat at the time:

> No, it was my duty to inform my Headquarters that I was entering a wholly new phase of operations, so that's exactly what I did. I have personal feelings on my own, but *it was my ethical duty to inform them.* Now, many people say: 'Well, ok, when you got the answer 'no', why didn't you just do it [the operations] anyway?' Because command of UN forces is different than one's own national forces. Those troops are only lent to me, so *I can't start fiddling with the mandate with those guys when their countries are keeping the squeeze on them.* It's [the job of national] contingent commanders to do it. So one reason was ethical, and two: it would have put those guys in an impossible situation.[67]

Following the Rwandan drama, the Brahimi report has endeavoured to tackle both those structural constraints mentioned above, i.e. the bureaucratic distinction between peacekeeping and peace-enforcement, and the vagueness of the terms of mandates.[68] The following statement by one Secretariat official aptly demonstrates one crucial asset from which UNAMIR was unable to benefit, namely the clarity of the terms of mandates:

> If in the [mandate of] first UNAMSIL [United Nations Mission in Sierra Leone] they had a few lines, then clearly with the Liberia mission it is a few pages where it is exactly spelt out what the mandate of the mission is. And then based on the mandate we provide very detailed rules of engagement to

the force commanders directly spelling out in what circumstances he is allowed to use what sort of force. So by now it will be much clearer for a force commander than back in the mid-nineties.[69]

The force commanders cited above benefited from the luxury of hindsight when denouncing Dallaire's action from a 'post-Brahimi' viewpoint; such criticism cannot, however, do justice to Dallaire's conduct in the 'pre-Brahimi' context. The vagueness of the terms of mandates in the 'pre-Brahimi' era rendered force commanders dependent on UN Headquarters and on national contingents in interpreting their mandates, which diminished their discretionary powers to use force.

Tribalisation and the statist paradigm of Western thinking

The general consensus among those of us watching the pictures and those who had taken them was that Rwanda was a madhouse, a primitive torture chamber where rival tribes were busy settling ancient scores.

(Keane 1996: 6)

The African 'barbarian' is thus not just a savage – and certainly not a noble savage, as in the early view of the South American Indians – but the imagined dark side of the Western 'rational man'.

(Chabal 2000: 826)

The role of Western normalisation, much as that of cognitive dissonance analysed in the third section, has remained largely unexplored in the previous literature on Rwanda. However, Western normalisation takes a central role in conflict management, as it has the potential to hamper peacekeeping operations and may even generate a 'body-bag syndrome' by compounding the lack of political will to intervene in conflicts portrayed as 'anarchic', 'mad' and 'tribal'. This section will demonstrate the disturbing impact of Western normalisation on conflict management, using the Rwandan case as an illustration, whilst the next chapter will draw upon the experiences of Darfur in order to outline counterstrategies to tackle this problematic relationship. This section will examine two aspects of Western normalisation by reflecting on various theoretical accounts, particularly those offered by Michel Foucault, Bhikhu Parekh and Michael Ignatieff. These novel dimensions of the Rwandan drama are intelligible in the 'tribalisation' of African conflicts and the statist paradigm of Western thinking.[70] Chapter 3 endeavoured to emphasise that Western-centred conflict management is often epitomised by a normalisation process, through which African conflicts are stereotypically portrayed as mad, tribal and ethnically motivated, permitting no possibility of resolution by rational means. As the picture of the African 'Heart of Darkness' prevails in the popular imagination of the West,[71] it would be interesting to examine how this Conradian image was reproduced in the UN's *external* relations with the public sphere and the media.

Documentary sources disclose that during the initial days of the genocide, a paucity of information and the 'fog of war' contributed to the creation of trite images of the Rwandan conflict. On 7 April 1994, Spokesman for the Secretary-General, Joe Sills, issued a press briefing, in which the situation in Rwanda was described as 'confused'.[72] However, lack of information was not a significant factor in the tribalisation of the Rwandan conflict, as an accumulation of information on the crisis failed to alter Western clichés conveyed through the Secretariat's press briefings. On 12 April, Sills again provided the media with a picture of a 'chaotic situation', and 'random killing' and 'looting' in Kigali.[73] These examples epitomise what Michael Ignatieff refers to as a 'chaos narrative' that arose at the end of the Cold War:

> [T]he narrative that has become most pervasive and persuasive has been the 'chaos narrative,' the widely held belief, only reinforced by the end of direct colonialism, that large sections of the globe, especially in central Africa and the fiery southern edges of the former Soviet empire, have collapsed into a meaningless disorder, upon which no coherent pattern can be discerned. The 'chaos narrative' demotivates: it is an antinarrative, a story that claims there is no story to tell and therefore no reason to get involved.
>
> (Ignatieff 1998: 289)

This 'tribalisation' of the Rwandan conflict was performed by deployment of what Michel Foucault terms '*normalisation technologies*'. On this reading, 'technology' refers to the joining of power and knowledge, while 'normalisation' signifies the distribution or organisation of agents around a norm with the aim of including 'normal' objects or agents and excluding deviant ones (Rabinow 1984: 17–20). Through such a normalising act, Rwanda became constructed as an 'abnormal madhouse' excluded from the concerns of the international community. The conflict there was portrayed as a 'mindless' one with no possibilities of resolution. As for linkages between communication and power, Foucault advises that social science 'should not concern itself with power at the level of conscious intention or decision' (quoted in McCarthy 1990: 448). Rather than asking, 'Who has power?' or 'What intentions or aims do power holders have?', the Foucauldian approach queries, 'How do things work at the level of on-going subjugation?' (Smart 1983: 83). It is agreed here, as Heikki Patomäki asserts, that the main originality of Foucault's approach lies in the idea that subjugation and power relations are not only produced through the intentional planning of agents. Exclusion is also carried out through unintentional activity which, in Patomäki's words, 'often escapes the horizon of actors' (Patomäki 2002a: 113).

Foucault's conception of power relations sheds some light on the way in which the image of the Rwandan conflict as anarchic and mindless was not only produced in the UN by Western states, such as the US and the UK, which were politically motivated to produce such stereotypical images *intentionally*. The Secretariat, and even some African countries devoid of any interest in reducing

UNAMIR, *unintentionally re*-produced these images. The third section explained this phenomenon by an appeal to the cognitive dissonance of organisational learning (internal relations of the UN), but this section maintains that the 'tribalisation' of Rwanda also resonated with the Western-centred popular image of African conflicts (external relations of the UN with the media). Another dimension of the Foucauldian approach which this book finds relevant to the Rwandan case is the notion of power as a pervasive object that exerts influences not only in political and military spheres, but also in expert communities, family relationships, architecture and so on. Power is something that 'runs through' all social networks (Foucault 1976: 114). At first glance, the Secretariat's reports to the Security Council and its briefings to the media seem to constitute nothing more than apolitical expert statements; from a Foucauldian perspective, however, they appear as instruments of power similar to the Security Council's presidential statements and resolutions.

Western normalisation operated not only in the UN's external relations but also *within* the UN system, in at least three respects. First, Bhikhu Parekh notes that the conception of humanitarianism is not universal but culturally specific, and therefore humanitarian interventions are always biased towards those cultural specifics (Parekh 1998: 147). Parekh explores the deep structures of Western civilisation and concludes that one factor in particular has dominated Western political life for the past three centuries, namely, a statist manner of thinking. This view resonates with Critical Theory in International Relations which maintains that the 'state' prevails as the organising concept of international relations and has primacy over human individuals as the referent object of security. More disturbing still, the 'state' tends to subjugate human-centred thinking in international politics.[74] This ontological bias produced concrete and tangible implications for the Tutsi population of Rwanda: the Secretariat's three options for UNAMIR's future as well as the Security Council's discussions throughout April 1994 were focused not on creating safe havens for Tutsi civilians (the level of human individuals) but on a political settlement to re-implement the Arusha agreement (the level of state). The organising concept and referent object of assessment for a possible intervention in Rwanda was not the human suffering of individuals. Instead, the primary concern was the restoration and reconstitution of the state, the organising unit of international relations, in the aftermath of the collapse of Rwandan state institutions on 6 April 1994.

A further consequence of the statist paradigm for humanitarian intervention is witnessed in the disjuncture between the effects and accountability of intervention. On the one hand, intervening states feel primarily *accountable* to their domestic sphere to justify their actions. If an intervention leads to casualties among the troops constituting the intervention forces, intervening states typically confront substantial domestic pressure to withdraw their forces. On the other hand, the *effects* of such a withdrawal are visited on those outside the national borders of intervening states. A moral dilemma thus arises when the withdrawal of intervening forces places thousands of civilians at risk, for the intervening state is not primarily accountable to the endangered civilians, but to its domestic electorate. 'If, say, twenty soldiers or civilians of the intervened country have to be killed in order to save the life of a single soldier of the intervening country', as Parekh illustrates, 'that is considered morally legitimate' (1998: 151). At the heart of Parekh's notion is the idea that the disjuncture between the effects and accountability of humanitarian intervention reflects less the political unwillingness of individual states to sacrifice their troops, than it exposes a commonly accepted norm in Western-dominated international politics.[75]

How, then, did such a moral disjuncture emerge in the Rwandan case? In an informal meeting of the Security Council on 15 April 1994, the representative of the US opined that priority must be given to the safety of UN peacekeepers in Rwanda, therefore maintaining the presence of UN personnel in the hazardous security environment of Rwanda would be irresponsible.[76] On the one hand, this statement should be understood in the context of the death of ten Belgian peacekeepers on 7 April. On 12 April, the Belgian government had announced the unilateral withdrawal of all its peacekeepers from UNAMIR, and subsequently proceeded to actively lobby the US government for the complete abolition of UNAMIR. Belgium required the total withdrawal of UNAMIR in order to conceal its unilateral abandonment of Rwanda. On the other hand, the *Realpolitik* of Belgium and the US does not constitute an exhaustive explanation of the uncompromising prioritisation of UN security concerns over the lives of Rwandan civilians, as the Security Council as a whole and the Secretariat tacitly approved this line of reasoning. Although Nigeria did emphasise in the Council that Belgium's call for the total withdrawal of UNAMIR formed part of its national politics and that the Council was not obliged to follow it, on 13 April, the Nigerian representative concurred with the rest of the Council that its primary responsibility was to ensure the security of UN personnel.[77] This view was strongly underlined by the Secretariat. On 11 April, the Secretariat's representative noted in an informal meeting of the Council that the first priority was the protection of UN personnel and the evacuation of foreign nationals.[78]

A further flaw in the argument that political unwillingness alone was responsible for the Security Council's prioritisation of the safety of UN peacekeepers at the expense of that of Rwandan civilians is discernible in the fact that none of the Council members actually had any of their own national troops in UNAMIR. In this regard, the policy of state representatives and UN officials was determined less by national interest than by the *presumption of a general norm in international society*. This norm was a statist one which gave precedence to the accountability of states to their domestic electorates over the effects of the withdrawal of peacekeeping troops on (Rwandan) civilians. The following example clarifies this argument. Only a few hours before the Council took the crucial vote on reducing the strength of UNAMIR, Military Adviser to the Secretary-General Maurice Baril briefed a group of non-permanent members of the Council. Baril explained to ambassadors that UNAMIR soldiers were exhausted, confused and constantly in fear. The Nigerian Ambassador Gambari, who participated in the briefing, assessed its impact:

I think it had a very big impact, because on the one hand we didn't want to put the lives of the troops, *other* troops, in jeopardy …. We had the responsibility for the safety of UN troops, we the Non-Aligned Countries that applied these troops, as you know: Bangladesh, Ghana, and so on…. *Then again, the principal duty of an ambassador is to protect the welfare of their troops that they had contributed to a UN peacekeeping operation.*[79]

This statement reveals a two-fold dysfunction of the statist paradigm. First, the Security Council's deliberations were determined by a *presumption* regarding the policies of other states, not necessarily by the actual policies pursued by the states in question. For example, Nigeria's presumption that Ghana was concerned for the welfare of its troops in UNAMIR did not quite correspond to the reality of Ghana's policy, as the Ghanaian government actually retained its UNAMIR contingent throughout the genocide, despite the deaths of three of its soldiers in action between April and July 1994.

Ultimately, the moral disjuncture between the locus of accountability and effects of humanitarian intervention boils down to a Western-biased conception of humanitarianism epitomised by 'double standards'. As Chapter 3 demonstrated by drawing upon Huntington's theory, Western-dominated international society tends to employ different yardsticks by which to assess the humanitarian needs (and value) of Western and non-Western peoples. Ironically, the only context in which the words 'humanitarian operation' were employed in the Security Council's informal discussions in April 1994 was in connection with the evacuation of Western expatriates, not the protection of Rwandan civilians. The term 'humanitarian operation' was introduced by the French representative in the informal consultations on 9 April 1994 when France informed other Council members that a French unit of 190 troops had taken control of Kigali airport.[80] France emphasised that this unit would serve to evacuate only the French expatriate community and other foreigners. It had nothing to do with UNAMIR,[81] or, in other words, with the protection of Rwandan civilians. The French decision was welcomed by other members. In fact, the terms 'humanitarian operation' and 'humanitarian aim' became synonymous with the evacuation of foreign nationals, a phenomenon discernible, for example, in statements from the US[82] and Brazil.[83]

These examples reflect the Western-centric nature of the word 'humanitarian' at its starkest. When questioned as to whether France's use of the term 'humanitarian operation' was ironic, the Czech Ambassador Kovanda replied: 'No, I understand that a nation is first and foremost interested in saving its own nationals.'[84] This statement again illustrates an inter-subjective structure which facilitated the indifference of the Security Council towards Rwandan civilians: the problem did not reside only with French or other states' egoism, but also with a presumption of, and acquiescence in, Western-centrism and the widely accepted 'double standard' of international society. Even though France was legitimately selfish in safeguarding its own nationals, this still begs the question as to why no member state liaised between the French evacuation forces and UNAMIR in order to come up with a deal: the French unit could, and should, have supported UNAMIR as a reciprocal gesture of goodwill, as UNAMIR for its part assisted the French evacuation operation by providing escorts to expatriates and sacrificing valuable time and resources, which could have contributed towards the saving of Rwandan lives. The only response to such events appears to contradict the presumption underlying human rights declarations: 'humanity' was not equally applicable to Western and non-Western peoples, and all member states acquiesced in that inequality.

Conclusion

This chapter has enlarged the picture of the causal complex of the UN's failure in Rwanda by adding three mechanisms, namely bureaucratic rationalisation, organisational learning and Western normalisation. It is already possible to conclude at this stage that the Rwandan drama was more complex than previously imagined; the tragedy was generated by the intersection of various 'levels' or 'planes' of reality, namely by the *interaction* between mechanisms (the relationship between early warning and bureaucratic rationalisation analysed in the first section), the working of bureaucratic rationalisation and Western normalisation in the *social stratum* (the second and fifth section), and the operation of psychological mechanisms in the *human stratum* (the third section). Such psychological factors are summarised in Figure 6.1, which depicts the mechanism of organisational learning.

It is unsatisfactory, however, to explain the Rwandan tragedy by reference to 'human factors' alone. The mechanisms of social construction, namely bureaucratic rationalisation and Western normalisation, also contributed to the UN's failure in preventing or halting the genocide. An interesting conclusion drawn from the analysis of this chapter is that large-scale human suffering as such cannot meet the threshold necessary to launch a humanitarian intervention unless

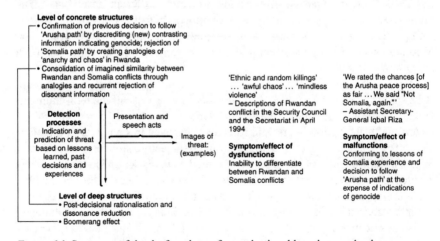

Figure 6.1 Summary of the dysfunctions of organisational learning mechanisms.

it is backed up by bureaucratic needs. Risking the lives of UN peacekeepers in Rwanda would have required a 'grand strategy' instituted by the UN bureaucracy. The protection of civilians as such was simply considered to represent an unrewarding 'middle option', and a risky one. The key consideration in the UN was less the rescue of civilians than the decision over whether an intervention in Rwanda would bestow credit or disgrace, success or failure, on the organisation. Figure 6.2 encapsulates the principal arguments of this chapter concerning bureaucratic rationalisation, although space constraints do not permit all of its relevant points to be presented here.

The fourth section of this chapter demonstrated that certain dysfunctions of the mechanism of bureaucratic rationalisation, such as the strict separation between peacekeeping and peace-enforcement, could have been eliminated or transformed via social construction by UN officials and diplomats. Such transformations could have been conducted at specific crucial moments in the conflict prevention process, for example during the processing of the January cable, which marked the crossroads between the 'Arusha path' of traditional peacekeeping and more robust peacekeeping.[85] Another, even earlier, window of opportunity to transform relevant structures emerged when Boutros-Ghali's *Agenda* was commissioned in 1992. As demonstrated in Chapter 3, the *Agenda* envisaged the creation of a 'middle ground' (peace-enforcement units) between peacekeeping and coercive military action. Such structural transformations could have contributed to the prevention of the Rwandan genocide. Moreover, in light of 'post-Brahimi' achievements, it is no exaggeration to argue that the contemporary UN system is better placed than in past years to prevent 'another Rwanda'. However, this hypothesis will be tested in the next chapter.

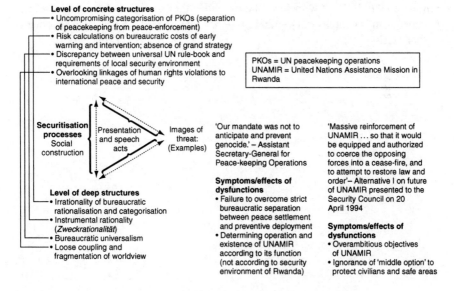

Figure 6.2 Summary of the dysfunctions of bureaucratic rationalisation.

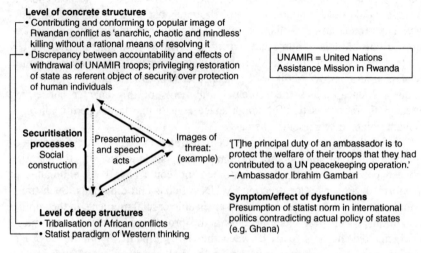

Level of concrete structures
- Contributing and conforming to popular image of Rwandan conflict as 'anarchic, chaotic and mindless' killing without a rational means of resolving it
- Discrepancy between accountability and effects of withdrawal of UNAMIR troops; privileging restoration of state as referent object of security over protection of human individuals

UNAMIR = United Nations Assistance Mission in Rwanda

Securitisation processes
Social construction

Presentation and speech acts

Images of threat: (example)

'[T]he principal duty of an ambassador is to protect the welfare of their troops that they had contributed to a UN peacekeeping operation.'
– Ambassador Ibrahim Gambari

Symptom/effect of dysfunctions
Presumption of statist norm in international politics contradicting actual policy of states (e.g. Ghana)

Level of deep structures
- Tribalisation of African conflicts
- Statist paradigm of Western thinking

Figure 6.3 Summary of the dysfunctions of Western normalisation.

The picture of the Rwandan disaster would remain incomplete without a reference to the plain truth that the UN's actions were racially biased. Based on the conclusions of the fifth section, it would not be an exaggeration to claim that the UN Security Council's discussions have been underlain by racial prejudice: the possibility of establishing safe havens to help black Rwandans, or even mentioning the term 'humanitarian intervention' in the same sentence as 'Rwandan civilians', was off radar screen of the Council, whilst it simultaneously decided to reinforce UNPROFOR with several thousand extra troops in order to assist white Europeans in safe areas in Bosnia. Figure 6.3 summarises the principal argument of that section.

7 Future visions of conflict management

Introduction

The half-hearted reaction of the international community to the plight of Darfurians has been widely perceived to be indicative of the sorry state of current intervention mechanisms. 'Too late, too little' was the blunt statement of Human Rights Watch concerning international action in Rwanda (Human Rights Watch 2004b). Lieutenant-General Roméo A. Dallaire, commander of UN troops in Rwanda at the time of the genocide, formulated his verdict as follows: 'Looking at Darfur, seeing Rwanda' (Dallaire 2004). This chapter, however, will claim that the international response to Darfur should not be assessed against the yardstick of Western greater missions. That is simply because such operations have either existed only as unrealistic, arrogant visions or deceptive paper tigers, as Alternative I in the Rwandan case, or have engendered a disastrous number of casualties, irresponsible withdrawals and unsustainable activities, as in UNOSOM II. The 'new yardstick' proposed here is the degree of structural transformation with regard to the operation and strategy of peacekeeping. By applying this new unit, or level, of analysis, the case of Darfur may appear in a less pessimistic light than in previous literature. Such an analysis could reveal various strategies by which future PKOs avoid potential pitfalls that have plagued UN peacekeeping since the early 1990s. The greatest benefit of an approach based on critical realism lies in the opportunity it offers both to uncover underlying forces or 'troublemaking' mechanisms constraining PKOs and to devise strategies through which their effects can be counterbalanced or diminished.

The first section will suggest that 'body-bag syndrome', triggered and aggravated by Western normalisation, can be assuaged or even eliminated by a 'new division of labour' between regional actors. Darfur serves as a laboratory for a new arrangement of cooperation in which richer organisations of developed countries, such as NATO, contribute material equipment and logistical support, while African organisations provide troops. The second section will claim that UN and AU engagement in Darfur indicates another innovative strategy, namely a pragmatic turn with regard to peacekeeping in general and the protection of civilians in particular. As demonstrated in the previous chapter, PKOs have been prevented from conducting civilian protection by rigid bureaucratic categories, such as the uncompromising distinction between peacekeeping and peace-enforcement, and by grand strategies pursued by international organisations that have diverted their attention away from practical means of protecting civilians. Although civilian protection has not yet become the guiding star of peacekeeping, the case of Darfur reveals several useful, though piecemeal, measures that together imply a pragmatic turn in peacekeeping by dint of which the protection of civilians can gradually become an integral component of any PKO.

The third section will claim that the case of Darfur reveals another innovation in humanitarian intervention, namely an increased synchronisation between mechanisms that aim to monitor and control genocidal governments. In opposition to the common presumption, this section will demonstrate that avoidance of the term 'genocide' indicates less political unwillingness to respond to atrocities in Darfur than a careful balancing act between the requirement to exert diplomatic pressure on the Sudanese government and the need to ensure its compliance in protecting Darfurian civilians. On the one hand, the condemnation of the Sudanese government's actions would necessitate the use of the term 'genocide'. On the other, diplomats have pragmatically calculated that use of the term would jeopardise the government's co-operation with the AU and UN operations and thus hinder their civilian protection functions, especially in light of the harsh security conditions in Darfur, which make it impossible for AU and UN troops to disarm the *Janjaweed* without the government's consent and co-operation.

The final three sections of this chapter will build upon the lessons learned of UN conflict management in order to outline future visions for the Organisation. The UN has been confronted by a disturbing, yet necessary, question as to its proper role in the international security architecture. In the 1990s, this question was prompted by the side-lining of the UN in Kosovo and the devastating failures of UN peacekeeping, not least in Bosnia and Rwanda. During the first decade of the new millennium, the question has re-emerged in connection to the failure in Darfur. At the same time, the UN's prestige has been further undermined by suggestions for possible substitutes to the UN, such as the League or Concert of Democracies, which would provide an alternative platform for democratic governments to deal with various multilateral problems ranging from HIV/AIDS to the conflict in Darfur.[1] This chapter will identify two ways in which the UN could deliver indispensable value added vis-à-vis other international and regional organisations, and fill a unique niche in the international security architecture. These two paths – or, to be accurate, parallel lanes – are the visions of the UN as a defender of the baseline of humanity and as a wheelwork of knowledge-producing mechanisms which could generate objective information for the 'consumption' of universal audiences. The main impetus that can push the UN forward into that direction is an unorthodox and innovative way to think out of bureaucratic boxes and categories.

New division of labour as a counterstrategy for 'body-bag syndrome'

Although it would be premature to evaluate the success of UN–AU–NATO–EU partnership in Darfur, an analysis of the initial stages of their co-operation reveals not merely a tendency to devolve the leadership and main responsibility for the protection of targeted civilians in Darfur to the AU, but also an unprecedented willingness of all organisations to coordinate their activities in Sudan. Such inter-organisational synergy materialised immediately in the wake of the authorisation of the United Nations Mission in Sudan (UNMIS) on 24 March 2005. Security Council Resolution 1590 adopted that day requested that the Secretary-General outline options for the provision of the UN's assistance for the AU, including logistical and technical support and reserve capacity.[2] The EU chose to provide a financial support package worth $120 million to AMIS, which covers almost half the costs of the operation (*USA Today* 2005). Similarly, NATO's North Atlantic Treaty Council pledged a substantial contribution for AMIS. On 8 June 2005, it decided to airlift additional AU troops to Sudan. This was a momentous decision in that for the first time in NATO's history, it launched a substantial co-operation scheme with the AU, and, also for the first time, began operations in Africa. The first NATO airlift took place on 1 July 2005 when Nigerian troops were moved to Sudan, followed by the transfer of personnel from Gambia, Kenya, Nigeria, Rwanda, Senegal and South Africa through July, August and September (*NATO Update* 2005b). Furthermore, NATO undertook to assist in the training of AU officers in managing intelligence and headquarters functions, such as command and control, logistics, and planning (*NATO Update* 2005a).

The increased inter-organisational collaboration has been generated not merely by individual policies pursued by each organisation in order to meet its objectives at the level of *concrete structures*, such as the transformation of the UN system, which aims to give more responsibility for the maintenance of peace and security to regional organisations in accordance with the Secretary-General's *In Larger Freedom* report[3] and Chapter VIII of the UN Charter. The increased coordination and distribution of labour between organisations has also been necessitated by certain *deep structures* prevalent in Western society. Briefly, organisational synergy has emerged partly as a result of either an intentional or, which is more likely, an unintentional strategy to counterbalance and avoid the side-effects of Western normalisation, the tendencies, benefits and drawbacks of which will be examined below.

At first glance, attributing the increase in organisational co-operation to any racial factors appears somewhat strange. Upon closer examination of figures, however, the growing engagement of the AU in peacekeeping seems to be merely a part of a wider tendency, namely, a racial shift in the composition of PKOs. Towards the beginning of 1991, eight of the ten main contributing countries of UNPKOs were from the developed world. A decade later, in August 2003, all of the ten main contributors were developing countries except Ukraine.

Four of these were African, namely Ghana, Kenya, Nigeria and South Africa. Whilst only a dozen African countries had ever contributed troops or police to UNPKOs before 1988, since then that number has tripled (Harsch 2003: 15).

The racial shift in UNPKOs reflects an increased ownership of African countries. This has been welcomed in the West, not only because the lion's share of all post-Cold War conflicts have afflicted Africa, but also due to the engagement of Western states in the war on terror and the consequent overstretch of their military expenditure. Those Western countries that spearheaded the so-called 'normative shift' in international society in the 1990s, calling for solidarity in protecting civilians targeted by genocidal governments, have found it difficult to dispatch troops to Darfur or elsewhere due to their simultaneous operations in Iraq and Afghanistan (Wheeler and Morris 2006: 444–63). On the other hand, the war on terror and consequent strain on Western defence budgets cannot fully explain the racial shift in UNPKOs, as the latter phenomenon began long before the terror attacks of 11 September 2001.

It is suggested here that the racial shift in peacekeeping can be explained not only by increased African ownership and the recent war on terror but also by the new division of labour between 'the West and the Rest', whose concrete embodiment is the partnership between the AU and NATO within the framework of AMIS: when African states have pledged to provide the manpower, i.e. troops and police, to peacekeeping operations, Western countries have agreed to offer hardware, i.e. logistical, technical and financial support. Most crucially, such a division of labour has served as a counterstrategy to deal with the 'dark side' of Western normalisation that scourged UN peacekeeping in the 1990s, particularly the chaos narrative about African conflicts that often triggered 'body-bag syndrome'. The following examination elucidates this 'counterstrategy' in more detail.

On 3 October 1993, eighteen US Rangers were killed in the single most lethal incident of UNOSOM II. The corpse belonging to one murdered US soldier was filmed by the CNN as he was dragged through the streets of Mogadishu. The 'body-bag syndrome' ensuing from the Somalia debacle had serious repercussions not only for the US but also for the whole UN peacekeeping system. It engendered a normalisation process that produced a widely shared (mis)perception of *all* African conflicts, most notably that of Rwanda following the UNOSOM II incident, as a Somalia-type of unmanageable, mad and tribal chaos. Even worse, it served to recall the lesson well-learnt in Somalia that peacekeeping and particularly peace-enforcement would be highly dangerous in Africa (see, for example, Piiparinen 2005: 209–26). Such images created the false impression that no grounds for intervention existed in what was described as a senseless and irrational chaos in Africa presenting insurmountable difficulties and considerable risk of casualties.

How, then, could the new division of labour in peacekeeping reduce or eliminate the effects of the above-mentioned 'chaos narrative'[4] of African conflicts and the related 'body-bag syndrome'? The answer is quite straightforward: by shifting their support from manpower to hardware for the sake of troop-protection, Western troop-contributing countries can *avoid* the emergence of 'body-bag syndrome' altogether. Perhaps the greatest benefit of diminished involvement of Western troops concerns the disjuncture between the effects and accountability of their intervention, as demonstrated in the previous chapter (Parekh 1998: 151). In Rwanda, the disjuncture between the effects and accountability of Western intervention provoked complete disregard for the humanitarian costs of UN withdrawal, which was mainly triggered by the 'body-bag syndrome' following the killing of ten Belgian peacekeepers by Hutu extremists on 7 April 1994. The accountability of member governments to their domestic electorates was uncompromisingly prioritised over the consequences of UNAMIR's withdrawal for the vulnerable citizens of Rwanda.

A pragmatic turn in peacekeeping

The following examination will explore the various ways in which structural adjustments can facilitate the protection of civilians. It will be claimed that the case of Darfur represents a continuum in the gradual transformation of the UN system, away from the rigidity of bureaucratic norms towards a more pragmatic direction. One key area of transformation in the UN peacekeeping system concerns the mandates of PKOs, which have been previously characterised by inflexibility. An instructive example in this regard is the way in which senior UN officials dealt with early warning signals emitted from Rwanda in January 1994, three months prior to the beginning of genocide. As demonstrated in the previous chapter, the UN system has recently transcended the aforementioned bureaucratic barrier between peacekeeping and peace-enforcement, through its frequent inclusion of elements from Chapter VII of the UN Charter within the mandates of PKOs.

The aforementioned shift in the UN peacekeeping strategy is clearly reflected in the mandate of UNMIS, which is based on Chapter VII of the UN Charter.[5] This opens up manoeuvring space for the UNMIS Force Commander to authorise the use of force against potential spoilers of the Comprehensive Peace Agreement and against those who plan crimes against humanity. Such discretionary powers were not available to force commanders at the time of the Rwandan genocide, as the events of January 1994 demonstrated. Furthermore, the risk of the so-called 'mission creep' from peacekeeping to the waging of war is reduced by the meticulous wording of the mandate of UNMIS which sets the clear and unambiguous parameters, objectives and powers of the operation, thus preventing the mission from launching enforcement actions beyond its intended scope. This move away from the uncompromising distinction between peacekeeping and peace-enforcement, in which the aims of PKOs rather than bureaucratic norms determine their functions, could be termed a 'pragmatic turn' in peacekeeping.

One structural change in the UN system that seems relevant to Darfur in particular concerns the responsibility to protect civilians. In the 1990s, this duty was absent from the mandates of UNPKOs. As demonstrated in the previous chapter, the protection of civilians currently belongs to the mandates and tasks of *all* operations. Security Council Resolution 1590, adopted on 24 March 2005, which established UNMIS, confirms the aforementioned new development regarding the protection of civilians. In Operational Paragraph 16, the Security Council 'Decides that UNMIS is authorized to take the necessary action ... without prejudice to the responsibility of the Government of Sudan, to protect civilians under imminent threat of physical violence'.[6] Furthermore, civilian protection is mentioned in other relevant paragraphs of the mandate of UNMIS, backed up by reference to Chapter VII of the UN Charter, i.e. the authorisation of peace-enforcement. In AMIS, the protection of civilians is effective not only as potential powers to use force, as in UNMIS, but also as a core function currently performed by peacekeepers, namely the guarding of camps for internally displaced persons (IDPs). The inhabitants of these camps had been subjected to recurrent assault and rape by pro-government militia.

The transfer of command and control functions from UN Headquarters to the level of regional organisations may constitute another 'pragmatic turn' inaugurating more effective decision-making in peacekeeping. The structural weaknesses and inadequacies of command and control functions executed by UN Headquarters have been extensively analysed in previous literature (Gordon 2001: 25). The transfer of command and control functions from UN Headquarters to the regional level offers a means of avoiding these problems. This section has examined three aspects of bureaucratic rationalisation that seem pertinent to peacekeeping, namely the mandates of PKOs, the responsibility to protect civilians, and the level of command and control functions. Although this falls short of an exhaustive analysis of PKOs, both AMIS and UNMIS display major improvements in these three areas compared to PKOs of the 1990s. The bureaucratic rationalisation of peacekeeping works through command and control structures at the headquarters, but the initial decision to launch humanitarian intervention is also dependent on other mechanisms that operate beyond the sphere of military expertise. One such mechanism is early warning, which can both generate and decrease political will to intervene (see, for example, Piiparinen 2005: 265–6). The following section will analyse the role of early warning as well as knowledge-building of conflict prevention in general in the case of Darfur, with a view to predicting the development of peacekeeping in the future.

A functional shift in control mechanisms

It will be argued in this section that synchronisation between control mechanisms, particularly between those of early warning and bureaucratic rationalisation, has been improved since the Rwandan genocide, a development that will be termed a 'functional synchronisation' or a 'functional shift' in decision-making on peacekeeping. Plainly rendered, the 'functional shift' refers to pragmatic trade-offs between different values in order to ensure the precedence of the most crucial function, which in humanitarian intervention is the protection of civilians. In the case of Darfur, this phenomenon has been reflected in a sophisticated balancing act between the detection, recognition and announcement of genocide (early warning) and other bureaucratic aims (bureaucratic rationalisation), such as the need to ensure the co-operation of the Sudanese government in civilian protection. At times, such calculations have obliged the suppression of diplomatic condemnations of the Sudanese government for the benefit of the pragmatic function to protect civilians.

As demonstrated in Chapter 4, the previous literature on Rwanda argues that aversion of the term 'genocide' served no function other than to constitute a cover for the inaction of major powers. However, the findings of this book indicate that even if the UN had possessed the independent 'UN fire brigade' envisaged by Sir Brian Urquhart, i.e. a 5,000-member brigade at the Secretary-General's disposal independently of states, the Security Council and the Secretariat would still have been reluctant to send such a rapid-deployment force to Rwanda. This is accounted for by the fact that the 'troublemaking' mechanisms within the UN system induced all actors, even Secretariat officials, to portray the Rwandan conflict as unmanageable chaos posing a considerable risk to the UN bureaucracy as a whole. The avoidance of the term 'genocide' was thereby a product of dysfunctional synchronisation between control mechanisms, notably between bureaucratic rationalisation (risk calculations) and early warning (detection of genocide). In Darfur, by contrast, such avoidance reflects functional synchronisation between these mechanisms; it has served functions that have been prioritised by the UN bureaucracy, most notably the Sudanese peace process and the protection of civilians.

With regard to the first function, the processing of early warning signals emitted from Darfur has been crucially affected by the development of the Naivasha peace process. The latter concerns the conflict between SPLM/A and government forces in southern areas such as Abyei, the Nuba mountains and the southern Blue Nile, rather than Darfur as such. Statements by US Secretary of State Colin Powell and other Western leaders explicitly demonstrate an intentional calculation that excessive pressure on the Sudanese government could lead to internal problems in Sudan which may in turn shatter the Naivasha agreement (the Comprehensive Peace Agreement), in which both Western and African countries had invested much political capital (Williams and Bellamy 2005: 38). This assessment may seem heartless from the perspective of Darfurian civilians targeted by pro-government militia. However, within the 'bigger picture' of the Sudanese conflict, such calculations are more supportive than undermining of humanitarian efforts, for two reasons. First, the southern conflict, the longest civil strife in Africa, has claimed approximately two million lives over two decades. In the stakes of human suffering, it almost constitutes a *sui generis* supreme humanitarian emergency,[7] which legitimises its prioritisation over the crisis in Darfur.

Second, and most importantly, Rwanda has supplied a fundamental lesson about the severe consequences of an excessive political pressure against a weak government. Under the banner of democracy and minority rights, international society attempted to push for the implementation of the power-sharing arrangement between the Hutu and Tutsi sides imposed by the Arusha agreement. Scant attention was turned to the severe effect of that relentless pressure on the increasing resentment felt by Hutu extremists, which ultimately triggered the genocide. In the case of Darfur, however, the main lesson of the drawbacks of excessive political pressure did not emanate from memories of Rwanda but from media images of violence, looting and chaos in Khartoum, triggered by the death of the SPLA leader John Garang on 30 July 2005. The attention of Western audiences immediately shifted from the excessive use of force by the Sudanese government in Darfur to the contrasting issue of whether the government possessed *sufficient* force to balance the security situation in the country. Hence, Western observers who had previously called for stronger censure of the Sudanese government soon realised to undermine its status with uncompromising denunciation would, in fact, be counterproductive and detrimental to the maintenance of peace and stability in the region.[8]

Mainstreaming RtoP and thinking out of bureaucratic boxes

It is now time to address the 'Beyond'-part in the title of the book, that is, the development of UN conflict management since its engagements in Darfur and Rwanda. One of the most encouraging developments in terms of the prevention of 'future Rwandas' is the emergence of the Responsibility to Protect (RtoP), a concept coined by the International Commission on Intervention and State Sovereignty (ICISS 2001). RtoP holds that the responsibility of international society to protect civilians threatened by genocidal regimes embraces three elements: responsibility to prevent the occurrence of massive human rights violations; responsibility to react to them; and responsibility to rebuild societies in order to repair the damages inflicted upon them by intervention and prevent the recurrence of violence (ICISS 2001: xi; Roberts 2004: 94–5).

According to an influential researcher on humanitarian intervention and the UN, Thomas G. Weiss, RtoP represents one of the most significant normative developments since the inception of the Genocide Convention. 'With the possible exception of the 1948 Convention on Genocide', Weiss argues, 'no idea has moved faster in the international normative arena than "the responsibility to protect"' (Weiss 2007: 1). This may not be an overstatement, as the inclusion of RtoP in the UN World Summit Outcome of 2005 signifies its universal endorsement by over 150 heads of state and government. This was a hard-won victory for humanitarianism when considered alongside the fact that RtoP has grown out from the more robust and Western-centric idea of 'humanitarian intervention', and RtoP has consequently been suspected of Western hidden agendas by the United Nations Non-Aligned Movement (NAM) and the G77 at the UN consisting of over 130 mostly developing countries. Furthermore, RtoP stands for one of the few actual successes in UN reform alongside the establishment of the Human Rights Council and the Peacebuilding Commission as part of the comprehensive reform package agreed in 2005. Yet, there is considerable ambiguity as to the *ontological nature* of RtoP, which has led to a wide range of interpretations of its meaning. Some accounts[9] consider RtoP as a normative step in tackling four grave and large-scale crimes, i.e. genocide, ethnic cleansing, crimes against humanity and war crimes.[10] David Scheffer terms these 'atrocity crimes' (quoted in Evans 2008a: 13), while UN Secretary-General Ban Ki-moon and his Special Advisor on RtoP Edward Luck describe them as the 'most egregious mass violations of human rights'.[11]

It is claimed here that RtoP could, in fact, be best described as a nascent control mechanism that aims at preventing and managing the 'atrocity crimes', particularly genocide. This is evidenced by three factors. First, unlike any previous convention or norm, RtoP determines the appropriate *order* of measures to be taken in conflict management: peaceful means should be exhausted prior to the application of forceful collective action. As explained in Chapter 2, such structured processes are termed 'mechanisms' in critical realist philosophy. Second, there are apparent similarities between RtoP and the former UN Secretary-General Kofi Annan's *Action Plan to Prevent Genocide*, which was published at the commemorative event of the Rwandan genocide on 7 April 2004. Both of these instruments are dynamic, programmatic and structured processes, i.e. control mechanisms, as opposed to norms and more static judicial devices. Furthermore, they deal with almost the same themes and aim at similar outcomes. The Special Advisor of the UN Secretary-General for RtoP, Edward Luck, has identified four programmatic dimensions of RtoP:

1   capacity building and rebuilding;
2   early warning and assessment;
3   timely and decisive response; and
4   collaboration with regional and sub-regional arrangements.[12]

Most of these dimensions are distinctly similar to the five points outlined in the Action Plan to Prevent Genocide:

1   the prevention of armed conflict;
2   the protection of civilians;
3   the ending of judicial impunity;
4   the strengthening of information-gathering and early warning; and
5   the implementation of swift and decisive action.[13]

Only a quick comparison reveals that RtoP and the Action Plan envisage similar actions such as early warning, prevention and early action to protect civilians.

Third, the comparison between RtoP and the action plan on genocide is apposite also in another respect: it reveals the raison d'être of RtoP, namely, the elevation of the most shocking 'atrocity crimes' above all the rest in the bureaucratic and normative ladders of international society. The 'RtoP puzzle' concerns not only the lack of clarity of its ontological meaning, but also its vagueness regarding the value it adds to conflict management. The latter mystery is exacerbated by the fact that the crimes 'introduced' by RtoP are explicitly determined in already existing norms of international humanitarian law, human rights law, refugee law and international criminal law which have been in effect for decades or centuries, such as the Geneva Convention on humanitarian law signed in 1864. In fact, the vastly expanding literature promoting RtoP is engaged more in self-explanation and sometimes frantic efforts to squeeze out the value added by RtoP ('insider account'), often without a success, than in explanation of how that concept helps in conflict management ('outsider account'). In order to open up the latter, outsider dimension, it is suggested here that RtoP functions as a securitisation mechanism. The Copenhagen School defines securitisation as a political act that raises an issue above the normal routines of everyday decision-making.[14] In the case in point here, the invoking of RtoP could be understood as a securitisation act whose purpose is to *make* the most horrendous crimes, particularly genocide, so extraordinary that the international community becomes concerned and sensitised, bearing in mind the plain truth that these crimes cannot become extraordinary for everybody by themselves.

Indeed, the uncomfortable truth becomes evident when considered alongside the fact that genocides tend to disappear, not only in the Hobbesian jungle of disinterested states, but also, rather unexpectedly, in two additional jungles of our own making: the normative one, embodied in fruitless judicial debates of experts and non-experts of international law on the applicability and remits of terms like 'genocide' and 'crime against humanity' while human suffering is continuing, and the bureaucratic one, embodied in artificial conceptual boxes of organisations that are impenetrable to real-life phenomena. For example, the former Secretary-General Kofi Annan's outstanding performance in preventing atrocities in Kenya in spring 2008 and complex UN peacebuilding in Burundi would most likely have gone unnoticed, unless they were labelled 'RtoP situations'. The stories of Annan's success in Kenya and the similar accomplishment in Burundi are brought back to life by expert statements and numerous reports produced and reproduced by the research centres worldwide that have only recently been established to promote RtoP.[15] What makes such analyses unique is that they give evidence to the real cause–effect connection between quiet UN diplomacy and the prevention of genocides, a relationship which would otherwise be easily overlooked in the media and elsewhere, simply because it is not visible through massive deployments of troops by intervening forces. RtoP gives a voice to silent peacemaking and mediation efforts of the UN, which frequently escape the attention of the international media.

We should not take for granted the rationality of international audiences or even experts to make such distinctions, for their perception is often guided by what Mika Aaltola terms the 'post 9/11 hysteria',[16] a phenomenon in which scandalous events appearing on television screens trigger sympathies and lead to action at the expense of less visible, but equally or more deadly, situations that would deserve more attention on humanitarian grounds. Indeed, RtoP is much about knowledge-production: many emerging research institutions such as the Global Centre for the Responsibility to Protect in New York and regional RtoP centres as well as NGOs are already combining their forces to form an epistemic community,[17] i.e. an expert network that produces credible information in order to bring perspective into the current information-flow on human suffering. The 'RP2 network' serves as a long anticipated counter-balance to the so-called CNN effect. Hence, the greatest potential of RtoP for changing the international security architecture cannot be found in its possible transformation into a norm of customary international law, but in creating an epistemic community for knowledge-production on conflicts. In this sense, RtoP can bring some order to the chaotic network of overlapping mechanisms of international conflict management by distinguishing acts that shock the conscience of mankind from lesser crimes.

This development could eventually lead to a form of a 'global triage' system similar to the medical triage, in which the most serious and 'solvable' life-threatening cases are treated with greater urgency than less serious or incurable ones. Drawing upon Jean-Hervé Bradol's account, Peter Redfield notes that the current international order is based on a degree of human sacrifice, i.e. an acceptance that certain populations can die in the quest for stability, a better world or some other greater pursuit. Set against this, 'Triage has the advantage of representing a system of prioritization based on the facts of suffering themselves' (Redfield 2008: 197). Moreover, it is apposite here to bring to mind Boutros Boutros-Ghali's statement referred to in Chapter 5, which pointed to difficulties to fully understand the gravity of the Rwandan situation at the time: 'Today it is easy, but on the spot, we did not have that vision to [distinguish] the bigger crime from a smaller one.'[18] Boutros-Ghali's remark confirms the conclusion of Chapter 5 that the material limitations of human resources in early warning should be taken seriously because of the complexity of the decision-making environment in multilateral organisations. RtoP serves as one useful 'servo-mechanism'[19] to manage these multifaceted situations and to fulfil the function of distinguishing the most serious atrocities from the variety of less urgent cases.

The above achievement marks a significant step towards the creation of a credible knowledge-producing system on atrocity crimes. The lack of such a system has thus far provided bullets for the political realist critique against the solidarist conception of humanitarian intervention, particularly for the articulation of the problem of abuse. According to the political realist suspicion, the crux of the problem resides in the impossibility of separating humanitarian interventions from those types of intervention in which humanitarianism is abused. Those cases in which humanitarianism merely serves as a cover for selfish motivations of states include proxy humanitarian justifications presented by Hitler's regime for its intervention in Czechoslovakia in 1938 and the similarly bogus humanitarian aims of the US intervention in Cuba in 1898. Thomas M. Franck and Nigel S. Rodley provide an eloquent formulation of this political realist objection to humanitarian intervention in their 1973 article:

> One of the problems not resolved by those who argue for a right of states individually or collectively to use force to ameliorate the oppression of peoples by their own regimes is that they cannot devise a means that is both

conceptually and instrumentally credible to separate the few sheep of legitimate humanitarianism from the herds of goats which can too easily slip through.

(Franck and Rodley 1973: 284)

RtoP provides one useful, albeit insufficient, mechanism to separate the sheep and goat cases; the complete fulfillment of this task requires a continuing debate on just war and humanitarian intervention.

A control mechanism alike to RtoP entails a teleological plan or desired end-state.[20] Paddy Ashdown, the former High Representative for Bosnia and Herzegovina, terms that final outcome an 'intervention end state' and considers it categorically important in all conflict management and peacebuilding missions. According to Ashdown, the intervention end state should be clearly defined in every mission implementation plan, for it provides accuracy and predictability for interventions. 'Our biggest mistake in past interventions', Ashdown explains, 'has lain in our failure ... most particularly to think and plan *through* the war phase to what follows *after* the end of the fighting...' (Ashdown 2007: 131). However, Ashdown tends to consider interventions from the viewpoint of Western operations alone, particularly those conducted by NATO and the EU in the Western Balkans. As demonstrated in Chapter 2, the teleological plan or desired end state of a control mechanism may not materialise because of intervening variables emanating from the material and social reality surrounding that mechanism. It is crucial to note that the UN typically has fewer, or next to no, material resources at its disposal than NATO to fulfil the stated end states of interventions, and thus always holds a greater risk of failure to meet its objectives. In theoretical terms, control mechanisms of the UN are more exposed to the intervening variables of the surrounding environment and thus more at risk of backfiring than those of Western organisations, simply because the former are sustained by weaker structures.

It is suggested here that, in place of 'intervention end states', two factors should be considered as the most important and distinctive elements of *UN* conflict management, namely structural constraints inherent in virtually all UN operations, and the consequent prudency to mainstream key principles for humanitarian action in the UN system. We should not deterministically prescribe such actions and their outcomes in advance. Instead of determining rigid end states, which often backfire because of complex and unforeseen circumstances beyond the UN's control, and which may even jeopardise the credibility and whole existence of the UN, we should adopt a more flexible strategy and *mainstream* important principles, such as the protection of civilians, in all activities of the UN. Plainly rendered, a control mechanism akin to RtoP should be considered more as a mindset than a mission statement.

On the one hand, RtoP serves as a useful argument to justify more resources from member states to conflict prevention and early warning capacities of the Department of Political Affairs of the UN Secretariat. Secretary-General Ban Ki-moon has already suggested the strengthening of UN early warning mechanisms as a means to operationalise RtoP.[21] Such proposals seem like old wine in a new bottle, or, rather, the repackaging of already existing innovations: early warning was vigorously advocated in the former Secretary-General Boutros-Ghali's *An Agenda for Peace*, and the 'atrocity crimes' constitutive of RtoP have actually been defined much earlier by the Geneva Conventions and the Genocide Convention. On the other hand, Secretary-General Ban's initiative reflects a genuinely innovative means to *mainstream RtoP in all functions of the UN*, which is already seen in his groundbreaking speech on RtoP in Berlin on 15 July 2008: 'Our goal is not to add a new layer of bureaucracy, or to re-label existing United Nations programmes; it is to incorporate the responsibility to protect as a perspective into ongoing efforts.'[22] The cornerstone of Secretary-General Ban's 'deep' conception of RtoP is the comprehensive use of all UN prevention and protection mechanisms as well as the engagement of regional, sub-regional and civil society partners of the UN. This mainstreaming of RtoP marks a significant shift in the mindset of UN conflict management from bureaucratic rationalisation towards a more holistic and pragmatic approach. In the latter, conflict prevention and protection of civilians are not 'boxed' in separate bureaucratic categories, isolated from other sections of UN action, but integrated in everything the UN does. As demonstrated in Chapter 6, bureaucratic categorisation, embodied in rigid and fixed procedures, wrought devastating effects on Rwandans. The mainstreaming of RtoP has the potential to provide important new social and mental optics to identify genocides. This will increase sensitivity of all actors to detect early warning signals of impending large-scale conflicts, even those to whom bureaucratic procedures do not explicitly assign such functions.

Secretary-General's Special Advisor Edward Luck has attempted to integrate RtoP in the whole UN system, especially in the work of the Peacebuilding Commission. On the one hand, these efforts illustrate the scarcity of the Special Advisor's own resources to operationalise the RtoP concept. NAM has strong doubts towards RtoP, which is widely, but erroneously, viewed by developing countries as an attempt by Western countries to interfere in the internal affairs of less-powerful states in the Third World.[23] Such suspicions have hindered the resourcing of Special Advisor Luck's office in the ACABQ (the Advisory Committee on Administrative and Budgetary Questions) and the Fifth Committee of the General Assembly. Luck's efforts to link the PBC and RtoP, which were also advocated by the EU Presidency under France's tenure, could be explained by the strong support NAM has given to the PBC, and the possible wishful thinking of senior UN officials that such positive attitude of NAM could somehow spill over from the PBC to RtoP if these two mechanisms were linked. The endorsement of the PBC by NAM stems from the fact that the operations of the PBC are based on national ownership, and its objective is to strengthen the capacity of countries themselves in preventing the relapse to conflict (the so-called 'second pillar' of RtoP denoting consent-based action), not to launch interventions without the consent of target countries (the 'third pillar' of RtoP). Senior UN officials may thus view the PBC as a useful, or at least politically harmless, instrument to promote RtoP; the instrumentalisation of peacebuilding for the cause of RtoP, i.e. the protection of civilians, sends a comforting political message to NAM countries that the focus of both the PBC and RtoP lies in consent-based capacity-building, not military intervention. This logic, however, raises the question as to whether the linkage between the PBC and RtoP merely represents a tactical and symbolic gesture – a 'fast track', or, more cynically, 'cheap trick' – in promoting RtoP. Currently there is an almost complete lack of vision of concrete ways in which RtoP could be promoted in the PBC, and how RtoP could reciprocally benefit the PBC.

On the other hand, Special Advisor Luck's attempts to mainstream RtoP may, importantly, illustrate a deeper shift in the culture of UN decision-making from rigid bureaucratic categories to a more holistic approach. In the Rwandan case, bureaucratic rationalisation formed a cognitive prism through which the 'form' (obedience to bureaucratic categories) was ultimately viewed holier than the 'function' it served (protection of civilians). With the help of mainstreaming RtoP in the whole UN system, this irrational order of things could be reversed; the 'form' could increasingly follow 'function', to paraphrase David Mitrany's adage (Mitrany 1975). In contrast to bureaucratic categorisation, the approach of RtoP based on mainstreaming no longer gives primacy to adherence to bureaucratic categories over the aim to protect civilians. Such mainstreaming is already visible in regional organisations, too. On 26 November 2008, the first substantial debate on RtoP was held within the EU since the 2005 Summit. Some member states already spoke of 'RtoP mainstreaming'. There was widespread agreement among members to include RtoP in the revision of the European Security Strategy drafted in 2003 and in ESDP missions, and to adopt it on agendas of thematic and geographical working groups of the EU. By mainstreaming RtoP in its own system, the EU aims to set an example to be followed by other regional groups, notably the African Union.

The bureaucratic barriers that continuously hamper vital UN functions such as early warning and protection of civilians are sometimes merely symptoms of deep-seated political discrepancies. Although the above paragraph painted a rather rosy picture of the attitude of NAM towards the PBC, the UN peacebuilding architecture has also been victimised by the suspicions of NAM, which increasingly views the UN and its organs as Trojan horses of Western interventionism. At the inception of the UN peacebuilding system in 2005, early warning was excluded from its mandate for political reasons. Developing countries suspected the PBC would evolve into an intelligence-gathering tool of Western countries, designed to support their interference in internal affairs of less-affluent countries. The exclusion of early warning from the radar screen of UN peacebuilding is absurd in light of its purpose and mandate, i.e. the prevention of lapse or relapse to conflicts in countries on its agenda (Piiparinen 2007c: 356–60). Early warning capacities of the PBC and its supporting institution, Peacebuilding Support Office (PBSO), would significantly enhance the strategic planning and awareness-raising capability of the UN peacebuilding architecture to fulfil its mandate to prevent (re)lapses to conflicts. However, from the viewpoint of bureaucratic rationalization, such a bizarre arrangement seems perfectly logical;

in the bureaucratic mindset, conflict prevention and post-conflict peacebuilding are viewed as strictly separate phases, or, metaphorically, separate bureaucratic boxes.

Developments in autumn 2008 indicate an increasing tendency to think across and out of these predetermined, and often artificial, mental boxes produced by bureaucratic mindsets. One senior UN official has noted a clear shift in the political atmosphere at the UN towards an approach in which conflict prevention is increasingly seen as part and parcel of peacebuilding. Researchers on the topic have added the theoretical rationale by reminding that conflict prevention is an inherent element in peacebuilding. Some member states such as Brazil have already advocated early warning as part of peacebuilding. However, the debate in the General Assembly on the PBF held in October 2008 may suggest otherwise; conflict prevention was mentioned only in a few speeches by member states. Nevertheless, the vision of linkages between early warning and peacebuilding may well materialise in coming years.

The history of UN peacebuilding is shorter than the memory of the Rwandan genocide. It would be interesting to learn whether the UN peacebuilding architecture could have contributed to conflict prevention and management in Rwanda, had it been in place already in the 1990s. At first sight, the hypothetical input of the PBC, PBF and PBSO to conflict management in Rwanda appears rather limited, and potentially even misleading and counterproductive. As of September 2008, approximately one-third of all PBF contributions was channelled to the security sector of countries on its agenda,[24] such as the rehabilitation of barracks in Burundi and the training of police forces and armies. The emphasis on the security sector in the PBF's work mainly stems from the lessons of so-called 'fragile states', whose conflict potential typically emerges from the weakness and possible collapse of state structures. However, Chapter 1 demonstrated that the Rwandan case was actually almost an exact opposite of the syndrome of state fragility. While the four countries on the PBC's agenda, i.e. Burundi, Sierra Leone, Guinea-Bissau and the Central African Republic, are all fragile states, Rwanda in the early 1990s possessed a fairly strong central administration and security structures. The answer then might be that the hypothetical effect of UN peacebuilding on the situation in pre-genocide Rwanda would, in fact, have been counterproductive, assuming that the PBF would have adopted the typical approach and focused on supporting the Rwandan security forces, which were complicit in planning and implementing the genocide.

However, the hypothetical impact of the PBC, PBF and PBSO on preventing the Rwandan genocide seems far more positive when their overall philosophy and working methods are considered; UN peacebuilding could have brought crucial value added by changing the technique of conflict management from rigid bureaucratic categorisation to a more open mindset. The first step in framing this more positive answer is the understanding of the underlying philosophy of UN peacebuilding, namely its bottom-up approach. In the words of one member in the PBF Advisory Group, the PBF's main purpose is to develop 'home-grown' solutions to local problems of target countries. This pragmatic approach has two significant benefits. First, it provides the PBC, PBF and PBSO with universal legitimacy and support from the whole UN membership; the emphasis on national ownership ultimately saves these organs from the worst fears of NAM regarding Western interventionism, although some doubts persist, as was demonstrated above. Instead of externally imposed solutions, which NAM vehemently resists, UN peacebuilding emphasises the guiding principles of national ownership and sovereignty of target countries. The outcomes of a prominent research project conducted in the Ralph Bunche Institute for International Studies at the City University of New York even reveal that the PBC has contributed significantly to reaffirming and disseminating the norm of state sovereignty, or 'furthering of the sovereignty agenda' (Jenkins 2008: 15), in the world arena.

Second, and perhaps most importantly, the 'home-grown' solutions sought by the UN peacebuilding architecture effectively resist 'bureaucratic universalism' described in the previous chapter. This bottom-up approach replaces rigid bureaucratic categories with a different mode of thinking, or philosophy, which opposes the illusion that 'one size fits all' in conflict management and peacebuilding; instead, the selection of the most fitting solution is always guided by the requirements of particular local conditions in each and every target country on the agendas of the PBF and the PBC, not by any universal bureaucratic model (see, for example, Call 2008: 13). In the pre-genocide and post-Arusha Rwanda, this mindset could have generated beneficial outcomes by providing an additional social prism through which the root causes of the Rwandan problem were viewed, in addition to the existing social prism that operated through the three-phased causal chain from UNAMIR to UN Headquarters and the Security Council examined in Chapter 5. This social prism was largely reductive, as it overtly limited the scope of examination to the civil war aspect, i.e. the conflict between the RPF and the Rwandan government forces, without addressing deeper structural violence such as the spread of hate rhetoric by the media and the spill-over of ethnic violence from Burundi to Rwanda. The UN peacebuilding architecture is designed to address particularly these types of structural 'root causes' of violence that were overlooked in Rwanda.

In order to test the above hypothesis, I asked one member of the Advisory Group, Dan Smith from the International Alert, about the potential impact of UN peacebuilding on preventing the Rwandan genocide. Smith's answer confirms the argument put forward here: 'The PBC and the PBSO will continue, both by their simple existence and through what they do, to encourage and facilitate a *mode of thinking* and of policy development that could have prevented 1994.'[25] Smith's answer implies that neither the UN peacebuilding architecture nor any other UN institution can provide an automation of accurate early warning information; rather, their impact mainly lies in their cross-cutting potential to affect the mindsets of decision-makers. Such mental impact also has a historical dimension. The UN peacebuilding architecture has grown out of the Rwandan tragedy and similar experiences, such as the failure of 1991 Bicesse Accords and the consequent relapse into a devastating war in Angola, as well as ten-to-fifteen years of scholarship. 'The new components of the UN's peacebuilding architecture,' Smith continues, 'do not exist in isolation. They come out of the credibility that peacebuilding has earned and they give it more credibility.'[26] Hence, the UN peacebuilding architecture is both a product and producer of the history of UN conflict management as a whole. By their sheer existence and operations, the PBC, PBF and PBSO serve as memorials of past painstaking failures, and, like war memorials, they constantly remind us of the omnipresent possibility of war and carnage even in the aftermath of the signing of peace accords. In this sense, they help us to save ourselves from wishful thinking. Such reminders could have made a difference in preventing the Rwandan genocide in the aftermath of the Arusha Peace Accord of 1993, which generated misleading and short-lived optimism in conflict management. As explained in Chapter 6, the decision-making of UN officials and diplomats was guided by a misguided, albeit common, focus on the intent of the signatories of the agreement; however, what mattered most was the intent of the potential spoilers of the peace treaty, which were ignored by the Arusha agreement and other conflict management mechanisms.

In order to summarise the main points of this section in more general terms regarding the future vision of the UN, Ashdown's metaphor of conflict management as a seamless garment seems an instructive starting-point:

> We need to start looking at these three phases – prevention, war fighting and post-conflict reconstruction – as a single seamless garment, where each piece pre-shapes and flows into the next and where, throughout all three phases, the overall aims remain unchanged.
>
> (Ashdown 2007: 130)

In terms of the production of knowledge on conflicts, Ashdown's metaphor encourages thinking across and out of the three separate bureaucratic boxes of prevention, conflict management and peacebuilding. In this regard, the value added by the PBC, PBF and PBSO resides both in their awareness-raising of hidden conflict potentials and in deeper analytical thinking regarding the *root causes* of conflicts.[27] The latter term particularly refers to the structural causes of violence. While the international community concentrated on addressing short-term symptoms of interstate conflict between the RPF and the Rwandan government, it largely overlooked worrying structural problems in Rwandan society. These factors included the history of ethnic violence and highly regarded social values of obedience and hierarchy, which together formed an explosive mixture and necessary raw materials for the implementation of genocide. The causes of the Rwandan genocide were complex, multi-level and diverse, but the eyes and ears of UN conflict management were focused narrowly on the civil war aspect. As opposed to this reductive and superficial approach, today's UN peacebuilding aims to identify structural causes of violence and to apply 'home-grown solutions' without political or bureaucratic prejudices. In this regard, UN peacebuilding could be described as a tabula rasa which allows the problem on the ground, not any universal bureaucratic model, to guide the selection of the most effective solution to be applied.

Defending the baseline of humanity as a future vision of the UN

As demonstrated in the previous chapters, the UN is going through a steep learning curve in conflict management. The existing literature and political analysts have not fully appreciated this development, as their focus has been on the UN's shortcomings, not its gradual achievements and structural changes. UN decision-makers seem to be learning from the 'troublemaking' mechanisms of the 1990s, including the drawbacks of Western normalisation which have provided an important lesson to avoid unrealistic missions and 'greater pursuits' under the guise of humanitarian intervention. An illustrative example of these recently learned 'counter-strategies' to Western normalisation is Secretary-General Ban's conception of RtoP, which he describes as 'narrow but deep'. As will be demonstrated below, the narrowing down of RtoP to the four gravest crimes that shock the conscience of humanity can save RtoP from the Western moral hubris and, simultaneously, from the suspicions of non-aligned countries that RtoP is a vehicle of such hubristic missions.

According to the groundbreaking definitions of RtoP in the 2005 Summit Outcome and Secretary-General Ban's statement, RtoP calls for action to prevent and manage genocide, ethnic cleansing, crimes against humanity and war crimes, but does not extend to other calamities and threats such as natural disasters, climate change and nuclear proliferation. On the one hand, Ban's rationalisation for the limited conception is based on a prudent and pragmatic assessment that the overstretching of the term would ultimately render it useless: 'Extending the principle ... would undermine the 2005 consensus and stretch the concept beyond recognition or operational utility.'[28] Secretary-General Ban's assessment is supported by Gareth Evans, who functioned as the Co-Chair of the influential International Commission on Intervention and State Sovereignty (ICISS): 'If R2P [RtoP] is to be about protecting everybody from everything, it will end up protecting nobody from anything' (Evans 2008a: 65). These statements confirm the argument presented in the previous section that RtoP is, by nature, a *control mechanism*, that is, an operational technique which aims at a desired end state, the protection of civilians.

On the other hand, Secretary-General Ban's rationalisation for the narrow conceptualisation of RtoP reflects a deeper philosophy in which the UN is regarded as an implementer or 'super-structure' of the most fundamental principles of humanity, i.e. the 'deep-structure' upon which the UN is based. This 'thin layer' of a limited number of underlying principles is enshrined in normative devices akin to RtoP, and it necessitates a certain degree of exclusion in order to deserve the description 'fundamental principles': humanity is for everyone, but not everything anyone wants it to be. Moreover, the UN should not be understood as a value in itself but merely as an implementer of deeper values based on humanitarianism.[29] In this sense, the UN should adopt a self-image as a defender of the most vulnerable groups and the most basic tenets of humanity and civilisation, now that it has experienced the rise and fall of the grand strategies of the 1990s exemplified by UNOSOM II and Alternative I of UN engagement in Rwanda, which both provided hard lessons of unrealistic and hubristic missions. The order between 'super-structure' and 'deep structure' proposed here actually confirms Dag Hammarskjöld's famous statement that the UN cannot be holier than the principles it serves: 'The principles of the Charter are, by far, greater than the organization in which they are embodied, and the aims which they are to safeguard are holier than the policies of any single nation or people' (quoted in Traub 2007: 12–13). According to Hammarskjöld's other famous adage, the UN was created not to take humanity to heaven but to save it from hell. At the same time, the narrow conception of RtoP invalidates suspicions of NAM that RtoP serves some greater pursuits of Western countries beyond its original conception outlined in Paragraphs 138 and 139 of the 2005 Summit Outcome. Perhaps it is not true that 'RtoP needs to be reinvented by non-aligned countries' in order to fully materialise, as one diplomat has quite pessimistically observed. Nevertheless, it is certainly true that the only way to transform RtoP from an aspiration to reality is the ownership of the concept by the whole international community, which can be achieved only by multilateral bridge-building diplomacy between geographical groups, not by unilateral, aggressive or hubristic campaigns by Western countries.

The prudency of strict restriction of RtoP to the core humanitarian values, and the necessity of simultaneous exclusion of other valuable pursuits such as the protection of environment from its scope, is confirmed by the preference of governments to separate RtoP from a more encompassing principle of 'responsible sovereignty'. The latter term refers to a wider set of global responsibilities concerning, for example, nuclear proliferation, terrorism, environmental protection, abuse of biotechnology and threats posed by biological weapons.[30] States even have reservations in expanding RtoP to other crimes that directly affect humans, such as the negligence of governments to assist victims of natural disasters. The latter prospect became a subject of intense international debate when French Foreign Minister Bernard Kouchner suggested the application of RtoP in helping the victims of the tropical cyclone Nargis in Burma in April and May 2008. The military junta had effectively blocked assistance offered by foreign aid organisations for thousands of Burmese civilians whose lives were affected by the disaster and who were in urgent need of supplies of food, medicine and shelter. There is a morally strong and legally valid argument to include the victims of natural disasters under the remit of RtoP in those cases where the rejection of aid, and the consequent starving of people, constitutes a crime against humanity, one of the four 'triggers' of RtoP. In this sense, a starvation campaign could be interpreted as a large-scale attack targeted against a civilian population, and hence a crime against humanity liable to be treated as a breach of RtoP (see, for example, Evans 2008c). Although there is no legal precedent to confirm this interpretation, it may well emerge in the near future.

Nevertheless, the previous literature and political statements have largely overlooked the fact that the Nargis case already offers a positive precedent of RtoP considering the fact that Secretary-General Ban launched a rapid and quite effective diplomatic campaign to convince the Burmese junta to allow foreign-aid deliveries in the country. Secretary-General Ban personally travelled to Burma while the crisis was still pending and the Security Council was incapacitated to deal with the question because of political discrepancies. This example perfectly captures the proper procedure of RtoP: peaceful diplomatic means should be used and exhausted before a military intervention is launched to deliver aid packages to suffering victims. Unfortunately, this positive precedent has been overshadowed by a more negative assessment of the Nargis case, which is restricted to the analysis of assertive and counterproductive arguments for forceful intervention during the crisis. The performance of Secretary-General Ban should be appraised as a positive precedent of RtoP similar to, although somewhat less effective than, the former Secretary-General Kofi Annan's successful efforts in the prevention of the spread of ethnic violence in Kenya in spring 2008.

RtoP embodies the ongoing discussion of international society on humanity in general and the rights and responsibilities of states to protect their populations in particular. The limits of RtoP almost directly correspond to the limits of humanitarianism in world politics, as interventions to the debate on the boundaries of RtoP either attempt to include certain groups within the protective umbrella provided by RtoP, or to exclude them from care of the international community. Such continuous redefinition of the scope of humanity culminates in the fluctuation of two concrete aspects of RtoP, namely the 'crime against humanity' and post-conflict peacebuilding. These are more changeable concepts than typically thought. There is, for example, an ongoing debate as to whether situations in countries like North Korea and Zimbabwe constitute 'crimes against humanity'. One report commissioned by the former Czech President and other eminent persons suggests that the North Korean government is committing crimes against humanity in two respects, namely its food policy that sustains famine in the country and its treatment of political prisoners. Hence, RtoP is considered applicable in the situation, sufficient to trigger international action against the North Korean government.[31] It is evident that the main reason behind such arguments derives from political motivations of individual states. In the case in point here, the US–Czech affiliation can immediately be detected behind the argument for an intervention in North Korea. Interestingly enough, two years later, while the Israel Defense Forces were conducting a military campaign in Gaza and the question arose as to possible external intervention to stop it, the Czech President noted: 'The Czech government will not support external interventions into the domestic affairs of sovereign countries. We should resist being seduced by philosopher-king ambitions' (Klaus 2009). There seems to be a clear shift in the tone of the above arguments regarding forcible RtoP, and these differences seem to be explained by the political context (North Korea versus the Middle East) in which they were made. While RtoP was endorsed in one context, it was rejected in another, depending more on political affiliations than on substantial thinking on RtoP, dubbed as a 'philosopher-king' viewpoint. At the same time, however, other states, particularly in the EU, were not only invited to debate the question but also forced to contemplate its implications to a consistent use of RtoP. Although such debate is, inevitably, imbued by mixed motivations in which political considerations are enmeshed with genuine humanitarian concerns, the most important aspect is that the debate is kept alive and the question remains as to where the exact boundaries of RtoP should be drawn.

Peacebuilding represents another sector in which the scope of RtoP – and humanity, for that matter – has been revised. In the original conception of RtoP outlined in the ICISS report, peacebuilding concerns, first and foremost, the *repairing* of damages inflicted upon societies by intervention (ICISS 2001: xi). In half a decade, however, this specification has largely disappeared from diplomatic language. Today, the third dimension of RtoP, alongside prevention and action, denotes peacebuilding in all forms, whether the repairing of damages left behind by military interventions or other measures to prevent (re-)lapses to conflicts. In fact, it is revealing that all countries on the agenda of the PBC, an organ into which the Special Advisor Edward Luck and many governments try to 'export' RtoP, have not experienced any robust military intervention in the past, perhaps with the exception of Sierra Leone. Peacebuilding in those countries does not aim at repairing damages of intervention, but, on the contrary, damages of non-intervention.

The argumentation here has thus far dealt with RtoP, including peacebuilding as one of its instruments. Nevertheless, UN peacebuilding per se offers another instructive example of the emerging focus on the 'baseline of humanity' in the UN's work. It is claimed here that the establishment of the PBC and PBF in 2005 illustrates, first and foremost, the aspiration of the international community to reclaim the basic function of the UN – that is, saving lives. Virtually all UN member states at the time agreed to the establishment of the PBC and PBF, which stands out as a rare moment of universal consensus and progress in UN reform. The philosophy behind these two organs is quite simple, yet fundamentally important for humanitarian causes: saving lives through the prevention of lapse or relapse to conflict. That responsibility of the UN, saving lives, belongs not only to peacekeeping operations but also to all other sectors of the UN, even those that are typically not regarded as 'life-saving', such as development assistance or multilateral UN diplomacy. Indeed, diplomatic manoeuvres in UN corridors or transactions of donations to the PBF are less obvious life-savers than blue helmets. However, the multilateral diplomacy between the thirty-one member states of the organisational committee of the PBC in New York and its country-specific configurations, as well as development assistance provided by governments to the PBF, can and will save lives indirectly. Charles T. Call provides revealing figures that indicate the way in which the UN peacebuilding organs can play an important role in saving lives:

If the implementation of only two peace agreements – the 1991 Bicesse Accords for Angola and the 1993 Arusha Accords for Rwanda – had not failed, some 2 million people, roughly one-third of all civil war victims during the 1990s, would not have died in subsequent internal violence.

(Call 2008: 1–2)

Although UN peacebuilding, which is by default less visible and more static than peacekeeping, is doomed to receive less recognition in the media for preventing future Rwandas than they deserve, saving lives will remain the crux of UN peacebuilding.

How, then, is the safeguarding of the baseline of humanity visible in the operations of the PBC and PBF? Perhaps the most revealing feature of these organs is the limitation of their agendas to a group of small African states. On the one hand, such reduction is one symptom of the lack of resources at the UN, a problem that does not similarly bother the organisations of affluent Western states. As a resource-starved, and sometimes incapacitated, institution, whose own Headquarters is in urgent need of renovation outlined in the Capital Master Plan, the UN has more realistic possibilities to produce positive outcomes in peacebuilding in smaller states such as East Timor, Sierra Leone and Burundi, than in larger and more challenging, albeit equally devastated, countries such as Afghanistan and the Democratic Republic of Congo. Also, geopolitical considerations and power politics count in the equation; while peacebuilding in Afghanistan and the Western Balkans has, to a large extent, rested on the shoulders of affluent Western states contributing to ISAF, EUPOL Afghanistan and EULEX Kosovo, smaller African states are often located outside the radar screen of Western donors and thereby fall into the safety net of UN peacebuilding. This is, in fact, the new global division of labour between international organisations, a simple strategic arrangement in which the UN constitutes the safety net of conflict management and peacebuilding for all those cases which other organisations are not concerned with. The mandate of the PBF assigns it to launch critical interventions in order to bridge those peacebuilding needs that are not covered by other funding mechanisms. These overlooked 'blind spots' on the strategic map of international donors that the PBF aims to cover include thematic sectors such as the improvement of youth employment, which has a strong negative correlation with conflict potential.[32] The frequently ignored sectors the PBF operates in also include the so-called aid-orphans, i.e. those countries, minorities or other vulnerable groups that traditionally receive scant attention from the donor community.

In the media, the vision of the UN as a safety net is sometimes portrayed in pejorative terms; the UN will be called in to solve all kinds of complex or nearly impossible problems which other international actors would not even contemplate. The ongoing *MONUC* operation (United Nations Mission in the Democratic Republic of Congo) is a conspicuous example of a situation in which the UN is confronted by forces well beyond its control and, instead of a singular conflict, it is more apposite to speak of a system of multiple conflicts at national, regional and international levels, and in political, ethnic and economic sectors.[33] *MONUC* stands out as a striking example of the UN's role as a 'safety net' for the most vulnerable groups that no other international or regional security organisation would assist. In such a dilemma, the UN lacks a moral option to answer 'no' to the demands to alleviate human suffering when the most elementary part of humanity is endangered. James Traub appositely describes this phenomenon as the 'UN's inevitability' and 'indispensability', using the UN's engagement in Darfur as an example: 'For a long, agonizing period, no one else, no other neighbor or regional body, wanted any part of the disaster' (Traub 2007: xv). Richard Gowan also draws attention to a peculiar discrepancy between the UN's indispensable contributions and ingratitude, or even ridicule, it arouses in conducting such tasks:

> Western analysts take a dim view of UN forces: heavily reliant on Asian and African troops, they are low-tech and do not match visions of twenty-first century warriors. Yet these are often the only forces available for trouble-spots like Liberia...
>
> (Gowan 2008)

Although placing the safeguarding of humanity at the centre stage of UN activity would, inevitably, further nourish this derogatory prejudice of the UN as a willful cleaning house of what are portrayed as the worst sewage systems of the world, at the same time it would render expectations of the UN more realistic and, consequently, might finally provide the UN with a moral possibility to turn its back on those secondary tasks which fall outside its core mandate, saving lives.

The original, but often forgotten, vision of the UN peacebuilding architecture was not to become another instrument of development assistance that would contribute to Millennium Development Goals,[34] but to limit its focus to eliminating conflict potential. The PBC and PBF are mandated to prevent (re)lapses to conflicts, without engaging in greater, and often hubristic, missions to develop societies. The overblown expectations of UN peacebuilding should therefore be challenged by noting that its raison d'être is nothing more than to defend human security. In fact, the mere existence and operations of the PBC and PBF serve to counter the 'grand strategies' often implied in Western greater missions.[35] I was confronted by these pervasive and well-justified doubts of Western greater pursuits when I worked as a desk officer on the PBF in the Ministry for Foreign Affairs of Finland. The evaluation written by one expert regarding my project proposal for a financial contribution to the PBF specifically raised the question as to why the PBF was supporting the energy sector in Sierra Leone, while the Bretton Woods institutions were in a better position to launch and manage such infrastructure projects with much greater financial resources. The statement grippingly described the PBF as a Danish sandwich table, an indirect jab aimed at the lack of any clear thematic focus or common denominator in existing PBF projects, which vary from security-sector reform to the improvement of youth employment. I was confronted by the pertinent question as to whether the PBF itself was complicit in unrealistic and pretentious greater missions it was prescribed to oppose.

Such suspicion, however, is gravely misguided in terms of the PBF, as arguments made in this and previous sections have demonstrated: the singular objective of UN peacebuilding is to save lives by preventing (re)lapses to conflicts, by *any* practical means at its disposal. The operations and projects of UN peacebuilding cannot therefore fit neatly in any predetermined bureaucratic 'boxes', such as the rule of law or youth employment, but they necessarily overlap a variety of sectors ranging from hard security to stabilisation of economy. Perhaps counter-intuitively, however, experts of development co-operation are likely to prefer the traditional bureaucratic approach, because their savoir-faire is organised in separate bureaucratic boxes; transcending these boxes would require walking an extra mile to grasp new sets of information, and might, professionally, mean a leap into darkness. Yet, the new yardstick for evaluating the performance of the UN proposed here is premised on the prudent logic that the function should always precede the form. In other words, the transformation of the UN should be based on substantive logic, not on subjective preferences of bureaucrats.

I decided to test the above hypothesis and presented the metaphor of the sandwich table to Ambassador Frank Majoor, the Permanent Representative of the Netherlands to the UN, who was working as the chairman of the PBF's country-specific meeting (CSM) on Sierra Leone. My question to Ambassador Majoor concerned the value added by energy-sector projects for peacebuilding in Sierra Leone. Ambassador Majoor mentioned, quite surprisingly, that there had been no intention to support the energy sector in the framework of the PBC before he travelled to Sierra Leone in his capacity as the CSM chair. Infrastructure appeared more as a long-term development issue than as a peacebuilding priority. The prospect of including it in the peacebuilding strategy emerged only in Sierra Leone, when the CSM was briefed on the local conditions. Ensuring electricity supplies of Freetown, or at least some reconstruction of its network infrastructure which was in a dismal state in the aftermath of civil war, appeared a useful way to deliver peace-dividends to the people of Sierra Leone; it could demonstrate that peace was real, effective and life-changing, a condition that could crucially improve people's daily lives after the destructive civil war.[36] This example illustrates the advantages of the 'bottom-up' approach of UN peacebuilding, whose solutions may, at first, seem unorthodox and counterintuitive from the viewpoint of bureaucratic rationalisation and models. However, 'on the ground', such unconventional and multifaceted devices of the PBC and PBF, sometimes even dubbed a 'sandwich table', turn out to be the best available means to produce tangible results. The PBF has much value in that it seeks to address a significant gap in the existing peacebuilding approach. It allows for critical interventions that *ideally anticipate* integrated strategies to bring war-torn countries on their feet, and that can have an immediate impact. PBF projects can be critical in preventing the worst possible scenarios, i.e. (re)lapse to conflict, by innovative, smart and carefully targeted solutions that lay the basis for more strategic and sustainable support for peacebuilding in critical areas.

It would be interesting to further elaborate the latter point, according to which the UN should focus on *critical* interventions, and to refine this argument to a more general theory. First, we ought to abandon the seductive but false presumption that the UN could take on the role of a 'big brother' of failed and fragile states in the same way it did during the trusteeship system, when it supervised the liberation of colonised countries after the Second World War. A nostalgic effort to transform the UN peacebuilding architecture into a form of trusteeship system would be a fatal pretension, because it implies wholesale strategies to develop societies, an idea at odds with the critical realist logic. Instead, the UN should strictly limit its actions to the identifying and tackling of those critical cause–effect relationships, or 'red lines', that are crucial to the maintaining of the baseline of humanity. There are, however, contrasting arguments to the 'red lines' approach outlined here. In terms of peacebuilding, Michael Barnett *et al.* suggest that we should be more concerned with the *degree* of state than the *kind* of state that is rebuilt. According to Barnett, international society has been too preoccupied with the latter aspect, exporting the liberal ideal of a democratic state under the banner of state-building. Therefore, the priority in peacebuilding has been given to certain themes integral to the Western liberal vision, particularly the strengthening of the rule of law, human rights, democracy and transitional justice. At the same time, the enlargement of the extent of state institutions and their control, authority and service infrastructure ('the degree of state') has been neglected (Barnett *et al.* 2007: 36). Barnett is right to draw attention to the downsides of the mechanism of Western normalisation, which was explored in the previous chapter, but overlooks another 'troublemaking' mechanism, namely *Zweckrationalität*. As will be analysed in more detail below, *Zweckrationalität* effectively counters or nullifies any attempt at enhancing the 'degree of state' in peacebuilding; the resource-starved UN in particular cannot engage in any grandiose scheme to rebuild the whole infrastructure and service base of an entire state. Instead, it needs to limit its efforts to implementing smart interventions aimed at the prevention of relapses to conflicts.

On the one hand, the smart interventions described above probably bestow less political credit to the UN than greater undertakings by Western organisations, which can muster massive capacities to reconstruction efforts from their affluent member states. On the other hand, Western organisations enjoy 'geomoral' freedom that enables them to limit their concern to those areas which are geopolitically or otherwise close to the interests of Western populations. That option will naturally be preferred and chosen, in the same political realist way that the AU is not expected to show any greater sympathy to the suffering on other continents than Africa. The UN, on its part, will remain in the moral prison of its own making in the sense that it will have no other way than to embrace the whole world, metaphorically speaking. As already explained in Chapter 3, the Secretariat and the Security Council often find themselves obliged, in accordance with the description of their remit in the UN Charter, to become involved in almost all erupting conflicts, even the most complex ones. This gives a further reason for the UN to limit its precious (read 'scarce') capacities to the most fundamental 'red lines' of humanity. Moreover, the UN has always been, and will always remain, severely constrained by *Zweckrationalität*, i.e. an ever-present potential of failure and the consequent possibility of its reputational destruction, the 'risk factor'. The UN should therefore prudently limit its actions to a narrow, but humanly deep, sector that can be managed.[37] All too often this reality is admitted only after it is too late to bridge the widening gap between the responsibilities entrusted to the UN and its scarce resources. Consider, for example, Boutros-Ghali's pessimistic statement in 1995 that, 'It would be folly to attempt to do [peace-enforcement] at the present time when the Organization is resource-starved and hard pressed to handle the less demanding peacemaking and peace-keeping responsibilities entrusted to it.'[38] UN conflict management was in a dead-end; it could not release sufficient resources to tackle urgent crises because of the lack of prioritisation and the consequent stretch of peacekeeping, which led to an unbearable level of risk in UN operations.

The 'risk factor' will always haunt the UN. With regard to the PBF, its first independent evaluation conducted by the OIOS (Office of the Internal Oversight Services at the UN Secretariat) identified a remarkable risk in the PBF's operations. At its third meeting, the PBF Advisory Group was puzzled over the term 'unacceptable risk' used by the OIOS in assessing the PBF's work, and considered this as an overstatement. The OIOS clarified that such risk was actually not financial but reputational. This crucial clarification implies that the original term used by the OIOS was perhaps not an exaggeration after all, but a realistic assessment of the current state of the PBF's affairs.[39] The reputational risk stems from the mismatch between stated objectives and resources to achieve them: thus far, none of the fourteen states on the PBF's agenda, and none of the four countries on the PBC's agenda, have relapsed into conflict. At the same time, however, the number of PBF target countries has risen from eight to fourteen in only a year (by the end of 2008). The UN, or any other organisation for that matter, cannot possibly secure total control over preventing conflicts in all of these countries. Every new target country adopted by the PBC or the PBF poses a considerable risk for the UN, because a relapse into conflict in any of these states would signal the failure of the PBC and the PBF in performing their duties. Such a failure would be a blow, possibly a fatal one, to the UN's credibility.

The successful military takeover in Guinea in December 2008 and an attempted coup d'état implemented by mutinous soldiers in Guinea-Bissau in November 2008, in which the PBC and PBF have been engaged since spring 2008, perfectly capture the predicament. The attack against the residence of President Joao Bernardo Vieira failed in its objective, but the alternative outcome was extraordinarily close. It is arguable how big an impact the hypothetical overthrow and consequent relapse to violence would have had on peace-building, as politicians and military officials in Guinea-Bissau have been implicated in corruption and the drug trade, but it certainly would have damaged the UN's credibility as a whole. Guinea-Bissau would have been viewed as the first clear failure of the UN peacebuilding architecture, a stain on the UN's record. It is only a matter of time before the UN will, for the first time, be confronted by a (re)lapse into conflict in a country under its consideration, and chances for that are continuously increased by the enlargement of the agendas of the PBC and the PBF. And the UN will be the usual suspect to be blamed, because neither the donor community nor the larger public possesses sufficient expertise to make an informed judgement that such failures should, in fact, be mainly attributed to the complexity of conflicts, not to the UN's performance. In this regard, it is interesting to note that the PBF Advisory Group actually suggested the addition of the description of the complex environment in which the PBF was operating in its revised Terms of Reference. The UN needed help in saving itself before it could save anyone else.

Instrumental rationality emerges when an organisation faces a difficult choice as to whether to engage in or to back off from a risky situation. An organisation may even be confronted by a 'hard choice' as to whether to trump all other values in order to preserve the most precious one, namely its own success and survival. It would be an interesting topic of future research projects to examine differences between the UN and other international organisations in their susceptibility to instrumental rationality. There is no doubt that all organisations would prefer to avoid instrumental rationality and disgraceful hard choices altogether if they could, which would be a prudent evasion move, but is the UN more defenceless and prone to face such thorny issues in which instrumental rationality emerges? The answer proposed here is 'yes': the UN is more exposed to instrumental rationality, because it represents universality and does not therefore have moral freedom to silence or tacitly ignore the most complex cases anywhere in the world that pose great risks of failure. For other organisations, it is morally justifiable to disregard large-scale suffering that happens outside their geopolitical radar screen, such as Darfur for the EU, or Georgia for the AU. Such advantage allows officials in these bureaucracies to be more selective. At the same time, 'geopolitical rationality' offers a perfect cover to ignore the most complex and risky engagements eliminated from the agendas of these organisations, and consequently no 'hard choices' emerge in the first place. That is the moral luxury the UN can never afford.

Another challenge to UN conflict management and peacebuilding, like almost any other activity of the UN, is the impossibility of achieving quick wins that would be rewarded by the international community and thereby remedy the credibility of the UN. Paddy Ashdown notes that 'Peacemaking and state-building are measured in decades, not years' (2007: 104). As opposed to swift and astounding triumphs, if there ever has been one in the UN's history, its gradual victories will be achieved unnoticed by a greater public and without much credit given to the UN. Perhaps the problem is compounded by the nature of UN actions, which usually combine economic, humanitarian and political means and development assistance with military capacities in integrated peacekeeping missions. In that sense, they are less spectacular and more invisible than military endeavours by great powers and their alliances whose firepower is designed to generate shock and awe in both opponents and in spectators.[40] As Ashdown reflects, UN actions are 'non-kinetic' (2007: 130). Such description reveals the common sentiment of many spectators, which quite unfairly pictures UN conflict management as somewhat static: the invisibility and the consequent lack of respect for UN operations has allowed a widespread misperception that UN peacekeeping is ineffective, expensive and in urgent need of reform. However, there is mounting evidence that suggests the opposite is true. Two studies published by Rand Corporation in 2004 and 2005 argue that UN-led operations are more successful and less costly than US-led interventions. Based on these and other influential research projects, Andrew Mack makes an important conclusion:

> The quiet successes [of UN peacekeeping] in Namibia, El Salvador, Mozambique, Eastern Slovenia, East Timor and elsewhere went largely unheralded, as did the fact that the United Nations' expertise in handling difficult missions has grown dramatically …. U.N. peace-building operations had a two-thirds success rate. They were also surprisingly cost-effective. In fact, the United Nations spends less running 17 peace operations around the world for an entire year than the United States spends in Iraq in a single month. What the United Nations calls 'peacemaking' – using diplomacy to end wars – has been even more successful.
>
> (Mack 2005: A21)

Peacemaking thrives in secrecy and behind-the-scene negotiations. Therefore many commendable and successful efforts of UN peacemaking, which may prove critical to end conflicts, often escape the eye of outside observers. Simple as it may sound, we should bring to mind the critical realist axiom that reality is more encompassing than mere observations of events. For the UN, this ontological principle seems to have turned into a predicament; it might, to a large extent, explain the somewhat unjustified criticism directed at the UN as a whole and the Secretary-General Ban Ki-moon in particular. While some media reports have criticised the Secretary-General for his low profile and even ridiculed him as an 'invisible man', they have largely overlooked his silent successes in persuading governments to engage in tackling long-term threats such as climate change and global food and energy crises. His low profile and persistent diplomacy also paid off in the Nargis case (Lynch 2008: A15).

Indeed, the succeeding generations will base their final assessment of Secretary-General Ban's performance on his ability to *prioritise* issues which are most crucial for the mankind, not on his media appearance. Such prioritisation actually seems to have worked quite well, as food security and helping victims of natural disasters exactly deal with the essence, or baseline, of humanity. The future years and decades will also show whether the UN as an institution, and not merely its Secretary-General, will follow that path that some NGOs have already taken. *Médecins Sans Frontières*, for example, seeks to reclaim the value of life by emphasising the concept of 'human dignity'. As Peter Redfield explains, this concept 'stands in as a baseline of value inherent in human existence' (Redfield 2008: 203). The emphasis on human dignity is one way to eliminate or diminish the current culture of sacrifice in world politics, in which certain groups deemed less valuable are simply left to die.

Defender of truth: the second vision of a future UN

The use of the word 'truth' here is a purposefully provocative and, hopefully, thought-provoking move. Postmodernists often view images of reality as merely reflections of the inner world of the viewer himself/herself, i.e. what he or she wants to see; critical realists, by contrast, believe that such images can, in fact, be more or less accurate reflections of the outside world. It is understandable that postmodernists, and Critical Theory in general, typically adopts a suspicious stance on any statement on 'truth' or 'real things', which are considered as deceptive and vicious speech acts aimed at imposing 'our truth' on others. However, critical realist philosophy defends the opposite commonsensical view-point that truth can be searched and found, without, however, a possibility of ever grasping the absolute truth. The complete and final image of reality will always remain a desirable, albeit unachievable, object of our searching. In philo-sophy of science, this romantic view of knowledge is, rather unromantically, termed 'epistemological relativism', which denotes a belief in the multitude of approaches in apprehending reality. As explained in Chapter 2, epistemological relativism from the critical realist viewpoint is always held in check by 'judge-mental rationality', a belief in the existence of real objects independent of our imagination, which also provides a yardstick to assess different epistemological approaches. Hence, critical realism allows us to talk about 'truth' and 'real things'. Based on this conception, the UN could be understood as a wheelwork of knowledge-producing, or 'truth-producing', mechanisms, a vision that has not yet fully materialised. This is the second vision of a future UN outlined in this section.

As noted earlier in this book, critical realism entails an important principle based on critical naturalism that, despite our search for truth, nobody should *naively* take speeches, statements and narratives as objective truths, because they usually serve particular political purposes. This philosophical axiom has direct relevance in the 'real life' of international politics, in which truth equals power, and states are reluctant to relinquish any part of their capacity to control and manipulate the truth, i.e. power, to the UN. The creation of a knowledge-producing 'arm' of the UN would increase its powers and independence, which is precisely the reason for fierce opposition against it by most member states of the UN, unwilling to give up a bit of their authority and control to UN officials. Yet, the building up of the UN's capacity to produce knowledge has a huge potential for improving its functioning and global governance in general. The materialisation of this vision would require political courage on the part of both UN officials and member states in the face of ferocious political opposition it is likely to arouse. In terms of peacebuilding, the inclusion of conflict prevention and early warning functions in the mandate of the PBSO would significantly strengthen the UN's capability to prevent (re)lapses to conflicts. In the field of peacekeeping, the recent establishment of the assessment team[41] in the Office of Military Affairs in the Department of Peacekeeping Operations (DPKO) of the UN Secretariat is likely to increase its capacity to produce early warning information.[42] This team is the first office in the UN's history that can process intelligence at the strategic level, and represents one courageous step in building the information-base of that department. Although the DPKO is designed to perform functions almost comparable to those of defence ministries in terms of peacekeeping, it has been deprived of the necessary resources to develop those capacities, including information-gathering, which are essential in any defence ministry. The Brahimi report (2000) recognised this disturbing gap in the DPKO's capacity and proposed the formation of EISAS (Information and Strategic Analysis Secretariat), which, however, has never materialised.[43] The assessment team is likely to fill that vacuum, at least partially.

'Speaking the truth', that is, producing as objective and accurate images of reality as possible for the consumption of universal audiences, represents *the* function the UN should more vigorously and courageously undertake. This role stems from the UN's legitimacy as the universal organisation, a unique quality that distinguishes it from any other international organisation. The UN already provides an extensive *normative* framework for regional and national actors. Thierry Tardy notes that the UN has become an inevitable partner of the EU in crisis management, providing legality and legitimacy to EU actions: 'In the crisis management field, it has been assumed that any EU-led military operation that would imply a chapter VII mandate would have to be legally endorsed by a UN Security Council resolution' (Tardy 2008: 3). In future, this 'submission' under the UN's legitimacy and legality could be transformed into a wider *epistemic* framework within which military actions of regional organisations would be guided, or at least enabled and constrained, by knowledge produced by control mechanisms of the UN outlined in Figure 3.3 of Chapter 3.

The above vision entails a radical, and perhaps even idealistic, claim; it would require both the improvement of the control mechanisms of the UN and, perhaps most crucially, 'Hammarskjöldian' courage on part of UN officials to speak for the truth, even in the crossfire of differing political interests of member states as well as internal conflicts in the UN bureaucracy itself, particularly *Zweckrationalität*. Nevertheless, the adoption of this vision could interestingly transform the disadvantageous *Zweckrationalität* into a *beneficial* mechanism for the UN. The Organisation would benefit in the long run if the yardstick for calculating its credit and loss was shifted from 'insider' assessments based on the Secretariat's relations with great powers, which effectively hampered the Secretariat from telling the truth about the Rwandan genocide in the Security Council in April 1994, to 'outsider' assessments based on the credibility of the UN in the eyes of the world with regard to its performance in conveying the truth to the Council. In other words, the focus of instrumental rationality should be 'externalised' from the UN's internal relations between its organs to the external relations between the UN and its stakeholders.

The deceitful images of the Rwandan genocide as a 'civil war' and 'ancient tribal hatred' were calculated to minimise damages to the Secretariat's relationship with great powers, but actually they caused long-term damages to the UN's credibility as the provider of objective information in the eyes of the whole world. We can know about the untruthfulness of the images of the Rwandan conflict only afterwards through stories produced and reproduced by researchers and investigative journalists. Here the separation between the 'academic world' and the 'real world' turns out to be artificial: researchers can play a key role in the transformation of the UN. For example, the investigative journalist Linda Melvern reveals crucial information on the Security Council's informal discussions during the Rwandan genocide and thereby contributes not only to the Rwandan case but also to the building of a new vision of the UN. The analysis and awareness-raising of internal knowledge-production processes at the UN by researchers helps the transformation of instrumental rationality at the UN, simply because it forces the UN to be truthful to itself and to others in order to safeguard its *public* image. This conclusion calls for active participation of outside actors and 'watchdogs', particularly researchers, in the further analysis of the knowledge-production system of the UN.

Operationally, the UN and the EU have already practised close co-operation in civilian and military crisis management, for example in Kosovo, Chad and Eastern Congo. In this regard, Richard Gowan describes the EU and the UN as two inseparable partners uniting their forces and different special skills towards the same goal:

> Outside Europe, there is currently not one ESDP operation that is not co-deployed alongside some form of UN presence .... The UN and EU are the Obelix and Asterix of international security: one handling big, slow missions while the other concentrates on smaller, flexible, operations.
>
> (Gowan 2008)

Thierry Tardy provides innovative suggestions for the further development of the relationship between the UN and regional organisations. Those forms of co-operation that have not yet materialised include the modular approach, in which an EU component operates under the UN command, and a joint or hybrid operation (Tardy 2008: 6). These are, in fact, concrete examples of the way in which the epistemic framework outlined above could function in practice: the UN could provide informed political and strategic guidance to regional organisations, and, most importantly, determine how conflicts are perceived and conceptualised, which is an important source of power.[44] However, it should be re-emphasised here that these UN control mechanisms are underdeveloped at the moment and may therefore produce equally devastating outcomes. They are powerful both in positive and negative senses. The confusing conceptualisation of the Rwandan conflict as a civil war, as opposed to genocide, virtually nailed the coffins of 800,000 Rwandans, or at least played a crucial part in the disaster; it (mis-)led decision-makers to apply those instruments in conflict management that were not suitable to the situation at hand. Here the knowledge was, indeed, pure evil power, to paraphrase Francis Bacon.

How, then, would the EU benefit from the submission of its powers under the UN's authority? The question seems pertinent in light of the fact that the EU possesses stronger operational and planning capacities than UN Headquarters, which would seem to offer nothing but dead weight for the EU, if the two organisations engaged in hierarchical co-operation. The proposed answer here again points to the UN's special quality, universality. While the UN typically aims to base its activity on long-term commitment to alleviating human suffering anywhere, simply because it has to as a universal organisation, the EU is liberated from such moral obligation. In fact, governments in the EU cannot justify to their domestic electorate indefinite engagement in African conflicts, for example.[45] It is therefore no surprise that the EU has implemented mainly short-term interventions that have usually supported larger UN deployments. An illustrative example here is the EUFOR DRC operation, whose mandate was to support the larger UN mission in the DRC during the 2006 national elections. However, it would be more logical for the EU to place its short-term missions and capacities of conflict management, such as battle groups, under the strategic umbrella of the UN's long-term political and military engagements than to pursue separate strategic objectives that would probably endure for only a short period of time, a typical life-span of the deployment of EU troops. Moreover, close affiliation with the UN might allow the EU to tap into the same base of universal legitimacy that the UN currently enjoys on the ground, although such legitimacy has somewhat diminished by the Organisation becoming a target of international terrorism. Yet, the EU–UN affiliation might enhance the force protection or at least acceptability of EU troops on the ground.

The fourth section was concluded by Ashdown's metaphor of the seamless garment. In concluding this section, it seems more appropriate to speak of overlapping garments, the term 'overlapping' here referring to the co-operation of the UN with regional organisations and the consequent complexity of conflict management mechanisms which can provide 'checks and balances' to each other. If the arsenal of conflict management mechanisms at the UN's disposal in Rwanda had included not only UNAMIR but also the PBC, PBF and PBSO, there would have been a greater possibility for the UN to detect the root causes of the conflict potential prior to the eruption of the genocide. The advantages of such overlapping, or entanglement, of mechanisms should not therefore be underestimated by demands for clearer 'coordination' or 'streamlining', frequently used catchwords in diplomatic parlance. It is probably true that the diversity of new institutions has increased complexity in conflict management, but, as a reward, it has also provided 'checks and balances' and new social optics to existing ones. The International Criminal Court (ICC) has already indirectly contributed to conflict management in Darfur (Piiparinen 2007d: 84–6). As another example, UN Secretary-General's Special Advisor on the Prevention of Genocide Juan Méndez identified worrying media outlets in the Ivory Coast in November 2004 which incited hate rhetoric similar to the provocation by the *Radio Télévision Libre des Mille Collines* (*RTLMC*) in Rwanda (Ashdown 2007: 85). He issued a statement that condemned these acts, passing the referral on to the ICC, which stopped the incendiary media broadcasting. These examples demonstrate that the combination of judicial, military and political mechanisms may produce surprising achievements in conflict management.

Conclusion

This chapter has explored three new strategies that the international community has devised in Darfur in order to achieve sustainable peacekeeping. On the one hand, such strategies seek to reconcile humanitarian values with strategic considerations. On the other hand, they have the potential to counterbalance the deep-seated problems of PKOs that have generated quick-fix solutions, withdrawals and inaction since the 1990s, most notably in Somalia (UNOSOM II) and in Rwanda (UNAMIR). The first section assessed the possibilities of the new division of labour between organisations to overcome the 'body-bag syndrome', perhaps the greatest problem afflicting peacekeeping. Although the new division of labour could indicate increasing unwillingness of Western countries to send their peacekeepers to what has been portrayed as the African 'heart of darkness', if the arrangement becomes widely accepted and institutionalised it could also serve as a means of supplying the military wherewithal desperately needed by African organisations. The second section suggested that the pragmatic shift in peacekeeping may offer a solution to another problem afflicting PKOs, namely the rigidity of bureaucratic procedures, which has obstructed the protection of civilians in particular. The shirking of the term 'genocide' in connection with atrocities in Darfur should, therefore, not be solely conceived as a suppression of the early warning mechanism but also as an indication of the successful application of humanitarian realism.

The conclusion of the first section regarding the racial shift in UN conflict management and its benefits for countering the Western 'body-bag syndrome' may appear rather cynical. It immediately raises the question as to whether this implies that we should pay heed to political realism and sacrifice the UN's longer-term principles, such as equality in bearing the risks of peacekeeping. While an overwhelming majority of troops come from the Third World, the developed world seems to be exempt of the risks peacekeeping entails. Based on the equitable geographical distribution of risks, peacekeeping should be the duty of each and every UN member state. Researchers of conflict management widely criticise the current imbalance in UN peacekeeping, which is considered morally unacceptable, and which should be remedied by greater engagement by Western and EU troops in UN operations (see, for example, Tardy 2008: 10). The purpose of this chapter has not been to refute this conventional wisdom based on the criticism of the 'peacekeeping Apartheid'.[46] However, this chapter has emphasised that the transformation of UN structures and the balance of peacekeeping cannot be achieved overnight. Therefore, the most fundamental value, i.e. alleviating human suffering, can best be ensured not by advocating the false promises of idealism but by accepting the structural constraints of conflict management in accordance with critical realist philosophy.

It should be clarified here that the term 'racial shift' applied in this chapter does not refer to the skin colour of peacekeepers or those persons whom peace-keepers are supposed to protect, but the geopolitical reality that the centre of gravity of peacekeeping currently lies in Africa, in which approximately three-quarters of all UN peacekeepers are positioned. Western states and their regional organisations are not expected to solve those conflicts that flare up outside their geopolitical and moral radar screen. Only after such overpowering political reality is accepted, there comes the 'idealist moment' with the examination of alternative arrangements, the 'other world'. This continuation from realism to idealism is a fundamental methodological move in a critical realist research project. This chapter has suggested several alternative arrangements, notably the development of the division of labour between international organisations (the first section), the mainstreaming of RtoP (the fourth section), the prioritisation of the UN's work on the core values of humanity (the fifth section), and the strengthening of the knowledge-producing capacity of the UN (the sixth section).

Currently a lion's share of the energy of UN member states is consumed by their efforts to safeguard national interests at the UN, as opposed to the preven-tion and resolution of conflicts. This is explained, not by the selfishness or greed-iness of any individual state, as political realists assume, but by understandable social conformity to the 'rules of the diplomatic game', in which every state is expected to maintain the appearance of a committed, credible and, perhaps most importantly, *predictable* partner among equals. Any deviant behaviour from this expected norm, i.e. the pursuit of national interest, would cast the shadow of unpredictability and anomaly over individual officials and states they represent. Such a phenomenon is underlain not by material factors such as economic inter-ests alone but by *Zweckrationalität* in general, as Max Weber explains it in terms of the system of market relationships:

> The manufacturer who in the long run acts counter to these norms, will just as inevitably be eliminated from the economic scene as the worker who cannot or will not adapt himself to them will be thrown into the streets without a job.
>
> (Weber 2003: 54–5)

An overwhelming amount of time and resources of state representatives is directed at campaigning for memberships in various organs and boards of UN agencies, rather than dealing with substantial and pressing issues of human suf-fering around the world. The daily routines of diplomats and officials are filled with campaigning and drafting, not problem-solving. For example, campaigning for a seat as a non-permanent member in the UN Security Council typically carries on for over half a decade or even a decade, while the duration of the actual membership is only two years. The exchange of notes, demarching and trading of votes during the campaign actually requires much more effort than conflict management during the actual membership. State representatives unwill-ingly find themselves in the Weberian iron cage, or the golden cage of multilateral diplomacy, in which negotiations are guided more often by squabbling over national priorities of member states than by actual problems on the ground.

In light of the above rather depressing conclusions, it would be tempting to ask if there is any way out from the current draconian and exhausting political games which leave only little room for innovative policy-making. However, the formulation of this question is framed in prevalent political realist terms and pre-supposes an already determined answer: the tone of the answer would be either apologist and minimalist, if it was 'yes', or conformist to pessimistic thinking on International Relations, if the answer was 'no'. The answer would be less self-evident and more revealing if the logic of the question was turned upside down: is there any other way out to improved conditions apart from a small but import-ant fraction of current multilateral diplomacy, which holds such forward-looking initiatives as RtoP? We should not dwell in the pessimistic observation that the bulk of today's international politics merely reproduces the traditional political realist game, which espouses the business-as-usual in multilateral diplomacy. Instead, we should be encouraged by a set of innovative, albeit unorthodox, ideas that has already been presented to us, which offers the only way to improved conditions, the 'golden path'.

Since 1648, a sovereign state has been a hard but empty shell in the sense that it has possessed practically absolute and unqualified sovereignty within its borders, a licence to (ab)use its people, to commit inhuman acts against them and to neglect their rights without much protest from other states. RtoP is unprecedented in that it offers the first serious and universally accepted initiative to add certain necessary qualifications to the conception of sovereign nation-states without which speaking of 'sovereign states' would be meaningless. In the same way as 'potable water' loses its meaning when it evaporates in air, the term 'sovereign state' becomes void when a regime hiding behind the protective belt of that concept and its related privileges of diplomatic immunity commits atro-city crimes. The logic behind this viewpoint is that humanity is a constitutive and integral part of any state, in the same way as liquid is a constitutive element of potable water. When a state loses these attributes outlined in RtoP, particu-larly a capacity to protect its population from genocide, it becomes artificial and abnormal in the eyes of international society: labels such as 'rogue state', 'failed state', 'collective mad-house' or another description of abnormality are attached to it, which is followed by the severe disruption of its 'business-as-usual' rela-tions with the rest of international society.

By drawing upon Zygmunt Bauman and Carl Schmitt, Jef Huysmans appo-sitely notes that, '[T]he state system (the international society of the English School) does not aim at the elimination of enemies but at the destruction of strangers, or more generally strangehood' (Huysmans 1998: 242). RtoP serves as one effective instrument to project the vision of what constitutes normal state-hood as opposed to abnormal strangehood in the international system. In this sense, it could be described as an immune system: in the same way as those abnormal particles in blood circulation which do not belong to a normal healthy body activate the natural resistance to disease, RtoP serves as a process or instrument through which the 'body politique' of international society aims to eliminate those abnormal or strange 'particles', i.e. genocidal regimes, which threaten the well-being of the overall organ, i.e. humanity. The crucial questions then relate to what is considered abnormal in international relations and whether the commitment of atrocity crimes by an individual state, which previously was quite common and widely accepted by other states, has now become so abnormal that it triggers the resistance of the rest of international society. Secretary-General Ban Ki-moon's report on RtoP, written mainly by his Special Advisor on RtoP Edward Luck, provides a clear answer:

> The responsibility to protect, first and foremost, is a matter of State responsibility, because prevention begins at home and the protection of populations is a defining attribute of sovereignty and statehood in the twenty-first century ... the assembled Heads of State and Government confirmed these two fundamental truths.[47]

This assessment appears not to be an overstatement in light of the fact that there is currently no alternative vision of the defining attributes of statehood which would seriously challenge or compete with RtoP. This confirms the argument here that RtoP constitutes a 'golden path', the only available route to improved conditions for humanity.

It is precisely because of the uniqueness and preciousness of RtoP, hence the label 'golden', that neither the aforementioned Secretary-General's report nor the UN World Summit Outcome dares to envisage any grandiose strategy to promote RtoP, which may fail and thus prove counterproductive and harm the valuable concept itself. For example, neither document touches upon the so-called 'precautionary principles', such as the question of proportional means of military intervention, or 'legitimate authority' which are analysed at length in the original ICISS report on RtoP. The latter report crucially states that a regional organisation can have legitimate authority to justify humanitarian intervention when the UN Security Council has rejected the proposal for intervention, subject to its seeking of subsequent authorisation from the Council. The current UN Secretary-General has prudently assessed that opening a debate on this issue or on another sensitive subject that would imply the lessening of political power of any group, whether the permanent members of the Security Council, developing or developed countries, would only lead to a dead-lock and consume the limited time of state representatives at the expense of the consideration of other aspects of RtoP that have more realistic chances to succeed. It therefore seems that the sheer preciousness of RtoP prevents international society from actually making full use of it. This paradox was seen during the UN World Summit when the government of Canada, one of the architects of RtoP, decided to drop a significant part of its ambitions in promoting the concept in order to ensure its endorsement by NAM countries. This proved an astonishingly successful strategy.

The 'golden path' of RtoP 'promised' here is paved by a certain degree of determinacy[48] in world politics; governments will eventually opt for the new initiatives because of their ability of collective learning. This radical conclusion counters the 'anti-progressivist' approach by so-called Hobbesians and Machiavellians in favour of the Grotian approach, which believes that 'Social learning takes place as states develop conventions and understandings – a global constitution in short – for preserving international order' (Linklater and Suganami 2006: 118). In fact, the analysis here approximates to the Kantian position, as collective learning may lead to enhanced solidarity among states in their pursuit of common objectives of humankind. As demonstrated in this chapter in connection to the birth of UN peacebuilding, international society can and will learn from the lessons of painful mistakes, which not only enables the adoption of new mindsets, but also more or less powerfully leads it to a piecemeal progress in the international security architecture. Such golden paths are similar to the emergence of the Westphalian system of sovereignties in 1648, which was also a product of the collective learning process, namely that of the Thirty Years' War. These paths may, at the time, appear only as footnotes of the history of world politics, but eventually and gradually they will evolve into new normative orders. It is wisdom to foresee these new world orders as they begin to unfold. It is also wisdom to see that any new normative order can be born only at the truly universal arena, not in any regional or national arrangement. This makes the UN unique, always.

8   Conclusion

> Evil, then, is revealed by the argument not to be over...
>
> (Aristotle, *Metaphysics*, Book Theta, Ch-9, 1051a)

The sheer evilness of the Rwandan drama still remains to be explained. Thorough investigation of the UN's performance, however, has revealed another, perhaps even greater, evil pertaining to the deep structures of our society that regulate conflict management. Although the extent and intensity of the genocide, and the UN's failure to prevent it, have shocked international society, these structural 'dysfunctions' persist and have the potential to produce 'other Rwandas' at any moment, on an even greater scale. Aristotle's metaphor seems apposite here: anything with reason that is accounted for in terms of its potentiality has also a potentiality for opposites. Medicine is a potentiality for both sickness and health (*Metaphysics*, Book Theta, Ch-2, 1046b). 'The serious in actuality', Aristotle continues, 'is both better and more worthy of reference than the serious in potentiality' (*Metaphysics*, Book Theta, Ch-9, 1051a). In the same way, what is worse and logically more disconcerting than the UN's past shortcomings in Rwanda and Darfur ('the serious in actuality') is the fact that the propensity to produce similar outcomes remains ('the serious in potentiality') because of certain 'troublemaking' mechanisms still residing in institutional and other social structures. The evil was present when the UN stood by while rural people in Rwanda were efficiently mobilised, grabbing their 'tools' – hoes, axes and machetes – and 'working' for the common aim by hacking down their compatriots as if harvesting the crop. However, the evil persists today in an unexpected place, namely in international bureaucracies and in government offices where decision-makers are conducting their daily routines; we all play a part in reproducing the same Western prejudices and biases in our everyday lives, generating devastating consequences for those excluded from the concern of international society through our actions and inaction.

The meanings of the terms 'good' and 'evil' applied by Aristotle have naturally evolved since the times of Ancient Greece, but the Aristotelian philosophy reveals two important aspects often overlooked in current conflict management. First, actualised events always form merely a tip of the iceberg of reality.

Although the events in Rwanda and Darfur were exceptionally cruel, their importance lies not only in lessons regarding these dramatic cases per se and the number of people the UN failed to protect, but also in their status as 'moments of truth' revealing the structural condition of UN conflict management.[1] They instigated an unprecedented and important self-reflection process at the UN. Consequent 'lessons learned' reports, written in the UN Organisation and elsewhere, offer a unique window of opportunity for 'outsiders' to peek inside the UN system and obtain information of the past and present state of relevant UN structures.[2] Second, and most importantly, a considerable possibility for surprise resides in every turn of international politics. Indeed, the medicine and humanitarian aid provided by Western organisations to Rwandan civilians during the genocide functioned merely as a 'humanitarian alibi' for inaction; according to the Aristotelian logic, all actions of the 'Western rational man' which seem humanitarian at the surface level carry a potentiality for both good and evil. Although the conclusion here calls for a critical, or even sceptical, approach to international conflict management, this critical realist view should be balanced by an emancipatory inquiry into those alternative paths that could lead to incremental advances in the reform of the UN conflict management system. This book suggests one methodological tool to conduct that task, namely the method of double movement.

Andrew Sayer's and Roy Bhaskar's models were synthesised with the aim of designing an innovative critical realist approach to IR. The product of this synthesis, the method of double movement, informs the conclusions of this book in the following ways:

1   its *holistic ontology* employs a multi-causal explanation and informs us that decision-making is usually regulated by a complexity of mechanisms operating on various planes or at various levels of reality rather than by a single factor;
2   its *emancipatory impulse* aspires to transcend the dichotomy between theory and praxis and invites practical suggestions as to how international organisations could be transformed to avert 'future Rwandas'; and
3   it also contains an *ethical dimension*, as it aims to go beyond the dichotomy between fact and value by suggesting that morality and responsibility are embedded in material and social realities.

For these reasons, the method of double movement offers a promising and reflective methodological device that would repay further deployment in IR research on causality, decision-making, conflict management and the reform of international organisations.

This book has sought to demonstrate that the causes of the UN's failure in Rwanda were more complex than previously imagined. Initial chapters explored the philosophical and theoretical underpinnings of existing accounts of the subject and argued that the mainstream literature tends towards methodological individualism, in which the causes of the UN's shortcomings are attributed to a paucity of political will on the part of state actors and UN officials. Meanwhile, the socio-historical context of the Rwandan case has been largely ignored. This book has demonstrated that the Rwandan drama was not only self-inflicted by individual actors but also a product of certain socio-historical factors. In short, it can be deemed a child of its time, a mirror image of the ailing control mechanisms of the early 1990s, which interacted and combined with each other to produce a devastating result in Rwanda.

The latter part of the book has confirmed that individualist explanations of the Rwandan case are too reductive, for the lack of political will should be construed less as an explanatory factor per se than as a factor to be explained by reference to the 'troublemaking' mechanisms that produced and compounded it. Nor does the culpability of individual actors provide a satisfactory explanation, as their mistakes were generated and intensified by a complex network of mechanisms affecting *all* actors within the UN system. Chapters 5 and 6 uncovered a 'draconian communicative consensus' in the Security Council, which was evidenced, for example, by the prevalent stereotypical and racial image of the conflict as 'chaotic, mad and tribal' and in the dominant discourse emphasising civil war at the expense of genocide. This intersubjective consensus cannot be explained satisfactorily as emanating only from the political interests of individual states. Instead, its explanation must also incorporate reference to certain mechanisms that constituted the Council's discourse as a whole. This is a radical claim. It implies that causes lie deeper than previously believed: the lack of political will to intervene in Rwanda arose *in conjunction with* certain underlying mechanisms.

The above causal relationship between political will and the complex of control mechanisms has considerable implications for a novel understanding of the 'Somalia effect'. The latter has been previously equated to the 'body-bag syndrome'; member states of the Security Council were reluctant to dispatch their troops into harm's way in Rwanda following the Somalia experience in which the UN had suffered it heaviest casualties since the 1960s. Member states thus *intentionally* excluded the Rwandan conflict from the Council's agenda. However, Chapters 5 and 6 of this book have demonstrated that the Somalia effect was more complicated than that. It was, in fact, 'multi-layered', generated not only by intentional political calculations but also by a multiplicity of other mechanisms operative at various levels. These included cognitive dissonance in *organisational learning* at the *unintentional* or subconscious level, and the tribalisation of African conflicts and moral self-disillusionment produced by *Western normalisation* at the level of deep structures of our civilisation. In addition, *bureaucratic rationalisation* contributed to the Somalia effect, as the previous UNOSOM II operation in Somalia deprived the UN bureaucracy of the political capital required to launch any subsequent 'grand strategies' in Rwanda. Finally, the malfunctions of the early warning mechanism and information-production in general allowed diplomats and officials to mistake the genocide for a Somalia-type of 'anarchic, mad and tribal killing', i.e. an unmanageable chaos.

The acknowledgement of structural constraints, in turn, directly invokes an *understanding* position on the Rwandan case, which has been sidelined by dominant *descriptive* approaches in the existing literature. There is, of course, an obvious reason for the avoidance of the 'understanding' type of storytelling: where should the line be drawn between understanding and sympathising with those people who chose to stand by when the genocide was unfolding, despite their potential ability to stop it? In answering this question, Gérard Prunier's assertion may be useful: 'Understanding why [Rwandans] died is the best and most fitting memorial we can raise for the victims' (1998: xii). Furthermore, it is suggested here that understanding the failures of state representatives and UN officials by reference to the structures and mechanisms which underlay their abandonment of Rwanda is essential to bridging the gulf between theory and practice, i.e. to drawing lessons to prevent such a catastrophe from happening again in the future.

In this regard, critical realist methodology has proven particularly instructive: the dysfunctions of 'troublemaking' mechanisms exposed by this book not only constituted causes of the Rwandan drama, but also form *dormant potentials* awaiting activation by similar events yet to ensue in different contexts. Hence, this study serves to alert attention to those factors still residing in the deep structures of our society and in concrete structures of the UN that could produce 'another Rwanda', and has suggested options for transforming them in order to forestall such a disastrous eventuality. However, this book has applied the conceptual tool of 'possible' not only in the negative sense as dormant 'troublemaking' potentials to generate another Rwanda-like disaster, but also in the positive sense as *possibilities to transform the UN system*. To re-invoke the critical realist metaphor of reality as an iceberg, some indications of the improved performance of the UN demonstrated by the case of Darfur (Chapter 7) could be considered as an actual event forming merely a tip of the iceberg; it reveals only part of the possibilities to reform the UN. Most of the possibilities for structural improvements identified in Chapter 7 and some sections of Chapters 5 and 6 'wait' to be actualised. Therefore, the book has important implications for the future reform of the UN by identifying those areas in which structural reforms would be feasible.

Having underlined the abundance of structural dysfunctions, it appears prudent to enquire into their overall 'net effect'. Chapters 5 and 6 investigated the role of these structural constraints as well as emancipatory possibilities in relation to each of the four 'troublemaking' mechanisms, without considering their total effect. The findings of this research suggest that the overall net effect was felt most strongly in a 'perception gap': even the most concerned members of the Security Council were able to acknowledge the genocide fully only four days after the Council had withdrawn the bulk of the peacekeeping force from Rwanda. Such a perception gap was caused by the dysfunctions of both detection and securitisation mechanisms. The former refer to early warning and organisational learning, whilst the latter denote bureaucratic rationalisation and Western normalisation. Archival records confirm that the perception gap was bridged on 25 April 1994, which signifies the Security Council's recognition of the genocide. From that moment, however, the dysfunctions of securitisation mechanisms continued to 'cause trouble', by contributing to the Council's reluctance to acknowledge the genocide and use the term in public.

The above conclusion implies that both detection and securitisation mechanisms were relevant in order to effect the prevention of the Rwandan disaster. To this extent, the conclusion advanced here opposes the common view held by many scholars and practitioners that the malfunctions of detection mechanisms played no role. The former Secretary-General, the then Under-Secretary-General for Peacekeeping Operations Kofi Annan still maintains that 'The failures of the international community to intervene effectively in Rwanda and elsewhere were not due to a lack of warning' (Annan 1999: 11). However, even his predecessor Boutros-Ghali failed to use the term 'genocide' until 4 May 1994, almost a month after the beginning of the massacres. Furthermore, the role of detection mechanisms is accentuated in those cases in which conflict prevention concerns strategically or politically unimportant countries or areas. Consider, for example, the following statement by Secretary-General Annan in the UN Commission on Human Rights preceding Operation Allied Force by NATO in Kosovo:

This last Commission on Human Rights of the twentieth century is meeting under the dark cloud of the crime of genocide …. Though we have no independent observers on the ground, the signs are that it may be happening, once more, in Kosovo.

(Quoted in Thornberry 2001: 52)

Neither the UN General Assembly nor the Commission on Human Rights had by that time applied the term 'genocide' in connection with the violence committed by Serb irregulars against Kosovar Albanians (Thornberry 2001: 52). In other words, the Secretary-General could securitise the violence in Kosovo as genocide without recourse to overwhelming early warning information, because the political willingness of NATO powers to acknowledge the threat of genocide and thereby legitimate intervention *enabled* him to do so. This stands in stark contrast to the silence of the Secretary-General during the Rwandan genocide; here, the Secretary-General could not afford to perform such securitisation acts without the support of the early warning mechanism, i.e. without overwhelming proof of the potential for genocide, as Chapter 6 demonstrated in connection to *Zweckrationalität*. In sum, the importance of the early warning mechanism was accentuated in the Rwandan case in contrast to strategically more significant areas.

The above conclusion concerns not only the net effect of, and the internal dynamics between, mechanisms, but also the openness of the UN system to the external sphere of politics and its status vis-à-vis other actors and systems. Of all international organisations, the UN and the OAU (the Organisation of African Unity, currently the African Union) were perhaps most favourably positioned to tackle the crisis, as they had peacekeepers on the ground when the genocide commenced. The OAU inquiry refers to one expert who claimed that the Rwandan conflict was 'the most easily preventable genocide imaginable' (IPEP 2000: 69). However, the way in which the OAU allocates the blame for the disaster to Western powers, and to Belgium, France, and the US in particular (IPEP 2000: 100), still begs the question as to why the OAU itself did not strengthen its presence in Rwanda in order to tackle the 'most easily preventable genocide'. The Permanent Representative of the Czech Republic to the UN, Ambassador Karel Kovanda's observation may provide a clue to the answer. On 25 April 1994, Kovanda wrote to the Czech Foreign Ministry:

> The regional organization [the OAU] is viewing the situation from the point of view of the country's [Rwanda's] stability or from that of the government's legitimacy; it's trying to bring about a ceasefire, holds both parties at the same level. Isn't it as if we wanted Hitler to reach a ceasefire with the Jews?[3]

Thus, the possibilities for OAU intervention in Rwanda were severely restricted by an uncompromising respect for the sovereignty of its member states which was maintained even *during* the genocide. In the UN Security Council, by contrast, Rwandan sovereignty played no role *after* the eruption of the genocide and the collapse of its legitimate government. Although this interesting contrast between UN and OAU policies on sovereignty cannot be elaborated further due to limited space, its implication is that prevention of the genocide hinged primarily on the UN's capacity. These considerations touch upon the essence of the second principal conclusion of this book, concerning emancipation.

According to an emancipatory vision developed in this book, the UN Security Council works most efficiently only when its actions are both mediated through the surrounding normative and institutional structure of the UN system and multilateral – involving the Secretariat, which Howard Adelman and Astri Suhrke aptly call the 'sixth permanent member' (Adelman and Suhrke 2004: 497) – rather than unilateral (undertaken by individual permanent member states). Such a vision portrays the Council as an open system in the following way: early warning mechanisms could have produced signals about the forthcoming Rwandan genocide; UN institutions, such as the Secretariat, could have made these signals (e.g. the 'January cable') known to Council members; and states could thus have been lobbied to launch a multilateral 'hammer and anvil' peacekeeping operation.[4] This concrete utopia is preferable to the political realist image of unilateral actions taken by individual members of the Council, such as the French-led *Opération Turquoise*, because institutions and mechanisms accord legality and legitimacy to UN actions, whereas the (belated) French action was deemed illegitimate (Hutu-biased) by the RPF. The latter conclusion offers a methodological guide for future research which adopts a simple logic: if it were acknowledged that not only states but also institutions and control mechanisms are important legitimating power bases in the UN, then it would follow, *contra* political realists, that the great powers do not constitute the only 'powerhouse'.

What alternative routes of action could UN diplomats and officials have taken to save more Rwandan lives? The Related Powers model provides a clue to the answer by suggesting that the Council could have functioned efficiently only in relation to the institutions and control mechanisms of the UN. However, the more practical question remains as to the particular means and time sequence through which Council members and UN officials could have *transformed* their structural constraints. The term 'transform' is pivotal here. According to Bhaskar's Transformational Model of Social Activity, actors rarely create but usually transform already existing social structures. The thwarted attempt of an individual DPKO official to create the early warning structure by conjuring up the 'black file' or 'black box' aptly illustrates this point.

The first step in exploring the unexploited means by which the Rwandan tragedy could have been averted involves an acknowledgment of structural constraints, the first conclusion of the book. By underplaying these constraints, the existing literature tends to overestimate the capacities of individual actors. This study has sought to shift the focus of research away from such a voluntarist position towards a more structuralist direction. This implies that the main cause of the Rwanda debacle was less a *lack of political will* than a *lack of courage* in individual UN officials and diplomats to counter the structural constraints they faced. The expression 'lack of will' contains connotations that are inaccurate in two respects. First, it implies that all it would have taken to avert the tragedy would have been the mere willpower or a simple effort of will on the part of individual actors. Second, it overlooks the fact that certain individuals demonstrated considerable willingness to save Rwandan civilians but failed in their endeavour due to structural impediments.[5] Two individuals in particular manifested enormous courage in attempting to liberate themselves from the restrictions imposed by the UN system. An individual desk officer in DPKO endeavoured to overcome a paucity of early warning structures by calling attention to Dallaire's cables. Force Commander Dallaire, on his part, initiated a direct information channel between himself and UN Headquarters, in contravention of UN procedures. Despite the level of self-sacrifice these efforts required, both proved to no avail, which only underlines the severity of the structural constraints their authors encountered.

Tackling the Rwandan crisis thus required 'Hammarskjöldian courage' on the part of UN diplomats and officials to overcome social and material impediments. The term 'Hammarskjöldian courage' here recalls the efforts of Secretary-General Dag Hammarskjöld to mitigate human suffering in the Congo in the early 1960s. In September 1960, he described the situation in the Congo as a 'case of incipient genocide', thereby legitimating the interposing of UN troops between the Congolese Army and the targeted civilians in the Kasai province (Roberts 2002: 9). This example resembles the emancipatory vision of a hypothetical intervention in Rwanda constructed here in three respects. First, in both cases, UN troops were already stationed in the country when the intervention (would have) started. Second, in both cases, the intervening side encountered formidable obstacles in managing to have their descriptions of the situation as 'genocide' accepted; Hammarskjöld in terms of normative constraints of contemporary international law, particularly the non-intervention principle, and UN officials and diplomats in the Rwandan case in terms of dysfunctions of detection and securitisation mechanisms. Third, both Hammarskjöld and Boutros-Ghali faced a severe lack of political will on the part of member states *and* UN officials to engage in a risky mission to 'save strangers'[6] in Africa. In the Rwandan case, such reluctance was exacerbated by the dysfunctions of the aforementioned mechanisms, such as bureaucratic calculations (*Zweckrationalität*) of possible costs or the projected damage of proposing intervention for working relations between the Secretariat and great powers. This point is perfectly captured by Boutros-Ghali's statement, presented in Chapter 6, that 'Here is your responsibility: you are supposed to have enough energy [read: courage] to say, "No, in spite of this [opposition by member states] I will convene the Security Council." '[7]

Drawing together the above ideas, 'emancipatory windows' can be understood as *critical moments in which actors could have liberated themselves from structural constraints in order to save Rwandan lives*, given that such emancipation would have required efforts on the part of these actors or others before them to transform the 'troublemaking' mechanisms of the UN system. The existing literature tends to locate an emancipatory window within the time period between 7 April and 21 April 1994.[8] It is claimed here, by contrast, that this window of opportunity should be enlarged to include those *years* prior to the genocide when the early warning mechanism, which was of crucial importance in bridging the so-called 'perception gap' from 21 April to 25 April 1994, was being constructed. In fact, emancipation would not have been possible with a single window; such a process is not the work of a fleeting moment, for example a sudden 'change of heart' impelling great powers to intervene in Rwanda. Prevention would only have been possible by exploiting several emancipatory windows. In fact, this book has identified three such windows, as will be explained below.

The prevention of the genocide did not hinge solely upon the political will, or willpower, of UN officials and diplomats, but also depended on the early warning structures and control mechanisms these actors found at their disposal. Chapter 5 has demonstrated that such structures should have been established and developed long before the eruption of the Rwandan crisis, simply because it is unreasonable to expect actors to suddenly fabricate them during a genocide, as the incident of the so-called 'black box' or 'black file' tragically illustrates. In light of the above considerations, the first emancipatory window presented in Figure 8.1 (page 177) is located on 31 January 1992, i.e. the date of the commissioning of *An Agenda for Peace*, when the Security Council displayed the political commitment to construct, strengthen and streamline UN conflict prevention capacities. The other two emancipatory windows, located in closer proximity to the Rwandan conflict, represent what Luc Reychler calls 'proactive' and 'reactive conflict prevention' (Reychler 1997: 27). The initial window of proactive conflict prevention denotes possibilities for preventing the genocide from erupting, whereas the later window of reactive conflict prevention refers to the potential to prevent escalation and intensification of the crisis.

With regard to the emancipatory window at the proactive conflict prevention stage, the establishment of UNAMIR constituted the focal point at which the UN conflict management system materialised into a nascent, albeit not fully functional, 'related whole', combining the three necessary components, i.e. the material powers of state actors, the rational–legal powers of institutions, and control mechanisms. The Security Council's decision to adopt Resolution 872 on 5 October 1993 marks not only the contribution of 2,548 military personnel from various countries to the UN mission in Rwanda (material powers), but also the institution of a vital information channel of early warning signals from Rwanda to UN Headquarters and the inauguration of knowledge-production processes based on that information (control mechanisms). It also inaugurated the Secretariat's opportunity to present policy options and measures to the Council in accordance with such knowledge (rational–legal powers). Therefore, Figure 8.1 styles 5 October 1993 as the 'opening up' of the second emancipatory window through which the prevention of the genocide was possible. However, this possible course of action was constrained by a lack of political will and dysfunctional control mechanisms. On the other hand, Chapters 5 and 6 have identified various means by which such dysfunctions could have been eliminated or held in check by the transformative powers of social (re)construction.

With regard to the emancipatory window at the reactive conflict prevention stage, further obstacles 'shrank' the window. As Alan J. Kuperman points out, the speed of the killing and the limitations of airlifting were severe *constraints* (Kuperman 2000: 101; 2001: viii). Yet, if the window was reduced on the 'constraints-axis', it was also somewhat widened along the 'possibilities-axis': novel *possibilities* that became available to the Security Council included an increase of accurate information about the genocide and the potential to establish a 'hammer and anvil' type of peacekeeping mission composed of part of the 1,500 evacuation troops and numerous safe havens created by UNAMIR. Figure 13 draws upon Figure 8.2 (page 178) in order to illustrate these three 'emancipatory windows'.

The above figure indicates that emancipatory possibilities resided not in individual states as partisans of an atomistic ontology assume, but in co-operation between the Security Council and the Secretariat (relational ontology). As demonstrated in Chapter 4, previous accounts are epitomised by reductive argumentation, which provides only a partial picture of the 'related whole' of the UN conflict management system and cannot espy the relationships between its components. This book argues that subjecting the whole system to analysis provides not only more information but also a wholly new dimension to the Rwandan story, in the same way as the corner pieces of a puzzle alone cannot reveal its image. That picture emerges only once all the necessary pieces are in place. Although it is premature to provide a conclusive assessment of conflict management in Darfur, as the crisis is still ongoing, we can situate that case in the above model by stretching the Z-axis portraying time. As demonstrated in Chapter 7,

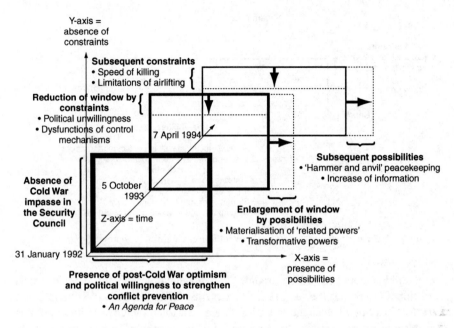

Figure 8.1 Emancipatory windows to prevent the Rwandan genocide.

the case of Darfur has revealed important novel possibilities, notably the new division of labour between relevant organisations and the functional and pragmatic shifts in the strategies of conflict management, which have enlarged the window of opportunity to intervene in potential genocides. Stretching further the axis portraying time, Chapter 7 identified the most promising possibilities opened up since the UN World Summit of 2005, which saw the establishment of the UN peacebuilding architecture (PBC, PBF and PBSO) and the inception of RtoP in the UN system. The PBC and RtoP, however, reflect achievements at the surface level of institutional arrangements only; perhaps the most important accomplishments have occured at the deeper level of bureaucratic culture and mindset, where the UN has taken the encouraging first steps in abandoning rigid and inflexible bureaucratic categorisations in favour of thinking outside of bureaucratic boxes, the prioritisation of the core values of humanity, and strengthening the knowledge-producing 'arm' of the UN. The latter three factors in particular form the future visions of the UN which should be pursued vigorously in order to prevent 'future Rwandas'.

The above considerations guide the formulation of the third and final conclusion of this book, concerning responsibility. Current debates on humanitarian intervention have engendered an emerging consensus which holds that the responsibility of international society to protect civilians threatened by genocidal regimes embraces three elements: responsibility to prevent the occurrence of massive human rights violations; responsibility to react to them; and responsibility

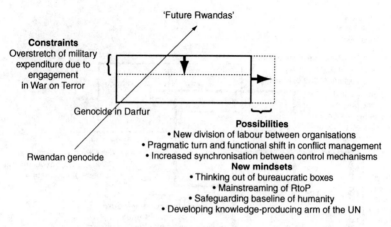

Figure 8.2 Emancipatory windows to prevent present and future genocides.

to rebuild societies in order to repair the damages inflicted upon them by inter-vention and prevent the recurrence of violence (ICISS 2001: xi; Roberts 2004: 94–5). This book has suggested a fourth element to be included in these notions of responsibility, namely the *responsibility to construct and transform* early warning structures and other control mechanisms in order to be able to prevent or halt genocides. As demonstrated in the earlier discussion on emancipatory windows, the necessary structures and mechanisms should have been developed long before the eruption of the Rwandan crisis, simply because actors did not have time to construct them during the genocide. In this sense, the UN's failure between January and May 1994 not only reflects 'damage in the making' but also 'damage done'. The responsibilities for the UN's breakdown should thus be apportioned not only to the actors in office during that period, but also to those who failed to set up the necessary structures prior to the genocide when such capacity-building was feasible, for example in the aftermath of *An Agenda for Peace.*[9]

The latter conclusion prompts further questions as to whether the respons-ibility to construct and transform UN control mechanisms has been acted upon since the Rwandan genocide, and to what extent such transformations have helped to prevent 'another Rwanda'. Although addressing these questions requires further research and cannot be answered here in any detail, the only sub-stantial investigation of the 'post-Rwandan' transformation of the UN system, namely John Borton and John Eriksson's *Lessons from Rwanda – Lessons for Today* published in December 2004, provides a pessimistic picture of the changes that have taken place. Most crucially, the report concludes that the Security Council did not discuss the genocidal killing in Darfur until March 2004, thirteen months after the outbreak of the conflict, and neither the Council nor the Secretary-General have recognised it as a 'genocide' (Borton and Eriks-son 2004).

At first glance, Borton and Eriksson's conclusions seem to stand in stark opposition to the argument advanced in this book according to which the current UN system is in a better position to prevent 'another Rwanda' due to its structural transformations. However, whilst this book agrees with Borton and Eriksson's claims concerning Darfur, there are two criticisms that can be levelled at their account which support the argument advanced here. First, more attention should be paid to the continuous development of UN control mechanisms which has generated gradual achievements in civilian protection since the Rwandan genocide. UN conflict management in the Ituri region of the Democratic Republic of Congo (DRC) provides an instructive example of the way in which the gradual transformation of the mechanism of bureaucratic rationalisation has created a 'grey area' between peacekeeping and peace-enforcement. This has enabled *MONUC* (United Nations Mission in the Democratic Republic of Congo) to use robust force against criminal elements, resulting in a decrease of militia activity and the withdrawal of armed gangs from *MONUC*'s zone of influence (Samuels 2004: 6). Such piecemeal progress has unfortunately been overshadowed by the UN's overall failure to prevent tragedy in the DRC and subsequent setbacks in *MONUC*'s operations in 2008, and in other African trouble spots. Michael Ignatieff's statement seems apposite here in highlighting the need to uncover and appreciate these 'hidden' achievements at the structural level, advancements which have been submerged by the 'failure-discourse' at the surface level of media coverage concerning the UN's overall record in Africa: 'We may be able to stop horror, but we cannot always prevent tragedy' (Ignatieff 1999: 96).

Second, Borton and Eriksson's report employs a different level of explanation than the critical realist methodology applied in this book. The former considers the lack of political will as a sufficient explanatory factor of the UN's failure, whilst this book has crucially argued that political will should be viewed more as a variable which is significantly influenced by the performance of the wider UN conflict management system. Borton and Eriksson base their entire comparison of Rwanda and Darfur on the following question: 'Has the international community become more willing to prevent or intervene against genocide or mass killing?' Conversely, a critical realist approach would inquire as to whether structural transformations have modified the willingness of states to intervene. By concentrating on indicators of political will as such, Borton and Eriksson manage to find similarities between the Rwandan and Darfur cases, but effectively fail to answer whether improved UN structures (would) have made a difference in preventing genocide.[10] At the same time, it should be acknowledged that political will is shaped not only by the UN but also by situational factors extraneous to the UN system, such as the Iraq war and the consequent political reluctance of governments to offer troops to any other operations.

By focusing on structural and situational factors overlooked by Borton and Eriksson, the conclusions of the final chapter of this book intimate changes in the operation and structure of PKOs, thereby providing hope for the future of peacekeeping. How, then, can the causal impact of such transformations be measured? UN Secretary-General Kofi Annan's *Action Plan to Prevent Genocide* provides a realistic and productive, though not exclusive, means of conducting such an assessment. As demonstrated in Chapter 7, the Action Plan outlines five points:

1   the prevention of armed conflict;
2   the protection of civilians;
3   the ending of judicial impunity;
4   the strengthening of information-gathering and early warning; and
5   the implementation of swift and decisive action.[11]

As will be argued below, the case of Darfur demonstrates that the UN system has thus far addressed four of these five points with both structural and pragmatic solutions.

As for Point 4 of the Action Plan, the transformation of the Security Council's briefing mechanism from a closed system to an open one and the establishment of the Secretary-General's Special Advisor on the Prevention of Genocide in particular provide useful additions to the parts of the UN system that aim to generate international concern for humanitarian intervention. As events in Darfur demonstrate, pragmatic means of protecting civilians form the crux of this new information-production system rather than labelling of conflicts as such. Perhaps an even more pertinent structural transformation relates to Point 3 of the Action Plan; Darfur sets a unique precedent not only for the ICC, as one of the first three judicial cases opened up by the Prosecutor of the ICC by June 2005,[12] but also for UN peacekeeping, as the first PKO in which the deterrent of ICC investigations has been effectively used as a tool to reduce further violence in its area of responsibility. Such a synchronisation between the judicial and operational functions within peacekeeping, whether intentional or not, can serve as an important precedent for future PKOs. The third major structural transformation concerns Point 2 of the Action Plan; the example of Darfur proves that the pragmatic shift away from the rigidity of bureaucratic norms and the new division of labour between relevant organisations can contribute effectively to the protection of civilians. With regard to Point 1 of the Action Plan, the application of the Naivasha agreement as an umbrella concept for the overall management of Sudanese conflicts has thus far proven pragmatic, viable and effective in resolving the crisis. This stands in stark contrast to the Rwandan case, in which the UN merely concealed its unwillingness to intervene in the genocide behind the application of the Arusha peace accord.

Perhaps the area in the current UNPKO system that most requires urgent attention and further transformation in order to enhance its conflict prevention capacity is Point 5 of the Action Plan, i.e. the ability to implement swift and decisive action, including military intervention. The tardiness of international response to the crisis in Darfur should not be downplayed: from the outbreak of violence in February 2003, more than a year passed before the first international organisation, the AU, decided to deploy a military operation to put down the massacres. It took two years until UN troops were deployed in Southern Sudan, with only a limited mandate to operate in Darfur. Ironically, the vanguard of the UN forces deployed in Sudan was composed of officers from the Standby High Readiness Brigade. The 'high' readiness of the UN to intervene in large-scale human rights violations still requires vast improvement.

Former Secretary-General Boutros-Ghali's statement on Darfur offers a particularly useful inspiration for formulating the concluding words of this book. When asked what lessons he would draw from Rwanda, Boutros-Ghali answered:

> I give you a very macro-interpretation: there is a basic discrimination *in the minds* between an event happening in Europe and an event happening in Africa. We were in Rwanda to protect the white people living there. We have the same problem today in Darfur. I had the same problem when they [member states] were spending five million a day in Yugoslavia, and they refused to give me five million for Africa.[13]

The phrase 'in the minds' is emphasised above because it aptly illustrates the main argument of this book that political unwillingness to intervene in Rwanda was not only an embodiment of *Realpolitik* but also a product of deeper (macro-) problems residing in our society, such as different values, stereotypes and prejudices attached to African and European people. Yet, Boutros-Ghali's statement furnishes only a partial conclusion, as it emphasises only one mechanism, i.e. Western normalisation. This book, by contrast, has considered the Rwandan failure as analogous to a syndrome, that is, a sum effect of various mechanisms, rather than a disease emanating from a single isolated cause. To close the whole argumentative circle of this study, Johan Galtung's famous metaphor can be paraphrased as follows: eliminating the Rwandan syndrome would have required not only addressing its symptom, i.e. political unwillingness, but also tackling its underlying causes, including the dysfunctions of UN control mechanisms.

Notes

Introduction

1 Although previous literature places an element of blame for the UN's failure in Rwanda, and especially for the mishandling of the so-called 'January cable', with the former head of the UN Department of Peacekeeping Operations (DPKO), Kofi Annan, there is no evidence that the operational performance of the DPKO per se has been significantly improved because of the departure (and promotion) of this individual.

2 On the concept of 'deep structure' in structural realism, see, for example, Buzan *et al.* (1993: 37–9).

3 Waltz states: 'Nations change in form and in purpose ... the similarity and repetition of international outcomes persist despite wide variations in the attributes and in the interactions of the agents that supposedly cause them' (1979: 67). Waltz proceeds to explain reasons for the focus on structures in his theory: 'A constancy of structure explains the recurrent patterns and features of international-political life .... Structural concepts, although they lack detailed content, help to explain some big, important, and enduring patterns' (1979: 70).

4 John Ruggie provides a useful description of the relationship between the level of phenomena and their underlying causes, i.e. layered structures: 'In a generative structure ... the structural levels closer to the surface of visible phenomena take effect only within a context that is already "prestructured" by the deeper levels' (Ruggie 1986: 150).

5 See, for example, Waltz (1979: 73).

6 Ontology here is understood as the theory of being and the nature of the research object, whereas epistemology refers to the theory of knowledge and how a researcher and people in general can know about the world (Lazar 1998: 10).

7 A previous account by the author aims to advance a deeper understanding of peacekeeping with regard to international intervention in Afghanistan. See Piiparinen (2007a: 143–57). This investigation explains successes and failures of provincial reconstruction teams (PRTs) of the NATO-led ISAF (International Security Assistance Force) by reference to differences in bureaucratic mindsets of civilian and military experts as opposed to the mainstream literature, whose explanation is typically based on a mere description of visible objects, such as the number of troops and their material capacities.

8 As Justin Cruickshank notes from the perspective of critical realist philosophy, all research projects are guided or underpinned by certain underlying meta-theoretical assumptions (Cruickshank 2002: 49). This book aims to expose such assumptions in the mainstream literature on Rwanda.

9 On early studies explaining the Rwandan case in these terms, see Boutros-Ghali (1996: 19); Destexhe (1995: 49); Leitenberg (1994: 6–11); Melvern (1995: 1–22); Vassall-Adams (1994: 56–8).

10 On recent studies explaining the Rwandan case in these terms, see Dallaire (1998: 79–80); Gourevitch (1999: 150); Power (2003: 329–90).

11 See Adelman and Suhrke (1996: 68); Jones (2001: 129); Melvern (2001a: 53); Willum (1999: 27); Ingvar Carlsson, Han Sung-Joo and Rufus M. Kupolati, *Report of the Independent Inquiry into the Actions of the United Nations during the 1994 Genocide in Rwanda.* UN Doc. S/1999/1257, 15 December 1999, p. 30.

12 The word 'betraying' here is derived from Linda Melvern's book, *The Ultimate Crime: Who Betrayed the UN and Why* (1995). While the initial twenty pages of the book touch upon the abandonment of Rwanda by the Security Council, the rest of the book, over 300 pages, describes the uneasy relationship between the UN and the great powers, and the US in particular, since the establishment of the UN. The 'betrayers' of Rwanda are thereby implicitly deduced from the 'historically proven fact', i.e. the selfishness of the great powers, which indicates an empiricist fallacy. Melvern's subsequent book provides a more elaborate and sophisticated account of the UN's failure in Rwanda, as it apportions the blame not only to the representatives of the great powers but also to UN officials. See Melvern (2000).

13 These negative experiences and the increasing unipolarity in world politics led to the tendency of states to bypass the Security Council by resorting to alliances and coalitions instead of collective security, for example in Kosovo (1999).

14 This problem is discussed in Suhrke (1997: 102).

15 See, for example, Wallace (2000: 34).

16 On the positivist way to separate objective facts from philosophical theories, values and interests, see, for example, Durkheim (1982: 159–63).

17 This book will devise the conceptual tool of 'possible' in three senses:

1 *methodologically* as a possibilistic methodology, which approaches the Rwandan case *indirectly* from its socio-historical context, revealing possible causes of the UN's failure in Rwanda;

2 *ontologically* as an investigation of both structural conditions productive of the failure *and* possibilities to transform and improve the UN system (emancipation); and

3 *epistemologically* as an inquiry, informed by an emotional intuition, into the state of mind of those actors who abandoned Rwandans ('How is it possible?').

18 This term is derived from Wheeler (2000).

19 With the term 'supreme humanitarian emergency', Nicholas J. Wheeler refers to extraordinary acts of killing and brutality, such as genocide. See Wheeler (2000: 34).

20 In this regard, this study is less concerned with 'efficient' than with 'permissive' causes. Whilst the former constitute *immediate* causes of the UN's failure, such as motivations, political unwillingness and national (dis)interest, the latter refer to the *background conditions* or *prerequisites* that must be present for the failure to occur. On the distinction between 'permissive' and 'efficient' causes, see Suganami (1996: 14–16). In fact, the research objects of this book could best be termed 'enabling and constraining causes', which have a broader meaning than 'permissive causes': whilst the latter have mainly normative connotations, 'enabling causes' refer more generally to structural causation. This type of causality has been overlooked in the previous literature on the UN's failure in Rwanda. Isaac A. Kamola's recent account introduces this term in investigating the causes of the Rwandan genocide. Drawing upon Louis Althusser's theory, Kamola analyses the way in which the coffee economy, including fluctuations in the price of coffee at global markets, produced the conditions for genocide in Rwanda (Kamola 2007: 571–92). In the same way, this book aspires to explore the structural causes that created the conditions for the UN's failure.

21 'United Nations, Facsimile from the Director of DPKO Hédi Annabi to Linda Melvern.' Extract from the *Linda Melvern Rwanda Genocide Archive*, The Hugh Owen Library, University of Wales, File: UN Secretariat/DPKO Kofi Annan.

22 An interview with Dr Boutros Boutros-Ghali in Paris on 15 April 2005.
23 This expression is derived from one account that represents the individualist and phenomenal type of explanations of the Rwandan drama, namely Power (2001: 84). Nevertheless, Power's account reveals crucial new information on the role of the US foreign administration in the Rwandan case.
24 The German word '*Vorstellung*' ('presentation' or 'performance') used by Marx perfectly encapsulates the logic of abstraction, the prefix '*Vor-*' meaning 'in front of' or 'before' and the term '*Stellung*' meaning 'position'. In other words, abstraction aims to go 'behind the setting' to explore what lies beyond the performances appearing in front of us.
25 At some points, the corroboration was performed in reverse order. As Paul Atkinson and Amanda Coffey point out, even official public records cannot be treated as firm evidence of what they report. See Atkinson and Coffey (1997: 47). For example, the official UN 'blue book' on Rwanda maintains that the information contained in the infamous 'January cable' was conveyed to the Security Council. See Boutros-Ghali (1996: 32). However, in Chapter 6 this claim will be countered by the results of an interview with the Czech Ambassador Karel Kovanda, who was acting President of the Security Council in January 1994.
26 United Nations Assistance Mission in Rwanda.
27 The permanent members of the Security Council. In accordance with Article 27(3) of the UN Charter, any of the permanent members – the US, the UK, Russia, France and China – has the power to veto a draft resolution or decision of the Council. The ten non-permanent members – six until the Charter amendment in 1965 – are elected for two-year periods by the General Assembly. See, for example, Kingsbury and Roberts (1993: 8).

1 Rwanda, the genocide of our time

1 In IR theory 'backward causalities' are discussed and problematised in the debate between David Campbell and Colin Wight. The latter defines backward causalities as retrospectively constituting causes to old changes (Campbell 1999: 321; Wight 1999: 315).
2 Convention on the Prevention and Punishment of the Crime of Genocide, 78 UNTS 277, Jan. 12, 1951, Article 2.
3 In contrast, the intent in the Cambodian killing fields was to eliminate possible *political* opponents, not the Khmer people as an ethnic, religious, national or racial group (Mendlovitz and Fousek 1996: 240).
4 Bhaskar's epistemological relativism states that every scientific account may be fallible. Nevertheless, by invoking *judgemental rationality* he provides a balance to this premise. Judgemental rationality maintains that not just any description or understanding will do, and some descriptions are better than others, because of the nature of particular structures and properties that exist independently of our understanding of them (Sayer 1992: 21).
5 Drawing upon Lemarchand, the term 'political tribalism' will be applied in this chapter, although it is more appropriate to call Hutu and Tutsi 'ethnic groups' rather than 'tribes'.
6 'International Criminal Tribunal for Rwanda, Case No. ICTR-96–7-I, The Prosecutor against Theoneste Bagosora, Amended Indictment'. Extract from the *Linda Melvern Rwanda Genocide Archive*, The Hugh Owen Library, University of Wales, Aberystwyth, File: Theoneste Bagosora, p. 2.
7 The figure is an estimate of Bhavnani and Backer (2000: 286). African Rights and Gérard Prunier estimate that 10,000 Tutsi were slaughtered between December 1963 and January 1964 (African Rights 1995: 12; Prunier 1998: 56).
8 Also the Organization of African Unity had established an observer mission (Neutral

Military Observer Group, NMOG) at the buffer-zone between the RPF-held territory and the rest of Rwanda in July 1992 (Boutros-Ghali 1996: 15).

9 *Linda Melvern Rwanda Genocide Archive*, File: Theoneste Bagosora, p. 37.
10 'Twenty Twenty Television, "United Nations, Rwanda", Interview with Dallaire.' Extract from the *Linda Melvern Rwanda Genocide Archive*, The Hugh Owen Library, University of Wales, Aberystwyth, File: Maj.-Gen. Roméo Dallaire. F.C. UNAMIR, p. 6.
11 Dallaire notes:

> As evidence, with the 450 men under my command during this interim, we saved and directly protected over 25,000 people and moved tens of thousands between the contact lines. What could a force of 5,000 personnel have prevented? Perhaps the most obvious answer is that they would have prevented the massacres in the southern and western parts of the country because they didn't start until early May – nearly a month after the war had started.
>
> (Quoted in Roberts 1995: 56).

12 This term is derived from Melvern (2000).
13 *Report of the United Nations High Commissioner for Human Rights and Follow-up to the World Conference on Human Rights: Situation of Human Rights in the Darfur Region of the Sudan*. UN Doc. E/CN.4/2005/3, 7 May 2004, pp. 15–16.

2 A critical realist approach to conflict management

1 For example, the sub-title of Linda Melvern's first book on the subject, '*Who Betrayed the UN and Why*', portrays the UN as being betrayed (by the great powers) rather than the betrayer (of Rwanda). Hence, the causes of the UN's failure are related to great powers, and the US in particular, rather than to the structural factors of the UN system as a whole. In this regard, the answers are given before the questions are even asked. See Melvern (1995). Melvern's subsequent accounts provide highly sophisticated and meticulous explanations of the Rwandan case.
2 As explained in the introduction, the initial chapters of this book will focus on the examination of *permissive* or structural causes of the Rwandan drama; that is, of the dysfunctions of the UN decision-making and conflict management system in the early 1990s. However, this analysis does not directly reveal the causal *strength* of such causes in relation to the case, i.e. whether they had a slight or major impact on the UN's failure in Rwanda. They will thus be termed 'possible' causes. Chapters 5 and 6 will proceed to interrogate their causal strength, i.e. the extent to which they contributed to the Rwandan tragedy, with the aid of causal weighting and empirical evidence.
3 This inclination is based on methodological individualism and atomistic ontology.
4 On the debate between positivism and post-positivism in IR theory, see, for example, Smith (1995: 1–37).
5 On the relationship between positivism and causal monism, see, for example, Wendt (2003: 494–5).
6 On the distinction between 'Why?' and 'How?' questions suggested by post-positivist approaches, see, for example, Fierke (1998: 5–6); Wendt (1987: 362–3).
7 This term is derived from the annual Cyril Foster lecture delivered by the former Secretary-General Javier Pérez de Cuéllar at Oxford University in 1986, quoted in Goulding (2004: 268).
8 Bhaskar's *Dialectic: The Pulse of Freedom* (1993) marks the third and arguably the latest development of critical realism as a philosophy. It deepens and enlarges the horizon of critical naturalism by showing that reality consists of things not only in the positive sense, i.e. what is present or produced through action, but also in the negative sense, that is, what is absent or produced through inaction, tacit acquiescence, neutrality

or indecision. The consequences of the absence of humanitarian intervention for the Tutsi during the Rwandan genocide dramatically demonstrate the equal importance of action and inaction in conflict management. Moreover, 'absences' may reveal certain essential features of the Western sphere of international politics, in which alternative views are often 'silenced', i.e. tacitly marginalised by defining them as irrational, deviant or mad. As Steve Smith notes, 'Silences are the loudest voices' (1995: 2). Dialectical critical realism has the prospect of giving insight into, if not voice to, those who have been excluded from the Western sphere of rationality. See, for example, Edgley (1998: 395); Patomäki (2002b: 343–65).

9 On the critical realist distinction between the necessary and contingent relations of objects, see, for example, Harré and Madden (1975: 8–26); Sayer (1992: 89).

10 An end product of double movement recalls Max Weber's notion of an 'ideal-type', which is generated by combining simple and one-sided elements into a more complex whole:

> An ideal type is formed by the one-sided *accentuation* of one or more points of view [cf. the first move] and by the synthesis of a great many diffuse, discrete ... *concrete individual* phenomena, which are arranged according to those one-sidedly emphasized viewpoints [cf. the second move].
>
> (Weber 1949: 90)

However, whilst Weber emphasises that an ideal-type is merely a 'synthetic construct' or 'utopia', which 'cannot be found empirically anywhere in reality' (1949: 89–90), from the critical realist perspective, a product of double movement appears as a representation of a *real* possibility belonging to what Bhaskar terms the 'domain of the real', although such a representation is indeed imbued with the researcher's own value judgements and subjective viewpoint.

11 Personal communication with Professor Andrew Sayer on 22 August 2003.

12 This book contends that the above reconceptualisation is not necessarily incommensurable with Bhaskar's presumption of regularities, as a sequence of events is frequently characterised by regularity. That is because the structures of generative mechanisms are usually of *longue durée* in nature, which ensures the continuity of the working of mechanisms. This, in turn, generates the regularity of events.

13 On the other hand, it is acknowledged that retaining Bhaskar's definition of the Humean, Lockean and Leibnizian levels and adding them to the method of double movement as such would serve the purpose of demonstrating that Humean positivism provides only a partial picture of reality: positivism restricts analysis to the domains of the empirical and actual, whereas the method of double movement provides a deeper exploration of the underlying domain of the real and then returns to the domain of the actual in the counterfactual world. Moreover, attaching the above-mentioned three 'big names' to Sayer's method would increase its comprehensibility, although Sayer is correct in stating that, 'They certainly do not give the method authority.' Personal communication with Professor Andrew Sayer on 22 August 2003.

14 The revised method of double movement also contains an ethical dimension, as it strives to bridge the gap between fact and value.

15 Translated by the author from an extract in Susiluoto (2002: 215).

16 The debate on the relationship between the 'part' (e.g. states) and the 'whole' (such as international system) is known by two names in International Relations theory: the so-called 'levels-of-analysis problem' has been debated mainly in American IR theory since the 1950s, whereas the 'agent–structure problem' has been discussed in the European IR tradition since the 1980s (see, for example, Carlsnaes 1992: 277; Singer 1961). However, this book will not examine these wide-ranging debates in any detail, but simply acknowledges, drawing upon Bhaskar's Transformational Model, that the levels of both agents and structures are necessary to explain events in international politics.

17 Emphasis added by author. According to Rule 1 of the (Provisional) Rules of Procedure of the Security Council, the President of the Council can call a meeting of the Council 'at any time he deems necessary', at the request of any member of the Council (Rule 2), following a recommendation of the General Assembly (Rule 3) or following a request by the Secretary-General under Article 99 of the UN Charter. See Provisional Rules of Procedure of the Security Council, as Amended 21 Dec. 1982. UN Doc. S/96/Rev. 7; Bailey and Daws (1998: 24).

18 The figure builds upon the Reflexive Social Cube (RSC) model by illustrating the way in which the scope of actors' decision-making is determined by the surrounding 'belt' of constraining and enabling structures. The RSC is presented in Piiparinen (2006b: 430–5).

19 Both the Secretariat and the UN Charter are considered here to constitute part of the 'structural belt', because the raison d'être of the former is the administration of UN institutions and the safeguarding of the principles established in the Charter. As the former Under-Secretary-General Marrack Goulding notes, 'The political functions entrusted to the Secretary-General [under Articles 99 and 98 of the UN Charter] obliged him to be the guardian of the Charter, independent of all member states and impartial in his dealings with them' (Goulding 2004: 268).

20 For example, a throat (structure) has possessed the causal powers of speech ever since the birth of the human species, but it has taken social learning (mechanism) for those causal powers to produce sophisticated communication systems, a relatively recent development in human history.

21 In critical realist accounts, mechanisms are often understood as processes, while structures are described as more stable, enabling entities (see, for example, Bhaskar 1998b: 170). Sayer also notes that mechanisms are often identified in ordinary language by transitive verbs thereby demonstrating their processual nature (Sayer 2000: 14).

22 The birth of the UN marked the victory of the Allied states, dominated by the West. The Organisation was established in the United Nations Conference in San Francisco on 25 April 1945 by fifty Allied states. The purpose of *their* UN was to maintain the post-war settlement following their victory in the Second World War (Howard 1993: 65). Characteristically of Western hegemony, the term 'United Nations' was coined by the President of the United States Franklin D. Roosevelt in the 'Declaration by United Nations' on 1 January 1942.

23 For a detailed account of the 'Related Powers' model, see Piiparinen (2009).

24 This view has been repeatedly expressed by Secretary-General Boutros Boutros-Ghali, although he attributes the UN's failure in Rwanda mainly to the unwillingness of great powers. At a news conference in New York on 25 May 1994, Boutros-Ghali said that, 'It is a failure not only for the United Nations; it is a failure for the international community. And all of us are responsible for this failure' (quoted in Lewis 1994).

3 UN conflict management of the 1990s

1 On the dependency of social mechanisms on particular socio-historical contexts, see, for example, Elster (1998: 45).

2 The Copenhagen School defines 'securitisation' as a 'means to present an issue as urgent and existential, as so important that it should not be exposed to the normal haggling of politics but should be dealt with decisively by top leaders prior to other issues' (Buzan *et al.* 1998: 29).

3 On the 'renaissance of the Security Council', or what is also described in the literature as the 'emergence of a new Council' in the post-Cold War era, see Wallensteen and Johansson (2004: 17–21).

4 An anthropocentric overtone nevertheless pervades Barnett and Finnemore's account.

The problem here does not constitute putting the cart (actors belonging to bureaucracies) before the horse (state actors), as Barnett and Finnemore do not regard bureaucracies as more powerful agents than states. Instead, they cannot see the wood (mechanisms working through bureaucracies) for the trees (actors belonging to bureaucracies). By emphasising that bureaucracies are 'purposive agents' and 'actors in their own right with independent interests' (Barnett and Finnemore 2004: 705), they fall into an anthropocentric fallacy, downplaying the way in which purposive decisions taken by bureaucrats are determined by bureaucratic procedures and mechanisms. In fact, Barnett and Finnemore's voluntarism is self-defeating, because the crux of Max Weber's theory is that everything, including a bureaucrat's own reason and purpose, is instrumental within a larger bureaucratic machinery.

5 The section states that, 'Preventive diplomacy ... needs early warning based on information gathering and informal or formal fact-finding' (Boutros-Ghali 1992: 13).

6 The hypothesis here posits that early warning mechanisms emerge primarily from the underlying layer of human resources in order to detect conflicts, and that the overload, or dysfunction, of these mechanisms is related to the limitations of human potential in predicting events and in 'covering' the perceived causal complex – in this case, the Rwandan genocide as part of a larger regional conflict system. In other words, the farther and deeper the causes of conflict extend, the more overloaded an early warning mechanism becomes. Gareth Evans also acknowledges this problem and therefore proposes the establishment of six 'regional preventive diplomacy centres' around the world that would be 'staffed by senior professionals expert in dispute resolution, closely familiar with the areas' (Evans 1998: 40).

7 An interview with Professor Klaus Törnudd in Helsinki on 26 June 2003. Törnudd was working as the Permanent Representative of Finland to the United Nations from 1989 to 1990, when Finland was a non-permanent member of the Security Council.

8 On the definition of cognitive dissonance, see Jervis (1976: 382).

9 The arrows representing those mechanisms that emerge from the human stratum are unidirectional. This indicates that brain capacities, Freudian defence mechanisms, cognitive dissonance and other such mechanisms exist and have causal effects independently of actors' conceptualisations and efforts to reproduce them.

10 Boutros Boutros-Ghali, *Supplement to an Agenda for Peace: Position Paper of the Secretary-General on the Occasion of the Fiftieth Anniversary of the United Nations*. Report of the Secretary-General on the Work of the Organization. UN Doc. A/50/60 – S/1995/1, 3 January 1995.

11 As many as 250 UN peacekeepers perished in Bosnia over four years. See Dorn and Matloff (2000: 39).

12 An interview with Professor Klaus Törnudd in Helsinki on 26 June 2002.

13 Impartiality could still be preserved in the new peacekeeping doctrine, because, as Goulding puts it, force would be used 'against armed persons because of what they do, not because of the side they belong to' (Goulding 2002: 17).

14 For example, cognitive dissonance seems to explain the obstinate resistance of Akashi to allow the North Atlantic Treaty Organisation (NATO) to call in air strikes against Serb forces in April 1994 after the latter had failed to comply with the NATO ultimatum to stop the shelling of the safe haven in Goražde. Such resistance had proven prudent in 1993 when Akashi had objected to calls for the UN to take military actions against the Khmer Rouge which had begun an offensive to sabotage the results of the 23 May 1993 elections. See Cohen (1994: 6). Thus, it was not only adherence to the bureaucratic rule of impartiality but also learning from past experiences that seems to have produced Akashi's miscalculation that standing firm to calls for military action was prudent during the crisis of Bosnian safe areas.

15 Michel Foucault's notion seems apposite here: 'We have yet to write the history of that other form of madness, by which men, in an act of sovereign reason, confine their neighbours ... through the merciless language of non-madness' (1989b: xi).

16 An interview with Under-Secretary-General and Special Adviser on Africa, Professor Ibrahim Gambari at UN Headquarters, New York, on 2 December 2003.

17 Social mechanisms, like those generating racial prejudice, exist only by virtue of actors' conceptualisations and efforts to reproduce them, whether intentionally or unintentionally. They are therefore represented by two-directional arrows.

4 Explanatory theories of the UN's failure

1 This chapter will utilise the theoretical framework established in Chapter 2 to criticise the existing literature on Rwanda. Although a critical stance will be taken towards certain elements of Alain Destexhe, Roméo A. Dallaire, Alison L. Des Forges and Linda Melvern's accounts, there is no intention of undermining the pivotal contributions that their descriptions have made towards solving the Rwandan mystery and exposing the perpetrators of the genocide. In addition, Force Commander Dallaire's actions exceed any literary contribution in importance, including this book. Showing enormous courage and self-sacrifice in their attempts to save innocent Rwandans, Dallaire and Destexhe contributed greatly to international efforts to alleviate suffering in Rwanda.

2 For example, Milton Leitenberg argued in 1994 that, 'The major reason for Security Council inaction was the criticism and opposition by the United States' (1994: 7).

3 Ingvar Carlsson *et al.*, *Report of the Independent Inquiry into the Actions of the United Nations during the 1994 Genocide in Rwanda*. UN Doc. S/1999/1257, 15 December 1999, pp. 20–2.

4 This expression derives from Toni Erskine's account (2004), which deems that in some contexts the Security Council can be held responsible both collectively and in terms of individual member states.

5 'Text of the January 11, 1994 Cable', in Adelman and Suhrke (1999: xxii).

6 Carlsson *et al.*, *Report of the Independent Inquiry*. UN Doc. S/1999/1257, 15 December 1999, p. 33.

7 UN Doc. S/1994/565, 13 May 1994.

8 UN Doc. S/1994/470, 20 April 1994.

9 UN Doc. S/1994/518, 29 April 1994.

10 The Joint Evaluation of Emergency Assistance to Rwanda describes the effect of the Somalia experience on UN conflict management in Rwanda as a 'shadow of despair' (Adelman and Suhrke 1996: 70).

11 UN Doc. S/1994/518, 29 April 1994.

12 'Statement on "The Security Council Role in the Rwanda Crisis" by Ambassador Colin Keating, Permanent Representative of New Zealand to the United Nations at Comprehensive Seminar on Lessons Learned from United Nations Assistance Mission for Rwanda (UNAMIR), 12 June 1996, Merill Lynch Conference Centre, Plainsboro, New Jersey.' Extract from the *Linda Melvern Rwanda Genocide Archive*, The Hugh Owen Library, University of Wales, Aberystwyth, File: UN Security Council/Colin Keating, p. 1.

13 This term is derived from Wheeler (2000).

14 Ironically, Boutros-Ghali expressed this view even before he himself uttered the term 'genocide' in the Security Council.

15 UN Doc. S/1994/518, 29 April 1994.

16 UN Doc. S/1994/640, 31 May 1994.

17 'United Nations, Facsimile from the Director of DPKO Hédi Annabi to Linda Melvern.' Extract from the *Linda Melvern Rwanda Genocide Archive*, The Hugh Owen Library, University of Wales, Aberystwyth, File: UN Secretariat/DPKO Kofi Annan.

18 For an extensive and in-depth inquiry into the role of France as a 'bystander' in the Rwandan genocide, see Kroslak (2002).

19 For example, the first in-depth inquiry into the role of the UK in the Rwanda debacle states that, 'During the genocide very little reliable information trickled out of Rwanda to the British High Commission in Kampala. The main source of information thus came through the UN Secretariat and Security Council in New York...' (Melvern and Williams 2004: 17). A paucity of first-hand information had already restricted UK decision-making during the pre-genocide phase; as the UK lacked an embassy in Rwanda, the British High Commissioner in Uganda visited Rwanda merely two or three times per year, while the Permanent Mission of the UK to the UN was not informed of the crucial 'January cable' by the Secretariat (a telephone interview with Lord Hannay on 15 March 2005).

20 Regarding the role of the Secretariat and the Security Council, the IPEP effectively repeats the findings of the so-called Carlsson Inquiry. See IPEP (2000: 99–112).

21 Willum uses only one page to justify his claim that the Secretariat pretended to be surprised, when the genocide struck, because admitting that it had prior information on genocide would have raised criticism against it (1999: 27).

22 Named after its chairman, Ingvar Carlsson, the former Prime Minister of Sweden.

23 Carlsson *et al.*, *Report of the Independent Inquiry*. UN Doc. S/1999/1257, 15 December 1999, p. 30.

24 Carlsson *et al.*, *Report of the Independent Inquiry*. UN Doc. S/1999/1257, 15 December 1999, p. 37.

25 Carlsson *et al.*, *Report of the Independent Inquiry*. UN Doc. S/1999/1257, 15 December 1999, pp. 30–52.

26 Certain supplementary knowledge has been provided subsequent to the Carlsson Inquiry by the International Panel of Eminent Personalities (IPEP), set up by the OAU. The final report of the IPEP was presented in May 2000.

27 The separation between explaining and understanding applied here refers to an outside/inside distinction seen in Heikki Patomäki's critical realist account, which is less restrictive than Hollis and Smith's original conception based on an uncompromising *Erklären/Verstehen* dichotomy. *Contra* Hollis and Smith, Patomäki's emphasis that reasons are also causes intimates that the examination of research objects from an outsider's viewpoint (termed here 'explaining'), such as the description of failures committed by individuals explaining the Rwanda debacle, must be supplemented by a deeper analysis from an (empathic) insider's perspective ('understanding'), such as reflecting on the reasons of individuals to abandon Rwandans by reference to the 'troublemaking' mechanisms which constrained their decision-making. In this regard, the examination of mechanisms requires *both* explaining and understanding, although in Hollis and Smith's conception it would denote only an *explaining*-type of research, like any other causal analysis.

28 The use of the word '*Realpolitik*' here is a means of illustrating the narrowness of the mainstream literature on the Rwandan crisis. David Forsythe, by contrast, expands the notion of international politics from 'realpolitik' (international power politics) and 'partisan politics' (national factional politics) to also include 'humanitarian politics', which in Forsythe's conceptualisation refers to 'the struggle to implement humanitarian values as official policy in the nations of the world' (quoted in Ramsbotham and Woodhouse 1996: 17). By approaching the Rwandan case from the viewpoint of 'realpolitik' and 'partisan politics' of states, the mainstream literature has largely neglected to consider the possibility of 'humanitarian politics' that could have emerged from UN structures and mechanisms and thereby mitigated the genocide. This exclusion of humanitarian politics from explanation has led to a one-sided, and non-emancipatory, examination of the Rwandan case. This book, by contrast, agrees with the 'Grotian' or 'solidarist' doctrine that international society is not only comprised of states with minimum purposes, but also exhibits solidarity or *potential* solidarity among states with respect to the enforcement of international law (see Bull 1966: 52).

5 Early warning

1 An interview with Under-Secretary-General and Special Adviser on Africa, Professor Ibrahim Gambari, at UN Headquarters, New York, on 2 December 2003.

2 Gambari was not alone in making this crucial distinction; his perception of the Rwandan conflict was almost identical to that of other non-permanent members. Ambassador Karel Kovanda, for example, directed attention to the separation even slightly earlier than Gambari. As Kovanda describes, 'I remember people [in the Security Council] arguing for a ceasefire, not realising that a ceasefire would play directly into the hands of the cutthroats. It was in this context that I made this distinction' (personal communication with Ambassador Karel Kovanda on 6 July 2004). However, the *Melvern Archive* demonstrates that 28 April 1994 was a crucial date in the sense that the distinction was applied not only in isolated statements but penetrated the Council's discussion throughout.

3 'Notes on the informal consultations of the Security Council.' Extract from the *Linda Melvern Rwanda Genocide Archive*, The Hugh Owen Library, University of Wales, Aberystwyth, File: Security Council/Informals/April–May 1994, p. 81.

4 *Linda Melvern Rwanda Genocide Archive* (henceforth: *LMRGA*), File: Security Council/Informals/April–May 1994, pp. 87–8.

5 *LMRGA*, File: Security Council/Informals/April–May 1994, p. 82.

6 *LMRGA*, File: Security Council/Informals/April–May 1994, p. 86.

7 An interview with Ambassador Karel Kovanda in London on 27 March 2004. Kovanda made the following statement in the Security Council's meeting on 5 May 1994: 'My delegation … has been shocked by the fact that neither the Security Council nor the Secretariat has so far managed to describe the massacres in Rwanda by the only word that fits them – namely, genocide.' UN Doc. S/PV.3375, 5 May 1994, p. 8.

8 An interview with Ambassador Karel Kovanda in London on 27 March 2004.

9 An interview with Ambassador Karel Kovanda in London on 27 March 2004.

10 This is an English translation provided by Ambassador Kovanda to the author of this book (personal communication with Ambassador Karel Kovanda on 8 July 2004). Kovanda's report to Prague is not published in English, but the original Czech version is presented in Kovanda (2004: 54). The English title of the article is 'The Czech Republic on the UN Security Council: The Rwanda Genocide, 1994'.

11 Personal communication with Ambassador Karel Kovanda on 8 July 2004.

12 An interview with Ambassador Karel Kovanda in London on 27 March 2004. The Czech draft implicitly criticises the Secretariat by noting that, 'The Security Council has considered information available from well-respected NGOs' (*Security Council – 28 April, 1994: A Draft Presidential Statement Presented by the Czech Delegation.* Document presented by Ambassador Karel Kovanda to the Rwanda Forum, Imperial War Museum, London, 27 March 2004). This 'indirect jab' at the Secretariat, however, was ultimately erased in the final version of the Presidential Statement on 30 April 1994. See UN Doc. S/PRST/1994/21, 30 April 1994.

13 *Security Council – 28 April, 1994: A Draft Presidential Statement Presented by the Czech Delegation.*

14 UN Doc. S/PV.3368, 21 April 1994, p. 3.

15 UN Doc. S/PV.3368, 21 April 1994, p. 2. The Nigerian and Czech delegations held similar views on the strengthening of UNAMIR and the Rwandan conflict. As Ambassador Kovanda said, 'Our thinking went along parallel lines' (personal communication with Ambassador Karel Kovanda on 8 July 2004). However, Kovanda was extensively briefed on the Rwandan situation by Human Rights Watch, and therefore he could avoid making such gross understatements of the Rwandan conflict as that made by the Nigerian delegation on 21 April 1994. For example, Kovanda reported to Prague as early as 20 April 1994 that 'According to Human

Rights Watch, some 100 000 people have been murdered [in Rwanda]' (Kovanda 2004: 54).

16 *Security Council – 28 April, 1994: A Draft Presidential Statement Presented by the Czech Delegation.*

17 *Security Council – 28 April, 1994: A Draft Presidential Statement Presented by the Czech Delegation.*

18 Personal communication with Ambassador Karel Kovanda on 6 July 2004.

19 On the intransitive and transitive objects of research, see Bhaskar (1997: 17); Bhaskar and Lawson (1998: 3).

20 A confidential telephone interview with a senior official of the UN Secretariat on 13 November 2003.

21 'Twenty Twenty Television, "United Nations", Interview with Ambassador Colin Keating.' Extract from the *Linda Melvern Rwanda Genocide Archive*, The Hugh Owen Library, University of Wales, Aberystwyth, File: UN Security Council/Colin Keating, pp. 25–6.

22 A confidential telephone interview with a senior official of the UN Secretariat on 13 November 2003; emphasis added by author.

23 According to some accounts, Booh-Booh forfeited DPKO's confidence and ultimately proved unequal to his tasks. See Dallaire (2003: 132); a telephone interview with Lord Hannay on 15 March 2005. One analyst, by contrast, has extensively examined the cable traffic between Booh-Booh and the Secretariat and comes to the conclusion that, despite Booh-Booh's shortcomings, his messages actually conveyed the same substantive information outlining a plot to murder civilians and to undermine the Arusha peace accord as Dallaire's faxes. A confidential interview with a member of the Joint Evaluation of Emergency Assistance to Rwanda (1996) on 26 February 2004.

24 A confidential telephone interview with a senior official of the UN Secretariat on 13 November 2003.

25 For this notion I am indebted to an anonymous reviewer of the book.

26 *LMRGA*, File: Maj.-Gen. Roméo Dallaire, 17 April 1994, Cable, p. 6; emphasis added by author.

27 *LMRGA*, File: Security Council/Informals/April–May 1994, p. 89.

28 On the concept of security complexes, see, for example, Buzan (1983: 106); Buzan *et al.* (1998: 12).

29 Until 1960, Rwanda, Burundi and Zaire were under the same colonial administration of Belgium. On linkages between these countries and their peoples, see, for example, Gachuruzi (1999: 51).

30 UN Doc. S/26757, 16 November 1993.

31 UN Doc. S/26927, 30 December 1993.

32 *LMRGA*, File: Security Council/Informals/April–May 1994, p. 118.

33 *LMRGA*, File: Security Council/Informals/April–May 1994, p. 81.

34 Personal communication with Ambassador Karel Kovanda on 1 April 1994.

35 *LMRGA*, File: Security Council/Informals/April–May 1994, p. 87.

36 Personal communication with Ambassador Karel Kovanda on 1 April 1994.

37 *LMRGA*, File: Security Council/Informals/April–May 1994, p. 131.

38 This term is derived from Adelman and Suhrke (1999).

39 In critical realism, counterfactuals are considered as one form of possibilities, which refer to something that would have happened if certain conditions, which did not in fact happen, had done so (Bhaskar 1986: 31).

40 For a detailed account of the 'black file', see Piiparinen (2006a: 335–9).

41 UN Doc. ST/SGB/2000/10, 15 May 2000, p. 2.

42 Personal communication with Ambassador Karel Kovanda on 9 January 2005. Consider, for example, the following reflection by Gambari on Booh-Booh's role: 'In terms of systemic difficulties or failure, we didn't have on the ground [in Rwanda] a Special Representative of the Secretary-General that was visible, that was influential,

that came to brief the Security Council directly like we now have.' An interview with Under-Secretary-General and Special Adviser on Africa, Professor Ibrahim Gambari, at UN Headquarters, New York, on 2 December 2003.

43 An interview with Lieutenant-General Roméo Dallaire in London on 27 March 2004.

44 An interview with Ambassador Karel Kovanda in London on 27 March 2004.

45 A confidential interview with an official of the Secretariat at UN Headquarters, New York, on 4 December 2003. It should be noted that the interview was made in 2003. Currently, there are two deputy SRSGs for example in the Democratic Republic of Congo.

46 This term is derived from the statement by Gregory Alex, who was working as the head of the emergencies unit of UNDP in Rwanda during the genocide (Frontline 1999a: 16).

47 An interview with Under-Secretary-General and Special Adviser on Africa, Professor Ibrahim Gambari, at UN Headquarters, New York, on 2 December 2003.

48 This team may include the Under-Secretary-General, the Assistant Secretary-General from the Office of Operations or from the Office of Mission Support, supplemented by a regional director, such as the Director of the African Division, the Military Adviser and the Civilian Police Adviser.

49 An interview with Special Assistant to the Military Adviser of the Secretary-General, Lieutenant-Colonel Ben Klappe, at UN Headquarters, New York, on 1 December 2003.

50 This hypothesis was presented by one participant in the seminar on the response of the UN to widespread and serious human rights violations held in London on 10 November 2004. The seminar was organised by the David Davies Memorial Institute of the University of Wales, Aberystwyth.

51 Personal communication with Special Assistant to the Military Adviser of the Secretary-General, Lieutenant-Colonel Ben Klappe, on 3 December 2003.

52 Yet, the lack of resources in DPKO is striking when considered alongside the fact that the corresponding number of military officers at the headquarters level in any UN member state would be considerably higher, if that institution would be responsible for over 100,000 soldiers on the ground, which is the current number of UN blue helmets.

53 An interview with Special Assistant to the Military Adviser of the Secretary-General, Lieutenant-Colonel Ben Klappe, at UN Headquarters, New York, on 1 December 2003.

54 An interview with Dr Boutros Boutros-Ghali in Paris on 15 April 2005.

55 This interviewee had also convened a working group in the UN on the implementation of the recommendations contained in the *Agenda*.

56 A confidential interview with a senior official of the Secretariat at UN Headquarters, New York, on 3 December 2003.

57 UN Doc. S/PRST/1999/34, 30 November 1999.

58 UN Doc. A/55/985-S/2001/574, 7 June 2001.

59 UN Doc. A/RES/57/337, 3 July 2003.

60 UN Doc. Press Release GA/10145, 3 July 2003.

61 For this notion I am indebted to an anonymous reviewer of the book.

62 An interview with Dr Boutros Boutros-Ghali in Paris on 15 April 2005. Boutros-Ghali proceeded to illustrate this point by reference to the drafting of his memoir which he constructed by the initial separation of each major conflict he dealt with into individual chapters. 'The editor told me this is not good,' Boutros-Ghali described, 'because what is important to show is ... that during the same period we were involved in four or five other operations.' The book was edited accordingly. In the case in question here, the chapter concerning Rwanda also includes passages on Bosnia, Haiti and (perhaps insinuating) Boutros-Ghali's discussions with President Clinton regarding the appointment of US nationals to senior UN positions, which

intertwined and clashed with their talks about the possibility of a US airlift of UN troops to Rwanda. See Boutros-Ghali (1999: 137).

6 Bureaucratic mechanisms

1 An interview with Ambassador Karel Kovanda in London on 27 March 2004.
2 The role of two other dysfunctions in the pre-genocide phase, namely bureaucratic universalism and the irrationality of bureaucratic categorisation, are extensively ana-lysed in previous accounts by the author. On 'bureaucratic universalism', see Pii-parinen (2007c: 355–78). On the 'irrationality of bureaucratic categorisation', see Piiparinen (2008: 697–724).
3 A confidential interview with a senior official of the Secretariat at UN Headquarters, New York, on 3 December 2003.
4 A confidential telephone interview with a senior official of the UN Secretariat on 13 November 2003.
5 In this regard, the interviewed UN official specified that bringing the January cable to the attention of the Security Council was not risky as such. The interviewee pointed out that the first step was to ask the Special Representative of the Secretary-General to deal directly with the Rwandan government in Kigali as well as the ambassadors of those countries that were involved, i.e. the US, France and Belgium (personal com-munication with a senior official of the UN Secretariat on 20 July 2004). However, the expression 'bringing the January cable to the Security Council' in this book refers to the powers of the Secretary-General to invoke his right to bring a potential conflict to the attention of the Security Council under Article 99 of the UN Charter, whereas the interviewee used this expression conversely, to refer to communication between the Secretary-General and permanent members of the Council. In the latter meaning, this book concurs with the interviewee that bringing Dallaire's fax to members of the Council did not involve a risk, as the Secretary-General functioned as merely a mes-senger to these states. However, on the former understanding such an act would have been deemed an early warning signal under Article 99, which would have put the credibility of the Secretariat at stake unless there was overwhelming evidence that genocide was about to occur.
6 UN Doc. S/RES/814 (1993), 26 March 1993.
7 A confidential interview with a senior official of the Secretariat at UN Headquarters, New York, on 3 December 2003.
8 China used this argument to justify its absence from a briefing by the High Represent-ative on National Minorities of the OSCE (Organisation for Security and Co-operation in Europe), Max van der Stoel. China described the High Representative's briefing to the members of the Council as 'inappropriate', because it concerned human rights. 'Notes on the informal consultations of the Security Council.' Extract from the *Linda Melvern Rwanda Genocide Archive*, The Hugh Owen Library, University of Wales, Aberystwyth, File: Security Council/Informals/April–May 94, p. 126.
9 Report by the Special Rapporteur on extrajudicial, summary or arbitrary executions in his mission to Rwanda, 8–17 April 1993. E/CN.4/1994/7/Add.1, 11 August 1993, Section 5, Paragraph 11.
10 Personal communication with Ambassador Karel Kovanda on 8 July 2004.
11 UN Doc. S/RES/794 (1992), 3 December 1992.
12 UN Doc. S/RES/688 (1991), 5 April 1991.
13 Dallaire has since said that he would have insisted on a larger peacekeeping force in Rwanda, if he had known about the human rights report (see Melvern 2004: 65).
14 An interview with Ambassador Karel Kovanda in London on 27 March 2004.
15 An interview with Major-General Henry K. Anyidoho in London on 27 March 2004; emphasis added by author.
16 An interview with Lieutenant-General Roméo Dallaire in London on 27 March 2004.

17 The identity of the Secretariat representative is not disclosed in this context, as the statement does not necessarily represent his/her personal opinion but the Secretariat's overall policy at the time.

18 *Linda Melvern Rwanda Genocide Archive* (henceforth: *LMRGA*), File: Security Council/Informals/April–May 1994, p. 87.

19 An interview with Special Assistant to the Military Adviser of the Secretary-General, Lieutenant-Colonel Ben Klappe, at UN Headquarters, New York, on 1 December 2003.

20 The identity of the Secretariat representative is not disclosed in this context and is replaced with the term 'Secretariat' for reasons mentioned in Note 17 above.

21 A telephone interview with Lord Hannay on 15 March 2005.

22 This term is taken in modified form from Nicholas J. Wheeler's concept 'supreme humanitarian emergency' in Wheeler (2000: 34).

23 An interview with Major Stefan Stec in London on 27 March 2004.

24 An interview with Major Stefan Stec in London on 27 March 2004.

25 *LMRGA*, File: Security Council/Informals/April–May 1994, p. 120.

26 *LMRGA*, File: Security Council/Informals/April–May 1994, p. 99.

27 Personal communication with Ambassador Karel Kovanda on 1 April 2004.

28 *LMRGA*, File: Security Council/Informals/April–May 1994, p. 131.

29 *LMRGA*, File: Security Council/Informals/April–May 1994, p. 132.

30 *LMRGA*, File: Security Council/Informals/April–May 1994, p. 132.

31 *LMRGA*, File: Security Council/Informals/April–May 1994, p. 133.

32 *LMRGA*, File: Security Council/Informals/April–May 1994, p. 134.

33 *LMRGA*, File: Security Council/Informals/April–May 1994, p. 152.

34 An interview with Lieutenant-General Roméo Dallaire in London on 27 March 2004.

35 An interview with Ambassador Karel Kovanda in London on 27 March 2004.

36 UN Doc. S/1994/470, 20 April 1994, p. 3.

37 UN Doc. S/1994/470, 20 April 1994, p. 3.

38 'UNAMIR, Outgoing Cable from Roméo Dallaire, UNAMIR, Kigali to Maurice Baril, United Nations, New York on 17 April 1994. Subject: The Military Assessment of the Situation as of April 1994.' Extract from the *Linda Melvern Rwanda Genocide Archive*, The Hugh Owen Library, University of Wales, Aberystwyth, File: Maj.-Gen. Roméo Dallaire. F.C. UNAMIR, p. 10.

39 An interview with Lieutenant-General Roméo Dallaire in London on 27 March 2004. The Deputy Force Commander of UNAMIR, Major-General Henry K. Anyidoho expressed a slightly divergent opinion: 'Personally I think that if we had got Chapter VII mandate, more robust mandate, that would have been better.' An interview with Major-General Henry K. Anyidoho in London on 27 March 2004.

40 *LMRGA*, File: Maj.-Gen. Roméo Dallaire, 17 April 1994, Cable, p. 10.

41 An interview with Major Stefan Stec in London on 27 March 2004.

42 The latter refer to the unpaid assessments of member states (first and foremost those of the US), which amounted to almost a billion dollars in peacekeeping.

43 An interview with Dr Boutros Boutros-Ghali in Paris on 15 April 2005; emphasis added by author.

44 The Czech Ambassador Karel Kovanda noted on the subject of the Secretariat's options:

> It was the second set of three alternatives [on 20 April 1994] where the substantial increase of UNAMIR was for the first time even discussed. Recently somebody asked me: 'Where did this proposal come from to increase the troops as the third alternative?' I don't know. In fact, I don't know it to this day.
>
> (An interview with Ambassador Karel Kovanda in London on 27 March 2004)

45 A telephone interview with Lord Hannay on 15 March 2005.

46 *LMRGA*, File: Security Council/Informals/April–May 1994, p. 121.

47 *LMRGA*, File: Security Council/Informals/April–May 1994, p. 121.
48 An interview with Major Stefan Stec in London on 27 March 2004.
49 In addition to bureaucratic categorisation and bureaucratic universalism, the interview with Boutros-Ghali indicated that the objection to the change in UNAMIR's mandate from peacekeeping to peace-enforcement might also have been underpinned by a third factor, namely *Zweckrationalität*, in which the avoidance of peace-enforcement was calculated to serve a greater bureaucratic objective, namely to appease troop-contributing countries in order to ensure the retention of their troops in UNAMIR:

> They [DPKO officials] would never ask General Dallaire to use enforcement. Just to give you an idea of the sensibility of this problem: to obtain the troops, you have to negotiate with the [troop-contributing] governments. And they will ask you: 'What will they [peacekeepers] do?' You say: 'They will only do peacekeeping, there's no danger for them, because they are not involved in peace-enforcement.' So you cannot change the mandate after you have received it. Why? Because if you do, immediately the country will say, 'I withdraw my troops', which happened with the Belgians in Rwanda.
> (An interview with Dr Boutros Boutros-Ghali in Paris on 15 April 2005)

However, Boutros-Ghali's statement should be assessed with caution, as it contradicts the real policy pursued by two main contributors to UNAMIR, namely Belgium and Ghana. *Contra* Boutros-Ghali's logic, the Belgian Foreign Minister Willy Claes did ask Boutros-Ghali for the reinforcement of UNAMIR's mandate to allow for enforcement action prior to Belgium's decision to withdraw its troops (Melvern 2000: 139), whilst the commander of the Ghanaian UNAMIR contingent similarly preferred a Chapter VII mandate (an interview with Major-General Henry K. Anyidoho in London on 27 March 2004). Hence, Boutros-Ghali's statement should be considered more as his personal misjudgement about the policy of troop-contributing countries or as an effort to defend his DPKO colleagues in retrospect, than as the epitome of instrumental rationality in the UN bureaucracy as a whole.
50 This description refers to 'blue helmets', that is, UN soldiers. See Goulding (1993: 459).
51 On the emergence of areas designated as 'safe havens' or 'safe humanitarian zones' in international politics in the early 1990s, see Yamashita (2004).
52 A confidential telephone interview with a senior official of the UN Secretariat on 13 November 2003.
53 The next section will demonstrate that the UN peacekeeping system has been reformed to allow not only impartial measures based on the consent of the parties of a peace agreement but also more robust peacekeeping.
54 *LMRGA*, File: Security Council/Informals/April–May 1994, p. 97.
55 *LMRGA*, File: Security Council/Informals/April–May 1994, p. 97.
56 An additional psychological factor deserving of attention in the UN's failure in Rwanda is groupthink, which is extensively investigated in Piiparinen (2006b: 443–5).
57 However, it should not be fatalistically concluded that psychological defects are doomed to occur, for these can be held in check through self-reflectivity. Irving Janis, for example, explores the ways in which groupthink can be avoided. It is perhaps telling, however, that all of his prescriptions for the prevention of groupthink use the verb 'should', not 'could' (1972: 207–24). This book, by contrast, prefers the latter formulation, as it aims to explore possible ways to *transform* the UN structure rather than to prescribe how actors should behave. In other words, its focus is more on social structures than on psychological factors, because the former can be transformed more flexibly than the latter.
58 An interview with Special Assistant to the Military Adviser of the Secretary-General, Lieutenant-Colonel Ben Klappe, at UN Headquarters, New York, on 1 December

2003. This development has also been noted by the recent assessment of the follow-up of recommendations suggested by the Joint Evaluation of Emergency Assistance to Rwanda (see Borton and Eriksson 2004).

59 A confidential interview with an official of the Secretariat at UN Headquarters, New York, on 4 December 2003.

60 A confidential interview with an official of the Secretariat at UN Headquarters, New York, on 4 December 2003.

61 The report dates back to March 2000, when Secretary-General Kofi Annan asked the Algerian Ambassador Lakhdar Brahimi to give recommendations on strengthening the UN peacekeeping system. Drawing upon lessons learned from the UN's failures in Bosnia, Somalia and Rwanda, the report recommends more robust mandates and rules of engagement for UN peacekeeping missions. See *Report of the Panel on United Nations Peace Operations*. UN Doc. A/55/305-S/2000/809, 21 August 2000, p. 10.

62 *United Nations Rules of Engagement: To Shoot or to Hold Your Fire, Use of Force from a Commander's Perspective*, p. 4. Confidential source.

63 Personal communication with Military Adviser to the International Peace Academy, Colonel Jussi Saressalo, on 1 September 2004; Samuels (2004: 5).

64 International Peace Academy and the United Nations, *Challenges in Peacekeeping: Past, Present and Future*. Seminar Report, UN Millennium Plaza Hotel, New York, 29 October 2002, p. 2.

65 A confidential interview with an official of the Secretariat at UN Headquarters, New York, on 4 December 2003.

66 An interview with Special Assistant to the Military Adviser of the Secretary-General, Lieutenant-Colonel Ben Klappe at UN Headquarters, New York, on 1 December 2003.

67 An interview with Lieutenant-General Roméo Dallaire in London on 27 March 2004.

68 See *Report of the Panel on United Nations Peace Operations*. UN Doc. A/55/305-S/2000/809, 21 August 2000, pp. 10–12.

69 An interview with Special Assistant to the Military Adviser of the Secretary-General, Lieutenant-Colonel Ben Klappe, at UN Headquarters, New York, on 1 December 2003.

70 Further disconcerting aspects of Western normalisation that seem pertinent to the Rwandan case, namely the pursuit of greater missions under the guise of Western interventions and the blaming of the 'Other' for self-inflicted failures as a consequence of Western moral self-disillusionment, are analysed in Piiparinen (2007c: 368–72).

71 On the way in which the international media constructed the popular image of the Rwandan conflict as 'unimaginable anarchy' and 'ethnic violence', see, for example, Lorch (1994: 12); Pottier (2002: 53–108); Wharton (1994: 21).

72 'Daily Press Briefing of Office of Spokesman for Secretary-General, 7 April 1994.' Extract from the *Linda Melvern Rwanda Genocide Archive*, The Hugh Owen Library, University of Wales, Aberystwyth, File: UNAMIR, p. 2.

73 'Daily Press Briefing of Office of Spokesman for Secretary-General, 12 April 1994.' Extract from the *Linda Melvern Rwanda Genocide Archive*, The Hugh Owen Library, University of Wales, Aberystwyth, File: UNAMIR.

74 One offspring of Critical Theory, the Welsh School based at the University of Wales, Aberystwyth, contends that the primary objective of security studies is the re-evaluation of what counts as security. The Welsh School views the reconceptualisation and replacement of the current referent object of security, 'states', with 'individuals' as an emancipatory project, which leads security studies away from the dominant and oppressive position of neo-realism based on state-centrism towards more human-centred conception of security (see, for example, Booth 1991: 340–2).

75 Boutros-Ghali's comment perfectly captures the argument advanced here that the statist paradigm is not merely a policy pursued by individual states but a more widespread embodiment of certain *deep structures* of Western societies, namely a culture that prioritises short-term public opinion and the long-term popular imagination (of the colonial past) over other motives:

> Governments cannot take responsibility to have their soldiers killed somewhere in Africa, because public opinion will never accept this. It needs a certain [alternative] culture to send my son to be killed somewhere in Angola, when our public doesn't even know where Angola is. Thus, it was easier to obtain troops from countries which had former colonies, Italians in Somalia and Portuguese in Angola, because the public still remembers the period of empire.
>   (An interview with Dr Boutros Boutros-Ghali in Paris on 15 April 2005)

Boutros-Ghali's statement reveals that the statist paradigm aggravated the Secretariat's *prejudice* against its possibilities of obtaining support for the option of a strengthened UNAMIR following the killing of ten Belgian soldiers, which partly explains why such an option was never realistically presented to states. In addition, the statist paradigm underlay the Secretariat's somewhat ill-advised and perilous decision to form UNAMIR's backbone from Belgian troops: the Belgian contingent came to be portrayed by Hutu extremists as a reincarnation of Belgium's colonial power. As a result, the whole UNAMIR mission faced severe resentment from the Hutu, which ultimately jeopardised UNAMIR's operations.

76 *LMRGA*, File: Security Council/Informals/April–May 1994, p. 137.
77 However, Nigeria specified that the Security Council should not only concern itself with the safety of UN troops and the lives of foreign expatriates, but must also safeguard the Rwandan civilians under its protection. *LMRGA*, File: Security Council/Informals/April–May 1994, p. 117.
78 *LMRGA*, File: Security Council/Informals/April–May 94, p. 87.
79 An interview with Under-Secretary-General and Special Adviser on Africa, Professor Ibrahim Gambari, at UN Headquarters, New York, on 2 December 2003; emphasis added by author.
80 The French task force was gradually building its strength up to 900 troops in total.
81 *LMRGA*, File: Security Council/Informals/April–May 1994, p. 71.
82 *LMRGA*, File: Security Council/Informals/April–May 1994, p. 73.
83 *LMRGA*, File: Security Council/Informals/April–May 1994, p. 79.
84 An interview with Ambassador Karel Kovanda in London on 27 March 2004.
85 Empirical evidence indicates that overcoming such bureaucratic barriers was not impossible. For example, the mandate of UNAMSIL underwent a rapid change from a traditional observer mission to a Chapter VII operation. A confidential interview with an official of the Secretariat at UN Headquarters, New York, on 4 December 2003.

7 Future visions of conflict management

1 For a more detailed account of the League of Democracies, see, for example, Carothers (2008).
2 *Resolution 1590 (2005) Adopted by the Security Council at its 5151st Meeting, on 24 March 2005.* UN Doc. S/RES/1590 (2005), 24 March 2005, pp. 4–5.
3 *In Larger Freedom: Towards Development, Security and Human Rights for All.* Report of the Secretary-General. UN Doc. A/59/2005, 21 March 2005, p. 52.
4 This term is derived from Ignatieff (1998: 289).
5 UN Doc. S/RES/1590 (2005), 24 March 2005, p. 6.
6 UN Doc. S/RES/1590 (2005), 24 March 2005, p. 6.
7 With the term 'supreme humanitarian emergency', Nicholas J. Wheeler (2000: 34) refers to extraordinary acts of killing and brutality, such as genocide.

8 For a detailed account of the synchronisation of control mechanisms, see Piiparinen (2007d: 81–4).

9 Gareth Evans, one of the most prominent experts on the subject, has on several occasions described RtoP as a norm. See, for example, Evans (2007; 2008b: 293).

10 Paragraphs 138 and 139 of the 2005 UN Summit Outcome, which established RtoP, define these four crimes: '[W]e are prepared to take collective action ... should peaceful means be inadequate and national authorities are manifestly failing to protect their populations from genocide, war crimes, ethnic cleansing and crimes against humanity.' UN Doc. A/RES/60/1, 24 October 2005, p. 30.

11 *Implementing the Responsibility to Protect: Report of the Secretary-General.* UN Doc. A/63/677, 12 January 2009, p. 28.

12 *Implementing the Responsibility to Protect: The Role of Regional and Sub-regional Partners.* Report on Wilton Park Conference 922, 11–13 July 2008, p. 1.

13 UN Doc. Press Release SG/SM/9197, AFR/893, HR/CN/1077, 7 April 2004.

14 The term 'securitisation' is defined by the Copenhagen School as a 'means to present an issue as urgent and existential, as so important that it should not be exposed to the normal haggling of politics but should be dealt with decisively by top leaders prior to other issues' (Buzan *et al.* 1998: 29).

15 See, for example, Global Centre for the Responsibility to Protect (2008: 4). Gareth Evans has also on several occasions hailed conflict prevention in Burundi and the political settlement in Kenya achieved by the mediation team led by Annan as victories for RtoP (Evans 2008b: 287–91).

16 Personal communication with Dr Mika Aaltola on 19 December 2008.

17 In International Relations theory, an 'epistemic community' is defined as a network of like-minded and impartial professionals that possesses recognised expertise and controls 'international problems', such as nuclear armament, ozone depletion, or, indeed, genocide threat (Adler and Haas 1992: 371; Haas 1992: 2–3).

18 An interview with Dr Boutros Boutros-Ghali in Paris on 15 April 2005.

19 On servo-mechanisms in decision-making, see Piiparinen (2006b: 431–2).

20 On the definition of 'mechanism' in critical realism, see Wight (2004: 288).

21 United Nations, Department of Public Information, *Secretary-General Defends, Clarifies 'Responsibility to Protect' at Berlin Event on 'Responsible Sovereignty: International Cooperation for a Changed World'*, UN Doc. Press Release SG/SM/11701, 15 July 2008.

22 UN Doc. Press Release SG/SM/11701, 15 July 2008. The speech was mainly written by the Secretary-General's Special Advisor on RtoP Edward Luck.

23 Therefore, Edward Luck prudently decided to consult closely not only the so-called 'Friends of RtoP' group in New York but also NAM and AU (African Union) countries, particularly Egypt and Jamaica, in the run-up to the finalisation of the Secretary-General's report on RtoP published in January 2009.

24 The exact figure presented in the first PBF Consolidated Annual Progress Report is 38 per cent. The report analyses the implementation of the 26 PBF projects approved for funding during 2007, the first year of operations of the PBF. UNDP Multi-Donor Trust Fund Office, *First Consolidated Annual Progress Report on Activities Implemented under the Peacebuilding Fund (PBF).* Report of the Administrative Agent of the Peacebuilding Fund for the Period 1 January to 31 December 2007, 16 June 2008, p. iv.

25 Personal communication with Dan Smith on 4 November 2008.

26 Personal communication with Dan Smith on 4 November 2008.

27 The potential of the PBF to address the root causes of violence was seen as one of its key functions and benefits in the third Advisory Group meeting of the PBF.

28 UN Doc. Press Release SG/SM/11701, 15 July 2008.

29 The forthcoming book of this author will study in more detail those deep structures upon which the international politics of the post-Cold War era is based. It will be argued that current world politics is characterised by new interventionism emanating

from four deep structures, namely the logic of anarchy, humanitarianism, pursuit of greater missions and ontological security.

30 The conclusions of the MGI (Managing Global Insecurity) project conducted in the Center on International Cooperation at the New York University advocate this wider conception of security implied in 'responsible sovereignty'. The statement by Kishore Mahbubani, the former Permanent Representative of Singapore to the UN and MGI Advisory Group Member, implies that 'responsible sovereignty' concerns the *outside* dimension of the actions of states, while RtoP mainly regards the *insider* account of the way in which states treat their populations:

> Responsible sovereignty – the idea that states must take responsibility for external effects of their actions – is a brilliant new idea whose time has come. No village can accept a home whose actions endanger the village. Neither can the global village accept the behavior of nations which endanger the globe.
>
> (Quoted in *A Plan for Action: A New Era of International Cooperation for a Changed World: 2009, 2010, and Beyond*. Report by Managing Global Insecurity, September 2008, p. 11)

31 DLA Piper US LLP and US Committee for Human Rights in North Korea, *Failure to Protect: A Call for the UN Security Council to Act in North Korea*. Report commissioned by the Honourable Václav Havel, Former President of the Czech Republic, the Honourable Kjell Magne Bondevik, Former Prime Minister of Norway, Professor Elie Wiesel, Boston University, 30 October 2006, p. ii.

32 The Nobel Peace Laureate of year 2008, President Martti Ahtisaari, pointed to this untapped potential in his Nobel speech:

> It is our task to create a future and hope for regions and countries in crisis where young people suffer from unemployment and have little prospects of improving their lives. Unless we can meet this challenge, new conflicts will flare up and we will lose another generation to war.
>
> (The Crisis Management Initiative 2008)

33 Yrjö Uurtimo and Tarja Väyrynen characterise the African Great Lakes region as the 'conflict system', in which 'it is difficult to distinguish between inter- and intra-state conflicts' (2000: 15).

34 For this notion I am indebted to Under-Secretary of State Marjatta Rasi, for whom I worked as a desk officer on the PBC and PBF in the Ministry for Foreign Affairs of Finland.

35 For a detailed account of 'greater missions' in Western interventions, see Piiparinen (2007c: 368–70).

36 Personal communication with Ambassador Frank Majoor on 29 December 2008.

37 A similar argument is made by Richard Gowan in terms of UN peacekeeping. Gowan convincingly argues that the UN currently faces a systemic and paradigmatic crisis in peacekeeping, because of which 'it may be able to achieve more limited but politically credible goals' (2008: 453).

38 Boutros Boutros-Ghali, *Supplement to an Agenda for Peace: Position Paper of the Secretary-General on the Occasion of the Fiftieth Anniversary of the United Nations*. Report of the Secretary-General on the Work of the Organization. UN Doc. A/50/60 – S/1995/1, 3 January 1995.

39 This argument reflects the author's personal assessment.

40 Secretary-General Ban addresses the problem of the UN's illusory invisibility in his article published in the International Herald Tribune, in which he notes that, 'The real UN, almost invisible to the general public, is the action-oriented UN. This real UN feeds 90 million people in more than 70 countries ... and vaccinates 40 percent of the world's children' (Ki-Moon 2008).

41 The formulation of the name of this team reflects one form of instrumental rationality

of bureaucracies: the UN aims to downplay or avoid any assertive tone in its terminology by branding, for example, early warning signals as 'assessment reports', which, however, de facto serve exactly the same function as 'intelligence reports'. In line with *Zweckrationalität*, that formulation is calculated to be politically more palatable for NAM countries which remain suspicious of any attempt by the UN to gather intelligence of their internal affairs.

42 However, the team is composed of only twelve military officials, which again reflects the chronic lack of resources at the UN Secretariat.

43 The establishment of EISAS could respond to the need to centralise the collection and analysis of early warning information at UN Headquarters, but this innovation has been stalled. On EISAS, see *Report of the Panel on United Nations Peace Operations*. UN Doc. A/55/305-S/2000/809, 21 August 2000, p. 12. However, the development of UN intelligence has been justified by separating intelligence as rationalised decision-support from espionage. As one peacekeeping expert observed in 2004, 'It is not a taboo anymore to mention the UN and intelligence in one sentence. Two years ago it was impossible'(personal communication with Military Adviser to the International Peace Academy, Colonel Jussi Saressalo on 1 September 2004).

44 The argument here concerns overall political and strategic guidance that could be provided to the EU by the UN, not the chain of command. Orders to EU operations are given by the Peace and Security Council of the EU.

45 This constraint is not only economic, deriving from the political responsibility of decision-makers so save tax-payers' money, but also a moral one, deriving from the accountability of decision-makers to those who voted them in the first place (see, for example, Piiparinen 2007b: 375).

46 This term is derived from De Coning (2006: 35).

47 *Implementing the Responsibility to Protect: Report of the Secretary-General.* UN Doc. A/63/677, 12 January 2009, p. 10.

48 The term 'determinism' is not applied here, as it would imply absolute certainty that actors will follow the 'golden path'. Instead, the formulation 'degree of determinism' refers to inclination of actors to follow that path. As demonstrated in Chapter 2, the critical realist idea of open systems opposes determinism by pointing to the omnipresent possibility of surprise in every turn of international politics. For example, Chapter 6 showed the way in which organisational learning, designed to guide decision-makers with the help of lessons derived from past experiences, actually misled UN officials by generating deceptive images of the Rwandan conflict coloured by fresh memories of Somalia.

Conclusion

1 Aristotle's argument calls to mind the method of double movement applied here: 'Clearly, then, discovery takes place by the bringing of the things that are in potentiality to actuality …. It follows that it is from the actuality that the potentiality is recognized…' (*Metaphysics*, Book Theta, Ch-9, 1051a). This Aristotelian logic underlies Bhaskar's model of scientific discovery and Sayer's method of double movement, in which the surface level of observations and events is considered as the starting point of abstraction, through which generative mechanisms can be explored.

2 The events in Rwanda and Darfur, however, should be considered more as *indicators* than mirror images of the UN's conflict management capacity.

3 This is an English translation provided by Ambassador Kovanda to the author of this book. Personal communication with Ambassador Karel Kovanda on 8 July 2004.

4 This type of mission would have been composed of UNAMIR soldiers already present in Rwanda ('anvil') and part of the 1,500 evacuation troops ('hammer') (Piiparinen 2007e: 56–62).

5 Whilst the existing literature tends to attribute the UN's failure to an *absence* of polit-

ical will, this book contends that it was also the *presence* of troublemaking mechanisms that obstructed the Council's decision-making. And, to stand this argument on its head, the emancipatory possibilities lay not only in *augmenting* political will, but also in *absenting* (eliminating) the troublemaking mechanisms via a transformation of the UN system.

6 This term is derived from Wheeler (2000).

7 An interview with Dr Boutros Boutros-Ghali in Paris on 15 April 2005.

8 A joint undertaking by the Carnegie Commission on Preventing Deadly Conflict, the Institute for the Study of Diplomacy at Georgetown University, and the US Army came to the conclusion that, 'A modern force of 5,000 troops, drawn primarily from one country [the US] and sent to Rwanda sometime between April 7 and 21, 1994, could have significantly altered the outcome of the conflict' (Feil 1998: 4).

9 Furthermore, it seems reasonable to place an element of blame for the UN's failure in Rwanda with those state representatives who signalled their political will to implement the *Agenda* but subsequently withdrew their support at critical moments. For example, Phyllis Bennis reveals that all of those twenty-three states which agreed to cooperate with Boutros-Ghali's SEPT (Standby Elements Planning Team) and to participate in the rapid deployment forces envisaged in the *Agenda* subsequently failed to send their troops to Rwanda in 1994 (Bennis 2000).

10 Their analysis does, however, include certain insights into the structural capacity of the UN to prevent genocides; for example the recently instituted Secretary-General's Special Advisor on the Prevention of Genocide.

11 UN Doc. SG/SM/9197, AFR/893, HR/CN/1077, 7 April 2004. United Nations, Press Release.

12 The other two cases concern the situations in Uganda and the Democratic Republic of Congo.

13 An interview with Dr Boutros Boutros-Ghali in Paris on 15 April 2005; emphasis added by author.

Bibliography

Adekanye, J.B. (1999) 'Conflict Prevention and Early Warning Systems', in S. Gibson, S. Klasen, E. Rothschild and L. Wohlgemuth (eds) *Common Security and Civil Society in Africa*, pp. 103–17, Uppsala: Nordiska Afrikainstitutet.

Adelman, H. (1998a) 'Difficulties in Early Warning: Networking and Conflict Management', in K. van Walraven (ed.) *Early Warning and Conflict Prevention: Limitations and Possibilities*, pp. 51–82, The Hague: Kluwer Law International.

Adelman, H. (1998b) 'Humanitarian and Conflict-oriented Early Warning: A Historical Background Sketch', in K. van Walraven (ed.) *Early Warning and Conflict Prevention: Limitations and Possibilities*, pp. 45–50, The Hague: Kluwer Law International.

Adelman, H. and Suhrke, A. (2004) 'The Security Council and the Rwanda Genocide', in D. Malone (ed.) *The UN Security Council in the Post-Cold War Era*, pp. 483–99, Boulder: Lynne Rienner.

Adelman, H. and Suhrke, A. (1999) 'Preface', in H. Adelman and A. Suhrke (eds) *The Path of a Genocide: The Rwanda Crisis from Uganda to Zaire*, pp. ix–xix, New Brunswick: Transaction Publishers.

Adelman, H. and Suhrke, A. (1996) *The International Response to Conflict and Genocide: Lessons from the Rwanda Experience. Study 2: Early Warning and Conflict Management*, Copenhagen: Steering Committee of the Joint Evaluation of Emergency Assistance to Rwanda.

Adler, E. and Haas, P.M. (1992) 'Conclusion: Epistemic Communities, World Order, and the Creation of a Reflective Research Programme', *International Organization*, 1, 46: 367–90.

African Rights (1995) *Rwanda: Death, Despair and Defiance*, 2nd edn, London: African Rights.

Annan, K. (1999) *Towards a Culture of Prevention: Statements by the Secretary-General of the United Nations*, New York: Carnegie Commission on Preventing Deadly Conflict.

Aristotle (1998) *Metaphysics*, London: Penguin.

Ashdown, P. (2007) *Swords and Ploughshares: Bringing Peace to the 21st Century*, London: Phoenix.

Atkinson, P. and Coffey, A. (1997) 'Analysing Documentary Realities', in D. Silverman (ed.) *Qualitative Research: Theory, Method and Practice*, pp. 45–62, London: Sage.

Bailey, S.D. and Daws, S. (1998) *The Procedure of the UN Security Council*, 3rd edn, Oxford: Clarendon Press.

Barnett, M. (2003) 'Bureaucratizing the Duty to Aid: The United Nations and Rwandan Genocide', in A.F. Lang (ed.) *Just Intervention*, pp. 174–91, Washington, DC: Georgetown University Press.

Barnett, M. (2002) *Eyewitness to a Genocide: The United Nations and Rwanda*, London: Cornell University Press.

Barnett, M. and Finnemore, M. (2004) *Rules for the World: International Organizations in Global Politics*, New York: Cornell University Press.

Barnett, M. and Finnemore, M. (1999) 'The Politics, Power, and Pathologies of International Organizations', *International Organization*, 4, 53: 699–732.

Barnett, M. and Weiss, T.G. (2008) 'Humanitarianism: A Brief History of the Present', in M. Barnett and T.G. Weiss (eds) *Humanitarianism in Question: Politics, Power, Ethics*, pp. 1–48, Ithaca: Cornell University Press.

Barnett, M., Kim, H., O'Donnell, M. and Sitea, L. (2007) 'Peacebuilding: What Is in a Name?', *Global Governance*, 1, 13: 35–58.

Bellamy, A.J. (2004) 'The "Next Stage" in Peace Operations Theory?', *International Peacekeeping*, 1, 11: 17–38.

Bellamy, A.J. and Williams, P. (2004) 'Introduction: Thinking Anew about Peace Operations', *International Peacekeeping*, 1, 11: 1–15.

Bennis, P. (2000) *Calling the Shots: How Washington Dominates Today's UN*, New York: Interlink Publishing Group.

Bercovitch, J. (1998) 'The United Nations and the Mediation of International Disputes', in R. Thakur (ed.) *Past Imperfect, Future UNcertain*, pp. 47–62, London: Macmillan.

Bhaskar, R. (1998a) 'General Introduction', in M. Archer, R. Bhaskar, A. Collier, T. Lawson and A. Norrie (eds) *Critical Realism: Essential Readings*, pp. Ix–xxiv, London: Routledge.

Bhaskar, R. (1998b) *The Possibility of Naturalism: A Philosophical Critique of the Contemporary Human Sciences*, 3rd edn, London: Routledge.

Bhaskar, R. (1997) *A Realist Theory of Science*, 2nd edn, London: Verso.

Bhaskar, R. (1993) *Dialectic: The Pulse of Freedom*, London: Verso.

Bhaskar, R. (1986) *Scientific Realism and Human Emancipation*, London: Verso.

Bhaskar, R. (1979) *The Possibility of Naturalism: A Philosophical Critique of the Contemporary Human Sciences*, 1st edn, Brighton: The Harvester Press.

Bhaskar, R. (1975) *A Realist Theory of Science*, 1st edn, London: Verso.

Bhaskar, R. and Lawson, T. (1998) 'Introduction: Basic Texts and Developments', in M. Archer, R. Bhaskar, A. Collier, T. Lawson and A. Norrie (eds) *Critical Realism: Essential Readings*, pp. 3–15, London: Routledge.

Bhaskar, R. and Norrie, A. (1998) 'Introduction: Dialectic and Dialectical Critical Realism', in M. Archer, R. Bhaskar, A. Collier, T. Lawson and A. Norrie (eds) *Critical Realism: Essential Readings*, pp. 561–74, London: Routledge.

Bhavnani, R. and Backer, D. (2000) 'Localized Ethnic Conflict and Genocide: Accounting for Differences in Rwanda and Burundi', *Journal of Conflict Resolution*, 3, 44: 283–306.

Bjurner, A. (1998) 'Security for the Next Century: Towards a Wider Concept of Prevention', in P. Wallensteen (ed.) *Preventing Violent Conflicts: Past Record and Future Challenges*, pp. 279–90, Uppsala: Department of Peace and Conflict Research, Uppsala University.

Booth, K. (1991) 'Conclusion', in K. Booth (ed.), *New Thinking About Strategy and International Security*, pp. 340–2, London: HarperCollinsAcademic.

Bourgi, A. and Colin, J. (1993) 'Entre le Renouveau et la Crise: L'Organisation des Nations Unies en 1993', *Politique Étrangère*, 3, 58: 581–96.

Boutros-Ghali, B. (1999) *Unvanquished: A U.S.–U.N. Saga*, London: I.B. Tauris.

Boutros-Ghali, B. (1996) 'Introduction', in United Nations, *The United Nations and*

Rwanda, 1993–1996, pp. 3–147, New York: United Nations, Department of Public Information.

Boutros-Ghali, B. (1992) *An Agenda for Peace: Preventive Diplomacy, Peacemaking and Peace-keeping*. Report of the Secretary-General Pursuant to the Statement Adopted by the Summit Meeting of the Security Council on 31 January 1992, New York: United Nations

Bryman, A. (2001) *Social Research Methods*, Oxford: Oxford University Press.

Bull, H. (1966) 'The Grotian Conception of International Society', in H. Butterfield and M. Wight (eds) *Diplomatic Investigations: Essays in the Theory of International Politics*, pp. 51–73, London: George Allen & Unwin.

Buzan, B. (1983) *People, States, and Fear: The National Security Problem in International Relations*, Brighton: Wheatsheaf Books.

Buzan, B., Jones, C. and Little, R. (1993) *The Logic of Anarchy: Neorealism to Structural Realism*, New York: Columbia University Press.

Buzan, B., Wæver, O. and de Wilde, J. (1998) *Security: A New Framework for Analysis*, London: Lynne Rienner.

Call, C.T. (2008) 'Ending Wars, Building States', in C.T. Call and V. Wyeth (eds) *Building States to Build Peace*, pp. 1–24, London: Lynne Rienner.

Campbell, D. (1999) 'Contra Wight: The Errors of a Premature Writing', *Review of International Studies*, 2, 25: 317–21.

Carlsnaes, W. (1992) 'The Agency-Structure Problem in Foreign Policy Analysis', *International Studies Quarterly*, 3, 36: 245–70.

Carr, E.H. (1995) *The Twenty Years' Crisis 1919–1939: An Introduction to the Study of International Relations*, 2nd edn, London: Papermac.

Carr, E.H. (1946) *The Twenty Years' Crisis 1919–1939: An Introduction to the Study of International Relations*, London: The Macmillan Press.

Chabal, P. (2000) 'Review Article: Is There a French Way of Explaining African Politics?', *International Affairs*, 4, 76: 825–31.

Clapham, C. (1998) 'Rwanda: The Perils of Peacemaking', *Journal of Peace Research*, 2, 35: 193–210.

Claude, I.L. (1996) 'Peace and Security: Prospective Roles for the Two United Nations', *Global Governance*, 3, 2: 289–98.

Coate, R.A., Forsythe, D.P. and Weiss, T.G. (2001) *The United Nations and Changing World Politics*, 3rd edn, Oxford: Westview.

Collier, A. (1995) 'The Power of Negative Thinking', *Radical Philosophy*, 69: 36–9.

Collier, A. (1994) *An Introduction to Roy Bhaskar's Philosophy*, London: Verso.

Collier, A. (1989) *Scientific Realism and Socialist Thought*, Hemel Hempstead: Harvester, Wheatsheaf.

Cox, R. (1981) 'Social Forces, States and World Orders: Beyond International Relations Theory', *Millennium: Journal of International Studies*, 1, 10: 126–55.

Cruickshank, J. (2002) 'Critical Realism and Critical Philosophy: On the Usefulness of Philosophical Problems', *Journal of Critical Realism*, 1, 1: 49–66.

Dallaire, R.A. (2003) *Shake Hands with the Devil: The Failure of Humanity in Rwanda*, Toronto: Random House Canada.

Dallaire, R.A. (1998) 'The End of Innocence: Rwanda 1994', in J. Moore (ed.) *Hard Choices: Moral Dilemmas in Humanitarian Intervention*, pp. 71–86, Lanham: Rowman & Littlefield.

De Coning, C. (2006) 'The Future of Peacekeeping in Africa', in H. Ojanen (ed.) *Peacekeeping – Peacebuilding: Preparing for the Future*, pp. 35–43, Helsinki: The Finnish Institute of International Affairs.

De Waal, A. (2004) 'Counter-Insurgency on the Cheap', *London Review of Books*, 15, 26: 2.

Des Forges, A.L. (1999) *'Leave None to Tell the Story': Genocide in Rwanda*, New York: Human Rights Watch.

Destexhe, A. (1995) *Rwanda and Genocide in the Twentieth Century*, London: Pluto Press.

Dorn, A.W. and Matloff, J. (2000) 'Preventing the Bloodbath: Could the UN Have Predicted and Prevented the Rwandan Genocide?', *The Journal of Conflict Studies*, 1, 20: 9–52.

Dreyfus, H.L. and Rabinow, P. (1982) *Michel Foucault: Beyond Structuralism and Hermeneutics*, Brighton: Harvester.

Durkheim, E. (1982) *The Rules of Sociological Method*, New York: Free Press.

Economides, S. and Taylor, P. (1996) 'Former Yugoslavia', in J. Mayall (ed.) *The New Interventionism 1991–1994: United Nations Experience in Cambodia, Former Yugoslavia and Somalia*, pp. 59–93, Cambridge: Cambridge University Press.

Edgley, R. (1998) 'Reason as Dialectic: Science, Social Science and Socialist Science', in M. Archer, R. Bhaskar, A. Collier, T. Lawson and A. Norrie (eds) *Critical Realism: Essential Readings*, pp. 395–408, London: Routledge.

Elster, J. (1998) 'A Plea for Mechanisms', in P. Hedström and R. Swedberg (eds) *Social Mechanisms: An Analytical Approach to Social Theory*, pp. 45–73, Cambridge: Cambridge University Press.

Erskine, T. (2004) ' "Blood on the UN's Hands"? Assigning Duties and Apportioning Blame to an Intergovernmental Organisation', *Global Society*, 1, 18: 21–42.

Evans, G. (2008a) *The Responsibility to Protect: Ending Mass Atrocity Crimes Once and For All*, Washington, DC: Brookings Institution Press.

Evans, G. (2008b) 'The Responsibility to Protect: An Idea Whose Time Has Come … and Gone?', *International Relations*, 3, 22: 283–301.

Evans, G. (1998) 'Cooperating for Peace', in R. Thakur (ed.) *Past Imperfect, Future Uncertain*, pp. 33–46, London: Macmillan.

Evans, G. (1997a) *Responding to Crises in the African Great Lakes*, New York: Oxford University Press.

Evans, G. (1993) *Cooperating for Peace: The Global Agenda for the 1990s and Beyond*, St Leonards: Allen & Unwin.

Fierke, K.M. (1998) *Changing Games, Changing Strategies: Critical Investigations in Security*, Manchester: Manchester University Press.

Finnemore, M. and Sikkink, K. (1998) 'International Norm Dynamics and Political Change', *International Organization*, 4, 52: 887–917.

Foucault, M. (1989a) *The Archaeology of Knowledge*, London: Routledge.

Foucault, M. (1989b) *Madness and Civilization: A History of Insanity in the Age of Reason*, London: Routledge.

Foucault, M. (1976) *Mikrophysik der Macht: Über Strafjustiz, Psychiatrie und Medizin*, Berlin: Merve Verlag.

Franck, T.M. and Rodley, N.S. (1973) 'After Bangladesh: The Law of Humanitarian Intervention by Military Force', *The American Journal of International Law*, 2, 67: 275–305.

Gachuruzi, S.B. (1999) 'The Role of Zaire in the Rwandese Conflict', in H. Adelman and A. Suhrke (eds) *The Path of a Genocide: The Rwanda Crisis from Uganda to Zaire*, pp. 51–92, New Brunswick: Transaction Publishers.

Gordon, S. (2001) 'Icarus Rising and Falling: The Evolution of UN Command and

Control Structures', in S. Gordon and F. Toase (eds) *Aspects of Peacekeeping*, pp. 19–41, London: Frank Cass.

Goulding, M. (2004) 'The UN Secretary-General', in David Malone (ed.) *The UN Security Council in the Post-Cold War Era*, pp. 267–80, Boulder: Lynne Rienner.

Goulding, M. (2002) *Peacemonger*, London: John Murray.

Goulding, M. (1993) 'The Evolution of United Nations Peacekeeping', *International Affairs*, 3, 69: 451–64.

Gourevitch, P. (1999) *We Wish to Inform You That Tomorrow We Will Be Killed With Our Families*, 2nd edn, London: Picador.

Gowan, R. (2008) 'The Strategic Context: Peacekeeping in Crisis, 2006–08', *International Peacekeeping*, 4, 15: 453–69.

Groom, A.J.R. and Taylor, P. (1978) *International Organisation: A Conceptual Approach*, London: Frances Pinter.

Gurr, T.R. and Harff, B. (1998) 'Systematic Early Warning of Humanitarian Emergencies', *Journal of Peace Research*, 5, 35: 551–79.

Haas, P.M. (1992) 'Introduction: Epistemic Communities and International Policy Coordination', *International Organization*, 1, 46: 2–33.

Harré, R. and Madden, E.H. (1975) *Causal Powers: A Theory of Natural Necessity*, Oxford: Basil Blackwell.

Harsch, E. (2003) 'Africa Builds Its Own Peace Forces', *Africa Recovery*, 3, 17: 14–20.

Heiskanen, I. (2000a) 'Sivilisaatioiden sodat, kulttuurikamppailut ja antiglobalismi. Osa II. Kulttuuriset kamppailut ja MES:n mahti', *Kosmopolis*, 4, 30: 7–37.

Heiskanen, I. (2000b) 'Sivilisaatioiden sodat, kulttuurikamppailut ja antiglobalismi. Osa I. Huntingtonia myötä- ja vastakarvaan', *Kosmopolis*, 2, 30: 7–24.

Hintjens, H.M. (1999) 'Explaining the 1994 Genocide in Rwanda', *The Journal of Modern African Studies*, 2, 37: 241–86.

Hirsch, J.L. and Oakley, R.B. (1995) *Somalia and Operation Restore Hope: Reflections on Peacemaking and Peacekeeping*, Washington, DC: United States Institute of Peace Press.

Hodder, I. (1994) 'The Interpretation of Documents and Material Culture', in N.K. Denzin and Y.S. Lincoln (eds) *Handbook of Qualitative Research*, pp. 392–410, London: Sage.

Hollis, M. and Smith, S. (1991) 'Beware of Gurus: Structure and Action in International Relations', *Review of International Studies*, 4, 17: 393–410.

Hollis, M. and Smith, S. (1990) *Explaining and Understanding International Relations*, Oxford: Clarendon Press.

Howard, M. (1993) 'The Historical Development of the UN's Role in International Security', in A. Roberts and B. Kingsbury (eds) *United Nations, Divided World: The UN's Roles in International Relations*, 2nd edn, pp. 63–80, Oxford: Clarendon Press.

Hulton, S.C. (2004) 'Council Working Methods and Procedure', in D. Malone (ed.) *The UN Security Council in the Post-Cold War Era*, pp. 237–52, Boulder: Lynne Rienner.

Human Rights Watch (2004a) *Darfur in Flames: Atrocities in Western Sudan*, 5, 16.

Huntington, S.P. (1996a) *The Clash of Civilizations and the Remaking of World Order*, New York: Simon & Schuster.

Huntington, S.P. (1996b) 'The Clash of Civilizations?', in S.P. Huntington (ed.) *The Clash of Civilizations? The Debate*, pp. 1–25, New York: Foreign Affairs.

Huntington, S.P. (1996c) 'The West: Unique, not Universal', *Foreign Affairs*, November/ December, pp. 28–46.

Huysmans, J. (1998) 'Security! What Do You Mean? From Concept to Thick Signifier', *European Journal of International Relations*, 2, 4: 226–55.

Ignatieff, M. (1999) *The Warrior's Honor: Ethnic War and the Modern Conscience*, London: Vintage.

Ignatieff, M. (1998) 'The Stories We Tell: Television and Humanitarian Aid', in J. Moore (ed.) *Hard Choices: Moral Dilemmas in Humanitarian Intervention*, pp. 287–302, Oxford: Rowman & Littlefield.

International Commission on Intervention and State Sovereignty (2001) *The Responsibility to Protect: Report of the International Commission on Intervention and State Sovereignty*, Ottawa: International Development Research Centre.

International Panel of Eminent Personalities (2000) *Rwanda: The Preventable Genocide*. The Report of International Panel of Eminent Personalities to Investigate the 1994 Genocide in Rwanda and the Surrounding Events, 29 May 2000.

Janis, I.L. (1972) *Victims of Groupthink: A Psychological Study of Foreign-Policy Decisions and Fiascos*, Boston: Houghton Mifflin.

Jenkins, R. (2008) *The UN Peacebuilding Commission and the Dissemination of International Norms*, New York: Ralph Bunche Institute for International Studies, City University of New York.

Jervis, R. (1985) 'Perceiving and Coping with Threat', in R. Jervis, R.N. Lebow and J.G. Stein (eds) *Psychology and Deterrence*, pp. 13–33, London: The Johns Hopkins University Press.

Jervis, R. (1976) *Perception and Misperception in International Politics*, Princeton: Princeton University Press.

Jones, B.D. (2001) *Peacemaking in Rwanda: The Dynamics of Failure*, London: Lynne Rienner.

Jones, B.D. (1999) 'The Arusha Peace Process', in H. Adelman and A. Suhrke (eds) *The Path of a Genocide: The Rwanda Crisis from Uganda to Zaire*, pp. 131–56, New Brunswick: Transaction Publishers.

Jones, B.D. (1995) '"Intervention without Borders": Humanitarian Intervention in Rwanda, 1990–1994', *Millennium: Journal of International Studies*, 2, 24: 225–50.

Jones, B.G. (2002) 'International Relations as Internal Relations', *Journal of Critical Realism*, 1, 1: 147–57.

Joseph, J. (2002) 'Five Ways in Which Critical Realism Can Help Marxism', in A. Brown, S. Fleetwood and J.M. Roberts (eds) *Critical Realism and Marxism*, pp. 23–42, London: Routledge.

Kakwenzire, J. and Kamukama, D. (1999) 'The Development and Consolidation of Extremist Forces in Rwanda 1990–1994', in H. Adelman and A. Suhrke (eds) *The Path of a Genocide: The Rwanda Crisis from Uganda to Zaire*, pp. 61–91, New Brunswick: Transaction Publishers.

Kamola, I.A. (2007) 'The Global Coffee Economy and the Production of Genocide in Rwanda', *Third World Quarterly*, 3, 28: 571–92.

Kanninen, T. (2001) 'Recent Initiatives by the Secretary-General and the UN System in Strengthening Conflict Prevention Activities', *International Journal on Minority and Group Rights*, 8: 39–43.

Karns, M.P. and Mingst, K.A. (2000) *The United Nations in the Post-Cold War Era*, 2nd edn, Oxford: Westview Press.

Keane, F. (1996) *Season of Blood: A Rwandan Journey*, London: Penguin Books.

Keohane, R.O. (1989) *International Institutions and State Power: Essays in International Relations Theory*, London: Westview Press.

Kingsbury, B. and Roberts, A. (1993) 'Introduction: The UN's Roles in International Society since 1945', in A. Roberts and B. Kingsbury (eds) *United Nations, Divided*

World: The UN's Roles in International Relations, 2nd edn, pp. 1–62, Oxford: Clarendon Press.

Klinghoffer, A.J. (1998) *The International Dimension of Genocide in Rwanda*, London: Macmillan Press.

Knight, W.A. (2001) 'Learning in the United Nations', in W.A. Knight (ed.) *Adapting the United Nations to a Postmodern Era*, pp. 28–40, Houndmills: Palgrave.

Koskenniemi, M. (1998) 'The Place of Law in Collective Security: Reflections on the Recent Activity of the Security Council', in A.P. Jarvis, A.J. Paolini and C. Reus-Smit (eds) *Between Sovereignty and Global Governance: The United Nations, the State and Civil Society*, pp. 35–59, London: Macmillan.

Kovanda, K. (2004) 'Ceska republika v Rade bezpecnosti OSN: Genocida ve Rwande, 1994', *Mezinarodni vztahy*, 3: 45–65.

Kratochwil, F. (2000) 'Constructing a New Orthodoxy? Wendt's "Social Theory of International Politics" and the Constructivist Challenge', *Millennium: Journal of International Studies*, 1, 29: 73–101.

Kroslak, D. (2002) *The Responsibility of External Bystanders in Cases of Genocide: The French in Rwanda, 1990–1994*, PhD thesis, Aberystwyth: University of Wales, Aberystwyth.

Kuperman, A.J. (2001) *The Limits of Humanitarian Intervention: Genocide in Rwanda*, Washington, DC: Brookings Institution Press.

Kuperman, A.J. (2000) 'Rwanda in Retrospect', *Foreign Affairs*, 1, 79: 94–118.

Kurki, M. (2006) 'Causes of a Divided Discipline: Rethinking the Concept of Cause in International Relations Theory', *Review of International Studies*, 2, 32: 189–216.

Lakatos, I. (1978) 'Introduction: Science and Pseudoscience', in J. Worrall and G. Currie (eds) *The Methodology of Scientific Research Programmes: Philosophical Papers, Volume I*, pp. 1–7, Cambridge: Cambridge University Press.

Lawson, T. (1998) 'Economic Science Without Experimentation', in M. Archer, R. Bhaskar, A. Collier, T. Lawson and A. Norrie (eds) *Critical Realism: Essential Readings*, pp. 144–86, London: Routledge.

Lawson, T. (1997) *Economics and Reality*, London: Routledge.

Lazar, D. (1998) 'Selected Issues in the Philosophy of Social Science', in C. Seale (ed.) *Researching Society and Culture*, pp. 7–22, London: Sage.

Lebow, R.N. (1984) 'Cognitive Closure and Crisis Politics', in R.O. Matthews, A.G. Rubinoff and J.G. Stein (eds) *International Conflict and Conflict Management: Readings in World Politics*, pp. 55–64, Scarborough: Prentice-Hall of Canada.

Leitenberg, M. (1994) 'Rwanda, 1994: International Incompetence Produces Genocide', *Peacekeeping & International Relations*, 6, 23: 6–11.

Linklater, A. and Suganami, H. (2006) *The English School of International Relations: A Contemporary Reassessment*, Cambridge: Cambridge University Press.

Lucas, J.R. (1990) 'Reason and Reality: Prolegomenon to Their Varieties', in R. Bhaskar (ed.) *Harré and His Critics: Essays in Honour of Rom Harré with His Commentary on Them*, pp. 41–7, Oxford: Basil Blackwell.

McCarthy, T. (1990) 'The Critique of Impure Reason: Foucault and the Frankfurt School', *Political Theory*, 3, 18: 437–69.

Marx, K. (1973) *Grundrisse: Foundations of the Critique of Political Economy (Rough Draft)*, Harmondsworth: Penguin Books.

Mayall, J. (1996) 'Introduction', in J. Mayall (ed.) *The New Interventionism 1991–1994: United Nations Experience in Cambodia, Former Yugoslavia and Somalia*, pp. 1–24, Cambridge: Cambridge University Press.

Mearsheimer, J. (1995) 'A Realist Reply', *International Security*, 1, 20: 52–61.

Melvern, L. (2004) *Conspiracy to Murder: The Rwandan Genocide*, London: Verso.

Melvern, L. (2001a) 'Is Anyone Interested in Rwanda?', *British Journalism Review*, 2, 12: 52–8.

Melvern, L. (2001b) 'The Security Council: Behind the Scenes', *International Affairs*, 1, 77: 101–12.

Melvern, L. (2000) *A People Betrayed: The Role of the West in Rwanda's Genocide*, London: Zen Books.

Melvern, L. (1995) *The Ultimate Crime: Who Betrayed the UN and Why*, London: Allison & Busby.

Melvern, L. and Williams, P. (2004) 'Britannia Waived the Rules: The Major Government and the 1994 Rwandan Genocide', *African Affairs*, 410, 103: 1–22.

Mendlovitz, S. and Fousek, J. (1996) 'Enforcing the Law on Genocide', *Alternatives*, 2, 21: 237–58.

Mitrany, D. (1975) *The Functional Theory of Politics*, London: Martin Robertson.

Morris, J. (2000) 'UN Security Council Reform: A Counsel for the 21st Century', *Security Dialogue*, 3, 31: 265–77.

Newman, E. (1995) 'Realpolitik and the CNN Factor', in D. Bourantonis and J. Wiener (eds) *The United Nations in the New World Order: The World Organization at Fifty*, pp. 190–212, London: Macmillan.

Niiniluoto, I. (1999) *Critical Scientific Realism*, Oxford: Oxford University Press.

Ohlson, T. (1998) *Power Politics and Peace Policies: Intra-State Conflict Resolution in Southern Africa*, Uppsala: Department of Peace and Conflict Research, Uppsala University.

Otunnu, O. (1999) 'A Historical Analysis of the Invasion by the Rwanda Patriotic Army (RPA)', in H. Adelman and A. Suhrke (eds) *The Path of a Genocide: The Rwanda Crisis from Uganda to Zaire*, pp. 31–59, New Brunswick: Transaction Publishers.

Ould-Abdallah, A. (2000) *Burundi on the Brink 1993–95: A UN Special Envoy Reflects on Preventive Diplomacy*, Washington, DC: United States Institute of Peace Press.

Outhwaite, W. (1987) *New Philosophies of Social Science: Realism, Hermeneutics and Critical Theory*, London: Macmillan Education.

Palmberg, M. (2001) 'Introduction', in M. Palmberg (ed.) *Encounter Images in the Meetings Between Africa and Europe*, pp. 7–19, Uppsala: Nordiska Afrikainstitutet.

Parekh, B. (1998) 'Rethinking Humanitarian Intervention', in J.N. Pieterse (ed.) *World Orders in the Making: Humanitarian Intervention and Beyond*, pp. 138–63, Basingstoke: Macmillan.

Parsons, A. (1993) 'The UN and the National Interests of States', in A. Roberts and B. Kingsbury (eds) *United Nations, Divided World: The UN's Roles in International Relations*, 2nd edn, pp. 104–24, Oxford: Clarendon Press.

Patomäki, H. (2002a) *After International Relations: Critical Realism and the (Re)construction of World Politics*, London: Routledge.

Patomäki, H. (2002b) 'From East to West: Emergent Global Philosophies – Beginnings of the End of Western Dominance?', *Theory, Culture & Society*, 3, 19: 343–65.

Patomäki, H. (1996a) 'How to Tell Better Stories about World Politics', *European Journal of International Relations*, 1, 2: 105–33.

Patomäki, H. (1996b) 'Maailmanpoliittisen mielikuvituksen rajat', in E. Lagerspetz, H. Patomäki and J. Räikkä (eds) *Maailmanpolitiikan moraali*, pp. 75–109, Helsinki: Edita.

Patomäki, H. (1995) 'How to Open Up World Political Spaces: The Possibility of Republican World Politics', in H. Patomäki (ed.) *Peaceful Changes in World Politics*, Research Report No. 71, pp. 28–80, Tampere: Tampere Peace Research Institute.

Patomäki, H. (1992) *Critical Realism and World Politics: An Explication of a Critical Theoretical and Possibilistic Methodology for the Study of World Politics*, Studies on Political Science No. 12, Turku: Department of Political Science, University of Turku.

Patomäki, H. (1991) 'Concepts of "Action", "Structure" and "Power" in "Critical Social Realism": A Positive and Reconstructive Critique', *Journal for the Theory of Social Behaviour*, 2, 21: 221–50.

Patomäki, H. and Wight, C. (2000) 'After Postpositivism? The Promises of Critical Realism', *International Studies Quarterly*, 2, 44: 213–37.

Peck, C. (2004) 'Special Representatives of the Secretary-General', in D. Malone (ed.) *The UN Security Council in the Post-Cold War Era*, pp. 325–39, Boulder: Lynne Rienner.

Peck, C. (1996) *The United Nations as a Dispute Settlement System: Improving Mechanisms for the Prevention and Resolution of Conflict*, The Hague: Kluwer Law International.

Pérez de Cuéllar, J. (1993) 'The Role of the UN Secretary-General', in A. Roberts and B. Kingsbury (eds) *United Nations, Divided World: The UN's Roles in International Relations*, 2nd edn, pp. 125–42, Oxford: Clarendon Press.

Physicians for Human Rights (UK) (1994) *Rwanda 1994: A Report of the Genocide*, London: Physicians for Human Rights.

Piiparinen, T. (2009, forthcoming) 'Related Powers of the United Nations: Reconsidering Conflict Management of International Organisations in Ontological Light', *Review of International Studies*.

Piiparinen, T. (2008) 'The Rise and Fall of Bureaucratic Rationalisation: Exploring the Possibilities and Limitations of the UN Secretariat in Conflict Prevention', *European Journal of International Relations*, 4, 14: 697–724.

Piiparinen, T. (2007a) 'A Clash of Mindsets? An Insider's Account of Provincial Reconstruction Teams', *International Peacekeeping*, 1, 14: 143–57.

Piiparinen, T. (2007b) 'The Lessons of Darfur for the Future of Humanitarian Intervention', *Global Governance*, 3, 13: 365–90.

Piiparinen, T. (2007c) 'Putting the Cart Before the Horse: Statebuilding, Early Warning and the Irrationality of Bureaucratic Rationalisation', *Journal of Intervention and Statebuilding*, 3, 1: 355–78.

Piiparinen, T. (2007d) 'Reconsidering the Silence over the Ultimate Crime: A Functional Shift in Crisis Management from the Rwandan Genocide to Darfur', *Journal of Genocide Research*, 1, 9: 71–91.

Piiparinen, T. (2007e) 'Rescuing Thousands, Abandoning a Million: What Might an Emancipatory Intervention Have Looked Like in Rwanda?', *International Relations*, 1, 21: 47–66.

Piiparinen, T. (2006a) 'Beyond the Mystery of the Rwanda "Black Box": Political Will and Early Warning', *International Peacekeeping*, 3, 13: 334–49.

Piiparinen, T. (2006b) 'Reclaiming the Human Stratum, Acknowledging the Complexity of Social Behaviour: From the Linguistic Turn to the Social Cube in Theory of Decision-making', *Journal for the Theory of Social Behaviour*, 4, 36: 425–52.

Piiparinen, T. (2005) *Producing Images of Genocide: A Critical Realist Reflection on the Conflict Management Expertise of the United Nations in Rwanda*. PhD thesis, Aberystwyth: University of Wales, Aberystwyth.

Popper, K. (1983) *Realism and the Aim of Science: From the Postscript to the Logic of Scientific Discovery*, London: Hutchinson.

Pottier, J. (2002) *Re-imagining Rwanda: Conflict, Survival and Disinformation in the Late Twentieth Century*, Cambridge: Cambridge University Press.

Power, S. (2003) *'A Problem from Hell': America and the Age of Genocide*, London: Flamingo.

Power, S. (2002) 'Raising the Cost of Genocide', in N. Mills and K. Brunner (eds) *The New Killing Fields: Massacre and the Politics of Intervention*, pp. 245–64, New York: Basic Books.

Power, S. (2001) 'Bystanders to Genocide', *The Atlantic Monthly*, 2, 288: 84–108.

Prunier, G. (1998) *The Rwanda Crisis: History of a Genocide*, London: Hurst & Company.

Rabinow, P. (1984) 'Introduction', in P. Rabinow (ed.) *The Foucault Reader*, pp. 3–27, New York: Pantheon Books.

Ramsbotham, O. and Woodhouse, T. (1996) *Humanitarian Intervention in Contemporary Conflict: A Reconceptualization*, Cambridge: Polity Press.

Redfield, P. (2008) 'Sacrifice, Triage, and Global Humanitarianism', in M. Barnett and T.G. Weiss (eds) *Humanitarianism in Question: Politics, Power, Ethics*, pp. 196–214, Ithaca: Cornell University Press.

Reychler, L. (1997) 'Conflicts in Africa: The Issues of Control and Prevention', in Commission on African Regions in Crisis, *Conflicts in Africa: An Analysis of Crises and Crisis Prevention Measures*, pp. 15–37, Brussels: European Institute for Research and Information on Peace and Security.

Reyntjens, F. (1996) 'Rwanda: Genocide and Beyond', *Journal of Refugee Studies*, 3, 9: 240–51.

Roberts, A. (2004) 'The United Nations and Humanitarian Intervention', in J.M. Welsh (ed.) *Humanitarian Intervention and International Relations*, pp. 71–97, Oxford: Oxford University Press.

Roberts, A. (2002) 'The So-called "Right" of Humanitarian Intervention', in *Yearbook of International Humanitarian Law*, 3: 1–42, The Hague: T.M.C. Asser Press.

Roberts, A. (1995) 'Proposals for UN Standing Forces: History, Tasks and Obstacles', in D. Cox and A. Legault (eds) *UN Rapid Reaction Capabilities: Requirements and Prospects*, pp. 49–66, Clementsport: The Canadian Peacekeeping Press.

Ruggie, J.G. (1986) 'Continuity and Transformation in the World Polity: Towards a Neo-realist Synthesis', in R.O. Keohane (ed.) *Neorealism and Its Critics*, pp. 131–57, New York: Columbia University Press.

Russett, B. (1998) 'A Neo-Kantian Perspective: Democracy, Interdependence and International Organizations in Building Security Communities', in E. Adler and M. Barnett (eds) *Security Communities*, pp. 368–94, Cambridge: Cambridge University Press.

Ryan, S. (2000) *The United Nations and International Politics*, London: Macmillan.

Sayer, A. (2000) *Realism and Social Science*, London: Sage.

Sayer, A. (1992) *Method in Social Science: A Realist Approach*, 2nd edn, London: Routledge.

Sayer, A. (1981) 'Abstraction: A Realist Interpretation', *Radical Philosophy*, 2, 28: 6–15.

Schechter, M.G. (2001) 'Possibilities for Preventive Diplomacy, Early Warning and Global Monitoring in the Post-Cold War Era; or, the Limits to Global Structural Change', in W.A. Knight (ed.) *Adapting the United Nations to a Postmodern Era*, pp. 52–64, Houndmills: Palgrave.

Schmitt, C. (1976) *The Concept of the Political*, New Brunswick: Rutgers University Press.

Sellström, T. and Wohlgemuth, L. (1996) *The International Response to Conflict and*

Genocide: Lessons from the Rwanda Experience. Study 1. Historical Perspective: Some Explanatory Factors, Copenhagen: Joint Evaluation of Emergency Assistance to Rwanda.

Sellström, T. and Wohlgemuth, L. (1995) *Rwanda – Ett Land i Kris*, Uppsala: Nordiska Afrikainstitutet.

Shawcross, W. (2001) *Deliver Us from Evil: Warlords & Peacekeepers in a World of Endless Conflict*, London: Bloomsbury.

Shotter, J. (1993) *Conversational Realities: Constructing Life Through Language*, London: Sage.

Silverman, D. (1998) 'Research and Social Theory', in C. Seale (ed.) *Researching Society and Culture*, pp. 97–110, London: Sage.

Singer, J.D. (1961) 'The Level-of-Analysis Problem in International Relations', in K. Knorr and S. Verba (eds) *The International System: Theoretical Essays*, pp. 77–92, Princeton: Princeton University Press.

Smart, B. (1983) *Foucault, Marxism and Critique*, London: Routledge.

Smith, M.J. (1998) *Social Science in Question*, London: Sage.

Smith, S. (2000) 'Wendt's World', *Review of International Studies*, 1, 26: 151–63.

Smith, S. (1996) 'Positivism and Beyond', in S. Smith, K. Booth and M. Zalewski (eds) *International Theory: Positivism and Beyond*, pp. 11–46, Cambridge: Cambridge University Press.

Smith, S. (1995) 'The Self-Images of a Discipline: A Genealogy of International Relations Theory', in K. Booth and S. Smith (eds) *International Relations Theory Today*, pp. 1–37, Cambridge: Polity Press.

Stromseth, J.E. (1993) 'Iraq's Repression of Its Civilian Population: Collective Responses and Continuing Challenges', in L.F. Damrosch (ed.) *Enforcing Restraint: Collective Intervention in Internal Conflicts*, pp. 77–117, New York: Council on Foreign Relations Press.

Suganami, H. (2002) 'On Wendt's Philosophy: A Critique', *Review of International Studies*, 1, 28: 23–37.

Suganami, H. (1996) *On the Causes of War*, Oxford: Clarendon Press.

Suhrke, A. (1997) 'UN Peace-Keeping in Rwanda', in G.M. Sørbø and P. Vale (eds) *Out of Conflict: From War to Peace in Africa*, pp. 97–113, Uppsala: Nordiska Afrikainstitutet.

Susiluoto, I. (2002) *Diplomatian Taiturit*, Helsinki: Gummerus Ajatus Kirjat.

Tardy, T. (2000) 'Le Bilan de Dix Années d'Opérations de Maintien de la Paix', *Politique Étrangère*, 2, 65: 403–22.

Thakur, R. (1998) 'Introduction', in Ramesh Thakur (ed.) *Past Imperfect, Future Uncertain*, London: Macmillan, pp. 1–14.

Thornberry, P. (2001) '"Come, Friendly Bombs…": International Law in Kosovo', in M. Waller, K. Drezov and B. Gökay (eds) *Kosovo: The Politics of Delusion*, pp. 43–58, London: Frank Cass.

Traub, J. (2007) *The Best Intentions: Kofi Annan and the UN in the Era of American World Power*, New York: Picador.

Uurtimo, Y. and Väyrynen, T. (2000) *Peace-building in the Great Lakes Region of Africa*, Occasional Papers No. 79, Tampere: Tampere Peace Research Institute.

Van Walraven, K. (1998) 'Inter-governmental Organizations and Preventing Conflicts: Political Practice Since the End of the Cold War', in K. van Walraven (ed.) *Early Warning and Conflict Prevention: Limitations and Possibilities*, pp. 19–44, The Hague: Kluwer Law International.

Vassall-Adams, G. (1994) *Rwanda: An Agenda for International Action*, Oxford: Oxfam Publications.

Wæver, O. (1996) 'The Rise and Fall of the Inter-paradigm Debate', in S. Smith, K. Booth and M. Zalewski (eds) *International Theory: Positivism and Beyond*, pp. 149–85, Cambridge: Cambridge University Press.

Wallace, B. (2000) 'The Rwanda Debacle', *Maclean's*, 2, 113: 34.

Wallensteen, P. and Johansson, P. (2004) 'Security Council Decisions in Perspective', in D. Malone (ed.) *The UN Security Council in the Post-Cold War Era*, pp. 17–33, Boulder: Lynne Rienner.

Waltz, K.N. (1979) *Theory of International Politics*, Reading: Addison-Wesley.

Weber, M. (2003) *The Protestant Ethic and the Spirit of Capitalism*, Mineola: Dover Publications.

Weber, M. (1949) ' "Objectivity" in Social Science', in E.A. Shils and H.A. Finch (eds) *The Methodology of the Social Sciences*, pp. 49–112, New York: The Free Press.

Weber, M. (1948) 'Politics as a Vocation', in H.H. Gerth and C. Wright Mills (eds) *From Max Weber: Essays in Sociology*, pp. 77–128, London: Routledge.

Weick, K.E. (1976) 'Educational Organizations as Loosely Coupled Systems', *Administrative Science Quarterly*, 21: 1–19.

Weiss, T.G. (2007) *Humanitarian Intervention: Ideas in Action*, Cambridge: Polity Press.

Wendt, A. (2003) 'Why a World State Is Inevitable', *European Journal of International Relations*, 4, 9: 491–542.

Wendt, A. (1999) *Social Theory of International Politics*, Cambridge: Cambridge University Press.

Wendt, A. (1987) 'The Agent-Structure Problem in International Relations Theory', *International Organization*, 3, 41: 335–70.

Wheeler, N.J. (2000) *Saving Strangers: Humanitarian Intervention in International Society*, Oxford: Oxford University Press.

Wheeler, N.J. and Morris, J. (2006) 'Justifying the Iraq War as a Humanitarian Intervention: The Cure Is Worse than the Disease', in W.P.S. Sidhu and R. Thakur (eds) *The Iraq Crisis and World Order: Structural, Institutional and Normative Challenges*, pp. 444–63, Tokyo: United Nations University Press.

Wight, C. (2004) 'Theorizing the Mechanisms of Conceptual and Semiotic Space', *Philosophy of the Social Sciences*, 2, 34: 283–99.

Wight, C. (1999) 'MetaCampbell: The Epistemological Problematics of Perspectivism', *Review of International Studies*, 2, 25: 311–16.

Wight, C. (1998) *The Agent-Structure Debate in International Relations Theory: A Critical Realist Reappraisal*, Aberystwyth: Department of International Politics, University of Wales, Aberystwyth.

Williams, P.D. and Bellamy, A.J. (2005) 'The Responsibility to Protect and the Crisis in Darfur', *Security Dialogue*, 1, 36: 27–47.

Willum, B. (1999) 'Legitimizing Inaction Towards Genocide in Rwanda: A Matter of Misperception?', *International Peacekeeping*, 3, 6: 11–30.

Wyn Jones, R. (1999) *Security, Strategy, and Critical Theory*, London: Lynne Rienner.

Yamashita, H. (2004) *Humanitarian Space and International Politics: The Creation of Safe Areas*, Aldershot: Ashgate.

Internet sources

Adelman, H. (2000) 'Genocidists and Saviours in Rwanda', *Other Voices: The (e)Journal of Cultural Criticism*, 2, 1. Available HTTP: www.othervoices.org/2.1/adelman/rwanda.html (accessed on 8 March 2002).

Borton, J. and Eriksson, J. (2004) *Lessons from Rwanda – Lessons for Today: Assessment of the Impact and Influence of Joint Evaluation of Emergency Assistance to Rwanda*, Copenhagen: DANIDA. Available HTTP: www.um.dk/Publikationer/Danida/English/Evaluations/Rwanda/index.asp (accessed on 15 May 2005).

The Crisis Management Initiative (2008) *President Martti Ahtisaari at Nobel Ceremony (10.12.2008).* Available HTTP: www.cmi.fi/?content=speech&id=107 (accessed on 3 January 2009).

Evans, G. (2007b) *The Responsibility to Protect: Creating and Implementing a New International Norm.* Address by Gareth Evans, President, International Crisis Group, to Human Rights Law Resource Centre, Melbourne, 13 August 2007 and Community Legal Centres and Lawyers for Human Rights, Sydney, 28 August 2007. Available HTTP: www.crisisgroup.org/home/index.cfm?id=5036&l=1 (accessed on 29 December 2008).

Feil, S.R. (1998) *Preventing Genocide: How the Early Use of Force Might Have Succeeded in Rwanda.* A Report to the Carnegie Commission on Preventing Deadly Conflict, New York: Carnegie Corporation. Available HTTP: www.ccpdc.org/pubs/rwanda/rwanda.html (accessed on 3 April 2002).

Frontline (1999a), *The Triumph of Evil: How the West Ignored Warnings of the 1994 Rwanda Genocide and Turned Its Back on the Victims.* Interviews: Gregory Alex. Available HTTP: www.pbs.org/wgbh/pages/frontline/shows/evil/interviews/gromo.html (accessed on 21 July 2004).

Frontline (1999b), *The Triumph of Evil: How the West Ignored Warnings of the 1994 Rwanda Genocide and Turned Its Back on the Victims.* Interviews: Iqbal Riza. Available HTTP: www.pbs.org/wgbh/pages/frontline/shows/evil/interviews/riza.html (accessed on 23 May 2002).

Global Centre for the Responsibility to Protect (2008) *Presentation to the Arria Formula Meeting December 1, 2008, Presented by Nicola Reindorp.* Available HTTP: http://globalr2p.org/pdf/related/GCR2PArriaFormulaPresentation.pdf, p. 4 (accessed on 24 December 2008).

Gowan, R. (2008) 'The EU Still Needs UN Peacekeepers', *euobserver.com*, 21 May 2008. Available HTTP: http://euobserver.com/13/26183 (accessed on 9 December 2008).

Human Rights Watch (2004b) *Too Little, Too Late: Sudanese and International Response 2004.* Available HTTP: http://hrw.org/reports/2004/sudan0504/8.htm#_Toc71531709 (accessed on 15 July 2005).

Jeffery, S. (2003) 'Key Quotes: Tony Blair's Speech to US Congress', *Guardian* (18 July). Available HTTP: http://politics.guardian.co.uk/print/0,3858,4715107–110878,00.html (accessed on 29 August 2003).

NATO Update (2005a) 'Green Light for NATO Support to African Union for Darfur', 9 June 2005. Available HTTP: www.nato.int/docu/update/2005/06-june/e0609a.htm (accessed on 15 July 2005).

NATO Update (2005b) 'NATO Starts Airlifting African Union Troops to Darfur', 1 July 2005. Available HTTP: www.nato.int/docu/update/2005/07-july/e0701a.htm (accessed on 15 July 2005).

USA Today (2005) 'NATO Considers Helping African Union Force in Darfur', 27 April 2005. Available HTTP: www.usatoday.com/news/world/2005-04-27-nato-darfur_x. htm?csp=36 (accessed on 15 July 2005).

Newspaper and magazine articles

Berkeley, B. (1998) 'Aftermath: Genocide, the Pursuit of Justice and the Future of Africa', *Washington Post Magazine*, 11 October.

Cohen, R. (1994) 'Man in the Middle Calls on Confucius', *New York Times*, 26 April, p. 6.

Dallaire, R.A. (2004) 'Looking at Darfur, Seeing Rwanda', *New York Times*, 4 October.

De Waal, A. (2004) 'Darfur's Deep Grievances Defy All Hopes for an Easy Solution', *Observer*, 25 July.

Evans, G. (2008c) 'Facing Up to Our Responsibilities', *Guardian*, 12 May.

Gourevitch, P. (1998) 'The Genocide Fax', *New Yorker*, 5 November, pp. 42–6.

Hilsum, L. (1995) 'UN Suppressed Warning of Rwanda Genocide Plan: Massacre Details Were Revealed Three Months in Advance', *Observer*, 26 November, p. 23.

Ki-Moon, B. (2008) 'The Real UN: More Than Just Talk', *International Herald Tribune*, 17 June.

Klaus, V. (2009) 'Do Not Tie the Markets – Free Them', *Financial Times*, 7 January.

Legum, C. (1995) 'Looming Tragedy', *New African*, February, p. 31.

Lewis, P. (1994) 'Boutros-Ghali Angrily Condemns All Sides for Not Saving Rwanda', *New York Times*, 28 May.

Lorch, D. (1994) 'In the Anarchy of Rwanda, Looters and Drunkards Rule', *New York Times*, 14 April, p. 12.

Lynch, C. (2008) 'Low-Profile U.N. Chief Struggles as Diplomatic Peacemaker', *Washington Post*, 29 September, p. A15.

Mack, A. (2005) 'Peace on Earth? Increasingly, Yes.', *Washington Post*, 28 December, p. A21.

Smyth, F. (1994) 'French Guns, Rwandan Blood', *New York Times*, 14 April 1994, p. 21.

Wharton, C.R. (1994) 'The Nightmare in Central Africa', *New York Times*, 9 April, p. 21.

Papers

Carothers, T. (2008) *Is a League of Democracies a Good Idea?*, Carnegie Endowment for International Peace, Policy Paper, May.

DLA Piper US LLP and US Committee for Human Rights in North Korea (2006) *Failure to Protect: A Call for the UN Security Council to Act in North Korea*. Report commissioned by the Honorable Václav Havel, Former President of the Czech Republic, the Honorable Kjell Magne Bondevik, Former Prime Minister of Norway, Professor Elie Wiesel, Boston University, 30 October.

Global Centre for the Responsibility to Protect (2008) *Presentation to the Arria Formula Meeting December 1, 2008, Presented by Nicola Reindorp*.

International Peace Academy and the United Nations (2002) *Challenges in Peacekeeping: Past, Present and Future*. Seminar Report, UN Millennium Plaza Hotel, New York, 29 October.

Kurki, M. (2003) *Re-engaging with Aristotle: Evaluating Critical Realist Philosophy of Causation in Aristotelian Light*. Paper presented to the Seventh Annual Conference of the International Association for Critical Realism, the University of Amsterdam, 15–17 August.

Langille, P. and Keefe, T. (2003) *The Future of Peacekeeping: An Experts' Discussion to Contribute to the Dialogue on Foreign Policy*. Draft Report of a Workshop Co-hosted by the Liu Institute for Global Issues, University of British Columbia, Centre for Global Studies, University of Victoria, The Canadian Centre for Foreign Policy Development and The Canadian Consortium on Human Security, 21 March.

Lemarchand, R. (1999) *Ethnicity as Myth: The View from the Central Africa*. Paper presented at the Centre of African Studies, University of Copenhagen, 4 May.

Samuels, K. (2004) *Use of Force in UN Peacekeeping Operations*. Report of IPA–UNDPKO Workshop, UN Millennium Plaza Hotel, New York, 6 February.

Tardy, T. (2008) *United Nations–European Union Relations in Crisis Management*. Paper presented at International Forum for the Challenges of Peace Operations.

UNDP Multi-Donor Trust Fund Office (2008) *First Consolidated Annual Progress Report on Activities Implemented under the Peacebuilding Fund (PBF)*. Report of the Administrative Agent of the Peacebuilding Fund for the Period 1 January to 31 December 2007, 16 June.

Interviews

Aaltola, M. (Academy of Finland Research Fellow, Finnish Institute of International Affairs), personal communication (19 December 2008).

Adelman, H. (Professor), personal communication (26 February 2004).

Anyidoho, H.K. (Major-General, Former Deputy Force Commander of UNAMIR), an interview in London (27 March 2004).

Boutros-Ghali, B. (Secretary-General of the United Nations 1991–6), an interview in Paris (15 April 2005).

Dallaire, R. (Lieutenant-General; Force Commander of UNAMIR 1993–4), an interview in London (27 March 2004) and personal communication (15 February 2005).

Gambari, I. (Professor, Under-Secretary-General and Special Adviser on Africa; Permanent Representative of Nigeria to the United Nations, non-permanent member of the Security Council 1994–5), an interview at UN Headquarters, New York (2 December 2003).

Haavisto, P. (Special Representative of the European Union for Sudan), an interview in Helsinki (4 August 2005).

Hannay, D. (Permanent Representative of the United Kingdom to the United Nations, permanent member of the Security Council 1990–5), a telephone interview (15 March 2005).

Klappe, B. (Lieutenant-Colonel, Special Assistant to the Military Adviser of the Secretary-General), an interview at UN Headquarters, New York (1 December 2003) and personal communication (3 December 2003).

Kovanda, K. (Ambassador, Permanent Representative of the Czech Republic to the United Nations, non-permanent member of the Security Council 1994–5), an interview in London (27 March 2004) and personal communications (1 April 2004, 6 July 2004, 8 July 2004 and 9 January 2005).

Majoor, F. (Ambassador, Permanent Representative of the Netherlands to the United Nations), personal communication (29 December 2008).

Malone, D. (Professor, Former President of the International Peace Academy), personal communication (28 May 2004).

Member of the Joint Evaluation of Emergency Assistance to Rwanda, a confidential interview (26 February 2004).

Official of the UN Secretariat, a confidential interview at UN Headquarters, New York (4 December 2003).

Saressalo, J. (Colonel, Military Adviser to the International Peace Academy), personal communication (September 2004).

Sayer, A. (Professor), personal communication (22 August 2003).

Senior official of the UN Secretariat, a confidential interview at UN Headquarters, New York (3 December 2003).

Senior official of the UN Secretariat, a confidential telephone interview (13 November 2003) and personal communication (20 July 2004).

Smith, D. (Secretary-General, International Alert), personal communication (4 November 2008).

Stec, S. (Major, former head of the humanitarian-assistance cell of UNAMIR), an interview in London (27 March 2004) and personal communications (31 March 2004 and 21 January 2005).

Törnudd, K. (Professor; Permanent Representative of Finland to the United Nations, non-permanent member of the Security Council 1989–90), an interview in Helsinki (26 June 2003).

Linda Melvern Rwanda genocide archive, University of Wales, Aberystwyth

Daily Press Briefing of Office of Spokesman for Secretary-General, 7 April 1994 (file: UNAMIR).

Daily Press Briefing of Office of Spokesman for Secretary-General, 12 April 1994 (file: UNAMIR).

International Criminal Tribunal for Rwanda, Case No. ICTR-96–7-I, The Prosecutor against Theoneste Bagosora, Amended Indictment (file: Theoneste Bagosora).

Notes on the informal consultations of the Security Council (file: Security Council/Informals/April–May 94).

Statement on 'The Security Council Role in the Rwanda Crisis' by Ambassador Colin Keating, Permanent Representative of New Zealand to the United Nations at Comprehensive Seminar on Lessons Learned from United Nations Assistance Mission for Rwanda (UNAMIR), 12 June 1996, Merill Lynch Conference Centre, Plainsboro, New Jersey (file: UN Security Council/Colin Keating).

Twenty Twenty Television, 'United Nations', interview with Ambassador Colin Keating (file: UN Security Council/Colin Keating).

Twenty Twenty Television, 'United Nations, Rwanda', interview with Dallaire (file: Maj.-Gen. Roméo Dallaire. F.C. UNAMIR).

UNAMIR, Outgoing Cable from Roméo Dallaire, UNAMIR, Kigali to Maurice Baril, United Nations, New York on 17 April 1994. Subject: The Military Assessment of the Situation as of April 1994 (file: Maj.-Gen. Roméo Dallaire. F.C. UNAMIR).

United Nations, Facsimile from the Director of DPKO Hédi Annabi to Linda Melvern (file: UN Secretariat/DPKO Kofi Annan).

Index

Aaltola, Mika 140
abstract objects 33
abstraction, method of 11, 33–6, 40–1, 46, 78
ACABQ (Advisory Committee on Administrative and Budgetary Questions) 143
Action Plan to Prevent Genocide 139, 180
Adekanye, J.B. 49
Adelman, Howard 64, 70, 74, 76, 85, 173
Advisory Committee on Administrative and Budgetary Questions (ACABQ) *see* ACABQ
African Great Lakes region 87–9, 200*n*33
African Group 89
African Union (AU) *see* AU
African Union Mission in Sudan (AMIS) *see* AMIS
'Agent–Structure Problem in International Relations Theory, The' 32
agent–structure relationship 38–9
Ahtisaari, Martti 200*n*32
Akashi, Yasushi 54
Akazu 20, 21, 64
Alternative I 109, 111, 112–13, 118
American IR theory 32
AMIS (African Union Mission in Sudan) 133, 136
An Agenda for Peace 2, 5, 6, 45, 48, 51–2, 84, 95, 114
Angola 116
Annabi, Hedi 115
Annan, Kofi 10, 66, 73, 90–1, 139, 140, 150, 172, 180, 182*n*1
Annan's initiative *see Towards a Culture of Prevention*
anthropocentric fallacy 30, 74, 75, 83
anti-realism 28, 32, 42
Anyidoho, Henry K. 104, 196*n*49

APROMOSA (Association for the Social Promotion of the Masses) 19
Arab League 86
Arendt, Hannah 14
Aristotelian philosophy 168–9
Aristotle 168
arms trade 56–7, 68
Article 99: UN Charter 38, 48
Arusha peace process 21–2, 63, 103, 115, 147
Ashdown, Paddy 142, 147, 157
Association for the Social Promotion of the Masses (*APROMOSA*) *see APROMOSA*
atomism 7
AU (African Union) 133, 134

backward causalities 15, 79, 96
Bacon, Francis 46, 47
Bagosora, Théoneste 21
Ban Ki-moon 139, 142, 148, 149–50, 158
Baril, Maurice 108, 115, 126
Barnett, Michael 4, 26, 44, 47, 53, 54, 74, 75–6, 155
Bauman, Zygmunt 165
Belgian colonial rulers 18
Belgium 68, 126
Bellamy, Alex J. 2
Bennis, Phyllis 202*n*9
Bhaskar, Roy 28, 29–30, 31, 33, 34, 36, 38, 40, 169, 174, 184*n*4
Bjurner, Anders 69
'black file' episode 91
Blair, Tony 69
'body-bag syndrome' 53, 75, 123, 133–5
Booh-Booh, Jacques-Roger 85, 92
boomerang effect 118
Borton, John 178, 179
Bosnia 49, 52, 54, 56, 108–9

bottom-up approach 146
Boutros-Ghali, Boutros 1–2, 5, 10, 45, 47,
    48, 51–2, 62, 63–4, 65–6, 82, 95, 96,
    102, 110–11, 141, 156, 181, 187*n*24,
    196*n*49
Bradol, Jean-Hervé 141
Brahimi report 44, 119, 122, 160
Brazil 89
briefings: by Gharekhan 93; as
    institutionalised practice 92
Brotherus, K.R. 37
bureaucracies: power of 47–8
bureaucratic categorisation 112–14, 143
bureaucratic indifference 4
bureaucratic rationalisation: aspects of 76;
    as control mechanism 45, *57*;
    dysfunctions during genocide 104–14;
    dysfunctions of 46, *129*; and early
    warning 99, 101–4, 136–7; and
    motivated biases 100; and organisational
    learning 117
bureaucratic universalism 54, 113, 146
bureaucratisation theory 47
Burke, Edmund 13
Burma 149–50
Burundi 22, 89, 140
Burundian massacres 88, 90
Burundian refugees 88

Call, Charles T. 151
Cambodia 54
campaigning: by state representatives 164
capitalism (Marx on) 41
Carlsson Inquiry 73
Carnap, Rudolf 30
Carr, E.H. 37
casualties: peacekeepers 52, 53, 120; *see
    also* 'body-bag syndrome'
causal complexes 16, 32
causal linkages 88
CDR (Coalition for the Defense of the
    Republic) 20, 21
chaos narrative 124, 134
Chapter VI: UN Charter 110, 120
Chapter VII: UN Charter 109–10, 120, 135
Chapter VIII: UN Charter 133
China 80, 89, 103, 111
Christopher, Warren 67
civil war: and genocide conflation 64,
    79–81
civilian protection 105–10, 120–1, 131–2,
    135–6
Claes, Willy 196*n*49
'*Clan de Madame*' 20

clash of civilisations theory 55
classification 48
Claude, Inis L. 57
clientship contracts (*ubuhake*) 17–18
closed systems 30
Coalition for the Defense of the Republic
    (*CDR*) *see CDR*
Coate, Roger A. 47–8
'cockroaches' 19; *see also Inyenzi* guerilla
    bands
coercive military action 52
coffee price crash 89, 103
cognitive dissonance 51, 54, 101, 114–18
collective political will 66, 67, 68–9
colonial Rwanda 18
concrete objects 33
conflict management: mechanisms 162;
    post-Cold War 46–8
conflict prevention 94, 145
Congo *see* Democratic Republic of Congo
constraints 36
'contexts' 32
contrastive explanation 100
control mechanisms: abstraction of 45;
    functional shift in 136–8; RtoP as 139;
    of Security Council 5–6; *see also*
    bureaucratic rationalisation; early
    warning; organisational learning;
    Western normalisation
costs: of peacekeeping 66
counterfactuals 31
coup d'état (1973) 19
Cox, Robert 2
creeping escalation 53
critical naturalism 10, 31, 159
critical realism: actors, structures and
    mechanisms 38–42; as alternative
    approach 8–10, 26; applications 31–2;
    and IR studies 27–8; and IR theory
    32–3; philosophic discussions 29–31;
    terminology of 3; and 'truth' 159
critical social realism 32
Critical Theory 125
Croatia 52
Cruickshank, Justin 182*n*8
Czech delegation draft presidential
    statements 81, 82–3
Czech Republic 61, 80, 83, 108, 150

Dallaire, Roméro A. 23, 63, 66, 67, 86, 92,
    104–6, 109–10, 115, 122, 131, 189*n*1
Darfur 23–5, 94, 131–8, 180–1
de Soto, Álvaro 50
Dedring, Jürgen 85

deep structures 1–2, 39–41, 45, *58*, *97*, 125, *128*, *129*, *130*, 180
'degree of state' 155
dehumanisation 14
Democratic Republic of Congo (DRC) 67, 89, 174, 179
Department of Humanitarian Affairs (DHA) *see* DHA
Department of Political Affairs (DPA) *see* DPA
Des Forges, Alison L. 65, 189*n*1
Dessler, David 32
Destexhe, Alain 15, 61, 65, 67, 189*n*1
detection mechanisms 45, 48–51, 76
deterrent effect: of peace-enforcement 119–20
DHA (Department of Humanitarian Affairs) 84, 91, 104
Dialectic: The Pulse of Freedom 186*n*8
'diminished responsibility' 100
discretionary powers 121–2
dissonance reduction 117–18
division of labour 133–5
Djibouti 111
donor fatigue 66
double movement, method of *see* method of double movement
double standards 55–6
DPA (Department of Political Affairs) 84, 91, 104
DPA Policy Analysis Team 85
DPKO (UN Department of Peacekeeping Operations) 63, 66, 84, 91, 93, 94–5, 104, 105, 115, 159–60, 182*n*1
DRC (Democratic Republic of Congo) *see* Democratic Republic of Congo

early warning: Annan's initiative 90–1, 95; assessment team 159–60; and bureaucratic rationalisation 101–4, 136–7; malfunction of 79–90, *97*; mechanisms 5–6, 11, 45, 48–50, 51, *97*, 142–3; signals 71–2, 85–6, 97, 101–2; training programme 91; and UN peacebuilding 144–5
EISAS (Information and Strategic Analysis Secretariat) 160
El Salvador 50
'emancipatory research' 3
emancipatory vision 6
emancipatory windows 37–8, 175–6, *177*, *178*
embassies, local 71
empiricist fallacy 4, 5, 8, 30, 60–1

epistemic communities 140–1
epistemic fallacy 28, 84
epistemological relativism 159, 184*n*4
Eriksson, John 178, 179
ethnicity 16, 18
EU: and UN co-operation 161–2
EUFOR DRC operation 162
European IR theory 32
evacuations 67, 105, 127
Evans, Gareth 148, 199*n*9, 199*n*15
ex post facto fallacy 15
explanatory approaches 9
extremism 20–1, 89
Eyewitness to a Genocide 4, 9, 74

failure of UN: events 61–4; 'first wave' explanations 64–9; 'second wave' explanations 69–74
FAR (Rwandan Army) 20, 22
Fashoda Syndrome 68, *75*
Finnemore, Martha 47, 53, 54
'first wave' literature 64–9
Former Yugoslav Republic of Macedonia (FYROM) 48, 52, 54
Foucault, Michel 56, 124, 188*n*15
fragmentation of worldview 6, 55, *57*, 76, 103, 104, *129*
France 56–7, 61, 66, 67–8, *75*, 89, 107–8, 127
Franck, Thomas M. 141–2
French representative 88
functional shift: in control mechanisms 136–8
FYROM (Former Yugoslav Republic of Macedonia) *see* Former Yugoslav Republic of Macedonia

G77 138
Gaddafi, Colonel 24
Galtung, Johan 181
Gambari, Ibrahim 57, 79, 81, 93, 126–7
Garang, John 138
Gaza 150
genocide: causal factors 16; and civil war conflation 64, 79–81; definition 15; scale of 83; use of term 81–3, 111–12, 137
Genocide Convention 76
'genocide fax' 63, 72, 96; *see also* 'January cable'
Ghana 67
Gharekhan, Chinmaya 87, 93
Global Centre for the Responsibility to Protect 140, 199*n*15

global responsibilities 149
'global triage' system 141
Goražde, Bosnia 108
Goulding, Marrack 49, 50, 53, 112, 119
Gourevitch, Philip 69, 70
Gowan, Richard 153, 161, 200*n*37
Grotians 27, 167
groupthink 196*n*57
Gruffydd Jones, Branwen 28
guerilla bands 19, 20, 67
Guinea-Bissau 156

Habyarimana, Agathe 20
Habyarimana, Jean-Pierre 68
Habyarimana, Juvénal 19–20, 22, 67
Hamatic thesis 18
Hammarskjöld, Dag 48, 149
'Hammarskjöldian courage' 174
Hannay, David 62, 63, 106, 111
Heiskanen, Ilkka 54, 55
Hempel, Carl 30
hermeneutics 9
Hintjens, Helen M. 16
Hobbesians 167
holistic approach 2–3
holistic ontology 40
Hollis, Martin 9, 190*n*27
human dignity 158
human resources: enhancement of 94–5
human rights violations 103
Human Rights Watch 62
humanitarian corridors 107–8
humanitarian intervention 23–4, 138,
    141–2
humanitarian operation 127
'humanitarian pockets' 23, 62, 105,
    106–10
humanitarianism 125, 127, 141, 148
Humean level 34
Huntington, Samuel 55–6, 127
Hutu government 68
Hutu group 17, 18–19
Hutu revolution (1959) 19
Huysmans, Jef 165

ICC (International Criminal Court) 162,
    180
ICISS (International Commission on
    Intervention and State Sovereignty) 148,
    151, 166
idealist level 34–5
ideal-type 186*n*10
identity cards 18, 19
Ignatieff, Michael 124, 179

Impuzamugambi 21
In Larger Freedom report 133
Independent Inquiry into the Actions of the
    United Nations during the 1994
    Genocide in Rwanda *see* Carlsson
    Inquiry
information: from non-UN sources 82, 87
information analysis 86–7, 94, 159–60
Information and Strategic Analysis
    Secretariat (EISAS) *see* EISAS
information mishandling 63–4, 69, 72
information sharing 90–2
institutional mismanagement 63–4
instrumental rationality 106, 157, 160,
    196*n*49; *see also Zweckrationalität*
intelligence failure 72, 86–7
Interagency Framework Team for
    Coordinating Early Warning, Prevention
    and Preparedness 91
Interhamwe militia 21, 22, 63
International Commission on Intervention
    and State Sovereignty (ICISS) *see* ICISS
International Criminal Court (ICC) *see* ICC
international intervention: literature on 1–4
inter-organisational collaboration 133
intervention end state 142
intransitive objects 84
intra-state conflicts 49–50
Inyenzi guerilla bands 19, 20, 67
IPEP report 71–2
IR theory: critical realism and 32–3
Iraq 113–14
'irrationality of rationalisation' 53–4
'Islamic Legion' 24
Israel 150
Ivory Coast 162

Janis, Irving 196*n*57
Janjaweed militia 24
'January cable' 87, 91, 96, 104, 115, 122,
    182*n*1, 1184*n*25; *see also* 'genocide fax'
Jeffrey, S. 69
JEM (Justice and Equality Movement)
    24–5
Jervis, Robert 100, 114, 115
*Joint Evaluation of Emergency Assistance
    to Rwanda, The* 65, 72
Jones, Bruce D. 72
Justice and Equality Movement (JEM) *see*
    JEM

Kamola, Isaac A. 183*n*20
Kangura 21
Kanninen, Tapio 90

Kantians 27, 167
Kayibanda, Grégoire 19
Keating, Colin 64, 79, 84–5, 117–18
Kenya 140, 150
Keohane, Robert 43
Kigali Weapons Secure Area 63
Klappe, Ben 195*n*19, 196*n*58, 197*n*66
Klinghoffer, Arthur Jay 68, 70
Knight, W. Andy 50
knowledge-production 140–1, 159–63
Kosovo 172
Kouchner, Bernard 149
Kovanda, Karel 80, 82, 83, 92, 99, 108–9,
    173, 191*n*2
Kuperman, Alan J. 176
Kurki, Milja 40

law-explanation orthodoxy 30
Lawson, Tony 100
League or Concert of Democracies 132
legitimacy 40, 160, 162
Leibnizian level 34
Leitenberg, Milton 189*n*2
Lemarchand, René 16
Lessons from Rwanda – Lessons for Today
    178, 179
'levels': Bhaskar 34; Wendt 32
Linda Melvern Rwanda Genocide Archive
    see Melvern Archive
literature: on international intervention 1–4
Lockean level 34
loose coupling 54–5, 103–4
Luck, Edward 139, 143, 151, 166

Machiavellians 27, 167
Mack, Andrew 158
Majoor, Frank 154
Managing Global Insecurity (MGI) project
    200*n*30
mandates: clarity of 122–3; of PKOs
    135–6
Marx, Karl 11, 33, 41
mass murder: mechanisms of 21, 22–3
material constraints 36
Mayall, James 120
mechanisms 5–6, 28–9, 32, 35, 39–42, 45;
    see also conflict management; control
    mechanisms; detection mechanisms;
    'troublemaking' mechanisms
Médecins Sans Frontières 65, 67, 158
Media, the 21
media portrayal: of UN 152
Melvern, Linda 62, 70, 111, 161, 183*n*12,
    189*n*1

Melvern Archive 12–13, 105, 111
Méndez, Juan 162
metaphysical arguments 29–33
method of abstraction 33–6, 40–1
method of contrastive explanation 100
method of double movement 3, 11, 12, 26,
    33–8, 42–3, 46, 78, 169, 201*n*1
method of falsification 73
methodological fallacies 4, 5
methodological individualism 4, 5, 60–1,
    69, 73, 74
MGI (Managing Global Insecurity) project
    200*n*30
Middle East 150
military force: use of 46
militias 21, 22, 24, 63
Millennium Development Goals 153
mission creep 53, 135
Mitrany, David 144
Mitterand, Jean-Christophe 68
modern civilisations 55
monitoring 5, 21
MONUC (United Nations Mission in the
    Democratic Republic of Congo) 152, 179
Morganthau, Hans 55
Morris, Justin 46
motivated biases 100
MRND (National Revolutionary
    Movement for Development) 20, 21, 22

Nagel, Ernest 30
Naivasha peace process 137
NAM (United Nations Non-Aligned
    Movement) 138, 143–4, 146, 149
Nargis cyclone case 149–50
national ownership 143–4, 146
National Police 22
National Revolutionary Movement for
    Development (*MRND*) *see MRND*
NATO 133, 142, 188*n*14
neo-liberal prism 6
'neo-neo debate' 57
Neutral Military Observer Group (NMOG)
    see NMOG
New Zealand 61, 89, 108, 117
NGOs (non-governmental organisations)
    see non-governmental organisations
Nigeria 61, 83, 89, 107
Nigerian representative 88
Nkongoli, Laurent 17
NMOG (Neutral Military Observer Group)
    184*n*8
non-governmental organisations 80, 82,
    86, 89, 94, 140

normalisation of deviance 56
normalisation technologies 124
North Korea 150

OAU (Organisation of African Unity) 172–3, 184n8
objects 33
Office for Research and the Collection of Information (ORCI) *see* ORCI
Office of the Internal Oversight Services at the UN Secretariat (OIOS) *see* OIOS
Ohlson, Thomas 87
OIOS (Office of the Internal Oversight Services at the UN Secretariat) 156
ontology 2
ONUC (United Nations Operation in Congo) 52–3, 62
'open systems' 27, 30, 40, 93–4, 99, 180
Operation Provide Comfort 108
Opération Turquoise 23, 173
ORCI (Office for Research and the Collection of Information) 84, 85
Organisation for Security and Co-operation in Europe (OSCE) *see* OSCE
Organisation of African Unity (OAU) *see* OAU
organisational learning 45, 50–1, 100, 101, 115, 117, *128*
OSCE (Organisation for Security and Co-operation in Europe) 194n8
Oversight Group 104
Oxfam 65, 70

Palmberg, Mai 56
Parekh, Bhikhu 125, 126
PARMEHUTU (Party of the Movement and of Hutu Emancipation) 19
Patomäki, Heikki 28, 32–3, 124, 190n27
PBC (Peacebuilding Commission) 143–4, 145–6, 147, 151, 152, 153
PBF (Peacebuilding Fund) 145–6, 147, 151, 152, 153, 156
PBSO (Peacebuilding Support Office) 144, 145–6, 147, 159
peace operations 52–3
peacebuilding architecture: UN 6, 144–7, 151–8; *see also* RtoP
Peacebuilding Commission (PBC) *see* PBC
Peacebuilding Fund (PBF) *see* PBF
Peacebuilding Support Office (PBSO) *see* PBSO
peace-enforcement 75, 113, 119
peace-enforcement units 51–2

peacekeeping 46–7, 52–3, 112–13, 119
peacekeeping budgets 66
peacemaking 158
Peck, Connie 85
People Betrayed, A 12
Perception and Misperception in International Politics 114
Pérez de Cuéllar, Javier 50, 84, 114
permissive causes 185n2
phenomenal level 34–5, 79–83
philosophic discussions 29–33
police forces 22
political pressure 137–8
political reforms 20
political tribalism 16, 18
political unwillingness 10, 66, 67, 68–9, 103, 125–6, 174–5, 181
political will 179
Popper, Karl 30
Popperian method of falsification 73, 111
positivism 6–8, 27, 30
Possibility of Naturalism, The 31
possible causes 26
'post 9/11 hysteria' 140
post-decisional rationalisation 115–17
postmodernists 159
post-positivism 27–8
Powell, Colin 137
power: of bureaucracies 47–8
Power, Samantha 61, 67
power relations 124–5
'precautionary principles' 166
precolonial Rwanda 17–18
Presidential Guard 21, 22
presidential statements 80, 81, 82–3
preventive deployment 89
preventive diplomacy 48, 84, 89
prioritisation 158
Programme Voisin 18
protection of civilians 105–10, 120–1, 131–2, 135–6
Prunier, Gérard 1, 14, 16, 18, 68, 171

racial bias 130
racial shift 133–4, 163–4
RADER (Rwandese Democratic Union) 19
Radio Rwanda 21
Radio Télévision Libre des Milles Collines (RTLMC) 21, 23
Rand Corporation studies 158
Rasi, Marjatta 200n34
rationality 53–4
rational-legal authority 47–8, 51, 70–1
'real': as a term 30–1

realist level 34–5
Realist Theory of Science, A 29–31, 34
Realpolitik 74, 75, 126
'red lines' approach 155
Redfield, Peter 141, 158
reductionism 8–9
reductive explanation 5, 6
reflection 43
Reflexive Social Cube (RSC) model 39,
    187*n*18
reforms, political 20
regional security complexes 87–8
reinforcement: of UNAMIR 104, 109–10,
    111
Related Powers model 40, 47, 174, 187*n*23
related wholes 40
Report of the International Panel of
    Eminent Personalities (IPEP)to
    Investigate the 1994 Genocide in Rwanda
    and the Surrounding Events 71–2
Resolution 1590 133, 136
Resolution 688 103, 113–14
Resolution 794 103
Resolution 814 102
Resolution 912 62
responsibility 177–8
Responsibility to Protect (RtoP) *see* RtoP
'responsible sovereignty' 149
Reyntjens, Filip 16
RGF (Rwandan Government Forces) 64,
    82, 110
risk calculation 101–2
risk factor 155–7
Riza, Iqbal 63, 115
robust mandates 119
Rodley, Nigel S. 141–2
RPA (Rwanda Patriotic Army) 20
RPF (Rwanda Patriotic Front) 20, 22, 23,
    64, 68, 110, 117, 173
RTLMC (*Radio Télévision Libre des Milles
    Collines*) *see Radio Télévision Libre des
    Milles Collines*
RtoP (Responsibility to Protect) 138–44,
    148–51, 165–7
Rubik's Cube analogy 42–3
Ruggie, John 182*n*4
'rupture approach' 37
Russet, Bruce 103
Russia 89, 108
Rwanda: colonial 18; precolonial 17–18
Rwanda Patriotic Army (RPA) *see* RPA
Rwanda Patriotic Front (RPF) *see* RPF
Rwandan Government Forces (RGF) *see*
    RGF

Rwandese Democratic Union (*RADER*)
    see RADER
Rwandese National Union (*UNAR*) *see*
    UNAR

safe havens 113–14; *see also*
    'humanitarian pockets'
Sahelian Arabs 24
Saressalo, Jussi 197*n*63
Sayer, Andrew 11, 33–4, 39, 42–3, 169
scale: of killing 83
Scheffer, David 139
Schmitt, Carl 56, 165
scientific discovery, levels of 34
'second wave' of explanations 69–74
Secretariat 62–3, 69, 70–1, 86–97, 107,
    115
Secretaries General 47, 48
Secretary-General's Special Advisor on
    the Prevention of Genocide 180
securitisation 45, 140
securitisation mechanisms 51–7, 76, 140
security complexes 87–8
Security Council: 1990s 45–6; and
    Burundian refugees 88; clash of
    civilisations 55–6; control mechanisms
    5; and loose coupling 55; as open
    system 40, 41; renaissance 46–7;
    Resolution 912, 62; Resolution 1590
    133, 136; Rwandan genocide and 3, 4
Security Council meetings: April 1994
    79–80
self-interest 55
Sellström, Tor 17–18
Senegal 67
Shotter, John 15
Sierra Leone 154
Sills, Joe 124
SLA/M (Sudan Liberation Army/
    Movement) 24–5
Smith, Dan 146–7
Smith, Steve 9, 27, 32, 190*n*27
Smyth, Frank 80–1
'social/causal complexes' 32
socially caused constraints 36
socio-historical mechanisms 45
Somalia 62, 64, 67, 76, 101, 102, 115, 134
sovereign states 165
Spain 61, 108, 111–12
Special Adviser on Genocide 94
SRSGs (Special Representatives of the
    Secretary-General) 92–3
state failure 49
state sovereignty 146

state-centrism 69
statist paradigm 125–7
Stec, Stefan 107, 110, 112
stratification 30–1
structural adjustments 135–6
structural level: early warning
    malfunctions 83–90
structural realism 1–2
structures: abstract 40–1; concrete 40–1;
    definition 39; and UN 38–41, 39–40
Sudan Liberation Army/Movement
    (SLA/M) *see* SLA/M
Suhrke, Astri 74, 76, 173
Supplement to an Agenda for Peace 45, 52

Tardy, Thierry 160, 161
taxonomy (Gouldings) 112–13
terrorism 162
Theory of International Politics 1–2
third wave of themes 74
totality 36–7
Towards a Culture of Prevention 90, 95
transcendental realism 30–1
Transformational Model of Social Activity
    38, 174
transitive objects 84
Traub, James 152–3
'tribal warfare' 56
tribalisation 123–8
tribalism 16
'troublemaking' mechanisms 36, 39, 73
'troublemaking' structures 39, 44
trusteeship system 155
truth 159
Tunisia 67
Tutsi: dehumanisation of 14, 24
Tutsi group 17, 18–19, 20–1, 22–3
Twa group 17

ubuhake (clientship contracts) 17–18
UK: costs of peacekeeping 62, 66; role of
    190*n*19; safe havens 113; and
    Secretariat 102
Ukraine 133
Ultimate Crime, The 183*n*12
UN: establishment 187*n*22; and EU
    co-operation 161–2; failure of *see*
    failure of UN; and loose coupling 55;
    media portrayal of 152; peacebuilding
    architecture 6; and regional
    organisations 161; Resolution 688 103,
    113–14; Resolution 794 103;
    Resolution 814 102; Resolution 912
    62; Resolution 1590 133, 136;

securitisation mechanisms 51–7; two
    UNs 57
UN Assistance Mission for Rwanda
    (UNAMIR) *see* UNAMIR
UN Charter: Article 99, 38, 48; Chapter VI
    110, 120; Chapter VII 109–10, 120,
    135; Chapter VIII 133
UN Commission on Human Rights 55
UN conflict–management architecture:
    transformation 44
UN Department of Peacekeeping
    Operations (DPKO) *see* DPKO
UN field offices 85
UN High Commissioner for Human Rights
    (UNHCHR) 91, 93–4
UN Observer Mission Uganda-Rwanda
    (UNOMUR) *see* UNOMUR
UN peacebuilding architecture 6, 144–5,
    151–8
UN World Summit (2005) 6
UNAMIR (UN Assistance Mission for
    Rwanda) 22, 23, 56, 61–3, 66–7, 71, 82,
    85, 86, 92–3, 104–5, 107, 109–10, 126
UNAR (Rwandese National Union) 19
UN-AU-NATO-EU partnership: in Darfur
    133
UNDP (United Nations Development
    Programme) 93
UNHCHR (UN High Commissioner for
    Human Rights) *see* UN High
    Commissioner for Human Rights
UNIFIL (United Nations Interim Force in
    Lebanon) 121
United Kingdom (UK) *see* UK
United Nations Development Programme
    (UNDP) *see* UNDP
United Nations Interim Force in Lebanon
    (UNIFIL) *see* UNIFIL
United Nations Mission in Sudan
    (UNMIS) *see* UNMIS
United Nations Mission in the Democratic
    Republic of Congo (*MONUC*) *see*
    MONUC
United Nations Non-Aligned Movement
    (NAM) *see* NAM
United Nations Preventive Deployment
    Force (UNPREDEP) *see* UNPREDEP
United Nations Protection Force
    (UNPROFOR) *see* UNPROFOR
United Nations Security Council *see*
    Security Council
United States of America (USA) *see* USA
universalism 55
UNMIS mandate 135

UNMIS (United Nations Mission in
   Sudan) 133, 136
unmotivated biases 100–1, 114
UNOMUR (UN Observer Mission
   Uganda-Rwanda) 21
UNOSOM II 102, 115, 134, 149, 170
UNPKOs 133–4
UNPREDEP (United Nations Preventive
   Deployment Force) 48
UNPROFOR (United Nations Protection
   Force) 52, 56
Urquhart, Brian 48, 137
Uruguay 67
US Rangers 134
USA (United States of America) 26, 60–1,
   62, 65, 66, 67, *75*, 79–80, 89, 111
Uurtimo, Yrjö 200*n*33
Uwilingiyimana, Agathe 22

van der Stoel, Max 194*n*8
Väyrynen, Tarja 200*n*33
Vieira, Joao Bernardo 156

Wallace, Bruce 69

Waltz, Kenneth N. 1–2
weapons embargo 68
weapons stockpiling 63
Weber, Max 47, 54, 164, 186*n*10
Weick, Karl E. 54–5
Weiss, Thomas G. 44, 138
Wendt, Alexander 28, 32
Western civilisations 55–6, 125
Western ideology 55
Western interventionism 144, 146
Western normalisation 45, 46, *57*, 123–8,
   130, 133, 148, 155, 181
Wight, Colin 5, 15, 28, 29, 32, 34
Wight, Martin 27
Williams, Paul 2
Willum, Bjørn 70, 73
'wise men' 37
Wohlgemuth, Lennart 17–18
Wyn Jones, Richard 36

Zimbabwe 150
Zweckrationalität 54, 76, 101, 110–12,
   155, 160, 196*n*49; *see also* instrumental
   rationality